9 75

TAILORING

TAILORING

ALLYNE BANE

associate professor of home economics
Ohio University

SECOND EDITION

McGRAW-HILL BOOK COMPANY   New York   St. Louis   San Francisco   Toronto   London   Sydney

PREFACE

Home-sewing enthusiasts of today contrast sharply with those of the past few decades. There was a time when the great majority of customers in fabric and pattern departments were either young students in high school classes or 4-H clubs or women of any age interested primarily in the economy that home sewing offered. Today the very young still shop for their first projects, but the adult customers reflect great changes in our society. Home sewing is no longer an economic necessity—today it is a luxury. Quite simply, most women sew today only because they want to. This book is written to serve the person with lasting enthusiasm—the person who wants to sew and who likes to sew. It does not offer a quick and painless method of finishing a dreaded assignment (as it might if it were written for those who sew for economic reasons only), but rather it offers techniques for meeting the special requirements of those who sew for the joy and the luxury of it.

Many women want to sew because they love and appreciate exclusive fabric and they know that beautiful fabric deserves excellent construction. Many want to sew in order to wear designs from the fashion centers of the world, and they know that high-quality design demands good construction. Many want to sew in order to wear superbly fitted garments, and they realize that superb fit requires a thorough understanding of the broad areas of clothing construction. Many want to sew in order to have a truly personalized costume, and they realize that a personalized costume is both intimate and revealing and therefore demands careful attention to every detail. And most women who sew for the luxury of it find great pleasure and satisfaction in sewing as a creative outlet; they sew with the urgency with which the artist paints. These women have learned that creative satisfactions are possible only if the resulting costume meets professional competition. Thus the joys and luxuries of home sewing are possible only with the time and patience and thought required for couturier methods and standards. This book is written to meet the demands of the home sewing enthusiast.

A book cannot replace the instruction sheet included with the commercial pattern; a book can only supplement the excellent directions given on the pattern. In general, the tailoring techniques recommended in this book are very similar to those suggested by all the pattern companies and are almost identical to those included with Vogue patterns. The explanations of fundamental techniques are more detailed and are fortified with more illustrations than is possible on an instruction sheet. The most typical construction is explained in depth, and the principle involved is discussed in great detail. In many cases, the basic principle is applied to other similar but less typical construction details. Because it is quite

impossible to cover every possible subtlety of construction, the instruction sheet of each pattern must supply the unique directions for that particular pattern. The reader must understand the principle involved—must understand it thoroughly so that it can be applied to ever-changing circumstances and designs. Space for elaboration on fundamental problems was gained by omitting construction details that are used infrequently; for example, pocket construction is not included because pockets are unique features that must be made according to the directions with each individual pattern. The author has a well-founded respect for patterns and pattern directions, a fact that will be obvious on almost every page of the book. When directions given here differ from those usually suggested on the pattern, the difference will be mentioned and explained, and in almost every case, the reader will see that the changes and improvements are possible because of the space for elaboration that a book allows; rarely, if ever, will the difference cast a bad light on the quality of pattern directions.

This edition of *Tailoring* bears little resemblance to the original one; it is, in reality, a completely new book. There are many more pattern alterations, and some of the new ones are remarkably effective. The chapter on fitting ("Fitting the Muslin Test Copy") has been greatly enlarged. The order of construction has been drastically changed. Each fundamental principle and basic construction detail is illustrated with examples of similar details on comparable designs. The section on skirt linings reflects several improvements of the last several years. The function and use of the complete interfacing and/or underlining, probably the most exciting and effective improvement in construction methods of the last ten years, are discussed in exhaustive detail. And throughout the book, there is an emphasis on the methods of testing and experimenting that are so important if the woman who sews is to keep pace with new developments in all those industries related in any way to fabric, findings, equipment, and construction technique.

The scope of this book is limited to construction techniques of tailoring. However, the reader must understand that a successful costume, whether it is made at home or purchased on the ready-to-wear market, is a result of careful study in broad areas of textiles and clothing. Artistic principles must be applied in the choice of color and color combinations, in the use of texture and texture contrasts, in the selection of pleasing lines for the individual figure, and in the effective use of proportion and balance. The fabric (its fiber content, weave, finish, etc.) determines the character, the wearing qualities, and the care of the garment. The influence of fashion is an important consideration. Thoughtful study of current fashion magazines and a careful survey of newsworthy fashion in large department stores and specialty shops will strengthen fashion know-how; reference books on clothing selection and wardrobe planning and a basic book on the fundamentals of textiles will be required.

New developments in fabrics and innovations in construction techniques, as well as improved features in commercial patterns, equipment, and findings, are a constant challenge to the woman who sews. Fundamental principles undergo little change, but each new development in any one of these related industries, as well as changes in fashion, creates the need to reevaluate old methods and invent new solutions. One of the best ways to be informed of the latest news in the home-sewing field is to study the monthly magazines published by the commercial pattern companies; these specialized magazines are concerned largely with new developments in all industries in any way associated with home sewing. Probably the most excellent way to keep up with the latest trends in construction techniques and to gain the advantage of the imaginative thought of the entire international fashion community is to use (or study) Vogue Paris Original and International Couturier patterns.

I am indebted to Mrs. Joseph Collins for her able assistance in the preparation of the manuscript; Donna is the kind of typist every author dreams about and seldom finds. Miss Katherine Smith deserves all the gratitude I have given her privately; she helped to check and proofread the manuscript (those never-ending details!), and her work was always accurate and always done with obvious devotion. It is impossible to mention all the persons (former teachers, professional friends, coworkers, and students at Ohio University) who have provided many of the inventive and original ideas that have become a part of my teaching and a part of this book; I have borrowed ideas from a great many people, and each one knows that I remember well the particular debt I owe her. My greatest debt is to my students at Ohio University for their inventiveness; for their suggestions, which have been a great help in writing this edition; and, perhaps more than anything else, for their enthusiasm which makes teaching such great fun for me.

ALLYNE BANE

CONTENTS

TAILORING

1

MAKE

IT

IMPORTANT

Home sewing offers many advantages: a saving in wardrobe costs, the opportunity to enjoy beautiful fabric within a modest income, the advantage of accurate and flattering fit for every figure, the satisfaction of a personalized costume, and, the greatest advantage of all, the thrill of creative expression. But these advantages, one and all, are dependent on the success of the costume. The ultimate success of a costume depends on excellent construction (entirely possible with experience and care and attention to directions) and on the thought, imagination, and good taste required in planning the costume. The planning of a costume must not be minimized. The designer of ready-to-wear makes a career of costume planning; she studies fashion trends and current customer reactions, she thinks of the role a costume will play in the lives of her customers, she chooses fabric that will meet these needs, she creates a design that will enhance the fabric (or perhaps she chooses a fabric to enhance the design), she experiments with color and texture, and she shops long hours for the right lining and the perfect accenting touches. These are only a few of the issues with which she is involved, but uppermost in her mind, always, is the search for those illusive qualities—good taste, smartness, elegance —for she realizes they hold the answer to customer satisfaction. If the woman who sews is to claim all the advantages of home sewing, she must meet the formidable competition of the professional designer, and in addition she must become increasingly aware of the greater competition of the designer of exclusive ready-to-wear. Eventually the woman who makes her own costumes can claim complete success as she reaches the couturier level of creativity.

PERSONAL
WARDROBE
NEEDS

The first step in planning is the consideration of personal wardrobe needs. The tailored costume can be as casual as a cardigan or as formal as a theater suit. Although one usually thinks of the tailored garment made in wool as being worn from fall into winter and spring, tailored costumes can be made in raw silk or interesting cotton suitings, so that the season of the year places no limit on costume choices.

The degree or level of fashion will be a basic consideration. Some readers will be willing to pay the high price in time and money for a costume that will be avant-garde fashion this season, realizing that the high style of the design will limit its life-span. Others, more practical, will choose something more basic in design in hopes that it will give many years of service. The lasting quality of a design is largely a matter of silhouette. Those designs which follow the basic body lines often stay in fashion's favor for five to ten years, providing there is no drastic increase in skirt or coat length. Lines that do not conform to body lines, such as exaggeratedly wide shoulders, the pegged skirt, the very flared back in a coat or jacket peplum, the leg-of-mutton sleeve, etc., are design lines that are relatively short-lived. Consequently, the matter of silhouette, since it is so responsible for seasonal wardrobe expenses, will be one of the more important considerations in planning for the tailored costume.

The woman who sews usually feels a special kind of devotion for a costume she makes, especially if it is a tailored one and more so if it is a first venture in tailoring. She will spend a great deal of time making it and will put a great deal of love into it, and she will very probably want it to last forever. For this reason, it might be well to plan the first tailored garment in a design with simple lines that are not tiring and in a somewhat basic silhouette so that it can be enjoyed for many years. However, even if the suit or coat is made in basic lines that will ensure a certain fashion stability, the costume can be planned for an important role in the wardrobe.

CONSIDERATION
OF CURRENT FASHION
AND INDIVIDUAL STYLE

Fashion has four components: (1) design (silhouette or line), (2) fabric (texture and texture combination), (3) color and color combination, and (4) details.

Changes occur in each of these components, but fashion rarely if ever changes in every one in one given season. One season the newsworthy change may be in fabric; another season the excitement may be in silhouette. Changes occur in more than one of the fashion components in a given season, but the really big news is usually confined to one segment of fashion. Changes in silhouette have the greatest impact on the fashion world simply because they are so very obvious. The woman who hopes to wear a costume for many years will confine her choices to basic silhouette lines and will plan for excitement in other ways.

The first step in wardrobe planning is the careful study of the current fashion picture. The woman who sews is wise to realize that her greatest competition and most excellent source of inspiration is the ready-to-wear market. The remarkably high standards of design and construction of clothes available at a reasonable price make them formidable competition indeed. There is no reason, however, to draw inspiration only from merchandise that one could afford on the retail market; it is far wiser and entirely possible to meet the demanding standards of the greater competition of exclusive, elegant costumes that one could not afford to buy ready-made. The quality of construction, even more than the quality of fabric, is obvious in exclusive ready-to-wear, and the little touches that make up quality construction are often quite simple to do. The woman who makes her own costumes is wise to visit exclusive departments for the purpose of establishing high standards and of "borrowing" tricks of the trade to add to her own collection. In other words, it is well to take advantage of the lessons to be learned from the most talented professional designers.

There are lessons to be learned from the buyer in the department store as well. She spends most of her budget on rather staple merchandise, while a much smaller percentage (approximately 10 percent) is allotted to current, exciting fashions. This smaller collection of high-fashion costumes is the prestige merchandise on which the fashion reputation of the store is based. The buyer, who must strive for fashion prestige, advertises these newsworthy fashions in window and departmental displays and features them in leading newspaper advertisements. Plan to see and study the ads and the displays because they give a capsule view of newsworthy fashion, interpreted by a professional buyer and chosen especially to meet the needs of a particular community and region of the country.

While making a market survey, take cues from the kind of ready-to-wear clothing you would buy. All too often, the woman who buys imaginative merchandise loses her courage when she selects a pattern and fabric and chooses an uninspired design that she would never have purchased ready-made. This understandable lack of courage is a result of limited experience in pattern and fabric selection. The solution is to try to retain normal confidence and to force yourself to use your usual imagination; each venture in home sewing will increase the skill of costume planning, and each imaginative costume will build confidence for future costumes.

In addition to considering current fashion, the shopper must give careful thought to her own individual style. Fashion is not a dictator—rather, the individual is the dictator and should use fashion to her own advantage. A woman need not be a slave to fashion as long as she stays within reasonable bounds; she cannot wear skirts 4 inches longer than those featured in current fashions, but she can wear them at a somewhat different length and still look fashionable. She can break one rule, and perhaps more, but she cannot break them all. A woman usually (and correctly) has a marked preference for a particular fashion trend because it is flattering to her (in terms of color, silhouette, etc.) or because she takes personal pleasure in it and finds it comfortable. If that preference is based on sound reasoning, the beloved fashion can be worn so often and so long that it becomes a "uniform." And if that fashion is artistically sound (the little Chanel suit is an excellent example), it can be varied and featured in every color and every fabric, and that very same fashion can make up an entire wardrobe for many years.

SUGGESTIONS FOR ADDING IMPORTANCE TO THE COSTUME

There are any number of ways of adding couturier touches to the tailored costume. Opportunities for creativity will be discussed by giving consideration to the components of fashion, and in addition, specific suggestions will be offered for linings and companion pieces.

DESIGN (SILHOUETTE OR LINE)
Even if the silhouette will be basic enough to enjoy fashion stability, the design lines of the pattern can be the outstanding feature of the costume. For example, the design lines of a Vogue Paris Original or International Couturier pattern may well be so interesting that every other component of the costume should be subordinate to design. The design should be, in the opinion of the author, one that is of sufficient complication to ensure the appearance of an obvious expenditure of time and effort. It is foolish economy in both time and money to make a suit "in a jiffy." The oversimplified construction details and design lines of the kind of suit that can be made in a very short time (no collar, no pockets, faced rather than lined) fool no one. One has but to visit the budget shop in a department store to see costumes of that description, priced so inexpensively that there would be no advantage in spending the time to make them. By contrast, costumes in the exclusive departments of the store feature subtle design surprises and intricate touches that look as if someone cared. The costumes we make at home should certainly show that someone cared, and the wise woman who sews will always keep in mind that every extra hour she spends in her workroom adds dollars to the apparent cost of the garment. The person who has become proficient in dressmaking and who is moving up the ladder to tailoring should not consider patterns planned for the novice. She is ready for more advanced work, and as soon as her experience warrants, she should consider Vogue Paris Original and International Couturier designs.

Many women commit the serious mistake of buying an attractive design and then subtracting all the excitement from it in an attempt to save time or effort. They rationalize that they do not need the pockets ("They aren't big enough to hold anything, anyway") or the buttons and buttonholes ("I never button a jacket") or the cuffs ("They get in my way when I type"), and it takes just one or two "subtractions" to turn a beautiful design into a carbon copy of bargain-basement merchandise. If the suit is to be a bargain in time and effort, it is far wiser to buy that bargain ready-made. There are no shortcuts to a professional costume, and the smart woman who sews holds one thought uppermost in her mind: *Extra hours mean extra dollars in apparent cost, extra hours mean more elegance, and extra hours mean far greater creative satisfaction.*

FABRIC (TEXTURE AND TEXTURE COMBINATION)

Because tailoring is a time-consuming process, the tailored costume deserves the very highest-quality fabric the consumer can afford to buy. Unfortunately there are very few bargains in fabric, and high quality demands a premium price. But there is no better way to add importance to the tailored costume than to make it of beautiful fabric; quality fabric gives pleasure to the beholder and wearer alike and, in addition, results in a garment that retains its beauty through hard wear and years of service.

The woman who has the ability and experience to ensure predictable, successful results can afford fabric of far better quality than she might be accustomed to buying. If home-sewn garments are to meet the competition of exclusive ready-to-wear, they must be constructed well and designed well, and they must be made of quality fabric. The first step toward ultimate success is to gain experience in construction and selection. A next logical move upward is to select a quality design. The last step upward (the final move because of the cost factor) is to buy quality fabric. The tremendous advantage of being able to afford an exclusive wardrobe on a mod-est income will have been achieved in these three logical steps forward.

The cost-comparison chart on page 6 may hold a pleasant surprise for some readers. It is based on prices of wool fabric, 54 inches wide, and on the amount of yardage required for a typical suit or coat. The three qualities of fabric listed might be considered minimum, average, and very good at present-day (1967) prices. The minimum-quality fabric would compare with that used in the $8.98 to $15.95 (possibly unlined) ready-made suit; the average-quality fabric could be compared with that used in the $49.95 to $79.95 ready-made suit; and the very good-quality fabric would compare favorably with that used in the ready-made suit priced at $79.95 and up to $125.

Obviously the differences in total cost are entirely dependent on the price of fabric, with all other costs remaining constant, but it is interesting to note that although the good-quality fabric costs three times as much as the lowest quality, the total cost of the suit only doubles. Assuming that the reader is sufficiently proficient in construction to meet the high standards of the better and exclusive ready-to-wear, it is revealing to see that for an additional $8 above minimum costs, she can move up to the $49.95-and-up bracket. Quality fabric is an excellent means of achieving wardrobe excitement, and the cost is not as prohibitive on a cost-per-garment basis as it appears to be from a cost-per-yard comparison.

The choice of fabrics suitable for tailoring purposes is not limited to wool, although wool does respond most beautifully to the molding and shaping required in excellent tailoring. Other fabrics which can be used for tailoring purposes are:

1 For the theater suit: brocade, satin, velvet and velveteen, simulated fur
2 For the summer suit: raw silk, linen, novelty suitings in cotton and man-made fabrics, some drapery fabrics
3 For the straight-line coat or jacket: corduroy, some upholstery fabrics, simulated fur and leather, suede

Each of these fabrics (and others not mentioned) can provide excitement for the tailored costume. Many of the fabrics listed (satin, velvet, simulated fur and leather, suede) will require special techniques of construction that only the

experienced person should undertake, and all of them will require some additional thought during construction to adapt tailoring techniques to fabrics lacking the qualities of wool. Discussion in this book will be confined to wool fabrics, and supplementary reading will be required if unique fabrics are to be used (see Allyne Bane, *Creative Clothing Construction,* McGraw-Hill Book Company, New York, 1966, for a discussion of the problems of sewing on many of the fabrics listed above).

The weight, the very thickness of the fabric, has a great deal to do with the success of the tailored costume. It is a distinct advantage to see the design shown in a photograph (Vogue Paris Original and International Couturier designs are always shown in a photograph) because it will be pictured in an appropriate weight and texture, chosen by a professional designer. The suit pictured in a nubby tweed coating will often be a disappointment if it is made in a flat,

COST-COMPARISON CHART

	MINIMUM QUALITY (estimated at $3 per yd)	AVERAGE QUALITY (estimated at $6 per yd)	VERY GOOD QUALITY (estimated at $10 per yd)
3 YD FABRIC	$10 (see note below)	$18	$30
PATTERN	$2	$2	$2
FINDINGS (zipper, thread, buttons, miscellaneous)	$3	$3	$3
JACKET LINING (rayon crepe at $1.50 per yd)	$3	$3	$3
SKIRT LINING (rayon crepe at $1 per yd)	$1	$1	$1
INTERFACING (muslin at 40¢ per yd)	$1	$1	$1
TOTAL COST	$20	$28	$40

NOTE   Some extra yardage is allowed for straightening and preshrinking.

lightweight flannel, and the suit pictured in the sleek lines of worsted crepe may well lose its charm if it is made in a sturdy tweed. The experienced person is able to make a wise selection of fabric appropriate for the design, but the inexperienced person needs the help of the photograph and of the list of suggested fabrics on the pattern envelope.

Certain fabrics and textures, by their very nature, are easier to handle and will result in a more professional-looking finished product. The inexperienced person should have the advantage of this kind of fabric, and the experienced person will find her talents multiplied if she chooses a fabric responsive to tailoring requirements. In brief, the fabrics most adaptable to tailoring have the following characteristics:

1 **they are firmly woven** Loosely woven fabrics, particularly some of the novelty weaves with long floats of thread on the surface, present a problem of raveling and stretching.

2 **they are somewhat pliable** Although gabardines, men's suiting, and similar rather stiff worsted fabrics make excellent tailored garments in the hands of the professional tailor, they do not ease well, they are more difficult to shape over curves, and they reveal every flaw of construction.

3 **they have some surface texture interest** The matter of surface interest is an important consideration for the novice. A very flat fabric, such as the typical dress flannel, shows every little detail of construction. Design lines will be prominent (and this is an advantage), but at the same time every flaw, every stitch, and the slightest mistake in pressing will be magnified. By contrast, a fabric with surface interest (nubby weaves, tweed, many of the

novelty weaves) will hide flaws of construction.

4 **the color is in the middle range** To some extent, a fabric in a light color presents the same problems as a flat-surfaced fabric, so the choice of a flat-surfaced fabric in a light color is a serious mistake for the novice. The very light colors and white tend to reveal every flaw of construction, and if the fabric is relatively lightweight, every seam and hem edge shows through to mar the beauty of the design. Black and other very dark colors are discouraging to some women because they shine readily with improper pressing and tend to pick up lint during construction.

5 **they are of a medium weight** The very lightweight fabrics show every construction flaw, and unusually bulky fabrics are difficult to handle at the machine and present a problem of bulk in heavy seam areas. Medium-weight fabrics can be used for a greater variety of designs because most patterns are planned for "average" circumstances.

COLOR AND COLOR COMBINATION

The choice of color is a very personal consideration, and rightly so. Color has tremendous powers of flattery (to the personal coloring of the individual, to the mood and personality of the individual), and the advantage of its flattery should be used in an individual way. In other words, unless one is working professionally in the fashion business in a capacity that requires dressing in fashions of the current season, it is wise to favor flattering color over fashionable color; color is not a demanding component of fashion for most women. In fact, if the color is fashionable and not flattering, the choice is so obviously fashion-oriented that even the fashion advantage becomes a disadvantage.

The mood of a color or a combination of colors and the effect those colors have on the individual are of far greater importance than their fashion rightness. Women (and men) are sensitive to the moods of color, subconsciously if not consciously, in a way that has nothing to do with the personal flattery that color provides, and this sensitivity to color is more important than fashion to the success of a costume. The best color to choose, therefore, is one that is flattering and one that pleases the wearer, fashion be hanged! If the flattering and pleasing color happens to be fashionable, consider that a happy little bonus.

It is fortunate that color does not have the dictatorial impact on fashion that silhouette has because fashions in color tend to change more often and more abruptly than fashions in silhouette. They change so quickly that it is quite impossible to keep in pace with color fashions if the costume is worn more than one season. For this reason there is questionable advantage in choosing a color that is not flattering for the sake of fashion alone; the fashion color will not be in favor for the lifetime of the costume. Fashions in color are not as demanding as those of silhouette for another rather interesting reason. There is far less agreement concerning color among the fashion leaders themselves. This phenomenon of fashion can be readily seen by comparing the fashions

in *Vogue* and *Harper's Bazaar* for any given month; although there will be a certain similarity of silhouette in both magazines, it will not be surprising if one favors hot pinks and oranges throughout the issue, while the other features sea colors in pale, cool tones. Color is, indeed, a very individual component of fashion.

The inexperienced person who may not have confidence in her ability to choose color and color combinations wisely has many sources of inspiration and assistance. The survey of the current market and the study of current magazines and prestige advertisements, mentioned earlier in this chapter, will be of great help. Displays in the yard-goods department will be particularly helpful because many of these displays will be planned around a coordinated color and texture theme, selected by the professional buyer. Fabric manufacturers, ever sensitive to fashion and customer needs, are providing a great service by offering fabrics in a wide range of coordinated colors and textures.

DETAILS

The details of fashion add great interest to the costume, but like color and to some extent like texture, fashions in details are not truly demanding. In other words, in most cases details add interest because they are interesting in and of themselves, not because they are fashionable. A relatively small percentage of women are aware of the seasonal fashions in "little touches." These details, then, offer fertile opportunity for individual preference and creative expression. Details are usually involved with little techniques of construction and the choice of accenting decoration, and although these details are a part of fashion, they need not be confined to a particular fashion season. The discussion of details is limited in this chapter because ideas for interesting accents will appear throughout the book. For example, button ideas appear on page 125, details to add interest to the skirt appear on page 169, and ideas for little details for the jacket or coat lining appear on page 301.

Every fashion magazine will picture interesting ideas that can be borrowed for future use. The woman who sews at home would be wise to collect pictures of unusual and appealing ideas to serve as an inspiration for future home sewing. An "idea scrapbook" should include suggestions for texture and texture combination, color and color combination, and details, for these three components of fashion will not be quickly outdated.

THE LINING
AS A SOURCE
OF COSTUME
INTEREST

There is no easier way to add a touch of magic and a custom look to garments made at home than to choose exciting lining fabrics. The costume look, which adds so much in apparent cost with very little expenditure of money, is easily achieved by the clever choice and use of these fabrics. The suit with a matching blouse and jacket lining and the coat with a companion dress and lining are favorites of fashion largely because of the pleasant impact of the coordinated look. The success of these costumes is not automatic, however; the blouse and the dress must have substance of design and detail to keep pace with the tailored costume; an understated shift dress or a mere shell of a blouse can cheapen an otherwise attractive tailored garment. Lining fabrics that will match some other item of clothing must be chosen with

extreme care. If the lining and blouse or dress are made of a gaudy print or in a design of poor taste, the fact that the two match will call obvious attention to the costume and thereby defeat the purpose. However, that is just a word of warning and is not intended to dwarf the imagination; imagination (the ability to dare a little and dream a little) is an essential for successful wardrobe planning.

The costumes listed below are described in some detail as an aid to integrating many of the thoughts included in this chapter, while at the same time serving as a stimulant to the reader's imagination. Note that the brief description of the design lacks interest and personality and that the same colorless description can inspire an important costume. Note the surprise element mentioned below; the fashion surprise should not be disregarded, for adults like surprises as much as children. Because the lining is seen only momentarily, it provides excellent ammunition for the surprise attack.

plaid suit with jacket lining and blouse in matching plain fabric The fabric: wool in a looped mohair in salmon pink with a mere suggestion of soft brown threads woven in for a hazy, plaid effect. The lining and blouse: salmon pink in rayon faille crepe.

full-length coat with skirt to give a walking-suit effect with lining and blouse in polka dots The fabric: suiting-weight linen in navy blue for the coat and skirt. The lining and blouse: Whipped Cream crepe with a navy background and white coin dots for the coat and (for a fashion surprise) the same fabric with a white background and navy coin dots for the blouse.

summer print coat with lining and dress in coordinated colors The fabric: a cotton drapery fabric with a white background splashed with rich purple and green in a geometric print. The lining and dress: rayon crepe in matching green for the coat lining and (for the person with fashion courage) linen in a harmonizing periwinkle blue for the dress.

practical car-coat-and-slacks suit in plain color with a striking lining The fabric: "Madison Avenue" gray flannel. The lining: simulated fur in zebra stripes. To be worn with sweaters and jersey pullovers in red, green, black, white, gold, etc.

a basic suit for the office and a five-o'clock date with jacket lining and blouse matching The fabric: charcoal gray double-knit wool, worn with any number of colorful tuck-in scarves during the day. The lining and blouse: a rayon brocade in champagne or off-white. The blouse: a brief little bolero overblouse, just short enough to reveal a cummerbund in emerald-green velvet.

The woman who is inclined to be extremely practical often resists any suggestion of a lining that will limit the use of every blouse in her wardrobe. It is true that the interesting costume cannot be entirely practical, but nonetheless it can be planned with many practical considerations. To illustrate: The zebra-striped lining for the car coat described above is, on the surface, an impractical

selection, but the black and white stripe offers unlimited combination with plain-colored blouses and sweaters. Probably the most impractical costume described above is the printed coat in white with rich green and purple. And yet the coat can be worn with the periwinkle blue suggested or a harmonizing lime green, as well as matching green or purple and white. The cautious woman can choose a suit lining with design interest, and if the background is white, the costume can be practical because it can always be worn with white blouses.

The coat lining attracts more attention than the suit lining. In most cases the coat must be a more versatile wardrobe item, and the lining must be chosen accordingly. Many readers will want the advantage of a matching lining in the coat; it can be interesting as well as practical. The choice of satin, with its subtle sheen and highlights, will add interest and a look of luxury, and it need not increase the cost if it is made of one of the better rayon satins. The use of satin need not be confined to formal garments; a satin lining is in good taste in many tailored costumes with the obvious exceptions of those made in sturdy tweeds, typical man-tailored garments, and sportswear. Some satin crepes, designed especially for linings, have a small woven-in design that adds subtle interest to the matching lining. There are several construction details, described on page 301, which will add interest and apparent cost to the coat lining.

FOR ADDITIONAL INTEREST: THE COMPANION PIECE

Companion pieces offer fertile opportunities for the imaginative woman. The blouse or dress coordinated with a coat or suit is such a companion piece. The go-with piece might be a hat, a purse, a stole, a belt to match the blouse or skirt, or any number of other "little" items. The companion accessory, if it is right, is a brilliant addition to the costume, but if it is wrong, it brings the entire costume down with it. The reader is urged to use the companion piece with imagination, while realizing that such pieces must be added with caution and with consideration to the several issues discussed in the following paragraphs.

There is a certain danger that the costume will look "homemade" if too many pieces are coordinated. This exaggeration will serve to illustrate: A suit with a blouse to match the printed lining, worn with a hat and purse in the suit fabric trimmed in the blouse fabric and with gloves dyed to match one of the colors of the printed blouse, would shout "homemade." This costume would be smart with a matching blouse and perhaps a hat of the suit fabric. But that is all. The hat should be trimmed with something that harmonizes in color and texture (ribbon, a cluster of fruit, a feather) rather than the blouse fabric. Accessories made in a harmonizing or coordinated fabric (velvet with a soft woolen suit or a coordinated plaid with a plain-colored suit) are often wiser choices.

Some fabrics, because of color or color combination or design, create so much interest that they must be used sparingly. One can imagine that a ruby-red coat with a lining and matching dress in a bold print of rich reds and greens would be stunning worn with stark black accessories, and it is obvious that the same costume would be grossly overdone if, in addition, the print were used for a matching turban and pouch bag. Likewise, a tailored suit in a large,

bold plaid (bright red and black) is a delightful addition to the wardrobe, but the same active plaid in a purse and matching beret, worn with the suit, would not be smart. However, the same plaid accessories would be attractive used with a suit in basic colors.

The quality of the companion piece must keep pace with and even surpass the suit or coat if the resulting costume is to look truly professional. No one is fooled by the fabric envelope, trying to be a purse, and yet the same envelope stiffened and padded professionally would enhance a costume. The hat based on a buckram frame (available at nominal cost in most large department stores) will add dollars in apparent cost to the total costume, and by contrast, a limp little pillbox would cheapen the costume. Decorations for the hat should have professional appeal. Trimming the hat is a problem because most of the trimmings available in the department store are basically dress decorations. If there is a very large city nearby, it is wise to shop in a millinery supply store to find appropriate accenting touches.

The companion piece will be a successful addition to the costume only if it is something that is currently fashionable, is being done by the leading designers, and is being worn by well-known fashionable women. This illustration will clarify the preceding statement: Ordinarily one could say that a little triangle of matching fabric, pretending to be a hat, would not keep pace with a lovely costume. And yet for a few seasons in the early 1960s, the little triangular head scarf was very fashionable, and one Paris designer, in presenting his 1963 fall collection, topped the entire collection (including the wedding gown) with little triangles tied in interesting ways. It is wise to study the market and copy only those accessory ideas which are currently fashionable.

ABILITY
AND
EXPERIENCE
IN CONSTRUCTION

It is good fun to make plans with the rosy glow of fashion in the air. But part of the planning must be directed to such workaday matters as making the most of personal strengths and minimizing weaknesses in the realm of clothing construction, giving consideration to the special problems tailoring presents. Tailoring is very similar to dressmaking, but there is much more handwork involved, with a subsequent increase in time and patience required. On the other hand, tailoring, especially with wool, is very rewarding, so that very often tailoring proves to be more fun for many persons than dressmaking, and therefore seemingly easier.

If the reader lacks patience for precision work, the pattern for the suit or coat should have fewer construction details; the shawl collar cut in one with the body of the garment is much simpler to construct than the separate or notched collar; the sleeve cut in one with the body of the garment is easier to construct than the regulation sleeve; patch pockets do not present the difficult problems of the various set-in or welt pockets. In the main, Vogue patterns involve more complicated work than the patterns of the other companies. A very simple rule is this: In general, the more expensive the pattern, the more difficult the construction details. These matters deserve consideration, but the woman who sews must keep in mind that construction details and complications add to the "someone-cared" look and therefore to the smartness of the costume. She should set her sights high and try to increase her abilities with every new project, in hopes that she can reach a couturier level of workmanship.

Chapters 2 to 5 are concerned with costume planning, for they contain specific, technical directions for pattern and fabric selection. The first five chapters of this book provide a background of information that must be mastered before it is time for the exciting business of selecting a pattern and fabric.

EQUIPMENT
AND
FINDINGS

Much of the equipment used for tailoring can be found in almost any home. Such items as straight pins, needles, scissors, and a yardstick are familiar to everyone. The excellence of the tools of tailoring adds a great deal to the quality of the finished product. Usually the scissors that have served ordinary household uses are not adequate to cut fabric well, and the straight pins that have served the occasional household purpose are not as thin and sharply pointed as lovely fabrics require. Sometimes these familiar items must be replaced with equipment of higher quality. In the main, sewing equipment is not too expensive, but it is expensive enough so that most of us must acquire it over a period of years. Certain items are essential, but other specialized tools can be purchased as interest and ability in construction increase.

It is assumed that most readers will have had some experience in dressmaking before undertaking a tailoring project and that it is not necessary, therefore, to discuss most of the items listed below. A few items which might be new to some readers are discussed below the chart.

CHART OF EQUIPMENT

essential items	helpful items for later purchase
scissors with 5″ to 7″ blades	
tape measure	scissors with 2″ to 3″ blades
yardstick	shears
6″ ruler	L square
gauges	pinking shears
tailor's chalk	pin marker
¼ lb of silk dressmaker pins	silk pins
assorted needles	seam board
thimble	buttonhole attachment
steam iron	zigzag attachment
Magic Mending Tape or Scotch tape	
ironing board	
machine	
zipper foot	
sleeve board	
tailor's ham	

SEAM BOARD

The seam board is simply a board about 1 inch thick, pointed at one end and mounted edgewise on a wooden base. The narrow surface with the pointed end makes it possible to press hard to reach seams right up to a square corner. This piece of equipment is so simple that it can be made in the home workshop, or an excellent substitute can be made by simply covering a tightly rolled magazine with muslin from which all sizing has been removed.

TAILOR'S HAM

The tailor's ham is shaped somewhat like an egg and measures about 10 by 14 inches. It is indispensable for pressing darts and curved seams. Cushions in a variety of sizes are available in many notions departments, but the woman who sews can make her own with little time and effort. Cut two ovals in the desired size from heavy muslin or duck from which all sizing has been removed. Seam them together, leaving an opening of about 5 inches. Turn right side out. Stuff the cushion tightly and smoothly with small scraps of wool or sawdust. Whip the opening edges together.

PRESS MITT

The press mitt is similar to, but smaller than, the tailor's ham and is made to slip over the hand. It too can be made at home, but it is inexpensively priced in most notions departments.

MAGIC MENDING TAPE

This tape will be used in pattern alterations to replace pins. It is very convenient to use; lines can be drawn over it with no difficulty, and the altered pattern will fold back into the envelope smoothly and easily. Scotch tape can be used, but it is not as easy to work with, and it will not take a pencil or pen mark. For the sake of brevity, directions in this book read "Scotch-tape this edge," but the Magic Mending variety should be used.

FINDINGS
AND
SUPPLIES

Findings and supplies for the tailored garment will be listed briefly on the envelope back of the pattern. They should be purchased at the same time the pattern and fabric are purchased to avoid unnecessary delay when work has begun. The findings will be familiar to most readers, although they may be put to new uses. The following brief discussion will be helpful to those readers who are making a first tailoring project.

THREAD

Many authorities recommend the use of silk thread for the structural seams of a wool costume because of the strength of silk. The author does not consider that silk thread is necessary and has found that mercerized thread works very well. If the reader would like to use silk thread, she must realize that the cost will be much higher because each spool of silk thread contains fewer yards than a spool of cotton thread. In the school laboratory situation, if silk thread is used in the tailoring class and cotton thread in other classes, the tension adjustment of both the bobbin and the top thread of the machine will have to be changed constantly; under laboratory circumstances, it seems wiser to use mercerized thread. However, the luster of silk thread is highly desirable for topstitched details and for stitching the lining if the fabric is silk or a very sheer fabric.

It is wise to purchase one spool of silk thread in a contrasting color to use for basting edges preparatory to pressing. If a basting thread must remain in the fabric during pressing, there is a danger that a heavier thread will press into the fabric, leaving little marks that are sometimes difficult to remove; the elasticity and fineness of silk basting thread will prevent this.

BUTTONHOLE TWIST AND BUTTONHOLE GIMP

In a mannish-tailored garment such as a blazer, the buttonholes will be hand-worked, in which case buttonhole twist is used for the hand stitches. Buttonhole

gimp, which is a cordlike thread, is required as a padding under the stitches to give the worked buttonhole a professional look as well as to provide the strength to withstand hard usage.

Very frequently the pattern will call for buttonhole twist for use in sewing on buttons. This heavier thread is most desirable if the tailored costume is made of very heavy fabric and/or is planned for hard service (such as a reefer in heavy tweed). However, if the fabric is light to medium in weight and if it is obviously a decorative rather than a serviceable costume, mercerized thread is preferable for this purpose.

Buttonhole twist is recommended frequently for topstitched details because the very thickness of the thread makes the stitching more prominent and the high luster of the thread adds a desirable accent.

COTTON-TWILL TAPE

This tape is firmly woven, is available in black or white, and comes in a variety of widths to serve many functional purposes. In the tailored garment it is used to strengthen and reinforce seams and areas that will receive hard wear. The ideal width is $\frac{1}{4}$ to $\frac{3}{8}$ inch. The choice of color is not an issue in most medium-weight, firmly woven fabrics and becomes important only in lightweight, loosely woven fabrics, where there is a danger of the color showing through; in extreme cases the white tape must be dyed to match the color of the interfacing or the garment. Cotton-twill tape shrinks a considerable amount, and therefore it must be washed in soap and hot water, dried, and pressed. The tailored coat will require approximately two 3-yard packages of twill tape. One 3-yard package is usually sufficient for a suit.

SHOULDER PADS

Fashions in shoulder lines make up one part, and an important part, of the silhouette picture. And because fashions in silhouettes are the most demanding, the issue of shoulder lines and shoulder pads becomes an important one. During World War II, the wide and square shoulder fashions ushered in shoulder pads that were all of 1 inch thick; the pads were essential to the success of the costume, and good ones were very expensive. In the years since 1950, and to the present time (1968), a natural shoulder line has been fashionable, and the shoulder pad has all but disappeared. The manufacturers of shoulder pads are constantly concerned with fashion, and as a result, shoulder pads available on the market are of a size and thickness to meet the current fashion needs. The woman who sews must be concerned with fashion in every detail. When shoulder pads are fashionable, she must be similarly concerned with the selection of the correct pad. If the pad plays a leading role, she must recognize its importance and be willing to spend more money for the right pad.

Shoulder pads serve many purposes, so that a pad may well be needed in those years when pads are not required by fashion. One purpose of the pad is to assure a smooth foundation on which the garment will hang. Persons with bony shoulders may need a thin pad to smooth the shoulder line. The pad can serve as a camouflage for shoulders that are too sloping or too narrow. Many persons have one shoulder higher than the other, and if the difference is extreme, extra padding can be added to the underside of one pad to compensate for the lower shoulder.

There are two basic styles of shoulder pads—square and round. See Figure 1. The square pad has a sharply defined angle at its outer edge. It is used for all garments with the usual set-in sleeve and regulation armhole. The round pad is smoothly molded and rounded at its outer edge. It is used for any garment which does not have a regulation armhole; for example, it is the correct choice for raglan sleeves, sleeves cut all in one with the body of the garment, and sleeves with a dropped armhole seam.

There are four sizes of shoulder pads; each is available in the round or square style. The size is determined by the amount of space the pad covers on the body and the thickness of the pad. See Figure 1. The sizes are blouse, dress, suit, and coat, and the amount of space the pad covers on the body and the height of the pad increase from blouse to coat. Blouse and dress pads are covered with fabric, usually white or black, and need not be covered with the fabric of the garment unless the addition of a nice touch to the inside of the garment or a better effect in a sheer garment is desired. Suit and coat pads are not covered with fabric because they are used in lined garments only.

Notice that all the pads except the coat model cover a triangular area on the body. Coat pads are made with a squared line in front and the usual diagonal line in back. This square shape in front allows the pad to cover a greater area, filling in the hollow between the shoulder and the bust for a smoother, better-tailored effect.

Shoulder pads vary greatly in price,

from a nominal cost of less than a dollar to several dollars in seasons when a padded shoulder line has fashion significance. A great deal of the success of the garment depends on the shoulder line, and a good pad will provide a professional-looking shoulder line. It is well to select inexpensive pads for utilitarian garments and to buy better pads for the more significant wardrobe items. Certainly the time, effort, and money that go into the making of a suit or coat justify the added expenditure of a well-made, smooth pad.

NOTE If a pad is to be used, it must be purchased at the time the pattern and fabric are purchased. It will be used for the fitting of the muslin copy and for every subsequent fitting on the jacket or coat.

ZIPPER

The traditional length of the skirt zipper is 7 inches, and in most cases this will be the length recommended on the pattern envelope. Some of the pattern companies suggest a 9-inch zipper for some utilitarian garments because the additional length will allow the woman with a small waist and larger-than-average hips to slip the skirt over her hips as she dresses; the 9-inch length, then, is recommended for practical purposes only. The woman with average waist and hip measurements can slip a skirt over her hips if it has a 7-inch zipper, so there is no advantage in the 9-inch zipper for the average figure.

We are accustomed to seeing a 7-inch zipper, and the 9-inch length (on any figure but the very tall one) looks very long. The total costume will look more attractive with the shorter zipper, even if it means that the skirt would have to be slipped on over the shoulders. So the 7-inch length is the appropriate choice for those costumes which are more

decorative than functional, while the longer length is acceptable for purely functional garments.

FINDINGS FOR THE WAISTBAND

The waistband construction recommended in this book is different from that suggested by the pattern and will require some findings that will not be listed on the pattern envelope. Before

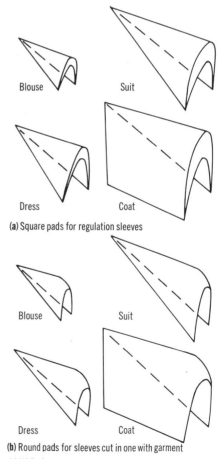

(a) Square pads for regulation sleeves

(b) Round pads for sleeves cut in one with garment
FIGURE 1

purchasing the fabrics and findings for the suit, it might be well to read through the waistband directions on page 201 for a better understanding of the supplies needed. The waistband will be stiffened with a strip of heavy Pellon (belting can be used if one prefers a waistband with exaggerated stiffness), and the underside will be finished with decorative ribbon, rather than the usual thickness of wool. The ribbon should be purchased in the width of the desired finished width of the waistband (probably about 1 inch). The ribbon can be grosgrain in a color matching the skirt or the lining fabric, or it can be one of the decorative ribbons with a woven-in design harmonizing in color and texture with the skirt and/or the lining. The ribbon will not be visible except to the wearer as she dresses, so this is a good opportunity to have some purely private fun with the costume.

RAYON BIAS SEAM BINDING

The pattern will probably recommend seam binding to finish the hemline of the skirt. Some skirts and most jackets and coats have linings attached to the hem of the garment. Because no raw edges are exposed, seam binding is not required for most skirts made by these directions. If the skirt has a pleat, some raw edges will be exposed, and seam binding will be used to finish them. Before the shopping trip, it would be well to glance through the directions for the skirt, paying particular attention to finishing the pleat edges (page 214). The finished skirt is pictured in Figure 57 on page 215; because the seam binding will be involved with the skirt fabric and the lining fabric, it could match either of

them. If the skirt fabric is a plain color, it should match that fabric, but there are circumstances under which it might better match the lining. For example, if the skirt is a black and white check and the lining is red, red seam binding would be a wiser choice than either black or white.

In some skirts and coats, the lining is hemmed separately and is not attached to the lower edge of the garment; in this construction, raw hem edges must be finished. This construction is used in garments with style fullness, and as an economy of fabric, the lining has less style fullness. Study the instruction sheet of the pattern selected to determine which method of construction is used. If the lining is free from the skirt or coat at the lower edge, rayon bias seam binding will be used to finish the garment hem, and if the lining fabric is heavy, rayon bias seam binding will be used to finish the lining hem.

NOTE The Hong Kong finish, described on page 149, is an attractive new way of finishing edges. If this finish is used, the rayon bias seam binding is not required; bias strips of lining replace the seam binding.

BUTTONS

It is not wise to purchase buttons on this first shopping trip. The choice of buttons for the jacket or coat is one of the most important decisions to be made, and careful testing should be done beforehand. Certain decisions can be made when the muslin copy is finished, and will be discussed later. More accurate decisions can be made when the garment has been basted together; testing out button ideas at that time will result in a far wiser choice than one could make on this first shopping trip. The issues involved with button selection appear on pages 125 to 129.

This metal chain is tucked under the edge of the lining of the finished skirt, jacket, or coat to add desirable weight to the garment. Although it is inserted in such a way that it is supposedly invisible, it does "peek out" as the jacket is slipped off, so that it adds a professional touch to the costume. Additional weight is the larger issue; weight may be required for the garment made of dress-weight woolen or for the jacket made for a person with rounded contours as an aid to creating smoother lines. These chains (in a choice of two weights) are available in notions departments for a nominal cost.

PATTERN SELECTION

Consistency of pattern size is of greater concern to the customer than any other characteristic of the pattern. Fortunately the administrators of the pattern companies are aware of this, and the major houses make consistently sized patterns (consistent within the companies themselves and consistent with sister companies) because these major companies base sizing standards on identical body measurements.

SIZING STANDARDS

The Measurement Standard Committee of the Pattern Fashion Industry has established standard body measurements which have been adopted by all the major pattern companies (Butterick, McCall's, Simplicity, and Vogue). The advantages of consistent sizing are so numerous that all the major companies cooperate with each other to make consistent sizing possible. The minor companies did not take part in the committee decisions but educators and customers alike continue to hope that they will adopt the sizing standards in the near future.

Each pattern company has a dress form in one size of each figure grouping, and each of the dress forms are made to specifications of the measurement standards of the pattern fashion industry. Each company makes a basic pattern to fit the standard dummy, and because the companies who conform to the standard are working on dress forms of identical size, the resulting basic patterns are remarkably alike. Since the basic pattern is the foundation for all the designs in the collection, all patterns of all major companies are remarkably consistent in size. The woman who sews may be assured that when her pattern size and figure type are established, all designs from companies using measurement standards of the pattern fashion industry will give comparable results. Furthermore, she may be sure that the pattern alteration required on one pattern will be correct for patterns from other companies who conform to the established standards.

the sizing change effective in January, 1968
Prior to January, 1968 all the major houses sized patterns consistently by using Government Bureau of Standards measurements. The Bureau's measurements were such that the customer usually required a pattern one size larger than she wore in ready-to-wear and this resulted in some confusion. What is more, the customer was hesitant to order a size 14 pattern when she thought of herself (and preferred to think of herself!) as a size 12, her size in ready-to-wear. In order to make pattern sizes correspond more closely to ready-to-wear sizing, a sizing change was initiated in January, 1968 and all designs appearing after that date have been made with standard body measurements developed and approved by the pattern fashion industry; with this

change the customer will probably wear the same size in a pattern that she buys in ready-to-wear. *wrong!!!*

comparison of "new sizing" and the former sizing based on bureau of standards measurements The new sizing does not result in an appreciable difference in fit. A comparison of new sizing measurement charts with those on an old pattern will reveal that body measurements are very much alike and that the main difference is that the measurements have been given a different and smaller size "tag." The customer will continue to buy dress, blouse, suit, and coat patterns by her bust size but, for example, she will find that a bust size of 34, formerly requiring a size 14 pattern, will require a size 12 if that pattern appeared after January, 1968.

There are a few changes in measurements but they are not extensive. Waist sizes in the new sizing are somewhat smaller. In Misses', Women's, and Junior figure types, hip measurements are slightly smaller (about ½ inch) in some sizes. Figure types remain the same with one exception: the former Teen, Pre-Teen, and Sub-Teen figure types have been replaced with one new figure type; it is called the Young Junior/Teen Figure type and is labeled "new size range" within a red circle. The "new sizing," labeled within a red box, is used for designs for the fashion minded group (the Young Junior/Teen age group and older), whereas the sizing of Men's and Boys' patterns remains the same; likewise Toddlers', Children's, and Girls' sizes have not been changed.

problems of the transition period During

the years 1968 and 1969 (when patterns sized by former standards and those sized with the new sizing standards will both appear in counter catalogs), *the customer must be especially careful to buy patterns according to her bust size.* The new sizing appears in a red chart in the catalogs while the former sizing is shown in a blue chart.

SLIGHT DIFFERENCES IN SIZING OF PATTERNS FROM DIFFERENT COMPANIES

FACTORS THAT DETERMINE SIZE

1 **body size** Body size is consistent in patterns from all the major companies because it is based on measurement standards established by the pattern fashion industry. *This is, however, the only factor of size controlled by measurement standards.*

2 **amount of livability (room to move and live in)** Each garment needs more size than mere body size to allow for action in each part of the body. This component of size is not decided by standard measurements (it differs too much with the costume) but is left to the discretion of each designer. Her opinion might differ from that of another designer, but it differs amazingly little. All designers must be, by training and because of their artistic talent, good judges of (a) the amount of livability allowance required for action and movement and (b) the amount of extra size required for attractive, becoming fit. One designer might think 6 inches is the appropriate amount

of allowance for livability at the bust of a semifitted suit, while another might favor 5½ or 6½ inches; their opinions differ so slightly that one is truly unaware of differences as a garment is worn.

The amount of livability allowance, particularly in the bust area, varies greatly in different types of garments (a) because some garments need to look larger to give the proper effect, (b) because garments are put to different uses, and (c) because of the variety of other garments over which they will be worn. The following is a list of average amounts of livability allowance recommended for the bust area by most designers and is included as an aid to understanding the issue of this component of size:

1 For a sleeveless dress, about 2 inches
2 For a fitted dress with sleeves, about 4 inches
3 For a blouse, from 5 to 8 inches
4 For a fitted suit, about 6 inches
5 For a semifitted suit, from 6 to 7 inches
6 For a boxy suit, from 7 to 9 inches
7 For a coatdress, from 6 to 9 inches
8 For a coat, a great variation from a minimum of about 8 inches to as much as 12 inches and even more

The reader must understand that these are generalities because fashion influences even this very functional matter of sizing. To illustrate: In some seasons the fitted dress is more closely fitted than in others, and a boxy coat may be quite trim in one season and become a "greatcoat" in another.

3 **style fullness** All garments must have the two factors listed above. Some garments have yet another component, style fullness. Style fullness is the extra size or fabric needed to make the garment look a certain way; it is obvious in such

features as the gathered skirt, the bat-wing sleeve, and the peg-top skirt. This component of size differs greatly from design to design, and each designer must judge the amount of fullness required for each particular design. This factor, more than any other, makes it seem that patterns differ in size. But each is based on the same body size, and if the customer buys her proper size she will be assured of the proper amount of livability and the ideal amount of style fullness, both decided by a talented designer.

RELIABILITY
OF
PATTERN
SIZE

Patterns are reliably sized, but it is perhaps understandable why a customer might have doubts about sizing that seem to be well founded. There are several reasons:

1 She may know very well that she has always worn patterns in size 12 and that they fit perfectly as long as she cuts them ½ inch wider at the side edge. She may not realize that a ½-inch addition may make the difference between one size and the next larger size and that the pattern in the correct size would fit better in many little ways than an altered pattern.
2 She may have been wearing her clothing too tight because her standards are not as educated as those of the trained designer. In other words, she may have been "stealing" some of the livability size and using it for body size. The livability amount at the bust of a fitted suit is about 6 inches, in the opinion of experts, but one could "get into" the suit if her size were 2 inches larger than the pattern. The suit would be judged a poor

fit by an expert because it would have only 4 inches of livability, but the inexperienced person might be satisfied with it.
3 She may have, perhaps without realizing it, always made garments with a great deal of style fullness, such as the shirt-waist, which is a popular beginning project. If considerable style fullness is involved, one can steal enough of it to make an additional 4 or 5 inches of body size. Stealing style fullness for body size is a serious mistake; there must be style fullness to give the design the character for which it was selected. But again an unknowing person might be honestly unaware that she had not achieved the proper effect.
4 She may have changed in size since she made the last garment; the size change may be an overall one, or it may be a change in distribution of flesh. Many women are unaware of gradual weight changes. It is advisable to take new body measurements before cutting each garment if there is any possibility of figure change.

THE TRUE TEST
OF PROPER SIZE
AND
FIGURE TYPE

The only accurate test of proper size and figure type is to make a garment with a dart-fitted bodice, regulation set-in sleeves, and a straight skirt. All the large pattern companies offer a basic pattern of this description. Such a basic dress, made in muslin or any inexpensive fabric, is a wise choice as a first project. This is a good test for size and figure type, required pattern alterations, and fitting requirements. When the best solution is attained, the customer can buy that size and make those alterations on any pattern from the major pattern houses.

FIGURE TYPES AND STANDARD MEASUREMENTS AS ESTABLISHED BY THE PATTERN FASHION INDUSTRY

Size is but one consideration; proper fit will result only if the pattern is purchased in the correct size and in the proper figure type. The pattern fashion industry has established several types of figures, and patterns in these figure types are offered by all the major companies. Selection of the best figure type is a more difficult matter than determination of correct size, and some experimentation will be necessary. Ready-to-wear is similarly typed into figure groups, and the figure type that is the best fit on the ready-made market will probably be right in a pattern too. A description of several figure types follows.

JUNIOR

Figure about 5'5", with high bust, quite well developed, and shorter-waisted than misses.

standard body measurements

Size	5	7	9	11	13	15
Bust	30	31	32	33½	35	37
Waist	21½	22½	23½	24½	26	28
9" Hip	32	33	34	35½	37	39
Back waist length	15	15¼	15½	15¾	16	16¼

JUNIOR PETITE

Figure about 5'1", fully developed, but small-boned and diminutive, and shorter-waisted than juniors.

standard body measurements

Size	3JP	5JP	7JP	9JP	11JP	15JP
Bust	30½	31	32	33	34	35
Waist	22	22½	23½	24½	25½	26½
7" Hip	31½	32	33	34	35	36
Back waist length	14	14¼	14½	14¾	15	15¼

MISSES

Figure about 5'6", fully developed, and longer-waisted than juniors. Misses sizes are planned for the average figure.

standard body measurements

Size	6	8	10	12	14	16	18
Bust	30½	31½	32½	34	36	38	40
Waist	22	23	24	25½	27	29	31
9" Hip	32½	33½	34½	36	38	40	42
Back waist length	15½	15¾	16	16¼	16½	16¾	17

WOMENS

An extension of the misses type cut in sizes for the larger, more mature figure; normal waist length.

standard body measurements

Size	40	42	44	46	48	50
Bust	44	46	48	50	52	54
Waist	36	38	40½	43	45½	48
9" Hip	46	48	50	52	54	56
Back waist length	17⅜	17½	17⅝	17¾	17⅞	18

HALF SIZES

Figure about 5'3", fully developed, but shorter in all ways than misses and womens; narrower shoulders and wider hips (compared with bust) than misses.

standard body measurements

Size	12½	14½	16½	18½	20½	22½	24½
Bust	35	37	39	41	43	45	47
Waist	28	30	32	34	36½	39	41½
7" Hip	37	39	41	43	45½	48	50½
Back waist length	15¼	15½	15¾	15⅞	16	16⅛	16¼

The major pattern houses offer a limited collection of somewhat basic patterns in proportioned lengths for short, average, and tall figures. The yardage charts state yardage differences for the three heights, and the pattern includes pattern pieces for each figure. It sounds like a wonderful idea, and indeed there are some advantages. However, the solution to problems of height is not as simple as these patterns would lead one to believe. These patterns are based on the assumption that a tall figure is tall in every portion of the body and that a short figure, similarly, is short in every way. Unfortunately, this is not true. A woman might be 6 feet tall, but her torso might be short; the short girl might have a longer torso than her 6-foot friends. Such cases are too frequent to be ignored. The proportioned pattern should be tested on the figure. A short person might well discover that she should use the average-length jacket, the longer sleeve, and the shorter skirt.

TO SELECT
AND PERFECT
THE CHOICE OF SIZE
AND FIGURE TYPE

1 Take bust, waist, and hip measurements over a slip and the undergarments you usually wear.

Blouses, dresses, suits, and coats are purchased by bust size (regardless of even very large hips). Separate skirts, slacks, and shorts may be purchased by either waist or hip size.

There are two exceptions to this general rule, which might make it advisable

to buy one size smaller than bust size. (*a*) The small-boned person with small shoulders and a full bust should buy the smaller pattern and then alter her pattern, as described on page 97, to compensate for her larger-than-average cup size. (*b*) The diminutive person might prefer a "greatcoat" in a size smaller than her bust size indicates; a coat cut with exaggerated fullness tends to engulf the slight figure, in which case it is advisable to steal some of the style fullness for body size.

2 Read the description of the figure types and select the one best describing your figure. A complete listing of figure types, and often a word description, appears in the back pages of the counter catalog.

3 Ideally, choose a basic dress for a first project as an aid in testing size, figure type, and pattern alterations. Perfect your sizing decision by keeping records of pattern alterations: Were they right? What should be done next time? Try another size or figure type if that seems advisable. With careful records, one should be established in the correct size and figure type by the second and certainly by the third project. It is assumed that the person undertaking a tailored garment has tested size previously and is quite sure of her size and figure type.

SELECTION
OF
PATTERN

It is well to survey the fabric offerings of the season and the store for inspiration before selecting the pattern or, if desired, to choose the pattern and get fabric inspiration from it. It is advisable for a novice to leaf through several counter catalogs, even if the experienced person may well go directly to her one favorite catalog. All customers should read the information in the yardage chart and any word description that might appear with the fashion sketch for a more accurate appraisal of the design. The ambitious person should select a design that will challenge her abilities —something new in construction details that will involve new learning.

The customer is allowed to examine the pattern envelope and instruction sheet before purchase, and she should request to do so. Although she cannot remove the paper pattern from the envelope, she can look over the instruction sheet and, by studying it and the information on the envelope back, can make a more informed purchase.

TERMS USED TO DESCRIBE TAILORED GARMENTS
One of the following terms will appear close to the fashion sketch and the pattern number in the counter catalog and will appear as a heading for the brief description of the design on the pattern envelope. The consumer tends to overlook these terms or, if she sees them at all, to misunderstand their implications; this mistake can result in a costume that is not sized properly. The differences between these tailored garments are involved with the amount of size allowed for livability (see point 2 on page 22). A suit requires a greater amount of livability allowance than a dress, and a coat requires more than a suit. With this thought in mind, the implications of these terms become evident.

suit-dress A costume so labeled is cut larger than a dress but smaller than a suit. Being dresslike in character, it should be made of dress-weight fabric or lightweight suiting, and although it might be made of medium-weight suiting, it would not be successful in a coating. The suit-dress is not intended for use with a blouse; it might be worn with a mere shell of a blouse, but it could never be worn over a sweater. It is not wise to buy a suit-dress pattern if the garment is to be used as a suit.

suit The suit is cut larger than a suit-dress but smaller than a coat. Most suits are designed for suiting-weight or medium-weight fabrics (except the car coat and its relatives) and would not be truly successful made of a coating. Most suits are designed to be worn with a blouse or lightweight sweater, but, except for the car-coat type of jacket, are not sized large enough to be worn with bulky sweaters.

coat-dress This garment, intended to lead a double life, is cut larger than a dress but much smaller than the conventional coat and is therefore designed to be made of medium-weight fabric, comparable to the typical suiting. It will serve as a coat if it is worn with very lightweight dresses, but it will not truly lead the double life its name implies because it is not sized large enough for wear with winter-weight dresses or sweaters and skirts. In order to lead a double life, it is sized slightly larger than is ideal for a dress. It is not wise to buy a coat-dress pattern if the garment is to be used as a coat.

coat The coat, which is sized larger than any of the others, is just what its name implies. It is designed to be made of heavier-weight suitings or any coating fabric and can be worn over almost any dress or medium-weight sweater. Not all coats are sized to be worn over heavy suits, however.

It is very important that the customer look for these descriptive terms because the differences in these garments are not necessarily evident in the fashion sketches. A suit-dress and a suit (and a coat-dress and a coat) will look strikingly similar in the illustrations.

THE ENVELOPE FRONT

The inexperienced person should select one view of the design as shown on the envelope front and carry it through without variation. The experienced person often decides to use this feature of one view and that of another, but if so, she should understand the subsequent problems of yardage, cutting, and construction. If a pattern can be perfectly matched in plaid, it will be pictured in plaid in at least one view on the envelope front, and the novice who wishes to use plaid should buy only a pattern so pictured.

THE ENVELOPE BACK

The line drawing on the back of the envelope reveals structural lines of the design more clearly than the fashion sketch. A word description will appear on the envelope back; it should be read carefully because it will reveal those features difficult or impossible to distinguish on the sketch. It might state that the design is a suit-dress rather than a suit or that the shoulders are slightly dropped or that the pocket is a simulated one. A scale drawing of the pattern pieces will appear on the envelope back or on the instruction sheet. To the experienced person, the pattern pieces reveal difficulty of construction and estimated time requirements. The novice can gain some help simply by using the number of pattern

pieces as a guide; in general, few pattern pieces (six instead of a possible twenty or more) indicate ease and speed of sewing. The number of markings (dots, notches) on the pattern is a criterion for judgment also. The notions and findings are listed on the back of the envelope. Notions should be purchased at this time; quite apart from the obvious saving in shopping trips, it is very discouraging to be in the mood to sew and to lack supplies needed. Appropriate fabrics for the design are listed on the envelope back under "Suggested Fabrics." The person with developed taste will not need this help, but the novice or the person who is not confident of her taste will find these suggestions invaluable. Special notes appear on the back of the envelope; such information as "Napped fabrics not suitable" or "Diagonal weaves not suitable" can make all the difference between success and failure.

One very important note appears on many patterns; it reads, "Extra fabric is required for matching plaids and balancing large design." Each plaid or large design, by size or nature, requires a different amount of extra fabric for matching purposes; the pattern company could not give a yardage amount that would be right for all the plaids or designs that the thousands of customers might choose. Therefore, the chart states the amount of fabric required for cutting the pattern pieces, and the customer must figure the extra amount required for matching her particular plaid. Figuring yardage for matching plaid is discussed on page 33.

The words "with or without nap" appear in the yardage chart. Fabrics with nap are those, like corduroy or velvet and napped woolens, which show shading differences when worn unless all pattern pieces are cut in the same direction. In general, such a layout requires more yardage. A more detailed discussion of napped and pile fabrics appears on pages 32 and 33.

THE YARDAGE CHART

The yardage chart is based on four factors which determine the amount of yardage required: (1) the view chosen, (2) the size of the pattern, (3) the width of the fabric, and (4) the nature of the fabric (napped, plaid, one-way design, etc.). The yardage chart is reliable, but a word of warning is necessary. Sometimes the customer must figure her own special yardage requirements; this is necessary for true accuracy because of some individual pattern alterations (additions in length, extreme additions in width), because of the special nature of the fabric, or because the fabric comes in a width not included in the yardage chart. Chapter 4 is devoted to the figuring of special yardage requirements. Information in that chapter should be studied before the fabric is purchased; if problems are encountered, a special layout must be made to avoid expensive mistakes *before the fabric is purchased.*

ASSISTANCE FROM THE STORE PERSONNEL

The staff in the pattern and fabric departments are willing to answer the customer's questions, but it is unfair to expect too much of a salesgirl's time. More than that, it is not wise to ask important questions of someone who may or may not be experienced and reliable. Customers tend to think that every girl in the fabric department is an expert in home sewing; some are truly expert, but others are not. Probably most customer questions are involved with figuring special yardage amounts (the very problems discussed in Chapter 4), and there is no quick, easy answer to any of them. The experienced salesgirl will confess that she does not know for sure but will offer to make an educated guess. As the customer learns more about home sewing, she will ask fewer questions of strangers and at the same time will learn to rely with confidence on the talented members of the sales staff. The best solutions to problems of home sewing can better be found through careful study of scientific information available in textbooks written by professionals.

FIGURING
SPECIAL
YARDAGE
REQUIREMENTS

There are many circumstances under which a special cutting layout must be made and special yardage requirements figured for the individual costume: (1) when fabric will be chosen in a width not stated on the pattern, (2) when two patterns are combined to make one costume or when features of two different views of the same pattern are combined into one, (3) when sections of the pattern are to be made in contrast not planned for on the pattern, (4) when the pattern is to be altered more than an inch or so in length or increased a substantial amount in width, (5) when pile or napped fabric is to be used with a pattern that does not include yardages for those fabrics, and (6) when estimating the extra amount of fabric required to match a specific plaid.

It takes such a small amount of time and effort to make a special layout that will result in accurate and economical yardage requirements that it is a foolish economy of effort to guess at yardage amounts for the special circumstances listed above. The economic advantage of the carefully executed special layout may result from a saving in the yardage (for the shortened pattern or for fabric in a width wider than the widths stated on the pattern) or from having enough but not too much extra fabric (for the lengthened pattern, for pile or napped fabrics, or for matching plaid). It is always a careless and costly mistake to guess at yardage requirements for special problems, and the mistake becomes more serious as the price of fabric increases.

GENERAL
DIRECTIONS
FOR MAKING
THE LAYOUT

The layout can be made in the school laboratory or in the home by methods very similar to those used in the yardage department of the pattern company. There the layout artist works on very long tables, marked off with crosswise lines in ⅛-yard divisions and with lengthwise lines denoting all the various fabric widths. Pattern pieces are placed down in various positions to determine the most economical arrangement, after which the total measurement (yardage needed) is recorded.

See Figure 1. With the relatively short table in the home situation, one may have to do certain sections of the layout, record that amount of yardage, and then start over again. Use yardsticks to mark off the appropriate width of fab-

ric or Scotch-tape a piece of string in the desired position on the table. Assume that one edge of the table is the lengthwise or crosswise fold. Place the pattern pieces on the table as economically as possible, observing "place-on-fold" and "straight-of-material" lines. Experiment for the best solution. It is well to study a pattern layout in a comparable width and view for a suggestion of arrangement and to study it again when the new layout is completed to see that all pattern pieces have been included and that each piece has been placed down the correct number of times.

Figure 1 pictures a small tabletop set up twice—once for certain sections to be cut on a lengthwise fold and again for certain portions to be cut on a crosswise fold. When all pieces have been placed on the table for the lengthwise fold, measure the edge of the table for the amount of fabric that segment of the layout will require. Then remove the pattern pieces and place down the remaining pieces for the crosswise-fold segment.

A word of caution: The measurement for the crosswise-fold segment must be doubled because the fabric will be folded over for a double thickness, thus requiring twice the length.

For example, if the pattern pieces take up 1¼ yards of table space on the lengthwise-fold layout, 1¼ yards will be required for that portion of the pattern. However, if the pattern pieces require 1 yard of table space for the crosswise-fold layout, twice that amount, or 2 yards, will be required for that segment. The total amount of yardage required would be 3¼ yards.

NOTE Make a rough sketch of the layout to be used during cutting.

FOR A FABRIC WIDTH NOT GIVEN ON THE PATTERN

The general directions given above should be followed for this special problem. One bit of advice: If the fabric is a few inches wider than any yardage listed on the pattern, the wise consumer will make a new layout, for although the extra width may not save any yardage, it is truly surprising how much yardage can sometimes be saved (depending on the shape of the pattern pieces) by the addition of a few inches in width. Many woolens are being made in 58- and 60-inch widths, rather than the traditional 54-inch width, and although many patterns give yardages for these wider widths, a majority of them do not at this time; the saving in length if 60-inch fabric is used can be as much as ½ yard in some patterns.

FOR COMBINED PATTERNS OR COMBINED VIEWS

The general directions given on page 30 should be followed for these special problems, but extra caution must be used in checking the finished layout. No one layout on the pattern will serve as a guide

for checking to be sure that all pieces have been placed on properly; you must check your own work very thoughtfully.

FOR SECTIONS IN CONTRAST

The general directions given on page 30 should be followed for this problem. One mistake is commonly made in cases of this sort (see the sample layout in Figure 2). For example, if the front facing and upper collar are desired in contrasting fabric, most persons would lay out the two pieces to determine the amount of contrasting fabric required, but many would neglect to make a new layout for the remaining pieces and would buy the amount of fabric stated on the pattern for the main body of the suit. This is a costly mistake. Note that if the upper collar and front facing are removed from the layout, the under sleeve may fit into the position where the front facing is pictured, in which case the under collar could be moved into a position opposite the jacket side, possibly resulting in a saving of ¼ yard of fabric.

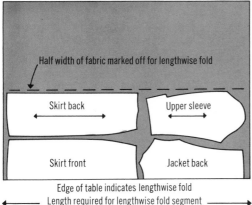

Half width of fabric marked off for lengthwise fold

Skirt back

Upper sleeve

Skirt front

Jacket back

Edge of table indicates lengthwise fold
← Length required for lengthwise fold segment →

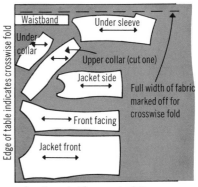

Edge of table indicates crosswise fold

Waistband

Under sleeve

Under collar

Upper collar (cut one)

Jacket side

Full width of fabric marked off for crosswise fold

Front facing

Jacket front

Length required for crosswise fold
← segment (must be doubled) →

FIGURE 1

FOR PATTERNS TO BE ALTERED A SUBSTANTIAL AMOUNT

Refer to Figure 2 below. Extra fabric for increases in length or a saving in fabric for the shortened pattern (even if changes in length are substantial) can be estimated in most cases by studying the layout to be used, without making a special layout. For example, assume that the suit in Figure 2 must be lengthened 2 inches in both skirt and jacket length. An additional 2 inches will be required in four positions on the layout (for the skirt pieces, for the jacket back, for the jacket front and the front facing, and for the jacket side). Therefore, an extra 8 inches or ¼ yard (9 inches) must be purchased. No special layout is required, and this kind of problem can be worked out in the store as soon as the pattern is purchased. Figuring the yardage for a shortened pattern is done in a similar manner. However, some layouts are arranged in such a way that this simple method could not be used with accurate results, and if the layout is unusually complicated, the pattern should be altered, after which a special layout should be made, using directions given on page 30.

Problems resulting from a substantial addition in width cannot be figured with accuracy by this simple method, and in these cases the special layout is required. Refer back to Figure 2 and note the space between the two skirt pieces. There is no way to determine exactly how much space is there by looking at the sketch; it may vary from ¼ to 1 inch or even more. It so happens that there is usually an extra inch between pattern pieces (thanks to the law of averages), so problems seldom arise if an extra ½ inch is added to each side edge. *But this is not always true.* Certainly if an inch or more will be added to each side edge, the pattern should be altered, after which a special layout should be made. In the pattern pictured in Figure 2, pattern pieces would have to be arranged quite differently, and undoubtedly more fabric would be required if the widened skirt pieces did not fit side by side on the same length of fabric.

FOR NAPPED OR PILE FABRICS

These fabrics have a different appearance and color if all pieces are not placed on the fabric in one direction (with the upper edge of all pattern pieces toward one end of the fabric); these fabrics require a one-way layout. If the layouts on the pattern have not been planned for napped or pile fabrics, it is probable that some pattern pieces have been laid in

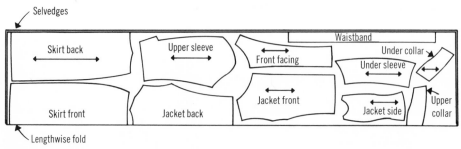

Selvedges

Skirt back · Upper sleeve · Front facing · Waistband · Under collar · Under sleeve · Skirt front · Jacket back · Jacket front · Jacket side · Upper collar

Lengthwise fold

FIGURE 2

opposite directions because they fit more economically in that arrangement; therefore, in most cases the special layout will require more fabric. Refer back to Figure 2. Note that the upper edge of most of the pattern pieces is placed toward the left end of the fabric—only the skirt pieces and the upper sleeve face in the other direction. This layout cannot be used for napped or pile fabrics until certain changes, which will require a special layout, are made. Some of these changes cause no problems, and a special layout is not needed. For example, the two skirt pieces can be turned around; they will fit into the same space and will create no problems. However, the position of the upper sleeve in the sample layout creates the need for a new layout. It appears that there is not sufficient width to turn that piece around. One possible solution is to move the under sleeve into the area where the upper sleeve is pictured and to change the position of the waistband, thereby obtaining what seems to be sufficient width for the upper sleeve. However, because the upper sleeve is longer than the under sleeve and because space must be found for the waistband, more fabric may be required; a special layout is needed. This example illustrates the value of following a layout on the instruction sheet for the size, width of fabric, and view to be used and of changing only those pieces which must be changed.

NOTE Other fabrics need a one-way layout also —any fabric with a one-way design, uneven plaids, and many of the simulated furs.

FOR PLAID FABRICS

Plaids are woven in even and uneven designs. An even plaid is one in which the four quarters of the design are identical, so that the design is the same when viewed from either end of the fabric.

An uneven plaid is one in which the four quarters of the unit of design are different. Therefore, the uneven plaid requires a one-way layout like that used for napped or pile fabric. If the plaid to be purchased is an uneven one, the first step in figuring yardage amounts is to make a one-way layout, according to the directions given above. If the plaid is an even one (the far wiser choice for the inexperienced person or for the first plaid costume), any layout on the instruction sheet can be used.

The yardage stated on the pattern (or the yardage as figured in a special layout) is the amount of fabric required for cutting the pattern pieces in the proper position, but does not include allowance for matching the plaid design. It is quite impossible for the pattern company to state the extra yardage needed for matching purposes because the extra amount is dependent on the size of the design unit in a particular plaid. For example, the amount required for matching a plaid with a 2-inch unit would be approximately half that required for matching a plaid with a 4-inch unit. Even when one knows the size of the unit in the plaid to be used, it is not possible to estimate the extra fabric required with absolute accuracy before the pattern is placed on the fabric. However, a reasonably accurate estimate can be made by working with the particular size of the design unit on the particular layout to be used.

Refer back to Figure 2. Each time pattern pieces are placed on one area of the fabric (in the sample layout the skirt pieces are placed on one area, and the upper sleeve and jacket back are placed on another), there is a chance that extra fabric will be required for matching. And at the very left end of the layout, as the first pieces are placed down, there is a chance that fabric will be lost as a result of locating the plaid unit in the desired position on the skirt pieces. So count the spaces between the areas, including one at the left end, for the number of times extra fabric might be required; in the sample layout, the total number is five. Each time there is a possible need for extra fabric, the amount required might be almost as much as the size of the plaid unit. Therefore, if the plaid unit is 3 inches, it is possible that almost 3 inches will be lost five different times. However, it is not at all likely that the maximum amount of fabric would be lost each time; sometimes the pattern will fit on in such a way that no fabric will be lost. The law of averages makes this a good rule to follow: *Figure the maximum amount that might be needed for matching and then buy about half that amount of extra fabric.* In the example given above, 15 inches (5 times 3 inches) is the maximum amount, and so, with average luck, 7½ inches should be sufficient; therefore,

¼ yard (9 inches) of extra fabric is a good educated estimate.

This illustration serves to point out that the amount of extra fabric for matching purposes is dependent on the number of pattern pieces (the number of spaces between areas on the layout) and on the size of the design unit.

There are other problems of matching plaids that cannot be solved before the fabric is purchased, and these problems may result in a need for still more extra fabric. The estimates above take into account matching the crosswise lines on the plaid. But it is impossible to predict the problems that might arise as a result of matching the lengthwise lines until the actual pattern pieces are placed on the fabric. For example, in the sample layout in Figure 2, the design unit should be centered in the center position (directly down from the shoulder position) of the upper sleeve. But without knowing the exact width of the two pattern pieces located in that area of the layout, it is impossible to be sure that the design can be centered on the sleeve in the space available. Problems of this sort may result in the need for a considerable amount of additional fabric.

NOTE Specific rules for laying pattern pieces on plaid can be found in many books on dressmaking; directions are given in detail in Bane, CREATIVE CLOTHING CONSTRUCTION.

FABRIC
SELECTION

The scope of this book does not include a study of textiles, although an understanding of the textile fibers and fabrics and their characteristics is essential to the consumer. It is assumed that the reader has taken the suggestions in the Preface and has armed herself with a fundamental knowledge of textiles from a recent and reliable source.

A REVIEW
OF WISE
BUYING
PRACTICES

REPUTATION OF THE STORE

Knowing the reputation of the store or merchant is the first step toward making any wise purchase. The store that stands in back of its merchandise with a sound refund policy is the only store in which an inexperienced person should shop. These merchants play a fair game, placing their reputations behind even the smallest purchase. Unfair practices exist in every business, and the fabric market is no exception. For example, there are some specialty shops where fabric is rewrapped on empty bolts to gain the advantage of information on the end of the empty bolt; in one typical case, a wool-nylon blend was wrapped on an empty bolt which read "100 percent virgin wool." Obviously, this merchant is known for his low prices. Large department stores would not jeopardize their nationwide reputations with malpractices of this sort; their future depends on continuing business. But the small merchant, especially in a city location, can make a reasonable profit on transient sales alone. The person who knows textiles well can shop anywhere with safety; the inexperienced person would do well to stay on the beaten path to the department store.

INFORMATION OF THE BOLT

Information on the end of the bolt of fabric includes a statement of the fiber content by percentage, and of finishes used, a statement of width, and often other information ("Drip-dry," "Permanent press," "Needs little or no ironing," "Less than 1 percent shrinkage," etc.) that is most helpful to the consumer. In addition, there is often a hangtag which gives suggestions for care and other pertinent information. The customer should check the width of fabric herself from the statement on the bolt; the salesgirl can make the human error of stating a width incorrectly.

EXAMINATION OF FABRIC

The customer has every right to examine fabric carefully; the wise buyer examines the entire length of fabric before it is cut from the bolt. Flaws in weaving or dyeing can occur without the knowledge of the merchant who purchased from a re-

liable fabric company. Loose threads on the underside are no disadvantage usually, but they do suggest an inspection of the area from the right side. If fabric has been on display in or near a window, evidences of sun fading may appear. Fabric left on display shelves for long periods of time may show age with dust or fading at the fold or selvedge edges. The customer must be cautious, the more so during clearance sales, for it is just such damaged goods that carry the more attractive prices at that time.

TENTERING AND FINISHING PROBLEMS

The process of tentering, which is rather like blocking curtains on a stretcher, should result in a fabric with lengthwise and crosswise threads in perfect right-angle position. The quality of the tentering process varies from excellent in many of the high-quality fabrics to very poor on some inexpensive fabrics. A variation of 1 inch from selvedge to selvedge is considered acceptable to most fabric finishers. See Figure 1 as an aid to understanding problems of tentering.

Fabrics that *have not been given one of the easy-care finishes* can be straightened, but they require effort and often result in a loss of yardage. If a poorly tentered fabric has been cut rather than torn from the bolt, the customer must buy extra yardage to compensate for the subsequent loss. Unfortunately, poorly tentered fabrics are often cut from the bolt (even those which could be torn with safety) because cutting makes the poor quality of tentering less evident. But the wise customer can learn to judge the quality of tentering before a purchase is made. If she can see the weave at all, she will sense the direction of the crosswise threads; they should be very close to a right-angle position, as shown in Figure 1a.

The matter of straightening poorly

tentered fabrics is complicated by various finishes which might have been applied to the fabric, and unfortunately these finishes are not always mentioned in the information given on the bolt. Many of the easy-care features we insist on today are a result of finishing processes which are heat-set at high temperature after the fabric is tentered; *the result is that the position of the lengthwise and crosswise threads is permanently locked in position, and fabrics so treated cannot be straightened.*

Although it is not possible without laboratory tests to be absolutely sure that one of the heat-setting treatments has been used, a few generalities may be helpful. High-quality all-wool fabrics are not usually so treated, whereas fabrics made of a combination of wool and nylon or wool and orlon and fabrics made of 100 percent nylon or orlon are more frequently treated. If the information on the end of the bolt states that the fabric is washable and will require little or no pressing (permanent press) or will retain crease lines well, it has been given one of the heat-setting treatments.

If the fabric was tentered off grain and if a heat-setting finish was then used, the finished fabric is locked into position and cannot be straightened. This is no great disadvantage in plain colors

(as long as the fabric gives visual satisfaction) because the fabric will not change with wear or dry cleaning and will hang properly during its lifetime. However, if the fabric is a woven plaid, the crosswise stripes will not be at right angles to the lengthwise stripes and cannot be straightened into the right-angle position required for matching. This condition is evident before plaid fabric is purchased; if a stripe on the upper layer of the folded fabric lies directly over the same stripe on the lower layer, the fabric is perfectly tentered and can be matched. If, however, the stripe on one layer angles off even a slight amount ($\frac{1}{2}$ inch), the fabric cannot be straightened, and the plaid cannot be matched properly. *It is well to confine the purchase of plaids and crosswise stripes to 100 percent wool fabrics, which have not usually been given the heat-setting finishes.*

Figure 1 pictures bolts of fabric as they appear in the store. Note the direction of the crosswise threads to see the variation from the proper right-angle position. The sketches show fabric which has been cut; if fabric has been torn

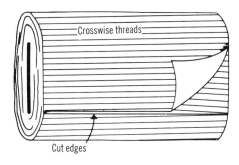

(a) Acceptable standard—fabric tentered with about a 1-inch variation from selvedge to selvedge

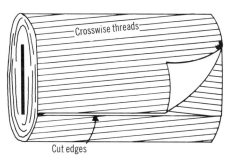

(b) Poorly tentered fabric with an off-grain variation of several inches

FIGURE 1

from the bolt, the direction of crosswise threads is more evident. Figure 1a shows fabric which meets an acceptable standard of tentering, with perhaps a 1-inch off-grain variation from selvedge to selvedge, while Figure 1b pictures fabric poorly tentered, with perhaps a 4- or 5-inch variation. The fabric shown in Figure 1a is a wise buy, providing:

1 It is a good-quality 100 percent wool, which has probably not been given a miracle finish, because it can be straightened into perfect position.
2 It is in a plain color in any fabric, because if the fabric has been given a heat-setting finish and cannot be straightened, it will hang well for its lifetime.

But this fabric is a poor purchase in plaid or a crosswise stripe or design if it has been given a heat-setting finish.

The fabric shown in Figure 1b, if it varies as much as 5 inches, is not truly a wise buy under any circumstances. If it has been locked into this position with the application of an easy-care finish, it is a poor buy because it will not give visual satisfaction, even in a plain color. If, however, it is 100 percent wool (with no claims of easy care), it probably can be straightened into proper position. If the fabric is inexpensive, a customer might decide to buy it, but she must realize that she will lose some yardage (the amount of the variation as she straightens this fabric) and that it might require professional blocking before it is ready for cutting. She must add the cost of an extra ⅛ yard of fabric and the possible cost of professional blocking (approximately 50 cents per yard) to the

original cost of the fabric. She may well decide it is wiser to put the extra money into better fabric.

EXTRA FABRIC FOR STRAIGHTENING AND PRESHRINKING

If fabric is poorly tentered, it must be straightened (see page 54), a process which will decrease the yardage by the amount of off-grain variation. If that variation exceeds 2 inches, the customer would be wise to purchase an additional ⅛ yard of fabric to compensate for the loss.

One of the great advantages of sewing at home is that fabric can be preshrunk before the garment is made, thereby ensuring adequate size and length for the lifetime of the garment. Preshrinking adds cost to the garment (1) because of the possible loss of yardage which must be compensated for, (2) because of the time required to do the process at home, and (3) because of the expense (about 50 cents per yard) of having fabric professionally preshrunk at the cleaners. In every case this is time and money well spent, an economy in the long run. Preshrinking at home is very tedious and time-consuming and, in most cases, will not meet the standards of the professional cleaners; it is wise to have preshrinking done by the reliable professional. Fabric carrying the label which reads "No more than 2 percent shrinkage" should be preshrunk for best results. Two percent of 1 yard is about ⁷⁄₁₀ of an inch; that means the average skirt could shrink about ½ inch. This amount is not great and is probably nothing to worry about in quickly constructed, staple garments, but such a loss would be very disappointing to the discerning person if the costume were an important one.

Wools which carry a label stating that they have been preshrunk may shrink somewhat when pressed or cleaned; again the amount of shrinkage is limited, but the demanding customer would be wise to ensure her investment in time and money by spending the additional 50 cents per yard to have the fabric put through the cleaning process.

Preshrinking is absolutely essential for both fabrics in the lined garment. In the lined garment, two fabrics must act as one; preshrinking will make this possible. It is entirely possible that the lining might shrink in the crosswise direction, while the fabric for the garment might shrink in the lengthwise direction; in such a case, the professional dry cleaners could not prevent, and should not be blamed for, the disastrous results in a completed garment.

It is impossible to state the exact amount of extra fabric required for preshrinking purposes because each fabric will respond in a different manner. An estimate of an additional ⅛ yard for a 3-yard length of fabric should be sufficient for most fabrics of average to high quality. Less expensive fabrics or loosely woven fabrics or crepes will probably shrink more than high-quality, firmly woven fabrics.

Specific directions for preparing fabric for preshrinking appear on page 55.

APPROXIMATE YARDAGES FOR BASIC GARMENTS
Although the wisest and most economical way to buy fabric is to buy the amount stated on the pattern (in other words, to buy the pattern and the fabric on one shopping trip), many persons like to buy fabric lengths to be used at future times. This is not really wise and certainly cannot be entirely safe, but there are times (sales or buying trips abroad) when it would be well to have a few estimates as guidelines. The reader who likes to buy ahead would be wise to make a little chart of estimated yardages,

based on her size, including several widths of fabric. A few minutes with a pattern catalog would enable her to make a simple little chart which she could carry in her wallet at all times. A chart similar to the one shown below, listing the kinds of garments she will probably make in the future, would be brief, workable, and as accurate as an estimate could be.

	35″	39″	45″	54″	60″
long-sleeved blouse					
sheath dress with sleeves					
straight skirt					
basic suit					
basic coat					

SELECTION OF MUSLIN FOR THE TEST COPY

Because of the expense and time that go into the tailored costume, a test copy of the jacket or coat (and for some figures, the skirt) is made in muslin to test pattern alterations, to solve problems of fitting, and as practice for new and difficult construction details. Muslin is traditionally used for test or sample garments because it is inexpensive, is firmly woven, and can be purchased in several weights.

The most important consideration in the selection of fabric for the test copy is the matter of suitable weight and body. The weight and character of the test fabric should be similar to those of the fabric to be used in the garment. The muslin for a skirt or suit jacket should be medium to heavy in weight; the muslin for a coat should be heavy in weight, and if the fabric to be used is especially thick and heavy (a true coating), muslin may not be heavy enough and a lightweight canvas, pillow ticking, or duck would be a better choice.

Muslin can be purchased in a bleached (pure white) or unbleached condition (somewhat yellowish). The unbleached type is recommended for use in test copies because it is less expensive and serves the purpose as well. Muslin is so inexpensive that there is no need to do a special layout to figure yardage amounts. Make a generous estimate of yardage (there are many uses for leftover pieces—interfacing, underlining, etc.). These estimates, based on 36-inch fabric, should be ample: for a skirt, 2 yards; for a suit jacket, 3½ yards; for a full-length coat, 5 yards.

Other firmly woven fabrics, similar in weight to the fabric to be used for the garment, may be used. In addition to duck, ticking, and canvas for use in coats, fabrics similar to heavy percale, Indian Head, and Tarpoon Cloth may be used for the suit jacket or skirt. If a more decorative fabric is used, the test copy may possibly, but not always, be made up into a serviceable garment; for example, the sample coat made of attractive ticking might be made into a housecoat. However, the reader must understand that she may need to cut into the test copy if unusual fitting problems arise and that it may not be in condition to be used later. The use of these more expensive fabrics is not recommended; unbleached muslin is the wisest choice under most circumstances.

SELECTION
OF
WOOL
FABRIC

Many issues involved in the selection of wool fabric have been discussed in preceding pages. Before studying the specific suggestions given below, review Chapter 1, pages 1 to 12; Problems of Yardage Requirements, pages 29 to 34; Wise Buying Practices, pages 35 and 36; and Tentering and Finishing Problems, pages 36 to 38.

SPECIFIC SUGGESTIONS

After the costume has been planned and the choice of fabric narrowed down to several possibilities, the following points should be considered before the ultimate choice is made:

1 Check the information on the end of the bolt for a statement of fabric width. Although most wools are woven in the traditional 54-inch width, it is dangerous to assume that every wool will be 54 inches wide. Many imported wools on the current market appear in quite unusual widths. For example, some homespuns from Scotland, which carry an attractively low price tag, are made in a 27-inch width, and twice the amount of yardage stated for 54-inch fabric will be required; challis, a dress-weight woolen, is usually imported and is woven in 36- and 42-inch widths; and many French imports are woven in 50- to 52-inch widths. Likewise, domestic woolens vary in width; many are woven in a 58-inch width, and the 60-inch width is becom-

ing increasingly popular. If the width of fabric varies from the widths stated on the pattern (wider or narrower by even a few inches), a special layout should be made; see Chapter 4.

2 Check the information on the end of the bolt for a statement of fiber content. The very best wools are 100 percent virgin wool, but on the other hand, some poor-quality fabrics are also made of virgin wool. In making a judgment of fabric, it is well to consider the fiber content and also the cost per yard (in a reliable store) for an indication of quality. Usually high-quality fabrics of 100 percent virgin wool have not been given a heat-setting finish, which means that they can be straightened into perfect position for cutting.

Many of the man-made fabrics (nylon, orlon, etc.) can be given an appearance similar to wool but will usually be less costly. These fabrics will not respond as well to tailoring, but they do have many excellent qualities, and many are almost as attractive as a fine worsted wool. These fabrics have often been given a heat-setting finish. They cannot usually be straightened if they have been poorly tentered, but they will have easy-care advantages, and they are non-allergenic.

3 Test the effect of all possible fabric choices before a mirror by holding a length of the fabric to the figure. The sales staff will not object to this; rather, they expect the customer to experiment and will, if time permits, help drape fabric on the figure in lines comparable to those of the design chosen. This test provides an opportunity to check the effect of color on the complexion and the effect of design on the figure. Study the effect of various possible choices in the mirror at close range and also at some distance; the effect of design is sometimes quite different when viewed from a greater

distance. If fabric is held to the figure in lines similar to the design lines to be used, the effect of weight and thickness of fabric can be studied as well.

4 Before making a definite decision, it is well to survey the market for other fabrics that will be a part of the total costume. Any contrasting fabric required, such as the lining fabric and companion blouse and dress fabrics, should be considered at this time. It is unwise to buy a tweed in tones of plum and red, no matter how lovely, without being sure that harmonizing colors are available in go-with fabrics.

5 If there is hope of using an accessory of a particular color (a favorite hat, a jeweled pin), the accessory can be taken to the store for study with the fabric, or a sample of the fabric can be tested with it at home before the final purchase is made. Likewise, if the fabric will require new accessories in unusual colors, a sample of the fabric should be tested with items in other departments. A successful costume is a result of careful consideration of all its parts, and no important matter should be left to chance.

SELECTION OF LINING FABRICS

NOTE Most of this section is devoted to the traditional lining fabrics used for suits and light-weight coats. Linings for added warmth are discussed on page 44.

Review Chapter 1 at this time, paying particular attention to the suggestions for adding costume importance with linings and companion pieces on pages 10 to 12. A descriptive chart of lining fabrics and appropriate uses appears on page 45.

SPECIFIC SUGGESTIONS

The effect of fabrics for linings and companion pieces must be tested for color and design with the wool fabric, as suggested in the preceding section. In addition, the following issues must be considered:

1 The following general rule of selection is an extremely important one: *Select a lining that will be subordinate to the fabric of the garment*—lighter in weight and of a softer hand so that it will not dominate the character of the costume. The wool suit or coat should look and act like wool; for example, if a lightweight wool were lined with a stiffer, heavier lining, the resulting costume would take on the character of the heavier and stiffer of the two fabrics. By this rule, taffeta is a poor choice for the lining of most costumes, and yet many women buy taffeta because they have seen it used so frequently in ready-to-wear costumes. Taffeta is used by the ready-to-wear industry not because it is ideal for the purpose but because it is inexpensive and easy to work with under manufacturing conditions.

EXCEPTION TO THE GENERAL RULE If the lining is to serve the additional purpose of acting like an interfacing to build out a silhouette (the A-line skirt), then it must have the dominant character of taffeta, etc.

2 The lining fabric should be pleasant to the touch—a smooth, soft fabric, whether it is silk, cotton, or rayon. The feel of the lining is important in skirts, jackets, and coats, and the smooth, somewhat slick lining gives a more pleasurable sensation than one with a fuzzy, sticky surface.

The lining fabric, ideally, should not be rough and fuzzy so that it will hang freely on the body. The skirt lining must not adhere to a girdle or a slip, and the jacket or coat must slip on easily over any fabric or sweater that might be worn with it. For this reason, the smooth and slick man-made fabrics, especially rayon, make excellent linings. Cotton and silk sheath-lining fabrics tend to cling more readily.

3 The lining should keep pace with the total garment in wearing qualities. Replacement of the lining of the jacket or coat and of the skirt (lined like a jacket) is possible, but it is a time-consuming process that might better be avoided. It is a foolish economy of time and money to buy a low-quality lining that will shred and pull out at the seams in one season of wear. The thin, sleazy sheath lining offered at minimum prices on the market is acceptable for lightweight garments, but will not withstand the kind of wear given to the typical tailored garment.

A good test of wearing qualities can be made in the store before purchase. Scrape a fingernail hard against the threads near the cut or torn edge at the end of the piece; then hold the fabric up to the light to see whether the threads have shifted and separated noticeably. If the threads have shifted out of line to any great extent under this kind of pressure, the fabric will not wear well and is not worth the time and effort that go into the tailored garment. This test will make the shortcomings of the sleazy sheath linings obvious; a slightly more expensive crepe will withstand the test much better.

4 The lining fabric must keep pace aesthetically with the garment. The obviously cheap lining is a very expensive mistake, for if the lining cheapens a $50 suit to the $25 level (and it can do just that), the lining is not economical but is expensive indeed.

The aesthetic and durable qualities of the lining become more important when there is to be a companion piece to match. A blouse or dress requires a higher-quality fabric than might otherwise be used for the simple lining; in this case it is better to favor the companion piece when making fabric choices. When a companion piece is involved, the fabric must be durable enough to withstand the most severe wearing conditions because the weaker link of the costume will limit the value of the stronger link.

5 If the lining is to be of a contrasting color or in a design of several colors, the color may show through loosely woven fabrics, especially if they are light in weight and color. The darker color of a print underneath a lightweight fabric in a light color may cast a muddy, spotty appearance over the garment.

NOTE The complete interfacing or underlining, discussed in connection with the construction of the skirt and jacket or coat, solves this problem. The addition of an extra layer of supporting fabric under the wool will prevent lining colors from showing through, and therefore lining possibilities are increased.

6 The lining fabric must be sufficiently heavy in weight to hide the raw edges and construction details inside the jacket or coat. These unattractive details will show through lightweight fabrics more readily; light-colored linings should be placed over the fabric to test the effect.

7 If the lining is to control stretch (as in the straight skirt), put pressure on the fabric in both lengthwise and crosswise directions by pulling it firmly against the hands. Pebbly crepes, although attractive in a jacket or coat, will stretch more readily than more firmly woven, flat fabrics.

8 The lining fabric should be of a quality that will assure visual satisfaction and durability, but it need not be expensive. For example, rayon crepes cost far less than silk crepes, and many are very attractive. Silk has a certain prestige value, and some persons like it because it is pleasant to the touch, but a silk lining greatly increases the cost of the tailored garment. If economy is an issue, it is probably wiser to put additional money into quality fabric for the garment and to buy a high-quality lining in one of the man-made fabrics; in these fabrics, the highest quality will cost less than the least expensive silks.

In matters of quality and beauty, the cost should increase as the importance of the lining increases. If there is a companion piece involved and if it is an important addition to the costume, a high-quality fabric is a wise and economical choice. A higher-quality, more durable fabric is required for the lining of the coat, which must withstand hard wear, than for the lining of a theater suit, which will have limited wear. If the jacket will be removed often, it must give more visual satisfaction than the lining of the suit-dress because the jacket will not be removed.

9 The skirt lining need not match the jacket lining, and although it must be as durable, it need not be as beautiful and may therefore be less expensive than the

jacket lining. Perhaps there is a certain pleasure for the wearer as she dresses if all linings match, but a less costly skirt lining is a wise economy and is recommended if the jacket or coat lining will be expensive.

10 The lining must serve a functional purpose, but one must guard against choosing a fabric that is so practical and functional that it becomes uninteresting. Linings can be replaced (the lining patterns should be saved for the lifetime of the tailored garment), and perhaps an unusual, even impractical, lining is the wisest choice if it provides the perfect accent. What is more, a new lining can give renewed zest to the costume, and many women will enjoy having a change in a few years. The author has recently replaced the shocking-green lining in a favorite navy-blue suit, which is now in its sixth year, and the new lining in a new color makes it seem brand-new.

SUITABLE LINING FABRICS

If the lining serves the functional and aesthetic purposes discussed above, there need be no other limitations on choice. For example, the lining can be cotton if it is smooth and silky, as many of the fine cottons are, and Whipped Cream is an excellent choice, especially if there is to be a companion piece that will be laundered.

EXTRA FABRIC FOR THE HONG KONG FINISH

The Hong Kong finish, a novel method of finishing seams and hems in skirts and unlined jackets and coats, requires the use of matching bias strips of lining to replace the usual seam binding. A unique way of finishing inner edges of front and neck facings makes the finish adaptable to the lined jacket or coat. Directions for finishing seams and hems appear on page 149, and directions for finishing facing edges in lined garments are given on page 325.

It would be well to study those pages at this time and to decide now whether this method will be used; extra lining fabric will be required if the Hong Kong construction is chosen and will not be required for traditional construction methods. Because of the very delicate nature of the finish, piecing seams in the bias strips must be avoided whenever possible. Ideally, the bias strips should be almost a yard long; ¾ yard of extra lining fabric would provide enough extra strips to bind all seams in a skirt, do the skirt hem, and finish the jacket and facing edges with a minimum of piecing. If, however, the skirt and jacket linings are different fabrics, about ¾ yard of each will be required.

LININGS FOR ADDED WARMTH

The winter coat, which must give protection against wind and severe temperature, can be "winterized" by using an interlining (an additional thickness of inexpensive cotton or wool fabric) or a lining fabric with special features for additional warmth. The true interlining is seldom used because of the greater ease of construction afforded by the combination lining fabrics discussed below.

For warmth without weight, fabrics with a Milium backing are the choice of many women. The satin face of these fabrics is very attractive and does not reveal the shiny aluminum back. The effectiveness of this lining as compared with the conventional lining is difficult to judge. Consumer reaction is colored by the freedom from bulky linings and the subconscious thought that it is supposed to be warmer; scientific tests have given varied results. This is the only special lining fabric that is sufficiently light in weight to be combined with medium-weight (suiting) fabrics.

All other fabrics for added warmth will very definitely give noticeable warmth, but they are all thick and therefore can be combined with only heavy-weight (coating) fabrics. Any conventional lining fabric can be quilted to an extra layer of interlining fabric at home. A limited number of quilted fabrics is available on the market. Depending on the quality of workmanship, the quilting process can greatly enhance the fabric. Sun Bac satin looks like a lovely satin on the face, but has a wooly backing which adds great warmth. Both of these linings will add noticeable bulk to the garment; the garment will seem perceptively

smaller after the lining is inserted, and allowance must be made for its additional thickness. Extra allowance for the thickness of fabric must be made when fitting the muslin test copy.

SELECTION OF SUPPORTING FABRICS (INTERFACING, UNDERLINING, BACKING)

The supporting fabrics play a backstage role in the tailored garment, but they are, nonetheless, so important to the to-

APPROPRIATE LINING FABRICS

	LIGHTWEIGHT FABRICS	MEDIUM-WEIGHT FABRICS	HEAVY-WEIGHT FABRICS
	wool crepe, dress-weight woolens, linen, suitings in cotton, silk, or man-made fabrics	any wool suiting or coating in medium weight, velvet, corduroy, upholstery fabric	heavy tweed, camel's hair, the true coatings, simulated fur
FOR SKIRTS	sheath lining in cotton or man-made fabrics, China silk, lightweight crepes	high-quality, heavier-weight sheath lining in silk or man-made fabrics, satin-back crepe, lightweight satin, taffeta (for purposes of supporting silhouette only)	same as for medium-weight skirt
FOR JACKETS	lightweight crepes in silk or man-made fabrics, smooth cottons, satin-back crepe, lightweight satin	satin-back crepe, lightweight satin	satin-back crepe, lightweight satin, satin with Milium backing, brocade, quilted lining fabrics, Sun Bac satin
FOR COATS	same as for jacket listed above	satin-back crepe, medium to heavy satin, satin with Milium backing	satin with Milium backing, heavy crepe, crepe-back satin, medium to heavy satin, brocade, quilted lining fabrics, Sun Bac satin, simulated fur

tal costume that the selection of the fabric and the construction details involved with the use of these fabrics make up a large part of any tailoring book.

The supporting fabrics serve many purposes: (1) to control stretch in the entire garment or in those portions which must withstand the greatest wear, (2) to add extra body to the fabric of the entire garment or to add body to certain portions of the garment, (3) to act as a cushion to bulky seams, and (4) to add sufficient body and stiffness to support unusual silhouette lines.

The one consideration that is of greatest importance in the selection of these fabrics is that of subordination versus domination. *The supporting fabric must be, in almost every circumstance, a fabric subordinate in weight and body to the fabric of the garment; it must add body without changing the character of the fabric selected for the garment.* The one exception to this rule has to do with the need to support silhouette lines which stand away from the body, possible only with a dominant interfacing; under these circumstances, the dominant interfacing is used in only that portion of the garment where support is required. For example, the exaggeratedly rounded hipline must be supported, but only the peplum area of the suit or coat would require the dominant interfacing, and a subordinate supporting fabric would be a wiser choice for all other areas of the garment. One thickness of the supporting fabric should be tested with one thickness of the wool chosen, and the two together should have essentially the same appearance (the same character) as the wool alone.

EXPLANATION OF TERMS USED ON THE PATTERN

There is some confusion concerning the terms used to designate the supporting fabrics; this is understandable, for the purposes of these fabrics overlap one another and often one fabric can act as an interfacing or as an underlining or backing or, to add further confusion, as a combination of both. Originally, the word "interfacing" meant a supporting fabric to be used in certain portions of a garment that would receive the greatest wear and require the greatest body—in other words, *an "interfacing" fabric was used to make a partial interfacing.* In recent years, the advantage of adding extra body to the entire garment has brought other terms into use—"underlining" and "backing." *These terms are used most frequently to describe an interfacing-like fabric, usually lighter in weight than the conventional interfacing, used to add some body to the entire garment.* In brief, then, "underlining" and "backing" are interchangeable terms used for the supporting fabric in a complete interfacing while "interfacing" is the term used for the supporting fabric in a partial interfacing. The terms "complete interfacing" and "partial interfacing" will be used in the discussion in this book.

METHODS OF CONSTRUCTION

Three methods of construction used for supporting fabrics are evaluated in detail in Chapter 12. Read pages 218 to 223 at this time and study the entire contents of Chapter 12 before selecting the method to be used and the supporting fabric that will be a wise choice. The pattern company may recommend one of several methods, whereas the reader who is experienced (or who has the benefit of an instructor) may prefer another method to serve her specific purposes. The following are brief statements of the recommendations in Chapter 12. Method 3 (although different from the method suggested by most patterns) is the wisest choice of construction for most tailored garments. Method 2 is preferred for full-length straight coats because it will create less bulk; method 2 is excellent for other similar problems as well. Method 1 (which is the original method of interfacing) is not recommended for high-quality garments, but is quite acceptable for "quick and easy" utilitarian garments. The fabric chosen for the complete interfacing (method 3) in a jacket or coat should combine the features of the conventional interfacing and those of an underlining or backing in that it should be heavier than the usual underlining or backing fabric and slightly lighter in weight than the traditional interfacing fabric.

DESCRIPTION OF SUPPORTING FABRICS

Supporting fabrics with sufficient body to be used for the partial interfacing and

to be used as a combination interfacing-underlining for the complete interfacing are listed below. Most of these fabrics are available in a variety of weights and grades.

unbleached muslin   This is an inexpensive, versatile cotton available in many weights. Muslin is an excellent interfacing even though it is the least costly of all.

sections of used sheets and pillowcases These household linens are made of a fine percale or a high-quality bleached muslin and are versatile in that the center sections, which have had more wear, will be of a softer hand than the edges, which may possibly have retained most

APPROPRIATE SUPPORTING FABRICS

	LIGHTWEIGHT JACKETS AND COATS	MEDIUM-WEIGHT JACKETS AND COATS	HEAVY COATS
FOR PARTIAL INTERFACING	lightweight muslin lightweight hair canvas Armo: green selvedge	medium-weight muslin medium-weight hair canvas Armo: blue or yellow selvedge	heavy-weight muslin wool hair canvas Armo: yellow or red selvedge
FOR COMPLETE INTERFACING (to be used as a combination of interfacing and underlining)	lightweight muslin percale in colors	medium-weight muslin percale or Indian Head in colors wool hair canvas	heavy-weight muslin Indian Head in colors
FOR UNDERLINING OR BACKING (to add small amount of body to entire garment, to be used with an additional partial interfacing)	Super-Siri Si Bonne Undercurrent in medium-soft finish in colors voile or organdy in colors	Siri Si Bonne Undercurrent in crisp finish in colors	lightweight muslin percale in colors

of the original crispness. They, like muslin, produce excellent results.

hair canvas   Tailoring canvases are made of cotton or a combination of cotton and other fibers, including wool and goat's hair. The fiber and hair content varies to produce interfacing fabrics of infinite variety. Armo hair canvases are woven with selvedge edges in special colors to indicate recommended uses: green, for lightweight fabrics; blue, for typical suitings; yellow, for medium-weight coatings; and red, for heavy coatings. All-wool hair canvas, although costly, has excellent draping qualities and will mold beautifully in collar and lapel areas; if wool hair canvas is used as a complete interfacing, it acts somewhat like an interlining because the extra layer of wool definitely increases warmth.

colored fabrics   For loosely woven woolens, a colored interfacing may be required. Cotton percale and Indian Head are available in a wide range of colors. These fabrics are similar in character to muslin and make excellent interfacings.

If a small amount of extra body is desired in the entire garment (the true underlining or backing) and a partial interfacing will be used for extra body in certain sections of the garment (method 2, page 219), the following fabrics are excellent choices for the underlining or backing.

Siri and Super-Siri   These fabrics, available in black and white, are made of spun viscose rayon. They are preshrunk and washable. Super-Siri is the softer and finer of the two and so is preferred for dress-weight woolens. Si Bonne is very similar to the Siris.

Undercurrent   These fabrics are made of 100 percent Avril (rayon), are preshrunk and washable, and are comparable in character to Siri. They come in crisp and medium-soft finishes and are available in a wide range of fashion colors, making them excellent choices for underlining loosely woven fabrics.

lawn and voile   These fabrics will add less body than either of the two mentioned above and would be used very rarely in the typical tailored garment. They might be used in a suit-dress or skirt of dress-weight woolen if the design features gathers, draping, or loose pleats.

The market is flooded with many interfacing and underlining fabrics far too numerous to mention. The increasingly prominent role these fabrics play in high-fashion costumes will be responsible for new and probably exciting fabrics in the future; the woman who sews must keep up with all these new developments. Other interfacing and underlining fabrics that may be used for special purposes are listed below.

organdy and silk organza   These fabrics can be used for lightweight summer suits if a degree of crispness and a little body are desired. They are not recommended for general use in tailored garments.

Staflex and Pressto   These are two of the press-on type of supporting fabric. Their advantage is that basting time is eliminated and that, when they are pressed on another fabric, the two truly act as one. There are disadvantages, however, and these fabrics are not recommended for use in tailored garments of high quality because they do not allow for the molding and shaping required in certain areas of the tailored garment. Trimming the press-on interfacing from seams to reduce bulk is difficult and very time-consuming. The press-on feature does save basting time, but these fabrics are recommended for quickly constructed, utilitarian garments only.

bonded and nonwoven types Pellon is the most familiar of the nonwoven interfacings. It is available in black and white and in a variety of weights. These fabrics have dominant characteristics (even those with the so-called bias feature); when combined with wool, the two together tend to take the stiff character of the Pellon rather than the softer character of the wool. Therefore, they are not recommended for general use as an underlining or an interfacing (they lack the subordinate character required for most uses), but can be used for building and supporting unusual silhouette lines. A heavy weight of Pellon is the perfect choice for stiffening waistbands, belts, and other flat, bandlike details.

SUGGESTIONS FOR BUYING

1 Study the envelope back and the instruction sheet of the pattern selected to find the method recommended. The yardage amount will be a good indication, as will be explained below, and the sketches on the instruction sheet will be a positive indication. *If the yardage amount stated for interfacing is obviously less than would be required to cut the whole garment*—if, in other words, the yardage amount is approximately 1 yard—the partial interfacing (method 1 in this book) has been recommended. More yardage will be required for a complete interfacing; an ample estimate can be made for inexpensive fabric, but if the interfacing is costly, a special layout should be made to determine the proper amount of yardage required (page 30). *If a yardage amount is stated for an underlining or backing and if that amount seems sufficient to cut the whole garment* (several yards perhaps), that yardage amount should be used for the underlining in method 2 and can be used for the complete interfacing, if method 3 is used.

2 Before making a selection, place a piece of wool fabric over the interfacing fabrics under consideration, testing one thickness of each to determine the effect of overall extra body. Then place one layer of interfacing between two layers of wool to test the effect for the collar and the faced and hemmed edges of the garment.

3 Many interfacings are available in a neutral tan or gray only, and many are offered in black and white only. If the wool fabric is loosely woven and there is a possibility that the color of the interfacing may show through, place a piece of interfacing under a portion of wool to compare the color with that of a portion that is not interfaced. If color differences are evident, choose percale or Indian Head (or Undercurrent) in colors; colors need not match perfectly to serve the purpose very well.

4 Be sure to check the width of interfacing fabrics because widths vary greatly. Many are available in 36- and 45-inch widths, but some (many of the canvases and usually wool hair canvas) are as narrow as 27 inches. Estimates of yardages are acceptable for inexpensive fabrics, but a special layout (page 30) should be made to figure proper yardage for costly fabrics.

5 If one must be practical, it is a wise economy to use one of the very excellent inexpensive interfacings (muslin, per-

cale, Indian Head) in preference to the more expensive canvases, for they will serve the purpose remarkably well and will not decrease the value of the finished costume. If there must be a choice, it is better to add extra cost to the wool and economize with muslin interfacing fabric.

6 Not all sections of one garment must be interfaced with the same fabric. Interfacings serve many purposes, and the experienced woman can make these fabrics serve her own particular needs by choosing several different ones. For example, muslin is a practical and excellent choice for the body of the garment; wool hair canvas molds beautifully and could be used for the collar and cuffs; and if muslin adds more body to the sleeves than is desired, Siri or Undercurrent could be used in the sleeves. In other words, make interfacings work for individual purposes and effects.

7 The interfacing fabric must be purchased at the same time the fabric and pattern are selected because, in the complete interfacing method (recommended in this book), it is used in the very first steps of construction.

PREPARATION
OF
FABRIC
FOR
CUTTING

BASIC
TERMS

The basic terms given below are used so frequently in all home sewing that the reader with sufficient experience to undertake a tailored costume should be well acquainted with them. They are included for review purposes, and if they are not a part of your working vocabulary, they should be memorized at this time. See Figure 1.

selvedge The selvedge (sometimes spelled "selvage") is the finished edge of the fabric running lengthwise on the bolt of fabric. There is a selvedge on each lengthwise edge of the fabric. The selvedge is woven differently, usually with stronger threads, from the body of the fabric.

lengthwise threads These are the threads running parallel to the selvedge. The lengthwise threads are usually stronger than the crosswise threads, and for this reason garments are cut in such a way that the lengthwise threads run lengthwise on the body. The words "straight-of-material," "straight-of-fabric," and "lengthwise grain" are used on the pattern to designate the direction of the lengthwise threads. Most fabrics will not stretch when pulled in a lengthwise direction.

crosswise threads These are the threads running at right angles to, or perpendicular to, the selvedge. These threads are usually slightly weaker than lengthwise threads, although they will not stretch noticeably. Sometimes the pattern layout will show a piece laid so that the straight-of-material line lies in a crosswise direction. This is done only on pattern pieces where maximum strength is not required or if it is necessary to work in a stripe design in a particular way.

true bias True bias is the diagonal of a perfect square of fabric. The bias line makes a 45° angle with the lengthwise and crosswise threads. The outstanding characteristic of the bias line is its elasticity. Any diagonal line on the fabric is bias and will stretch somewhat, but the maximum amount of stretch and "give" is obtained only with the true bias line.

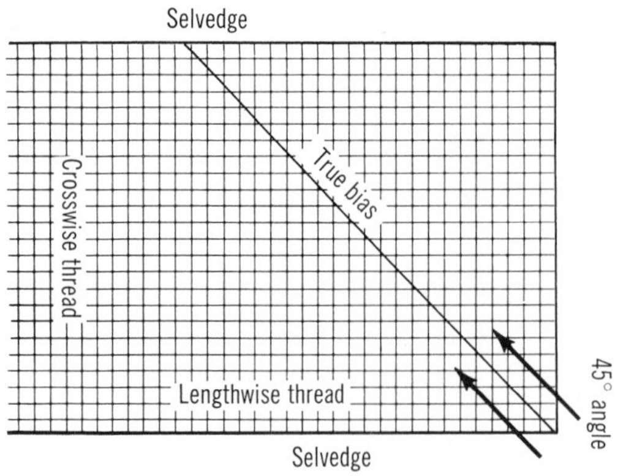

FABRIC FLAWS

After the fabric has been purchased, inspect it again for flaws. Inspect every inch of it. If there is a flaw—a heavier thread, a loose end of yarn, etc.—mark around the flaw with a basting stitch or make a chalk mark on the wrong side. Most small flaws can be avoided when the garment is cut.

TO EVEN FABRIC

Some fabrics can be torn from the bolt, while others must be cut. If fabrics are cut from the bolt, they should be cut carefully along a crosswise thread. However, this is time-consuming, and most salesgirls cannot spend the time required, except for very expensive fabrics; instead, they usually cut the fabric approximately at right angles to the sel-

Selvedge

Crosswise thread

True bias

Lengthwise thread

Selvedge

45° angle

FIGURE 1

vedge with little regard for the crosswise threads.

If fabric has been torn from the bolt, it need not be evened but must be straightened (page 54). If fabric has been cut from the bolt it must be evened, as described in the following section, before it is straightened.

METHODS OF EVENING FABRICS

There are several ways of evening fabrics, and one should choose the simplest method that will ensure proper results.

1 Very loosely woven fabrics, fabrics with a woven crosswise stripe (as in a stripe or plaid), or fabrics with some prominent crosswise threads (as in some novelty weaves) can be evened very quickly by cutting along the visible crosswise threads. These threads in a loosely woven fabric (even in a plain color) are quite easy to follow, although results may not be entirely perfect; raveling out a few threads will correct slight errors.

2 In some fabrics that are more firmly woven, the crosswise threads can be followed quite well if the fabric is held up to the light by an assistant. One can see the threads better and, with care, can cut along the threads with reasonably accurate results. The errors can be corrected by raveling out excess threads. This method is not a wise choice unless the threads can be seen quite well.

3 Clipping into a selvedge and then tearing the fabric is the very easiest and quickest method, but must be used with caution because most fabrics do not tear well; in some fabrics the lengthwise threads snag and distort to damage the fabric. Cotton fabrics made in a plain weave usually tear well, whereas novelty, Jacquard, and satin weaves will probably

be damaged by tearing. Soft woolens may be distorted if this method is used. This method is not advisable for most fabrics used in tailoring.

4 The most time-consuming method, but the one that is entirely safe for any fabric, is pictured in Figure 2. Clip into the selvedge near the cut edge of the fabric through a single thickness. Pull a crosswise thread, drawing up the fabric for a few inches. Then cut along this puckered line. Ravel out another thread and continue across the width of fabric. This procedure is easy or difficult depending on the nature of the threads. A strong, smooth crosswise thread in a loosely woven fabric can be pulled for perhaps half the width of fabric before it breaks; a weak, sticky, wooly thread in a tightly woven fabric may break when the puckered line is only ½ inch long.

NOTE Some wool fabrics that appear to be matted together (some of the camel's hair coatings) are almost impossible to even by any method.

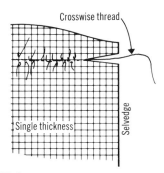

FIGURE 2

TO
STRAIGHTEN
FABRIC

NOTE Remember that fabrics with finishes permanently heat-set cannot be straightened; they must be cut in the condition purchased. See page 36 for a review of tentering and finishing problems.

When the fabric is evened, fold it in half lengthwise with selvedge edges together. See Figure 3. If the ends of the fabric (the crosswise threads) lie on top of each other and form a right angle with the selvedge, as they do in Figure 3a, the fabric is straight. If the ends of the fabric miss each other and do not make a right angle with the selvedge, as seen in Figure 3b, the fabric must be straightened.

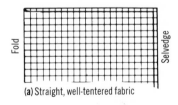

(a) Straight, well-tentered fabric

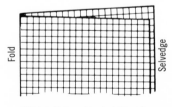

(b) Fabric that must be straightened, poorly tentered

FIGURE 3

Open up the fabric and place it on a table; flaws of tentering will show up readily in contrast to the square corners of the table. Figure 4 pictures three examples of poorly tentered fabric, shown in single thickness lying on a tabletop. Figure 4a shows the crosswise threads taking a diagonal direction across the entire width, which is the most common distortion. Figure 4b shows fabric that is in good condition in some areas, but needs attention in others. Figure 4c shows crosswise threads out of line, changing direction at the center line, where the fabric was folded. By pulling along bias lines in the direction required (study the arrowed lines in the sketches), the crosswise threads can be pulled into line. Move along about 6 inches between each bias line and always pull on the true bias line for maximum stretch. Test the fabric on the tabletop to check results; Figure 5 pictures fabric properly straightened. Sometimes fabrics must be stretched several times and the pressure must be increased before they are in proper condition.

If a wool fabric is poorly tentered with an off-grain variation of several inches, it can be straightened into a rectangular shape, as shown in Figure 5, but it may not lie smoothly on the table. Bubbles and diagonal ripples, as shown in Figure 6, may form, and no amount of smoothing out will correct the situation. In extreme cases of this sort, the fabric should be folded lengthwise with the selvedges and ends in proper position; then all edges should be basted prior to preshrinking. When this rippled fabric is put through the cleaning process, it will return in excellent condition; grain lines are readily aligned when the fabric is wet.

Selvedges may be out of line, or the fabric may have been folded inaccurately. When the fabric is folded lengthwise, selvedge edges should lie on top of each other or parallel to each other.

PREPARATION
FOR
PRESHRINKING

When the fabric has been evened and straightened, edges must be basted together so that the fabric is held in proper position for the dry-cleaning process. The right side of the fabric should be folded to the inside. If the two sides of the fabric look very much alike, the manufacturer will have folded the right side to the inside; if the wrong side is unattractive or if the right side of the fabric has a distinctive character, the manufacturer may have folded the right side to the outside. Study the cutting layout to be used and fold the fabric, insofar as it is possible, in the position in which it will be cut. In most cases fabrics are cut on a lengthwise fold, but if the cutting layout requires a crosswise fold, the fabric should be folded into that position at this time. If the layout features a combination layout, the fabric should not be cut at this time, but should instead be folded in the position required for the larger of the various segments of the layout.

Fold the fabric right sides together into the desired position and place it on a large table. Pin the corners in proper position and then work between the corners, pinning all edges together. Baste selvedge and fold edges and ends in position with long (1 to 1½ inches) basting stitches.

TO
PRESHRINK
WOOLENS

Many good-quality woolens purchased from the reliable dealer will not shrink

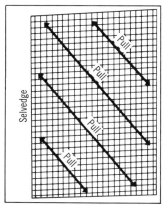

(a) Most common distortion

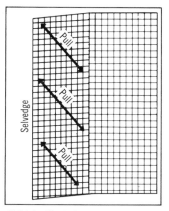

(b) Fabric off grain in some areas only

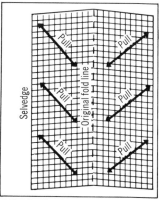

(c) Fabric off grain on each side of center (original fold) line

FIGURE 4

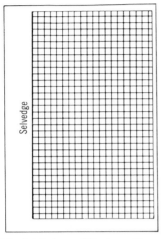

FIGURE 5 Fabric in condition for cutting: perfect grain-line position

appreciably if professionally dry-cleaned. Some carry a label such as "Ready for the needle" or "No preshrinking necessary." These statements are not entirely reliable, although certainly the fabric will shrink less than a fabric that does not carry such a label. The bargain wool from an unknown merchant should certainly be preshrunk, and it is a wise economy to preshrink all fabrics which will be dry-cleaned; the wise person who sews will take every precaution to ensure satisfaction.

Professional dry cleaners will preshrink wool at a nominal cost (50 cents per yard is average), and the saving in time is well worth the cost to many busy women. The home process includes rolling the wool in a wet sheet, allowing it to remain for about ten hours, and then pressing the fabric (see page 163 for techniques of pressing). The large-surface irons at the professional shop ensure a more satisfying result than home pressing with the smaller iron.

NOTE The coin-operated dry-cleaning machines may use a stronger cleaning solution than the professional dry cleaner. If garments will be cleaned by self-service, preshrink the fabric by the same method.

TO PRESHRINK LINING FABRICS

Lining fabrics should be evened and straightened in the general manner discussed above. However, because of the infinite variety of fabrics which might be used for linings, the reader should experiment and use caution. The crepe and crepelike linings that are ideal for

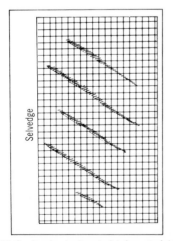

FIGURE 6 Poorly tentered fabric, straightened but still in poor condition

lining purposes will offer no problems of straightening. If an unusual lining is used —if, for example, a stiff taffeta or brocade has been chosen—problems may arise in straightening the fabric; some of these fabrics (rather like the fabrics with a heat-set finish) cannot be straightened into perfect position.

A lining fabric of high quality will probably not shrink in the dry-cleaning process, and the reader might decide not to have these fabrics preshrunk. However, inexpensive sheath linings that might be chosen for the skirt lining will shrink considerably; these fabrics should be put through the dry-cleaning process to ensure a successful costume. The experienced person working with expensive fabric and an intricate pattern will want to preshrink all lining fabrics.

PREPARATION OF SUPPORTING FABRICS

Interfacing and underlining fabrics can be evened and straightened in the general manner discussed above. They can be preshrunk by the professional cleaner, if the reader desires, but this step is not necessary. These fabrics do not shrink when the finished garment is dry-cleaned.

NOTE   Do not wash unbleached muslin because it becomes very stiff with one washing.

PREPARATION OF PATTERN FOR CUTTING AND PATTERN ALTERATIONS

There is something so exciting about a new pattern and new fabric that most women have an uncontrollable urge to start cutting immediately. It would be wonderful if one could get off to exciting business on this first wave of enthusiasm, but unless the pattern is properly prepared, the discouragement and difficulties of fitting which might arise later will be magnified. Clothing construction is a delight from beginning to end if it is done step by step so that the whole project (from cutting to fitting and finishing) moves along smoothly and successfully. Although the preparation, measuring, and pattern alterations described here will take some amount of time now, these preliminaries will save time and trouble in the long run.

GENERAL
SUGGESTIONS

1 A suit or coat pattern contains a surprising (and often confusing) number of pattern pieces. They should be sorted out in meaningful piles—the skirt pieces, the garment pieces, the interfacing sections, the lining sections, and perhaps the pattern pieces for a blouse. For the time being, only the pieces for the jacket or coat and skirt will be used. Place all other pieces—interfacing, lining, blouse— in separate labeled envelopes.

2 Pattern pieces should be pressed with a warm iron to remove creases and ensure more accurate cutting, and then they should be hung over a hanger and pinned securely in place. After they are pressed, they should not be folded up again before the fabric is cut.

3 Any pattern piece that is not cut on the fold has a straight-of-material line indicated; it is relatively short, usually about 5 to 9 inches long, depending on the length of the pattern piece. This line will be placed on lengthwise lines on the fabric and can be more accurately placed if it extends the full length of the pattern piece. Using a yardstick, extend the straight-of-material lines to the edges of all pattern pieces (Figure 1).

4 When working with a group in a home or a school laboratory situation, each person should put her name on each of her pattern pieces and on the instruction sheet.

TO
TAKE
BODY
MEASUREMENTS

See Figure 2. Body measurements should be taken over the undergarments that will be worn with the costume. The tape measure should be held flat against the body for snug, but not tight, measurements. The tape should be parallel to the floor. Whether an assistant takes these measurements (recommended) or whether you work alone before a mirror, accurate measurements will result only if the body is viewed from the front and also the side to check the position of the tape measure. An assistant should work at eye level for even more accurate results. The 3-inch hipline is especially difficult to measure because of the rounded contours in that portion of the body; be very careful that the tape does not slip up in the back.

Two measurement and alteration charts are included on pages 67 and 68: a skirt chart (adaptable to slacks and shorts) and a chart for jackets and coats. A copy of the appropriate chart should

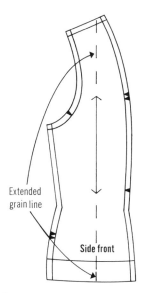

Extended
grain line

Side front

FIGURE 1

be made for each garment to be constructed; the classroom teacher will probably want to run off mimeographed copies. Select the appropriate chart and record your body measurements in parts 2 and 3 of the chart.

EXPLANATION OF MEASUREMENT AND ALTERATION CHARTS

If patterns are properly tested on the figure and accurate body measurements are compared with measurements of the pattern, it is possible to figure pattern alterations so that little or no fitting will be required. By keeping a record of alterations made and making notes of recommended changes in future gar-

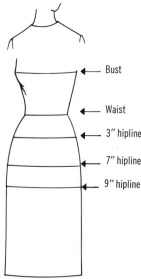

FIGURE 2 To take body measurements

ments, women with problem figures can attain such accuracy that eventually they can sew with little fitting. Fitting is the most difficult step in clothing construction for the experienced person as well as the novice, so every care should be taken to make fitting easier. Pattern measurement and alteration is not easy and is time-consuming, but making alterations is infinitely easier than fitting. The measurement and alteration charts are divided into three parts.

part 1 Pattern measurements involved with length and proportion are checked not really by measuring but by pinning the pattern together and testing it on the figure. This method is recommended only for length and never as a test for width or overall size because the paper will not bend around the body to give an accurate test of width or size.

part 2 Some measurements involved with width or size can be checked by comparison with the Body Measurement Chart. The standard Body Measurement Chart includes body measurements for the bust, waist, and 7- or 9-inch hipline (see Figure 2).

part 3 Certain important measurements of width and overall size must be made by measuring the actual pattern because no comparable measurement is stated in the Body Measurement Chart. The 3-inch hipline and the biceps line of the sleeve must be checked in this manner.

PART 1: TESTS ON THE FIGURE

PINNING THE PATTERN TOGETHER
Jacket or coat pieces, skirt pieces, and sleeve pieces must be pinned together

as they will be sewn; if in doubt, follow through the instruction sheet for the construction order. Facings, collars, pockets, etc., need not be included at this time. Pin in darts and fold in tucks and pleats. Turn under one shoulder edge on the seamline and lap it to the seamline of the corresponding shoulder.

Pin in the hems along designated hemlines in the jacket or coat, the sleeves, and the skirt. Pin the underarm seams of the sleeves, but do not pin the underarm seams of the jacket or coat or the side seams of the skirt; if the pattern is pinned at the sides, it will not bend around the body well.

TESTS FOR THE JACKET OR COAT

Have an assistant hold the pattern to your body, taking the following precautions: The shoulder line must lie on the top of the shoulder, center-front and center-back lines should be in proper position, and the neckline should fit the neck in the way it was intended for the particular design. The assistant should grasp one hand firmly over the shoulder so that the pattern cannot shift while the tests are made.

1 **overall length**   Wear a skirt comparable in design and length to the skirt that will be worn with the jacket. Study the effect of length to be sure the jacket creates attractive proportions on your figure (if the hems were not pinned up along hemlines earlier, pin them in place at this time). The pattern for a full-length coat should be tested over a dress the length of most garments to be worn with the

coat; the coat should be about 1 inch longer than those garments. Estimate any alteration required and record it in the appropriate measurement and alteration chart.

2 **position of waistline for fitted jackets and coats**   Have an assistant smooth the pattern over the front and bust area, with the shoulder line held firmly in proper position, to test the length of the waist area of the jacket or coat. Compare the waistline marking of the pattern with your waistline position. Estimate any required alteration and record it in the alteration chart.

Being careful to keep the pattern on the shoulder in the same position, smooth the back pattern down over the shoulders in the center-back area. The assistant must test the position of the waistline of the pattern and compare it with the position of your waistline. This test will determine alterations required for back length. Estimate any alteration required and record it in the alteration chart.

3 **position of underarm darts**   An underarm dart should be on a level with the high point of the bust, pointing directly to the high point of the bust. Likewise, any slanting dart, such as the typical French dart, should point in the direction of the high point of the bust. If these darts fall above or below this level, record the required alteration in the chart.

4 **tests for the sleeve**   These tests have a

certain margin of error, but it is not great, and no other method that might be used to test sleeve length would be more accurate. Have an assistant slip the sleeve over your arm and bring it up to the position it should take (this is the margin of error); try to hold the seam-line in the sleeve cap in the position it will take on the body.

NOTE Sleeves that gather to a cuff must have sufficient length to allow the bloused effect. The cuff should be pinned on the sleeve during this test to ensure the desired results.

With the hem pinned up, study the total sleeve length; if in doubt about the effect, experiment with different lengths at this time. Record any desired altera-tion in the chart.

The elbow dart of a fitted sleeve should create shape for the bent elbow. Bend the arm slightly so that an assis-tant can test the dart position. The two-piece sleeve (composed of an upper-sleeve and an under-sleeve section) does not have a dart, but is shaped by the seams. The elbow position is difficult to determine in these sleeves, and therefore any correction might better be done by fitting in the muslin copy. Record any required alteration in the chart.

5 **tests for decorative details** Other details that have to do with proportion (such as pocket flaps, band trims, etc.) can be pinned into place and examined for the effect of placement and size. Be sure to turn under seam allowances on these small pieces so that they will be the "finished size," that is, create the same effect that they will on the finished gar-ment. Make a note of desired changes.

Ideally, details of this sort can be tested much more accurately after the muslin copy is made, and in most cases, it is wiser to wait with changes on these small issues until that fitting. These tests are recommended as a pattern alteration only for very obvious problems. Slight and subtle corrections should be ignored at this time and made later as a fitting correction.

TESTS FOR THE SKIRT

Wear shoes similar in line and heel height to those which will be worn with the skirt. Have an assistant pin a tape measure around your waist and then pin the skirt pattern to the tape, with the seamline of the pattern on the lower edge of the tape.

With the hem pinned up, study the skirt length; if in doubt, experiment with different lengths at this time. Record any desired alteration in the chart.

NOTE Slacks must be tested for total length and also for length of the crotch seam. Tuck the pattern between your legs; the crotch seam should fall about 2 inches below the body. These patterns may need alteration in length in the torso area. Estimate the alteration, do the altera-tion, and retest on the figure for accuracy.

PART 2:
COMPARISONS
WITH THE STANDARD
BODY MEASUREMENT CHART

This part of the chart is very easy to fill in because it involves merely comparing measurements and then figuring the dif-ferences for the required alterations. Two points need clarification.

CONCERNING WAIST MEASUREMENT

The chart states that waist measurements should not be decreased by pattern alteration. This does not mean that the waist will remain too large in the finished garment; it means simply that the waist will be adjusted by fitting rather than pattern alteration.

CONCERNING THE HIP MEASUREMENT

This measurement stated on the charts is that of the fullest part of the hip; for shorter figure types (Half Sizes, Junior Petites, Young Junior/Teens) it is the measurement of hips 7 inches below the waist and for figures with a longer torso (Misses', Womens, Juniors) it is the 9-inch measurement.

If every figure were quite average in all-over shape, nature of body curves and posture, a comparison of the bust, waist, and hip measurements with corresponding measurements on the body would be sufficient to establish required pattern alterations. However, individual figures may have problem areas at other levels. Examples are: the bell-shaped figure with problems at the 3-inch hip level, the figure with large thighs that present problems below the usual hip level, the figure with a roll of fat in the midriff area, and the figure with large arms. These individual figure irregularities make it necessary to test additional levels on the pattern by taking actual pattern measurements and comparing them with corresponding body measurements.

PART 3:
TESTS MADE
BY TAKING ACTUAL
PATTERN MEASUREMENTS

These tests require taking measurements of the pattern with all seams, darts,

tucks, and pleats folded in as they will be in the finished garment. See the charts on pages 65 through 68. Note that the "measurement needed" must include allowance for livability as well as body size. Average livability amounts are included in the charts for the 3-inch hipline and the biceps line of the sleeve. Space has been allowed to record information at other areas that might present individual problems. The minimum livability amount for the midriff area of a fitted jacket is 2 to 3 inches.

NOTE The 9-inch hipline is included in the sketches to illustrate the method of taking the measurement. This 9-inch measurement is the one included on the measurement chart for taller figure types, but the shorter figure with problem thighs may need to take this additional measurement.

NOTE The issue of style fullness as a component of pattern size was discussed earlier, but bears repetition at this time. Pattern size is a result of three components: (1) body size, (2) livability allowance, and, in some designs, (3) style fullness. The measurement and alteration charts cannot include the style-fullness factor because it varies so much from design to design. Style fullness must be given attention for each particular design and is discussed in more detail on pages 22 and 114.

1 Most patterns pieces are made for the half figure, in which case the measurements must be doubled. Therefore, in the skirt pictured in Figure 3, *A* plus *B* plus *C* plus *D* doubled equals the 3-inch

hip measurement, and *E* plus *F* doubled equals the 9-inch hip measurement. Record these amounts in part 3 of the charts in the column headed Measurement of Pattern. Seams, pleats, darts, tucks, etc. (the shaded sections in the sketch), are not measured because they will not be a part of the finished size of the garment.

2 The technique is the same regardless of the type of pattern pieces involved. Figure 4 pictures pattern pieces for a typical semifitted suit with the 3-inch hip measurement indicated (*G* plus *H* plus *I* doubled). Note that the measurement of the jacket front was taken from the seamline to the center front only—the shaded extension on the buttoned front is not measured because it does not add to the finished size of the garment.

3 The biceps line of the sleeve is a line at right angles to the straight-of-material line, located at the base of the sleeve cap and extending the full width of the sleeve. See Figure 5. The sleeve pictured is the two-piece sleeve used so frequently in tailored garments. The base of the sleeve cap (the biceps line) begins at the underarm position in the undersleeve section, as shown. It is at right angles to the straight-of-material line and continues across the upper-sleeve section at the same level on the lengthwise seamlines. These two measurements (*J* plus *K*) make up the biceps measurement. Record the biceps measurement in part 3 of the charts under the column headed

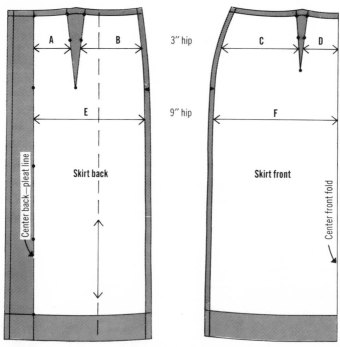

FIGURE 3 To take actual pattern measurements

Measurement of Pattern.

4 The matter of style fullness complicates the problem. Figure 6a shows a popular skirt design with style fullness created by loose tucks at the waist instead of a snug dart fitting. The broken lines in Figure 6a do not appear on the pattern and have been included on this sketch to clarify the issue of style fullness. The tuck lines are so short (less than 3 inches) that one might measure straight across the pattern at the 3-inch hipline, assuming that all the width was available for body size and livability allowance. This is a common and serious mistake resulting in an unattractive skirt in which the tucks (or gathers, as the case may be) poke out and form a sort of shelf below the waist.

The important thing to understand is that additional size must be estimated for style fullness if the garment is to have the desired effect. The broken lines in Figure 6a, formed by extending the tuck lines of the pattern, indicate the

allowance needed for style fullness; these tucks, then, are rather like long darts that will be stitched for a few inches only.

See Figure 6b. To make allowance for style fullness, fold in the extended tucks as if they were darts. Then take measurements across the shaped pattern. In the example shown, line L doubled equals the 3-inch hipline of the skirt front; in this example, the extended tuck lines converge at about the 9-inch hipline, so that hipline (line M in the sketch) could be measured with the pattern flat on the table. Add these measurements to those of the skirt back and record the total amount in part 3 of the charts in the column headed Measurement of Pattern.

It is impossible to give enough ex-

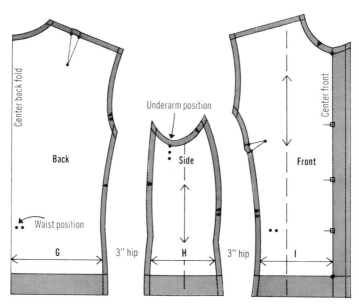

FIGURE 4 To take actual pattern measurements

amples to illustrate all the problems of style fullness that might arise in every possible design. The example given above illustrates the general principle: *Fold in amounts for style fullness and take measurements over the folded pattern.* This principle must be studied and applied to each new design.

INTRODUCTION TO PATTERN ALTERATIONS

If a pattern is purchased in the correct size and figure type, pattern alterations can be kept to a minimum. The alterations included in this chapter are those which are required most frequently and those which can be executed without danger of destroying the accuracy of the pattern. "Play it safe" is a good motto for the woman who sews. This does not mean that it is wise to cut a garment far too large or too long; it does mean that it is safer and wiser to cut the fabric a little larger and a little longer (rather than smaller and shorter) until exact

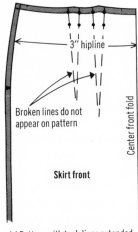

(a) Pattern with tuck lines extended

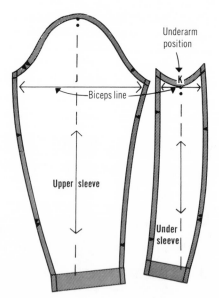

FIGURE 5 To take actual pattern measurements

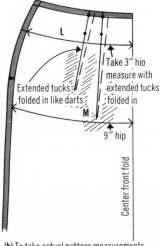

(b) To take actual pattern measurements when style fullness is involved

FIGURE 6

MEASUREMENT AND ALTERATION CHART FOR SKIRTS, SLACKS, AND SHORTS

PART 1
CHECK THE FOLLOWING BY PINNING THE PATTERN TOGETHER AND TESTING ON FIGURE

	ALTERATION REQUIRED
LENGTH OF SKIRT (or of slacks or shorts)	lengthen or shorten?_____
LENGTH OF CROTCH SEAM (slacks and shorts)	lengthen or shorten?_____

PART 2
CHECK THE FOLLOWING BY COMPARING YOUR MEASUREMENTS WITH THOSE GIVEN ON THE BODY MEASUREMENT CHART

	YOUR BODY MEASUREMENT	MEASUREMENT ON CHART	ALTERATION REQUIRED
WAIST			increase?_____ (do not decrease by pattern alteration)
FULLEST PART OF HIP			increase or decrease?_____

PART 3
CHECK THE FOLLOWING BY TAKING ACTUAL PATTERN MEASUREMENTS

	YOUR BODY MEASUREMENT	MEASUREMENT REQUIRED	MEASUREMENT OF PATTERN	ALTERATION REQUIRED
3″ HIPLINE		your body measurement plus 1″ is _____		increase or decrease?_____
SPACE FOR INDIVIDUAL PROBLEMS		your body measurement plus livability amount is _____		increase or decrease?_____

NOTE   This chart is adaptable for slacks and shorts, but in part 3, in the column headed Measurement Required, the measurement needed is 1 inch more for slacks and shorts: 2 inches at the 3-inch hip level.

MEASUREMENT AND ALTERATION CHART FOR JACKETS AND COATS

PART 1

CHECK THE FOLLOWING BY PINNING THE PATTERN TOGETHER AND TESTING ON THE FIGURE

	ALTERATION REQUIRED
POSITION OF WAISTLINE (for fitted garments only)	front: lengthen or shorten above waist?_____ back: lengthen or shorten above waist?_____
POSITION OF UNDERARM DART	move up or down?_____
SLEEVE LENGTH	lengthen or shorten?_____
POSITION OF ELBOW DART	move up or down?_____
LENGTH OF JACKET OR COAT	lengthen or shorten?_____
POSITION OF POCKETS	move up or down?_____

PART 2

CHECK THE FOLLOWING BY COMPARING YOUR MEASUREMENTS WITH THOSE GIVEN ON THE BODY MEASUREMENT CHART

	YOUR BODY MEASUREMENT	MEASUREMENT ON CHART	ALTERATION REQUIRED
BUST			increase or decrease?_____
WAIST			increase?_____ (do not decrease by pattern alteration)
FULLEST PART OF HIP			increase or decrease?_____

PART 3
CHECK THE FOLLOWING BY TAKING ACTUAL PATTERN MEASUREMENTS

	YOUR BODY MEASUREMENT	MEASUREMENT REQUIRED	MEASUREMENT OF PATTERN	ALTERATION REQUIRED
3″ HIPLINE		your body measurement plus a minimum of 2″ is _____		increase or decrease?_____
SPACE FOR INDIVIDUAL PROBLEMS		your body measurement plus livability amount is _____		increase or decrease?_____
BICEPS LINE OF SLEEVE		your body measurement plus a minimum of 2″ is _____		increase or decrease?_____

NOTE The amounts listed in part 3 in the column headed Measurement Required are absolute minimums. Many coats and jackets will require more size, especially if they are loose and boxy.

requirements have been established by making many successful costumes. Strangely enough, many persons dislike adding size to a pattern, often insisting that they know they will not need it. This is a serious mistake; it is so much better to add some extra size to the pattern as a safety measure and then baste the garment, if desired, along the original seamlines of the pattern. That is what is meant by playing it safe. If a garment is cut too small, it takes three times as long (or longer) to make it larger than to take in a garment that is too large. And the saving in time is the lesser of the two issues because the garment that is let out by using seam allowances is not as serviceable as the one in which proper seam allowances are used.

Keeping records of pattern alterations made and their degree of success is the way to perfect knowledge of requirements. If this is done for several garments, requirements can be so well established that one need not take measurements of figure or pattern, but can proceed to make the required alterations with confidence.

Pattern alterations solve problems of length and of width or overall size very effectively; by contrast, fitting is more involved with the difficult problems of shape and contour. Four types of alterations are discussed in this chapter: alterations in length, alterations in width, alterations for sleeve width and shoulder height, and alterations involved with changing the shape as well as the size of the garment (very effective alterations that are much more advanced and complicated).

INFLUENCES OF THE MUSLIN COPY ON PATTERN ALTERATIONS

The approach to pattern alterations is different if a muslin test copy will be made, and a muslin copy is an essential for tailored costumes because of their expense. If no test copy is made, the worker must make every decision very cautiously, and if in doubt, she must play it safe by being sure that she has sufficient size and length. By contrast, if a test copy is made, little issues can be temporarily dismissed, to be decided when the muslin test copy is made up. For example, if measurements indicate that a mere 1-inch addition in width might be needed in a certain area, the extra inch should be added to the pattern if no test copy is to be made, whereas with a test copy, if there is doubt and if the amount involved is very small, the addition need not be made as a preliminary pattern alteration, but can be made later, after the muslin fitting, if it is required.

A test copy will be made of the jacket or coat, and therefore subtle alterations need not be made before the muslin test copy is fitted. Understand that large and obvious alterations should be made at this time because the test copy should fit as well as possible at the first fitting; only little doubtful alterations can wait. By contrast, most readers will not make a muslin copy of the skirt (only those with serious figure problems), and so if there is a need for even a slight alteration in the skirt, it should be done now, as a pattern alteration.

With no test copy for the skirt, it is all the more important to play it safe.

When the muslin test copy is to be made, then, pattern alterations are done in two different steps. The large and obvious alterations are made before the muslin copy is cut; then, after the muslin test copy is fitted, fitting corrections are transferred to the pattern as pattern alterations at that time.

There is another way the making of a test copy influences pattern alterations. If no test copy is made, the pattern alterations are made on all corresponding pattern pieces at the same time; in other words, if a jacket is lengthened, the facing, interfacing, and lining pieces would be lengthened a corresponding amount immediately. But if a test copy is made, alterations are made on the structural pieces of the jacket only; then, after these alterations have been tested in the muslin test copy and any other alterations (suggested in fitting) have been made on these structural pieces, corresponding pattern pieces are altered accordingly at that time.

GENERAL SUGGESTIONS

The sketches in this book show only the structural pieces of the pattern. The lesser pieces are not pictured (in this book or on alteration sketches in the instruction sheet), but it is assumed that all corresponding pieces will be altered in like manner. It is well to place all pieces that will fit the same area of the body on top of one another; for example, when the jacket-front alterations have been decided, place the front-facing and front-lining pieces together, with corresponding edges even, and alter all remaining pieces accordingly.

If an addition in length or width is made, the sketches show a strip of paper Scotch-taped to the pattern (Magic Mending Tape is excellent for this purpose). Always take the time to add a strip of paper, which will call attention to the altered line as you cut, and resist the temptation to use the margin of the pattern for this purpose; there is a great danger that pencil lines on the thin tissue paper might be overlooked when cutting.

For alterations to change width or overall size of the pattern, the illustrations in this book show additions in size, rather than reductions. This has been done intentionally because *additions must be made as pattern alterations, whereas reductions in size can be made by basting seamlines in such a way that the reduction is taken care of at that time.* It is well to play it safe by being cautious of decreasing pattern size until many garments have indicated a need for less size. When figure requirements have been well established by several garments, reductions can be made by pattern alteration, following the general principles illustrated in Alterations for Changing Pattern Width. Until that time, decreases are made much more safely by basting edges with larger-than-⅝-inch seam allowances.

ALTERATIONS FOR CHANGING PATTERN LENGTH

A BRIEF REVIEW

Alterations in length are made in two different ways. The simplest method is that of adding a measured amount to, or trimming a measured amount from, the lower edge of the pattern. This method is usually used on rectangular pieces, but it can be used often on shaped pieces when making very small changes. The more complicated method is that of making a change within the body of the pattern by inserting a strip of paper to

lengthen and folding in a tuck to shorten. See Figure 7. If the pattern is not rectangular (the flared skirt pictured, a fitted sleeve, pieces for a fitted garment) and if the alteration is a sizable one, this more complicated and time-consuming method must be used. In these cases, lengthening-shortening lines will usually be printed on the pattern; these lines are drawn at right angles to the straight-of-material line or center lines. If the lines do not appear, draw them in a right-angle position.

These alterations must always be made on parallel lines—the tuck for shortening must be a parallel tuck, and any addition must be made on parallel lines. Parallel alterations are necessary so that the extended or shortened straight-of-material line will remain ruler-straight, as it was originally. This will happen automatically when a parallel tuck is taken at right angles to the straight-of-material line. The alteration for lengthening requires one additional step. See the lengthened pattern in Figure 7. Draw parallel lines on a strip of paper. Scotch-tape one section of the pattern to the strip, with the cut edge along one ruler line. Extend the straight-of-material line in the pattern to the strip of paper, as shown. Then place down the other section, along the remaining ruler line, with the straight-of-material line of the pattern over the extended line on the strip. If these steps are followed, the original straight-of-material line will be ruler-straight in the altered pattern.

This method of alteration is further complicated because the diagonal lengthwise edges of the pattern piece will be distorted. Both the lengthened and the

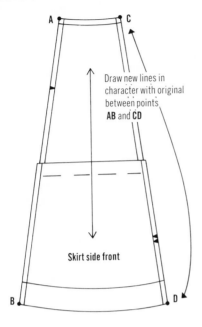

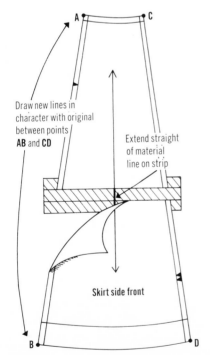

FIGURE 7 To correct distortion on vertical edges of diagonal or shaped pattern pieces

shortened patterns are equally distorted, although the distortion is more evident in the shortened pattern because of the proximity of lines. The distortion must be corrected in such a way that the altered line has the character of the original. In the illustration shown, the original line was ruler-straight, so new ruler-straight lines must be established between points *A* and *B* and points *C* and *D* (not drawn to avoid confusion).

Figure 8 shows a pattern with a diagonal line that was not ruler-straight originally. Notice that no distortion occurs at the front edge because that edge is parallel to the straight-of-material line; distortion occurs only on diagonal lines. In the example shown, line *AB* on the original pattern was a slightly curving line. A new line *AB* must be drawn in a similar curve to be in character with the original.

SKIRT ALTERATIONS

to change length at lower edge   See Figure 9. The simplest way to alter pattern

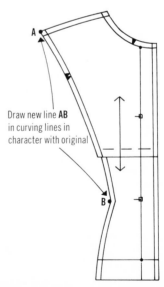

FIGURE 8 To correct distortion on vertical edges of pattern

length is by adding to, or trimming from, the lower edge. This quick method is recommended (1) for changing any piece that is rectangular or nearly rectangular in shape, providing no design detail complicates the problem, and (2) for changing many shaped pattern pieces a very slight amount.

to change length while retaining design proportions See Figure 10. Changing the length of a pattern piece at some level within the body of the pattern must be done, even for the rectangular skirt illustrated, if design proportions must be retained. Pleats and vents are design details that require alteration within the body of the pattern piece.

to alter length in a shaped pattern piece See Figure 11. If length must be altered in an area of the pattern that has shape (not rectangular), a strip of paper must be inserted or a tuck made. The example shown is the alteration for a person with a long or short torso. Note that the pattern curves to the notch (the 7-inch hipline) and is a ruler-straight line below; this line fits the average figure properly. This alteration is very helpful because it enables one to adjust the pattern so that the curved area is the same length as the

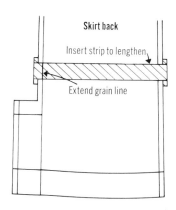

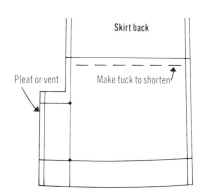

FIGURE 10 To alter length of rectangular pieces while retaining proportions of design features

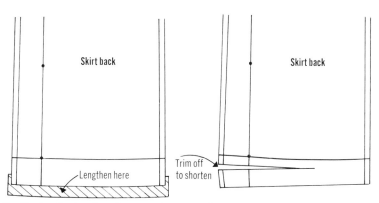

FIGURE 9 To alter length of rectangular or nearly rectangular pieces

corresponding curved area on the individual figure. These alteration lines are indicated on most shorts and slacks patterns, but are rarely indicated on skirt patterns; they can be drawn on the skirt pattern, if desired.

Another example of a shaped pattern piece is the flared skirt pictured in Figure 7, which should be altered by the method shown in that sketch if a considerable alteration is required; if several inches are added to the flared skirt, the width increase at the lower edge is so great that the pattern may not fit on the width of fabric, and if several inches are cut away, the altered pattern will be less flared (narrower) than the designer intended. If, however, the change is slight,

the alteration can be made at the lower edge, as shown in Figure 9.

JACKET AND COAT ALTERATIONS

The style line or silhouette of the jacket or coat dictates the method for changing length, just as in the skirt. Therefore, the rectangular straight-lined garment can be altered at the lower edge, whereas the flared garment may need to be altered within the body of the pattern. Retaining the proportions of design lines becomes a greater issue in jackets and coats, as illustrated in Figures 12 and 13.

to alter coat length at lower edge See Figure 12. The boxy coat can be altered at the lower edge, but any alteration in length suggests a possible change in the position of pockets or similar design features and respacing of buttonhole markings. If the pocket markings are simple, like those shown, they can be drafted easily into the desired position. These matters should be tested on the body

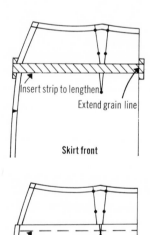

Insert strip to lengthen

Extend grain line

Skirt front

Make tuck to shorten

Skirt front

FIGURE 11 To alter skirt length in torso area

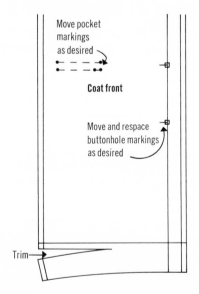

Move pocket markings as desired

Coat front

Move and respace buttonhole markings as desired

Trim

FIGURE 12 To correct proportions of simple design lines for the altered pattern

prior to pattern alteration or tested when fitting the muslin copy. A suggestion for the inexperienced person is this: Anticipate that better proportions will result if pockets at the hip level are moved up or down about one-half the amount of the alteration at the lower edge; for example, if 2½ inches was trimmed from the lower edge, move the pocket up 1¼ inches and test the effect. This suggestion illustrates that another solution to this problem is to make one-half the desired alteration in length at the lower edge and the other half in the body of the pattern, above the pocket or design markings.

to change length while retaining design proportions See Figure 13. In this example, the pocket lines are more complicated, and the finished pocket line is so close to the hemline that any change in length at the lower edge would seriously affect the proportions of the design. This example illustrates how a style line dictates the method of alteration needed. In this case, altering length within the body of the garment, as shown, is the only accepted method.

to alter length of fitted sleeve See Figure 14. The fitted sleeve, whether it is the one-piece sleeve shown or the two-piece sleeve frequently used in tailored garments, is intricately shaped to fit the contours of the bent arm. Therefore, it must be altered within the body of the pattern, perhaps on two different levels —above and below elbow position. The illustration pictures a sleeve shortened above the elbow and lengthened below to illustrate that different alterations can be made at different levels; even the average-length arm may be short in one portion and long in another.

to alter waist length for fitted and semifitted garments See Figure 15. The illustration

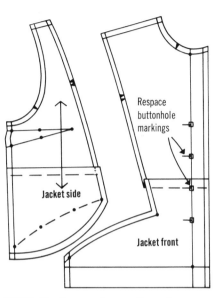

FIGURE 13 To correct proportions of more complicated design lines by pattern alteration

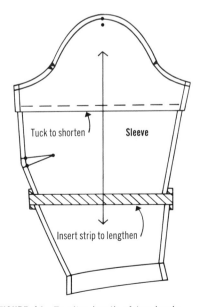

FIGURE 14 To alter length of two levels

shows a typical suit pattern designed on princess lines. The position of the waist is of great importance because there is no seam through which slight fitting corrections can be made, and the position is of greater importance in truly form-fitting, very nipped-in garments; the waist position must be at a proper level for the figure before the fabric is cut. This can be done by pattern alteration before the muslin test copy is made, but because great accuracy is necessary, additional corrections will undoubtedly be made when fitting the test copy. Because of this need for perfection of waist level, if for no other reason, a muslin test copy is always required for the truly fitted garment.

Figure 15 shows the fitted pattern lengthened an equal amount on all

pieces. An equal alteration (for lengthening or shortening) is quite simple, offering no greater problem than would be encountered with any shaped pattern piece. All vertical edges (except front and back edges) are somewhat diagonal or shaped, and so all will be slightly distorted by alterations in length; corrections must be made to give each line the character of the original pattern line (see Figures 7 and 8 on page 72). The person who needs an equal alteration is one with an average figure with average curves and posture, differing from the average in torso length the same amount in all parts of the figure.

But it is not at all unusual for a person to require different amounts of alteration in the front and back waist lengths; the unequal alterations are required more frequently because so many possible figure problems might be involved above the waist level. Examples of figure irregularities that will call for varying the amount of alteration in waist

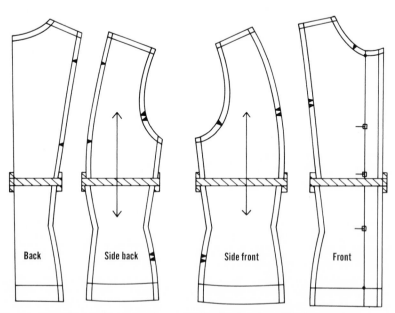

FIGURE 15   To alter waist lengths an equal amount—for fitted and semifitted garments

length are (1) the full-busted figure (more length in front), (2) the round-shouldered figure (more length in back), (3) the very straight back (less length in back), and (4) the figure with a waist that dips toward the back rather than dipping slightly toward the front (more length in back). Of course more than one of these irregularities may appear in the same figure. When the problems of posture are added to those of figure, alterations might multiply; for example, drooping shoulders offer the same problems as rounded shoulders, and the exaggerated "chest-out" posture will require extra front length. So do not assume that alterations in waist length will be equal; the odds favor unequal alterations.

Figure 16 pictures the same fitted suit with the waist length altered in varying amounts; the example illustrates the alteration for a figure of normal front length that is 1½ inches shorter than average in back length. Each piece must be altered on parallel lines (a parallel

tuck for shortening or a parallel insertion strip for lengthening) to retain proper grain line. If this kind of alteration is indicated, one can assume that the problem is a gradual one; the example shows the alteration for a figure that becomes gradually shorter from front to back.

It is very important to understand the basic principles shown here, for these general principles must be used to solve the problems of many different types of figures and must be applied to an infinite variety of designs. Try first to see the solution to the two large problems; note that the alteration has increased in gradual, even steps and that the pattern piece was lengthened at the lower edge the same amount it was shortened above the waist. So the two large problems have been solved—the waist level has been

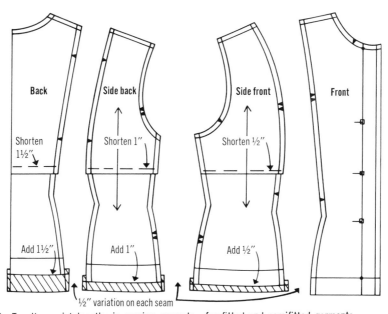

FIGURE 16 To alter waist lengths in varying amounts—for fitted and semifitted garments

corrected in a stair-step fashion, the total length of corresponding seams is the same, and corrected seams are identical to the length of the original seams.

There are some little inaccuracies that may be troubling the more experienced readers, and the following discussion should place them in proper perspective; they are really insignificant inaccuracies, after all. The inaccuracy that seems most serious at first thought is that the waist indentation on the pattern pieces will not coincide; the waist level on corresponding seams will be slightly different—it will differ by the amount of variation from one piece to another (in the example, the variation is ½ inch). This inaccuracy is so slight and can be corrected so easily as the seam is basted that it is of no concern. A simple paper sample will prove that this inaccuracy can be dismissed from your mind. See Figure 17. Place two identical pieces of notepaper together and cut one long edge in lines similar to the shaped lines of the pattern, as shown. Shift one piece

down the amount of variation on the pattern (½ inch in the example shown) and pin upper and lower edges together, cut edges even, as shown. Hold the sample up to the light to see the resulting difference in waist levels. You will easily see that when the seam is basted with the deepest indentation midway between the two levels of indentation on the pattern pieces, the problem is completely solved.

Another slight inaccuracy is that any notches appearing below the alteration line will not match, but will miss each other by the amount of variation between the two seams (in this case, the same ½ inch). This is no problem at all if the worker understands that the notches should not match; it becomes a problem only if she forces notches to match.

Additions were made at the lower edge in order to equalize the total length of corresponding seams. However, this addition may make the total length incorrect for some figures. But the addition is a way of playing it safe—the jacket or coat may or may not be too long, but it will not be too short, as it might be if other methods of evening off were used. Because the hem of jackets and coats is pinned up and tested on the figure, any excess fabric can easily be trimmed from the lower edge just prior to finishing the hem.

The alteration pictured in Figure 16 was chosen because it is a simple illustration of the logical progression of the unequal alteration in ½-inch variations. However, figuring the amount of variation on each pattern piece can be a more difficult problem if certain other amounts and certain more complicated figure problems are combined with a great variety of possible designs. A general formula can be used to serve every possible circumstance:

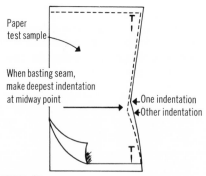

Paper test sample

When basting seam, make deepest indentation at midway point

One indentation
Other indentation

FIGURE 17

The total amount of variation from front to back divided by the number of corresponding seams equals the variation from one piece to another.

79

*PREPARATION OF PATTERN FOR
CUTTING AND PATTERN ALTERATIONS*

That formula applied to the alteration pictured in Figure 16 is 1½ inches divided by 3 equals ½ inch, the required variation from one piece to another.

Figure 18 pictures the pattern pieces for a semifitted suit. The shaping at the waistline of these designs is very subtle, but even so, proper alteration is required for an attractive fit, even if absolute perfection of waist level is not so much of an issue as it is in truly formfitting garments. This pattern is included to illustrate the use of the above formula, applied to a very different problem. This figure requires lengthening some pieces and shortening others, but regardless of the alteration, the formula gives the correct solution. In Figure 18, the total variation from front to back (1¼ inches)

divided by the number of corresponding seams (2) equals the amount of variation from piece to piece (⅝ inch). To make the pattern increasingly shorter from front to back, the jacket side is shortened ⅛ inch, thereby making the required ⅝-inch variation from piece to piece. In order to even off the lower edge and correct the length of corresponding seams, the total variation of 1¼ inches was added to the jacket back, and ⅝ inch was added to the lower edge of the jacket-side section.

to change level of horizontal and diagonal darts Figure 19a pictures an alteration for lowering the position of the dart; the procedure would be the same for raising

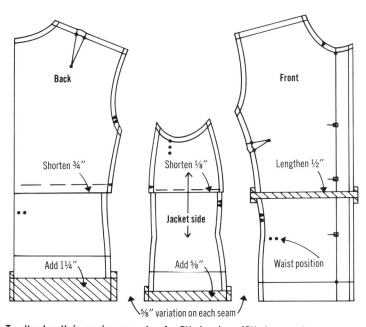

FIGURE 18 To alter length in varying amounts—for fitted and semifitted garments

the dart. Draw in new dart lines in the desired position (shown in broken lines in the sketch) so that they will be at a level with the high point of the bust; by making the new dart lines parallel to the original lines, the resulting dart will be the same width as the original. Figure 19b illustrates that a dart can be changed in length.

Whenever the position of a dart is changed, there is a slight distortion at the vertical seamline which is caused by the need for a new "jog" for the new dart. However, if the dart position is

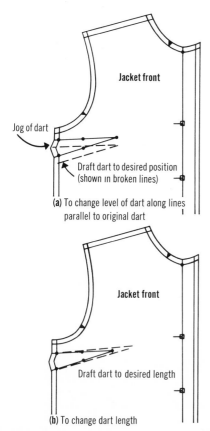

Jacket front

Jog of dart

Draft dart to desired position
(shown in broken lines)

(a) To change level of dart along lines parallel to original dart

Jacket front

Draft dart to desired length

(b) To change dart length

FIGURE 19

changed only a small amount (½ inch or less) and if the dart line is approximately at right angles to the vertical seamline, as shown in Figure 19, the slight distortion can be ignored. For larger alterations and diagonal darts, additional steps are necessary, as explained in the paragraphs below and illustrated in Figure 20.

See Figure 20a. This alteration is one in which the direction as well as the level of the dart has been altered. A change in direction might be made for two reasons: because the dart is so close to the seamline at the upper edge that it cannot be raised to the desired level (as illustrated in the example pictured) and because a different line is more attractive on the figure. If the direction of the dart is changed, the distortion at the vertical seamline will be such that a correction must be made. Any change in a diagonal dart (the French dart) will create serious distortion at the vertical seamline. Scotch-tape a strip of paper (preferably tissue paper) to the pattern in the dart area, as shown in Figure 20a.

See Figure 20b. Fold in the dart on the new dart lines and pin in place. Note the distortion on the vertical edge. Draw a new pattern line between points *C* and *D*; this line must be in character with the original (ruler-straight in this example) or in character with a curved line if the original line was curved. Cut along the new line, with the dart folded in; the distortion will be corrected, and a proper jog for the new dart will be formed.

ALTERATIONS FOR CHANGING PATTERN WIDTH (OVERALL SIZE)

GENERAL RULE 1: ALTER ONE-QUARTER OF THE DESIRED AMOUNT AT EACH SIDE EDGE

"Side edge" means not the two side

edges of each pattern piece but the edge of any pattern piece that will be at the side of the body when worn. See Figure 21, which illustrates this rule with the alterations for a figure that is slightly larger than average at waist and hip levels, becoming increasingly larger in the lower part of the body. Note that an identical alteration was made to the front and back; to alter overall size, make identical alterations on corresponding edges.

NOTE A most common error is to alter one-half rather than one-quarter of the desired amount. But keep in mind that most patterns are made on the half and will therefore be cut twice, so that an alteration of one-quarter of the desired amount will result in the proper amount when the complete garment is cut.

Figure 22 shows the side sections of a fitted jacket pattern with side edges altered according to the general rule stated above; the same alteration used for the skirt pieces in Figure 21 is shown. The inexperienced or careless person often neglects to alter jacket or coat hiplines even though she does alter the skirt pieces; the alterations at the side edges of the skirt and jacket or coat pieces must be identical.

Figure 23 pictures pattern pieces which will require an exception to the general rule. Note that the underarm or side position is located within the jacket-side section, making it impossible to alter at the side position according to the general rule. Alterations in patterns of this kind must be made on other vertical edges which will be slightly in back of, and to the front of, the side position on the body. Since there are two seams involved, making a total of four edges to be altered (and a grand total of eight edges when the pattern is doubled), one-eighth of the desired alteration must be

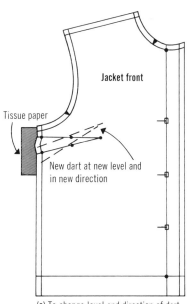

Tissue paper

Jacket front

New dart at new level and in new direction

(a) To change level and direction of dart

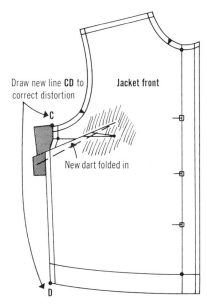

Draw new line **CD** to correct distortion

C

Jacket front

New dart folded in

D

(b) To correct distortion and create proper jog for new dart

FIGURE 20

made on the four edges involved, as shown. The alteration pictured will add extra size to both the front and the back for the figure that is somewhat too large in both areas, as is usually the case. However, there are figure problems which might suggest that the total addition be added to just the two back seams or to the front seams only. For example, if this extra size is needed because of a pad of flesh on the back hip, the addition could be made to the two back edges only, and if extra size is needed for unusually prominent hipbones, the total

addition (one-quarter of the desired amount) could be made on the two front edges.

GENERAL RULE 2: MAKE IDENTICAL ALTERATIONS ON ALL CORRESPONDING EDGES AND PATTERN PIECES

Of course, each pattern piece that will fit to the altered piece and to that part of the body which requires alteration must be altered identically. An addition to the waist of the skirt must be made on the waistband, an addition to the side edge of a jacket or coat must be made to the side edge of the lining pieces as well, etc. If one is not making a muslin test copy, those identical alterations on corresponding pieces and edges should be made at the time the structural pieces

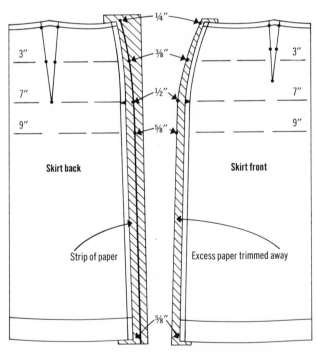

FIGURE 21 General rule 1. Alter one-quarter of the desired amount at each side edge. Example: addition of 1 inch at the waist, 1½ inches at the 3-inch hipline, 2 inches at the 7-inch hipline, and 2½ inches at the 9-inch hipline

are altered. However, if a test copy is made (as it will be for the tailored garment), corresponding alterations should be made after the basic alterations have been verified by fitting the muslin copy and after any additional alterations made during that fitting have been transferred to the structural pieces of the pattern.

GENERAL RULE 3: ALTERED LINES MUST BE IN CHARACTER WITH THE ORIGINAL PATTERN LINES
"In character" does not mean that the altered line should be identical to the original but that it should be similar enough to the original so that it does not distort the original. The original line at the side edge of a skirt curves slightly above the 7-inch hipline and is a ruler-straight line below the 7-inch hipline. After alteration, the corrected line must curve slightly (not abruptly) above the

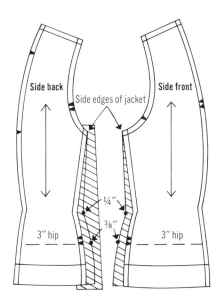

FIGURE 22 Illustration of general rule 1

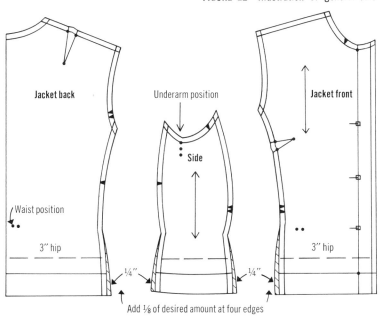

Add ⅛ of desired amount at four edges

FIGURE 23 An exception to general rule 1. Sample alteration: no addition at the waist and an addition of 2 inches at the 3-inch hipline

widest hip level, and it must be a ruler-straight line below that level.

Figure 24 illustrates this rule. Glance very quickly at the sketches, and you will see that although both side edges have been altered and are therefore not identical, the side edge in Figure 24a is a compatible, logical line, while the side edge of Figure 24b looks out of character.

These sketches have been included to serve a second purpose. There is some confusion in the minds of most women who sew about whether an addition at the hip levels should be continued in a parallel line to the lower edge, or whether the altered line can be brought back gradually to the original line at the lower edge, as it is shown in these sketches. If in doubt, the addition should be made on the whole length of the pattern, for it can easily be nipped in when the garment is fitted. *The general principle is this: The lower edge of the altered pattern must measure the same or slightly wider than the widest hip measure.* Three factors must be considered.

1 **the shape of skirt pieces** If the original skirt pieces are rectangular (Figure 24b), any addition at the hipline that is not extended to the lower edge will break the general rule and will make the skirt slightly pegged, and the altered line will not be in character with the original. If, however, the original skirt pieces are slightly flared at the side edge (Figure 24a), an addition can be made at the hiplines, and as long as the addition is small enough so that the altered hipline does not measure more than the lower edge, the addition can be narrowed

down to the original line at the lower edge without breaking the general rule.

2 **the amount of alteration involved** In Figure 24a, the alteration at the hiplines is very small and is less than the flare at the side edge of the skirt. However, to exaggerate the point, if 2 inches had been added to the side edge of the skirt, that great alteration would have made it necessary to continue the addition to the lower edge (as shown in Figure 21).

3 **the type of figure problem** The figure problem illustrated in Figure 24a is one of extra size in the area above the 7-inch hipline, but the thighs must not be large because no addition is needed at the 9-inch hipline. Therefore, movement of the thighs will not be a problem, and the alteration at the side edge can be narrowed back to the original line. However, the figure problem shown in Figure 24b is obviously one of larger-than-average hips and very probably larger-than-average thighs, as suggested by the fact that the greatest alteration is required at the 9-inch hipline. This figure will require extra size for movement of the thighs, and so any addition should be extended to the lower edge.

The slight curve above the 7-inch hipline has a great deal to do with the character of the side edges. The original pattern curved above the 7-inch hipline and was ruler-straight below because in the average figure, for which the pattern was made, the high point of the hip curve is near the 7-inch line. However, many figures differ: the bell-like figure may curve out the maximum amount at the high hip, the 3-inch level; and the figure with thick thighs may curve out the maximum amount at the lower hip, the 9-inch level.

So "in character" means that the side edges

should curve slightly above the high point of the hips (the 3-, 7-, or 9-inch hipline) and should be a ruler-straight line below that point.

See Figure 25 for three examples; in each case the required alteration (which results in a line that is not in character with the original) is sketched on the skirt back piece, and the proper alteration (in character with the original pattern line) is shown on the skirt front piece. The general rule of retaining the original character of lines is needed more in skirt patterns than in any other because the three hiplines, so close together and so close to the waist, may each require a different alteration.

The sketch on the left in Figure 25a shows the alteration problem marked off with dots and a broken line on a strip of paper. This figure is average in one respect—the high point of the hip is the 7-inch hipline—but the figure is larger than average. Examine the broken line to see that it looks strange; it is not in character with the original. The sketch on the right shows the problem solved with a slightly curving line above the high point of the hip and a ruler-straight line below. In this case, the line tapers back to the original line at the lower edge because the 9-inch hipline is normal, indicating that the figure does not have large thighs, and because the 7-inch hip measures less than the lower edge, extra width is not needed in the lower area.

The sketch on the left in Figure 25b shows the alteration problem marked off with dots and a broken line on a strip of paper. This figure is not average in that the high point of the hip is at the 9-inch hipline, and the figure is larger than average at that level. The broken line is not in character. The sketch on the right shows the problem solved with a slightly curving line above the high point of

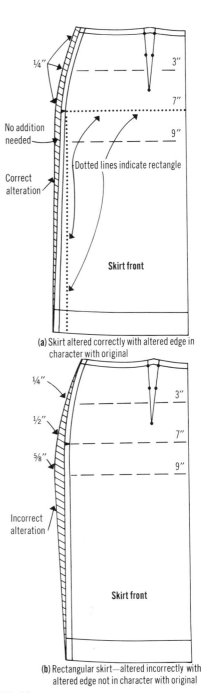

(a) Skirt altered correctly with altered edge in character with original

(b) Rectangular skirt—altered incorrectly with altered edge not in character with original

FIGURE 24

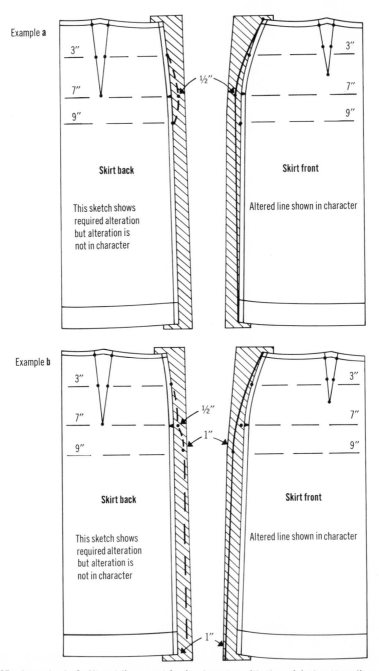

Example **a**

3″
7″
9″
½″

Skirt back

This sketch shows
required alteration
but alteration is
not in character

Skirt front

Altered line shown in character

3″
7″
9″

Example **b**

3″
7″
9″
½″
1″

Skirt back

This sketch shows
required alteration
but alteration is
not in character

Skirt front

Altered line shown in character

3″
7″
9″

1″

FIGURE 25 General rule 3. Altered lines must be in character with the original pattern lines

the hip and a ruler-straight line below. In this case, the additional width was added the full length of the skirt because the extra width required at the 10-inch hipline indicates that there is a thigh and leg problem and that this figure probably needs extra size in the lower area.

The sketch on the left in Figure 25c shows the alteration problem marked off with dots and a broken line on a strip of paper. This is the bell-shaped figure, very round at the upper hip level. The broken line is not in character. The sketch on the right shows this problem solved with a slightly curving line above the high point of the hip and a ruler-straight line below. In this case, the line tapers back to the original line at the lower edge because the 9-inch hipline is normal, indicating that the figure does not have large thighs and that extra width is not needed in the lower area.

This problem is more complicated

than the other two, and it involves another rule:

If more than ½ inch is added at each side edge (2 inches of total size) at the 3- or 7-inch hipline, an addition must be made to the waistline in order to keep the corrected line in character with the original.

This must be done even if the figure does not require extra size at the waist, as the illustrated problem shows. Note that the amount added is about one-half the amount that was added at the 3-inch hipline; enough width must be added so that the line curves slightly (not abruptly) above the 3-inch hipline.

If the waist does not require addi-

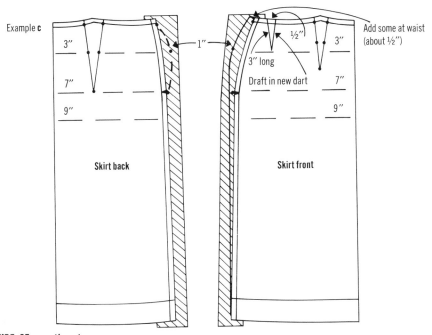

FIGURE 25 continued

tional width, this alteration has made the waistline too large. However, this extra waist size is a great advantage in fitting this type of figure because the figure that is more rounded than average needs extra dart shaping to give the extra shape needed in this rounded area. For the 1-inch addition at the 3-inch hipline, an addition of about ½ inch at the waistline was made. Draft in a new dart, ½ inch wide and 3 inches long, as shown. It is impossible to say exactly where this dart should be located. Darts create shape and should be located to create shape where the figure is most rounded. In figures of this bell-shaped type, a good estimate of placement is about 2 to 2½ inches from the original side seamline. This will be satisfactory for the time being; this dart should be basted in for a first fitting. During the fitting, the posi-

tion can be changed, and the dart can be lengthened or shortened as the individual figure requires.

All the general rules explained above can be applied to all pattern pieces. Figure 26 illustrates this rule, concerning the character of the altered line, applied to the side edges of sections of a fitted jacket or coat. The example given is the same as Figure 25c; study this sketch in relation to Figure 25c to see that the principle is exactly the same, applied to new circumstances. The dart, a temporary one to be tested for accuracy during the first fitting of the muslin copy, must be extended above the waist; a length of 5 inches is a good estimate.

ALTERATIONS
FOR CHANGING
SLEEVE WIDTH
AND SHOULDER HEIGHT

TO ALTER SLEEVE WIDTH FOR HEAVY ARMS

Heavy arms create a troublesome problem because width must be added, and yet it makes the cap of the sleeve fuller; the result can be a somewhat gathered sleeve cap. Of course, the greater the addition, the more gathered the effect. These alterations solve this problem to a large extent.

Figure 27 illustrates one way of gaining extra sleeve width, but this method is confined to those circumstances when extra size has been added to the jacket or coat at a corresponding position; in other words, if width has been added to the jacket or coat pieces in order to increase bust size, this alteration can be used. In the one-piece sleeve, the addition must be the same as that added to each side edge of the garment pieces. The addition can be extended to the lower edge, as shown, if the arm is heavy for its full length, but the addition can be gradually

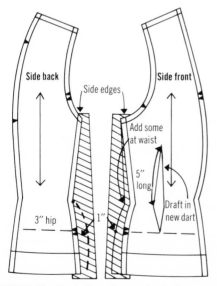

FIGURE 26 Illustration of general rule 3

(labels within figure): Side back — Side edges — Side front — Add some at waist — 5" long — 3" hip — 1" — Draft in new dart

tapered in to the original line at the lower edge if only the upper arm is fuller than average.

Only the under-sleeve section of the two-piece sleeve is involved in this alteration because the underarm position (corresponding to the underarm seams of the garment) is located in this sleeve section and marked by dots on the pattern. Because the addition will be made in one position only, it must be twice the amount added at each side edge of the jacket or coat. Slash the under sleeve at the underarm position on a line parallel to the straight-of-material line. The sketch pictures an insertion strip which gradually narrows down to the original width at the lower edge; this alteration will be correct for the figure with extra size in the upper-arm area only. If the arm is fuller than average for its total length, a parallel insertion strip should be used. Mark the new underarm position and a new grain-line position along the center of the insertion strip.

NOTE These general principles can be used to decrease sleeve width. Excess size can be trimmed from the vertical edges of the one-piece sleeve. For the two-piece sleeve, the same slash is made and the pattern edges lapped over each other to decrease width as desired.

If jacket or coat pieces have not been altered in size, an addition of sleeve width cannot be made at the underarm position as shown in Figure 27 and must be made in the body of the sleeve by methods shown in Figures 28 and 29.

Figure 28 shows a simple method of inserting an extension strip, which is quite acceptable if the addition will be less than ½ inch and if the fabric eases well (crepes, knits, soft woolens). Draw in the biceps line at right angles to the straight-of-material line; it will be used as a guideline. See Figure 5 on page 66 to establish the biceps line in the

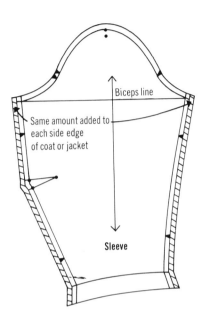

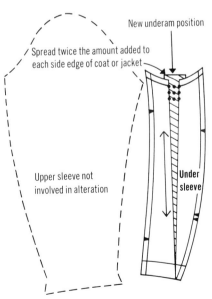

FIGURE 27 To increase sleeve width when bust size of jacket or coat piece has been increased

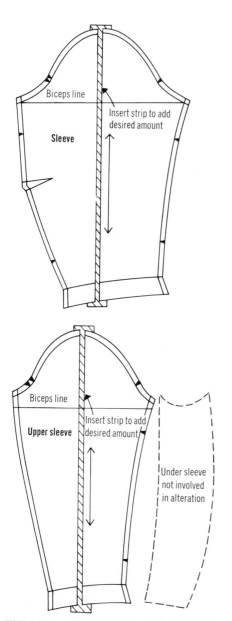

FIGURE 28 To increase sleeve width ½ inch or less in fabrics that ease well

two-piece sleeve. Slash the pattern from the shoulder position to the lower edge on a line parallel to the straight-of-material line. Be sure the right-angle guideline remains ruler-straight in the altered pattern. The shoulder position should be marked halfway between the original shoulder markings (at the center of the insertion).

Figure 29 pictures another solution, the wiser choice for an addition of about 1 inch and for all fabrics that do not ease well. The method is identical to the one described above, but with one addition. Draft in a dart on slightly curving lines, as shown. The dart position will act as a shoulder-line marking. This dart will be sewn in and will appear in the finished garment. This idea might meet with some resistance from the reader, but its great advantages far outweigh the one disadvantage that a dart in this position is somewhat unusual (designers use it occasionally, however). The addition of this dart makes it possible to gain the width required at the biceps line without having excess fullness to ease into the armhole; the dart is far less offensive than a gathered-looking sleeve.

Depending on the amount of width added by this type of alteration and depending on the size of the arm below the elbow, additional corrections must be expected during fitting. If a great deal of width is added and if the lower arm is quite average in size, the vertical seams will have to be fitted for a gradually narrowing effect at the first fitting of the muslin test copy.

TO ALTER SHOULDER HEIGHT

Figure 30 pictures garment pieces and the sleeve pattern and illustrates the alteration for shoulders that are squarer than average. The desired increase is added at the outer, armhole edge of the garment pieces and gradually tapers back to the original shoulder line at the neck edge. The same amount must be added at the shoulder position on the sleeve cap, gradually tapering back to the original pattern line at the notch position.

For shoulders that slope more than average, the alteration can be done in a similar way; in that case, excess is trimmed from the pattern. The alteration is not pictured because it seems wiser to take care of this correction in fitting, at least for the first several projects. When several garments have been tested and a need for the alteration is clearly indicated, a pattern alteration can be made safely.

TO ALTER SHOULDER WIDTH

See Figure 31a, which pictures the front and back pieces of the garment properly altered for additional width. Slash into the patterns from the shoulder line (about 2 inches in from the armhole edge) to the armhole seamline at approximately the notch position. Use an extension strip to gain the extra width. Pivot the small section out from the notch position to achieve the desired increase and Scotch-tape in place. This will distort the shoulder line very slightly, and it should be straightened with a ruler. The same method in reverse will decrease shoulder width, as shown in Figure 31b. Cut to the notch position and lap out the excess width. This alteration will result in very slight distortion of the shoulder line; even it with a ruler. The sleeve pattern is not affected in any way by this alteration.

ALTERATIONS FOR CHANGING PATTERN SHAPE AS WELL AS SIZE

WARNING The alterations included in this section are remarkably effective and will result in

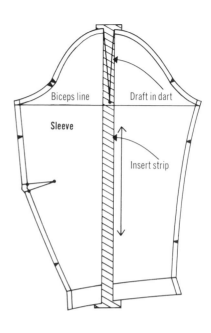

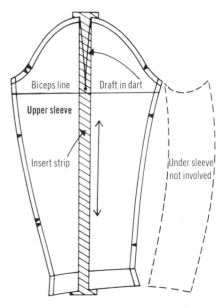

FIGURE 29 To increase sleeve width larger amounts; method recommended for fabrics that do not ease well

greatly improved fit for the figure that differs in shape from the average figure. However, each one requires an estimate (an educated guess) that cannot be completely scientific. So each altered pattern (skirt as well as jacket or coat) must be tested in muslin to verify the estimate. After many garments have been made and the estimate has been perfected, the alteration can be made with confidence without muslin testing.

TWO METHODS OF ADDING WIDTH

The section beginning on page 80 includes general rules for adding width or overall size. *The rules given there should be used for the figure that is quite average in general shape but differs in measurement from the average; they should be used for the figure that is smaller or larger than average in both front and back.*

The more complicated alterations in this section are involved primarily with shape. The following statement should help clarify the difference between the two methods: *If the problem is one of overall size quite equally distributed throughout the body, the general rules for adding width should be used; if the problem is one of shape in a specific portion of the body, these alterations should be used.*

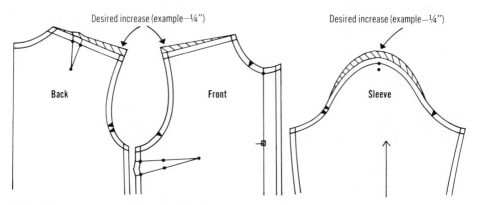

FIGURE 30 To increase height of shoulder line and sleeve cap for square shoulders

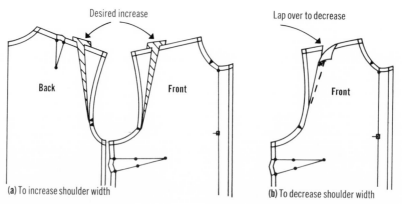

FIGURE 31 To alter shoulder width

The following figure irregularities have to do with shape in a particular part of the body, and the problems they create can be solved by the alterations in this section. Consider the fit of most of the garments in your wardrobe (those made with patterns and those ready-made); all were made for the average figure, and any misfit is a result of your own variation from the average. These brief descriptions explain how the garment, cut for the average figure, will look on a figure that is not average in shape.

protruding hips When viewed from the side, the side seams of the average skirt swing toward the back, rather than falling in a plumb line; the skirt juts outward at the center back. There may be some evidence of diagonal ripples leading from the high point of the hip curve diagonally downward toward the side seam.

prominent hipbones or stomach When viewed from the side, the side seams of the average skirt may swing toward the front, and the skirt may jut out at the center front. There will be evidence of diagonal ripples leading from the larger-than-average curve diagonally downward toward the side seam.

flat hips or smaller-than-average front curves The dart fittings in the average skirt create too much shape, and there will be puckers at the tip of the darts; the garment does not lie smoothly on the body.

round shoulders In the fitted garment, diagonal ripples form at the larger-than-average curve and lead diagonally downward toward the side seam or diagonally upward toward the outer edge of the shoulder.

flat shoulders or very straight back The dart fittings of the average garment create more shape than the figure requires, and the garment stands away (bows out) from the figure in the shoulder area; it does not lie smoothly over body curves.

larger-than-average bust curve In the fitted garment, diagonal ripples lead from the high point of the bust in any one of several directions: diagonally upward to the outer edge of the shoulder or to the neck edge, diagonally across to the armhole seam, or (the most common direction) from the high point of the bust diagonally downward toward the side seam. A boxy garment will have a "maternity-wear" look.

smaller-than-average bust curve The dart fittings of the average garment create more shape than the figure can fill out, and the garment stands away from the figure at the bust; it does not lie smoothly over body curves.

There is an issue of size in each of these problems, but the variation in shape is far more important. Ordinarily, problems of shape are solved by fitting rather than pattern alteration, but if they can be solved (or partially solved) by pattern alteration, fitting is greatly simplified.

THE PRINCIPLE OF THE DART
Shape is created in a garment by the use of seams and dart fittings, but in most garments, the dart fittings play the larger role. The principle of the dart is this:

The dart must end near the high point of the

curve it is to fit; the greater the curve, the wider the dart required to fit it properly, and the smaller the curve, the narrower the dart required.

This principle will be used for all alterations in this section (and will be used later when the garment is fitted).

Each alteration will alter dart width, and the problem (the estimate, the educated guess) is to decide exactly how much the width should change. Shape is difficult to pinpoint in scientifically obtained measurements. One can see that a prominent curve (bust or back hips) differs from average, but it is difficult to state the variation exactly. For this reason, the

muslin test copy is absolutely essential for testing every alteration in this section. The estimated alteration will be made, tested in muslin, and then corrected if necessary before the pattern is cut in fabric. Directions will include a spread of estimates for each alteration, but the reader must understand that they are educated guesses and that some other amount, slightly different, might be better for her particular figure.

A quick glance at Figure 32 will illustrate that while a change is being made in dart width and therefore in the shape of the garment, there is an additional advantage of a change in size. And the change in size, whether it is more or less, is made exactly where the problem figure requires the change. These two improvements, occurring simultaneously, are responsible for the very effective results of these alterations.

SKIRT ALTERATIONS FOR PROTRUDING HIPS OR PROMINENT FRONT CURVES

Figure 32   Draw a ruler line down the center of the dart to the lower edge. Slash along the ruler line to a point $\frac{1}{16}$ inch from the lower edge. Scotch-tape one edge of the pattern to a ruler-straight line on a strip of paper. Make an estimate of the extra width required at the hipline. The estimate might vary from $\frac{1}{4}$ inch for slightly protruding hips to an inch or more for exaggerated problems. Allow the pattern to spread the desired amount at the hipline, retaining the original width at the lower edge, and secure the remaining edge to the insertion strip, being sure to keep the pattern edge ruler-straight, as shown. Draft in a new dart from midway between the old dart lines at the tip to the original markings at the waistline, as shown. Note that this alteration has resulted in a wider dart, which will create more shape for the larger-than-average curve, and has

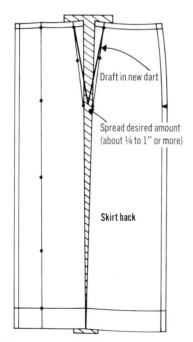

Draft in new dart

Spread desired amount
(about ¼ to 1" or more)

Skirt back

FIGURE 32   For protruding hips—to increase size and shape by enlarging existing dart

allowed extra width exactly where it is
required.

Figure 33   A change in a dart requires a
new dart jog in order that edges, when
sewn, will be even at the cut edge. To
make a jog for the new dart, fold along
the corrected dart line nearest the center
and bring that line to the remaining corrected dart line. Pin in place. Trim the
upper edge along the cutting line of the
pattern, with the dart folded in.

NOTE   This step is necessary if darts will be
pressed to one side and will remain their full
width in the finished garment. But this step can
be ignored in the tailored garment made of heavy
fabric because darts will be slashed and pressed
open and large darts will be trimmed to a narrower width, in which case the jog has no real
purpose.

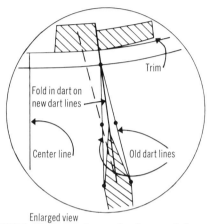

Enlarged view
FIGURE 33   To create new jog for new dart

Figure 34   This sketch shows the identical alteration done in a slightly different
way. Rather than increasing the width of
the existing dart, the pattern can be
slashed and spread to allow for an additional dart. The dart can differ in length
to create shape at any level desired. Additional shape and size have been created
by use of the same principle. The additional dart is a wiser choice when large
increases in width are required because
two darts create shape over a broader
area. Draft in a new dart with its tip
midway between the slashed lines at the
level of the most prominent curve, ending at the cut edges of the pattern at the
waistline, as shown.

Figure 35   The width of darts in the
front skirt can be increased in an identical manner. The existing dart can be increased (as illustrated in Figure 32), or
an additional dart can be added (as
shown in Figure 34). Figure 35 shows
the most complicated alteration for the

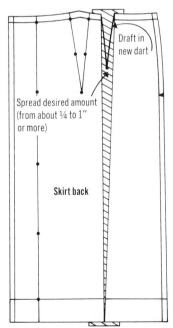

FIGURE 34   For protruding hips—to increase size
and shape by adding an additional dart

front skirt. The figure with very prominent hipbones requires shape at the high point of the hipbone. Hold the skirt in proper position to the figure and mark the high point of the hipbone on the pattern. Now slash this pattern from any desired position on the waistline through the marking for the hipbone, extending the line to within 1/16 inch of the seamline at the side edge. Scotch-tape one edge of the pattern to a ruler-straight line on a strip of paper. Allow the pattern to spread the desired amount at the position of the hipbone, retaining the original line at the side seamline. Secure the remaining edge to the insertion strip, being sure to keep the pattern edge

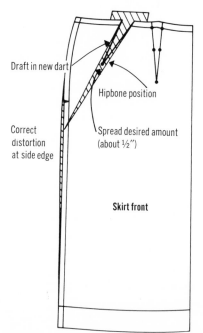

Draft in new dart

Hipbone position

Correct distortion at side edge

Spread desired amount (about 1/2")

Skirt front

FIGURE 35 For prominent hipbones—to increase size and shape by adding a dart

ruler-straight, as shown. An estimate of 1/2 inch, more or less, should be good for most figures. Draft in a new dart with its tip midway between the slashed lines at the hipbone position, ending at the cut edges of the pattern at the waistline, as shown.

This alteration has slightly distorted the side seamline—it is not in character with the original. Correct the distortion with a ruler line from the high point of the hip to the original line at the lower edge, as shown. To create the jog for a new dart, see Figure 33.

SKIRT ALTERATIONS FOR SMALLER-THAN-AVERAGE CURVES

NOTE Problems of flat hips or smaller-than-average front curves can be solved in a similar manner, worked in reverse. The sketch pictures a back skirt altered for flat hips; the front skirt can be altered in an identical way.

Figure 36 To decrease dart width, draw a line down the center of the dart to the lower edge. Slash along the ruler line to within 1/16 inch from the lower edge. Make an estimate of the desired decrease in width at the hip level. Estimates will be quite small—a 1/4-inch decrease for slight problems would be wise, and it would be rare if a decrease of more than 3/8 inch were required for very flat figures. Lap one cut edge over the other the desired amount at the hip level, retaining the original size at the lower edge; be sure to work with ruler-straight lines so that the pattern remains flat.

The sketch does not picture the new dart drafted in because the lines are confusing on a sketch. Note that the two dart markings at the waistline are now closer together. Draft in a new dart from midway between the markings at the tip of the old dart, returning to the original markings at the waistline. Note that this alteration has resulted in a narrower dart, which will create less shape for the smaller-than-average curve and also in less width and overall size. To create the jog for a new dart, see Figure 33.

JACKET OR COAT ALTERATIONS FOR SHOULDER CURVES THAT DIFFER FROM THE AVERAGE

NOTE The sketch shows the alteration for round shoulders, but this alteration can be worked in reverse for the figure with a very straight back. Figure 36 illustrates the principle that can be used for any pattern piece when less shape and size are desired.

Figure 37 Greater shape and extra width for round shoulders can be obtained by enlarging the existing dart (Figure 37a) or by creating an additional dart (Figure 37b). The alteration is made following the general principles used in skirt alterations; see the text accompanying Figures 32 to 34. The amount of spread required at the shoulder level will probably vary from ¼ inch for slightly rounded shoulders to ½ inch and perhaps as much as ¾ inch for very exaggerated problems. If the larger amount is required, it is wiser to create a new dart (Figure 37b) so that shape will be spread over a broader area.

A discussion of the problems of creating more or less shape in garments with princess lines appears on page 103, and the alteration for round shoulders (which is similar in principle to the problem shown in Figure 37) is shown in Figure 46.

JACKET OR COAT ALTERATIONS FOR THE BUST WITH LARGER-THAN-AVERAGE CURVES

The larger-than-average bust is the most serious figure problem, for it is one that cannot be solved completely after a garment has been cut; the problem must be solved as a pattern alteration. The pattern has been made for an average bust

line, which is really relatively small—an A or B cup size. The person who wears a larger cup size is larger than average and requires this alteration. The principle of increasing or decreasing shape is the same as that used for skirt alterations, but bust alterations are more complicated for three reasons: (1) bust curves vary more than any other curves on the body, (2) front patterns are more intricately cut to create design features, and (3) in some cases, the alteration involves a change on several pattern pieces. However, because the larger-than-average bust is the most difficult problem to solve in fitting, these alterations are especially valuable and are well worth the time and thought they require.

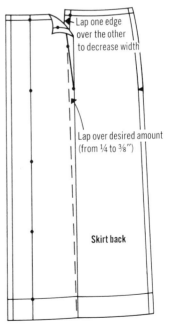

FIGURE 36 For flat hips—to decrease size and shape

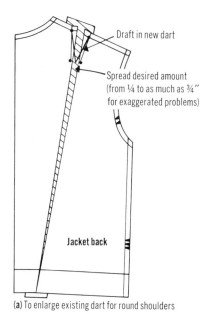

Draft in new dart

Spread desired amount
(from ¼ to as much as ¾"
for exaggerated problems)

Jacket back

(a) To enlarge existing dart for round shoulders

Draft in new dart

Spread desired amount
(from ¼ to as much as ¾"
for exaggerated problems)

Jacket back

(b) To create additional dart for round shoulders

FIGURE 37 For round shoulders—to increase size
and shape

The alteration problem would be simple if an estimate of the alteration could be based on cup size alone. However, there is another factor involved in bust shape; posture plays a large part. The person who holds herself erectly adds chest size to her bust curve; a Junior-A cup size and an erect posture may result in a figure that is larger than average; a D cup size and a sagging posture may result in average shape. It is this ambiguous factor of posture that makes any estimate included in these alterations little more than an educated guess. Muslin testing is absolutely necessary until the estimate has been perfected scientifically.

The following estimates of the amount of additional spread at the bust point must be considered quite general because of the posture issue:

1 For a size A cup with normal posture, undoubtedly no alteration is required, but if the posture is very erect, an additional ¼-inch spread may be required.

2 For a size B cup with normal posture, probably no alteration is required, but if the posture is very erect, a spread of ¼ to as much as ¾ inch may be required.

3 For a size C cup with normal posture, a spread of ½ inch may be required, but if the posture is very erect, as much as 1 inch may be required.

4 For a size D cup with normal posture, a spread of ¾ inch may be required, but if the posture is very erect, as much as 1¼ inches may be required.

Figure 38 The sketches show two examples of jacket or coat designs with darts in a somewhat vertical direction. All patterns can be altered following the general principles used in the skirt alterations. Draw a ruler line down the center of the dart for the full length of the pattern. Slash to within 1/16 inch of the lower edge or within 1/16 inch of the seamline. Scotch-tape one edge of the pattern to a ruler-straight line on a strip of paper. Estimate the desired spread at the bust level (see above) and secure the remaining edge to the insertion strip, keeping lines ruler-straight. Draft in a new dart from midway between the old dart lines at the tip to the original dart markings at the shoulder or waist, as shown. Note that this alteration has resulted in a wider dart for the larger-than-average curve and in extra width exactly where it is required. To create a new jog for the shoulder dart, see Figure 33.

Figure 39 Horizontal and diagonal darts create an additional problem. The principle of alteration is exactly the same as for the vertical darts discussed above. However, when the pattern is spread to create extra shape for the bust, the front edge of the pattern is distorted. The distortion must be corrected by drawing in a line in character with the original—usually the original line is ruler-straight, as shown. Note that the center-front line is similarly distorted and must be corrected; buttonhole markings must be relocated and respaced on the corrected center-front line because there will be a very slight dislocation of buttonhole markings.

This alteration has affected the front facing, which must be altered in a corresponding manner, as shown. Test the accuracy of the alteration by placing the altered patterns together and being sure that cut edges of the altered patterns are even.

Figure 40 The sketch illustrates an additional problem encountered when a horizontal or diagonal dart is altered in a pattern with a front facing cut in one with the garment. Compare this sketch

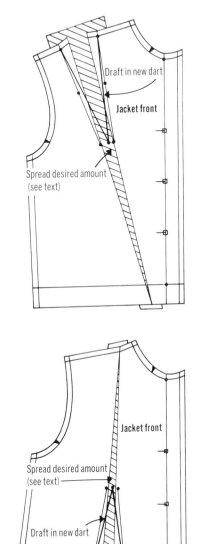

Draft in new dart

Jacket front

Spread desired amount (see text)

Jacket front

Spread desired amount (see text)

Draft in new dart

Waist position

FIGURE 38 For larger-than-average bust—to increase size and shape by enlarging existing dart

with the sketches in Figure 39 to see that the alteration is identical in general principle. The only difference is that this pattern must be slashed along the fold line before alteration is begun, and when both sections have been altered, the two sections must be combined again. Note that the new fold line is a ruler-straight line located midway between the altered, original fold lines.

Figure 41 Ordinarily, one does not add an additional dart to a jacket or coat front because it alters the design somewhat. However, there are circumstances under which one might need to create a new dart; the sketch shows an example that appears quite frequently. The de-

sign with a seam close to the bust, involving a side section to complete the front unit, is sometimes made with no dart fitting to allow definite shape right at the point of the bust, although shaping in the general area is created through the seam. If a design line is even a short distance over from the high point of the bust, the person with a larger-than-average bust must make a new dart for the shape she needs at the bust point.

At the present time, designers seem to favor a "no-dart" look; in all pattern books and especially in *Vogue* books, there are many designs which do not have darts to create shape directly at the bust curve. The issue becomes more serious when seams are a greater distance from the high point of the bust. General shaping can be created by seams, but the bust curve, particularly if it is larger than average, requires more than general shaping. The design pictured in Figure

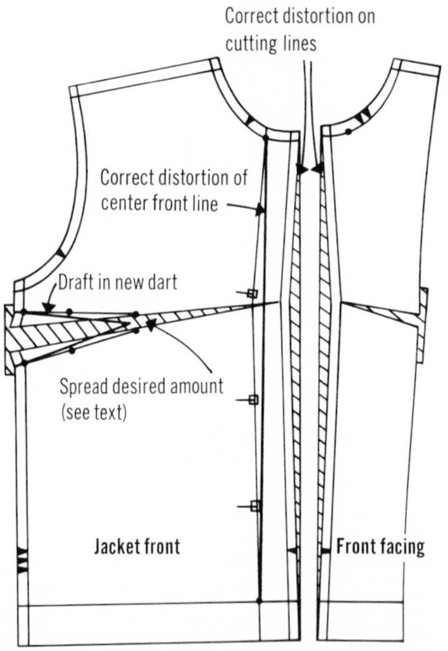

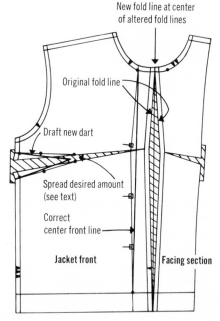

FIGURE 39 For larger-than-average bust—to increase size and shape by enlarging existing dart

FIGURE 40 To alter for larger-than-average bust when front and facing are cut in one piece

41 has a seam which appears to be about 2 inches from the bust point; shaping created by the seam is in the general area of the bust. However, in current pattern books, there are several designs with seams as far as 4 or 5 inches from the bust; there is not even subtle shaping in the bust area. It is unfortunate that the designers are favoring the no-dart look, for it does not result in a good fit for even the small-busted person and it results in a truly bad fit for the large-busted person. More unfortunately it has little if any real merit: A dart line is not offensive to design and often enhances it. Therefore, if good fit is important to the reader, she may want to use the alteration pictured in Figure 41, regardless of her bust size.

With the pattern pieces pinned together and fitted on the body, mark the point of the bust, as shown in the upper sketch. Slash the pattern from any desired position on the vertical seam through the bust point to within 1/16 inch of the seamline at the front edge. Scotch-tape one edge of the pattern to a ruler-straight line on a strip of paper. Allow the pattern to spread the desired amount at the bust. Draft in a new dart with its tip midway between the slashed edges at the bust, ending at the cut edges of the pattern at the vertical seam, as shown. To create a jog for the new dart, see Figure 33. Correct the distortion on the front edge and on the center-front line. Relocate and respace button markings on the corrected center-front line. Make corresponding alterations on the front-facing pattern, as shown in Figure 39.

ADDITIONAL ALTERATIONS FOR THE LARGER-THAN-AVERAGE BUST

A brief review of the several alterations in this section will be helpful at this

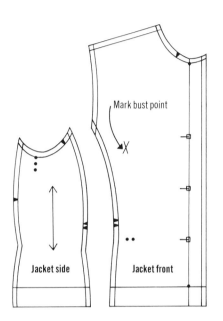

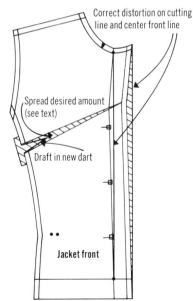

FIGURE 41   For   larger-than-average   bust—to create an additional dart

time. These alterations have changed the shape of the pattern by changing dart size and have resulted in a change in size (width) at the exact position where extra size is required; by contrast, the general rules for adding overall size on pages 80 to 88 result in extra overall size (width) in both the front and the back sections of the pattern.

The curve that is larger than average requires extra width, and of course it requires extra length to cover the larger curve, as well. Depending on the position of the dart which appears in the pattern, these alterations have resulted in extra width or extra length and have not resulted in both. Note that every alteration has resulted in a wider dart for

more shape but that the vertical darts shown in Figures 32, 34, 35, 37, and 38 have added extra width, while the horizontal darts illustrated in Figures 39 to 41 have resulted in additional length only. So all the alterations have taken care of the shape issue, while the issue of extra size at the point it is required is not entirely solved. This is not serious at all in the case of the vertical darts (in other words, it is not a serious problem if width has been obtained) because the extra length required in the pattern with vertical darts can be easily obtained by adjusting hem length on the finished garment. But the problem is more serious in the pattern with horizontal darts when no extra width has been obtained; the figure with a bust very much larger than average is in great need of extra width in the area very close to the bust point.

See Figure 42 for an example of the method of obtaining extra width for the larger-than-average bust on a pattern with horizontal darts. Refer back to Figure 41, where the first step of slashing and spreading the dart is pictured. Add an additional strip of paper to give extra width on the curved edge of this pattern. This need not be an exact amount (be sure it is ample) because it will not be incorporated into the fitting of the muslin copy. Mark the original seamline as shown; these dots will be tailor-tacked, and the muslin copy of the garment should be basted with this original seamline matching the seamline on the corresponding piece. Then during fitting, if a need for extra width arises, the seam can be ripped, and this extra allowance can be used. (See Figure 12, page 123, to see how this issue will be handled during fitting.) After that fitting, then, any extra width needed at this point can be transferred to the pattern as a scientific alteration.

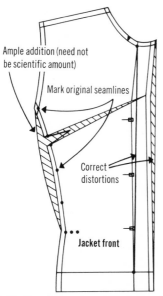

Ample addition (need not be scientific amount)

Mark original seamlines

Correct distortions

Jacket front

FIGURE 42 To allow extra width for a pattern with horizontal darts

ALTERATIONS FOR THE TYPICAL PRINCESS-LINE GARMENT

The typical princess-line garment has no darts, and the shape for body curves (front or back) is achieved by the use of shaped seams which serve the function of darts. See Figure 43, which pictures the two sections of a princess-line jacket front. The two pattern pieces have been placed in such a position that they almost touch each other at the bust level and the hip level; notice that the seamlines create shape that suggests the shape of a small shoulder dart and a small underbust dart. If something is done to move the pattern farther apart at the bust level, while keeping the same position at the lower edge, there will be a greater space between the pattern at the shoulder (try this with your own pattern), and it will be the same thing as creating a wider dart.

Figure 44 shows the alteration that will, in effect, create more shaping for the bust, while at the same time adding width at the bust level. An ample addition has been made at the bust level, gradually tapering back to the original pattern lines at the shoulder and waist. This need not be an exact amount (be sure it is ample) because it will not be incorporated into the fitting of the muslin copy. Mark the original seamline as shown; these dots will be tailor-tacked, and the muslin copy should be basted with this original seamline matching the seamline of the corresponding piece. Then during fitting, if the need for extra width arises, the seam can be ripped, and this extra allowance can be used. (See Figure 12, page 123, to see how this issue will be handled during fitting.)

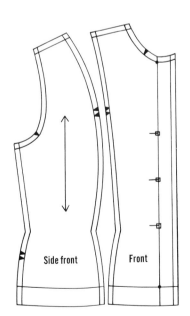

FIGURE 43 The princess-line garment has dart fitting created by shaped seams

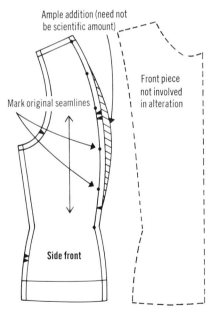

FIGURE 44 To alter princess-line garment for larger-than-average bust

After that fitting, then, any extra width needed at this point can be transferred to the pattern as a scientific alteration.

If the bust is very much larger than average (a D-cup figure), the above alteration can be combined with the alteration which adds an extra dart in the position where it is needed. See Figure 45. An extra dart can be added to the side front piece, as shown, just as the extra dart was added to the jacket front in Figure 41. Notice that the spread for an extra dart has distorted the grain line slightly, just as the similar alteration in Figure 41 distorted the center front, which was the grain line of that pattern piece. Correct the slight distortion by extending the straight-of-material line in the lower part of the pattern, as shown. Some extra shape has been created by

this extra dart, and more shape can be created by following the directions given in the preceding paragraph.

The principle of this alteration can be applied to the back pattern to correct round shoulders, as shown in Figure 46.

JACKET OR COAT ALTERATIONS FOR THE BUST WITH LESS-THAN-AVERAGE CURVES

The smaller-than-average bust is not a great problem because so many women who have the problem solve it very easily by wearing padded bras. If desired, the pattern can be altered, following the principles discussed in the text accompanying Figure 36; every alteration pictured in this section can be done in reverse to create less shape and size.

CORRESPONDING ALTERATIONS FOR LINING PATTERNS

If separate lining pieces are included with the pattern, alterations for shoulders

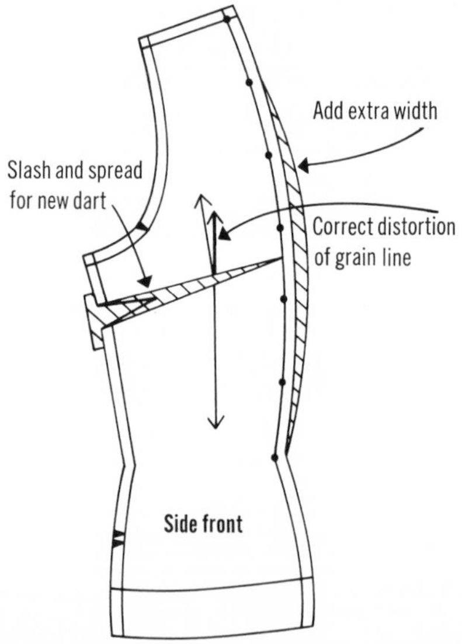

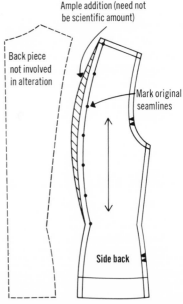

FIGURE 45 To alter princess-line garment for very large bust

FIGURE 46 To alter princess-line garment for round shoulders

or bust must be made on the lining patterns. These alterations should not be made immediately; alteration of the structural pieces should be tested in muslin before alterations are made on lining pieces.

Back-lining patterns are simple to alter because the dart arrangement is identical to that in the jacket pieces. But the dart positions in lining-front patterns are not always identical in every way to those in the jacket or coat sections, so it is often difficult to alter these pieces in an identical manner. For example, the lining pattern included with the commercial pattern may have a shoulder tuck or dart that does not appear in the garment, or there may be a tuck in the lining in

the position where a dart appears in the garment. It is difficult to make identical pattern alterations on pieces that do not have identical darts and seams. If the lining pattern is very different or if very complicated pattern alterations were made, it is simpler to make a new lining pattern than to alter the existing one. This can be done by copying portions of the altered pattern pieces for the garment; see To Make Lining Patterns on page 295.

FITTING
THE MUSLIN
TEST
COPY

The discussion in this chapter is confined to testing the jacket or coat. The test copy of the jacket or coat is required because these garments have intricate design features, because they are composed of intricately shaped pattern pieces, and because the figure in the bust and shoulder area is most difficult to fit.

However, a test copy of the skirt, as well as the jacket, is necessary under certain circumstances. If the skirt is intricately cut in unusual lines that may not be attractive on the figure, it is wise to make a muslin copy. The person with a problem figure should make a test copy of the skirt. The problem figure is not one that is larger or smaller in overall size (this can be taken care of easily by pattern alteration), but is one in which curves in particular areas are shaped very differently from those in the average figure. Examples are unusually large thighs, protruding hips, and prominent front curves. The figure with less curve than average does not require a muslin copy because corrections can be made safely by fitting in the wool fabric. The figure which is larger than average but quite average in shape is no great problem, providing the skirt is cut sufficiently large. Read Purposes of the Muslin Copy below to determine whether a test copy is needed. In addition, read Fitting the Skirt on pages 178 to 190, paying particular attention to the section on seam direction (Figures 10 to 17). If any of the flaws in seam direction pictured are problems you have encountered in ready-made or homemade garments, it would be wise to make a muslin copy of the skirt, using fitting directions on pages 178 to 191.

PURPOSES OF THE MUSLIN COPY

The purposes of the muslin copy are (1) to check the fit of the garment and the accuracy of pattern alterations, (2) to test design features for placement and proportions, (3) to test the appropriateness of the design on the figure and the degree to which the individual finds it comfortable and appealing, and (4) to allow practice on new and complicated construction details. These purposes indicate a great need for the muslin copy for the first ventures in tailoring. However, there are circumstances under which the muslin copy loses its value. If the figure is so average in size and shape that patterns and ready-made garments fit perfectly (the "straight-size" figure), there is no need to test the pattern for size and fit. If the figure is average in length as well as size, design features and proportions will be attractive. If the design is a

simple one in basic lines (completely "safe"—nothing to dislike), there is little reason to test its appeal to the individual. And of course, the person with much experience needs no practice on construction details.

If the muslin copy is to serve all purposes well, it must be made with high standards of accuracy. One must guard against the tendency to be careless; the tendency does exist because the worker realizes that she will not wear the garment and that she is working with inexpensive fabric. Extreme care must be taken when practicing intricate construction details. And if the muslin test copy is to present a true picture of the design, it must be constructed and pressed well so that it will be attractive.

CUTTING AND MARKING

NOTE For fitted garments only: If the garment will hug the body for a very trim effect, it is well to cut 1 inch beyond the edge of the pattern at the side position (the edge that will be at the side when the garment is worn). The side seam, then, should be basted in a 1⅝-inch seam allowance and the excess size used only if necessary. This is a wise precaution because these garments must fit so perfectly that they frequently require adjustment in size during fitting.

Only the jacket or coat pieces are used for the muslin copy. Pieces are cut in the usual way, although certain concessions can be made. Piecing as an aid to saving yardage is permissible under certain circumstances: (1) The long

inch) for doing intricate construction details such as collars and welt pockets. These design details are seldom changed during fitting, and the regulation stitch length will result in greater accuracy for practicing complicated construction.

front-facing piece of a coat can be pieced, if desired, at any place below the lapel level. (2) Pieces cut on a fold (upper collar, jacket or coat back) can be made with a seam if necessary. (3) If the pocket is an obvious feature of design (patch pockets), all pockets must be cut, but if there are two pockets hidden in a seam, only one need be cut in order to practice construction details. (4) If there are several welt pockets or pocket flaps, all welt and flap sections should be cut in order to test design proportions, but only one pocket must be completely finished as a practice for construction details.

Transfer all pattern markings to the muslin by using pencil marks. If a lead pencil is used, draw in the shape of the marking (triangle, square, large or small dots). Colored pencils, one for each shape of marking, can be used. Ruler lines (for darts and center lines) can be drawn on the muslin as an aid to accurate construction.

The muslin test copy must look much like the finished garment, but it is not a truly finished garment because only the necessary construction points are completed. Interfacing, tape, and padding stitches are not needed; buttonholes can be pencil lines or slashes in the fabric; buttons can be devised of circles of cloth or paper; and topstitching can be indicated with pencil lines. However, all structural parts of the garment must be basted with accuracy. It is necessary to follow through the order and directions on the instruction sheet and supplement them with the more detailed directions in the text (Chapter 13). Intricate construction details, such as gussets (page 259) and the typical tailored collar (page 264), should be followed very carefully from the text in order to gain full benefit from practice of construction. Pressing seams in the proper direction before proceeding to the next step is as important as it would be if the garment were to be worn. All directions and sketches in Chapter 13 include the interfacing, tape, and padding stitches, and the worker must simply skip sentences involved with those details and concentrate on the basic construction.

BASTING
THE
MUSLIN
COPY

The test copy can be basted by hand or machine as the worker desires. Machine basting should be done with the longest stitch on the machine and with no backstitching at the ends of darts or seams. If numerous corrections are anticipated, it is well to use thread in a contrasting color, which will be easier to remove.

NOTE   Use a shorter stitch (12 to 15 stitches per

If there are points to be reinforced (points that will be clipped or slashed before being seamed), the instruction sheet will include one of two methods of reinforcement. Read Reinforcing Corners on page 161 for more detailed discussion and directions, and if the circumstance calls for a very secure reinforcement (method 2), use a scrap of fabric on the muslin copy; reinforced corners are difficult to handle, and practice is required.

Do not try on the garment or attempt to fit any section or feature of it until the entire muslin copy has been completed. Even if there are obvious corrections to be made, the entire garment must be complete before it will hang properly on the body; for example, the collar greatly influences the fit of the entire shoulder area.

Turn up hems along the hemline as indicated by the pattern and pin in place temporarily. Press the finished muslin copy well. Pin in shoulder pads (directions on page 281) if they will be used. Be sure to have the center-front line clearly defined on the outside of the garment on both right and left fronts; use a marking-basting line or a pencil line.

PREPARATION
FOR
FITTING

Both persons involved with the fitting must know, before the fitting, what to look for during fitting and, in a general way, the solution to problems of misfit. Both persons, then, should study the remainder of this chapter before any fitting is undertaken.

The person to be fitted should wear the bra and foundation garment she will wear with the costume as well as any other item of clothing (blouse and skirt or dress, as the case may be) similar in line to the garments that will be worn with the costume. Shoes similar in design and heel height to those which will be worn with the garment will aid in giving a more accurate picture of the total effect. And for a psychological advantage, the person to be fitted should look her best and should comb her hair in a style similar to the style she will wear with the costume; a casual, windblown coiffure can make a sophisticated design look

unattractive, while an appropriate hair arrangement will enhance the costume.

FITTING
THE JACKET
OR
COAT

Fitting directions for length and width of the garment will be presented in the order used in the measurement charts and for pattern alterations in Chapter 7. As an aid to fitting, it is well to review the comparable pattern alteration in Chapter 7; fitting is similar to pattern alteration, with one being done on flat paper and the other in shaped fabric. Additional details of shape and contour will be discussed in the latter part of this chapter. It is well to make notes of every fitting correction made as fitting progresses.

There is no reason why the fitting must proceed in the exact order presented in this book. There *is* a reason to avoid disappointment and discouragement by correcting large, obvious errors of fit immediately. The total length of the garment often needs the most obvious correction, and so this may be the right place to begin, but there is no reason why the placement of a pocket or the removal of an unattractive design feature cannot be the first step.

CORRECTIONS IN LENGTH (PART 1 OF THE MEASUREMENT CHARTS)

for fitted garments only The position of the waist in snugly fitted garments is a most important issue and so should be

corrected before any other fitting is done.
Read To Alter Waist Length for Fitted
and Semifitted Garments on page 75.
Fitting corrections are done very much
like pattern alterations. Figure 1a shows
the method for shortening the garment
by pinning in a parallel tuck, and Figure
1b shows how to lengthen the garment
by slashing through the fabric and inserting a parallel strip of fabric. Figure 1c
pictures the more difficult problem of
alteration required if sections of the garment must be altered in differing
amounts. In this case, the vertical seams
must be ripped up to about bust level
so that corrections can be made on parallel lines. This fitting correction is rather
like the pattern alteration pictured in
Figures 7 and 8 on page 72.

Make a note of the fitting correction
required. When all fitting has been done,
this correction must be transferred to the
pattern in the form of a pattern alteration or a correction on a previous alteration. At that time, the lower edges can
be evened off. See page 77 to alter the
pattern for this correction.

check position of bust darts Horizontal
bust darts must end at a level with the
high point of the bust, and diagonal and
vertical darts must point in the direction
of the high point of the bust. The tips of
all darts must be close to the high point
of the bust in order to create shape
where it is needed. See Figure 2. Mark
the high point of the bust. Sketch in a
pencil line to establish the desired dart
position. The new dart can be parallel to
the original, as shown, or the direction of
the dart can be changed if desired; it

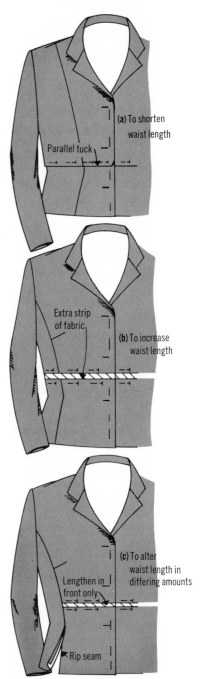

FIGURE 1 To adjust waist length of fitted
garments

can be an identical length or a different length. Remove bastings from the original dart and pin in a new dart the same width as the original but in the desired position; pin in the dart on the outside, as shown. The new dart can be transferred to the inside and basted for a second fitting to ensure proper fit.

NOTE Shoulder darts can be altered in an identical manner.

Make a note of the fitting correction required. When all fitting has been done, this correction must be transferred to the pattern in the form of a pattern alteration or a correction on a previous alteration. See page 79 to alter the pattern for this correction.

check position of elbow dart If it is a one-piece sleeve and there is an elbow dart, bend the arm slightly, bringing the hand up to about waist level, and check the position of the dart. The dart should end at the elbow position. The dart can be brought into proper position by taking a tuck in the sleeve (or inserting a strip of fabric, as illustrated in Figure 1b).

The two-piece sleeve does not have a dart, but there is subtle shaping at the elbow level. View the figure from the side to determine whether the curve of the sleeve and the shaping for the elbow are in the proper position. The sleeve should curve slightly forward from the elbow position. The elbow position can be brought to the proper level by the method illustrated in Figure 1.

Make a note of the fitting correction required. When all fitting has been done, this correction must be transferred to the pattern in the form of a pattern alteration or a correction on a previous alteration. See page 75 to alter the pattern for this correction.

correct length of jacket or coat The length of the coat is a matter of personal choice; the coat should be about ½ to 1 inch longer than the garments over which it will be worn. Jacket length is a matter of personal choice, but there is the important matter of proportion to be considered as well. Experiment with various lengths even if the jacket appears to be an attractive length; it is well to lengthen one side and shorten the other temporarily as an aid to seeing the effect of different proportions. Subtle changes in

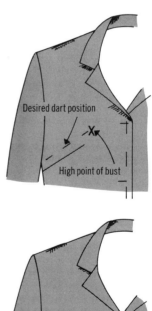

Desired dart position

High point of bust

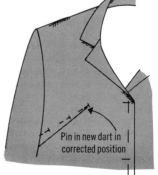

Pin in new dart in corrected position

FIGURE 2 To change position of bust dart

length can be made on the wool garment at a later date, if desired.

Make a note of the fitting correction required. When all fitting has been done, this correction must be transferred to the pattern in the form of a pattern alteration or a correction on a previous alteration. See page 74 to alter the pattern for this correction.

check position of pockets, belts, and other design details The position of a coat pocket should be such that it can be used easily.

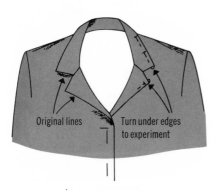

(a) To make collar and lapels narrower

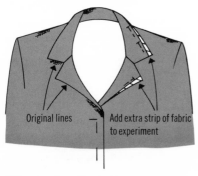

(b) To make collar and lapels wider

FIGURE 3 To test size and shape of collar and lapel lines

Bend the arm slightly, placing the hand in a comfortable position; this is an indication of the approximate position of the coat pocket. With this in mind, study the proportions of the garment to see that the pocket, if it is exposed, creates an attractive division of space. Experiment with various pocket levels.

Functional use of the pocket is less important in high-fashion costumes. A pocket can be in any position if it is to be an interesting design feature. *Vogue* has featured a walking coat with a pocket almost at the hemline and a jacket with a pocket in the underarm position above the waist. If the pocket is an obvious design innovation, check its position for proportions only, with no thought of its convenience.

Make a note of the fitting correction required. When all fitting has been done, this correction must be transferred to the pattern in the form of a pattern alteration or a correction on a previous alteration.

Experiment with the proportions of all design features such as belts or pockets. The level on the body is one matter to consider. Length and width of design details should be considered; even if the feature seems attractive, it is well to experiment because a change may be an improvement.

The garment has been designed in good taste and in good proportions, and most persons are not able to improve upon the work of the professional designer, but the effectiveness of that good design varies with individual differences. For example, the woman with large facial features will find that slightly larger design units near her face will minimize her features, and the person with very slim, delicate hands may find that very large cuff units will need modification. Figure 3 illustrates how to experiment with sizes and shapes of collar and lapel units, and these techniques can be applied to pockets, welts, cuffs, belts, etc.

Figure 4 illustrates that the unit can be changed in width or size and that it can be changed in other ways, as well. The broken line in Figure 4a illustrates that the collar and lapels can be widened, but in addition the front edge of the collar and the upper edge of the lapel have been changed to create a different angle as the two meet. When making changes on the collar, it is important to retain the original line at the corner point, as shown, although the person who understands patterns well can make certain changes at the corner if she desires. Figure 4b shows a collar and lapel made narrower and the slant of the front end of the collar changed, while retaining the original line at the upper edge of the lapel. Figure 4c is an example of how the character of the design unit can be changed.

Figure 5 pictures the pattern pieces involved with changes in collar design; the pattern alteration pictured is the one required for the change illustrated in Figure 4a. Note that changes are made on the outer edges—no change is made on the edge of the collar pieces that will join to the jacket. It is important to retain the original line of the pattern at the point where collar and lapel edges join and, in the jacket and facing pieces, at the level of the top buttonhole marking.

CORRECTIONS IN SIZE OR WIDTH (PARTS 2 AND 3 OF THE MEASUREMENT CHARTS)

There is a tendency to fit the muslin copy so that the width or overall size of the muslin garment gives the effect desired in the finished garment. One must guard against fitting too snugly at this time because the thickness of wool fabric at seams and in hem and facing areas, as well as the addition of a lining, will de-

(a) To widen and change design unit

(b) To narrow and change design unit

(c) To change character of design unit

FIGURE 4 Possible changes in design of collar and lapel lines

crease the size of the wool garment. It is a good general rule to fit the muslin copy in such a way that it is, at all levels, about 1 inch larger than the desired size of the finished wool garment.

As a test for width, pinch out the excess fabric so that the garment hugs the body; the excess which can be pinched out is the amount of livability and style fullness in the garment. Estimate the amount and compare that amount with the estimates of required livability amounts on page 22. This will be only a general indication of changes required because in addition to livability, the amount necessary for style fullness (if the design requires it) can be judged only by studying the garment on the figure.

The tailored garment, fitted or boxy, must hang from the shoulders without clinging too tightly to any other part of the body because if the garment is too tight, it will tend to ride up on the body, creating unattractive horizontal ripples. If horizontal ripples appear at any level

of the garment, they indicate that the garment is too tight in the region directly below that area. For example, horizontal ripples above the waist of a fitted jacket indicate that the jacket is too tight at the waist or high hip level, and horizontal ripples 2 or 3 inches below the waist are an indication that the garment is too tight at the 7- or 10-inch hipline.

NOTE In fitted or semifitted garments, horizontal ripples might indicate that the garment is too long above the waist, but it is assumed that the waist position has been corrected before any other fitting is undertaken.

Fitting corrections are very much like pattern alterations. Reread Alterations for Changing Pattern Width on page 80. Seams can be nipped in or let out just as the pattern alteration would be done. If it is necessary to let seams out more than ½ inch, see Figure 6. Rip the vertical seams in the trouble area and top-stitch an extra piece of fabric to corresponding seams in the area; note that this is just a lapped seam with the raw edge simply stitched to an extra piece of fabric. Now fit the garment, allowing the extra width needed.

Make a note of the fitting correction

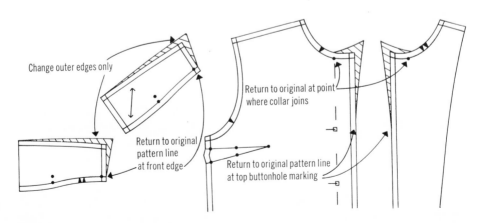

FIGURE 5 Sample pattern alteration for changes of collar and lapel designs

required. When all fitting has been done, this correction must be transferred to the pattern in the form of a pattern alteration or a correction on a previous alteration. See page 80 to alter the pattern for this correction.

CORRECTIONS FOR SLEEVES AND SHOULDERS

NOTE To correct sleeve width and shoulder height in garments where the sleeve is cut in one with the body of the garment, see Figures 9 and 10 and the accompanying directions on page 118.

The sleeve can be fitted in a manner similar to the pattern alteration for the same problem; study To Alter Sleeve Width for Heavy Arms on page 88 as an aid to understanding the fitting directions given below.

for slim arms See Figure 7. Begin work by ripping the armhole seam for a few inches at the top of the sleeve cap. Figure 7a shows how to fit the sleeve for slim arms. Pin in a parallel tuck on the lengthwise grain of the fabric. An absolute minimum of 2 inches of livability is needed at the biceps line in the sleeve, and 3 inches for a suit (and as much as 4 inches for a coat) is usually required.

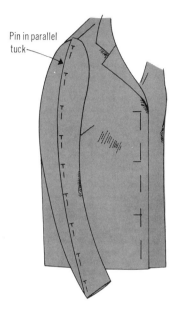

(a) To fit sleeve for thin arms

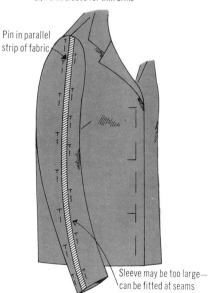

(b) To fit sleeve for heavy arms

FIGURE 7 To correct sleeve width

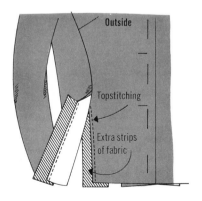

FIGURE 6 To add fabric for letting out seams

Be sure that the sleeve is comfortable when the arm is moved in the usual manner.

This correction must be checked carefully because any change in the sleeve becomes quite involved. Before proceeding, remove the sleeve from the armhole and stitch in the tuck, perfecting it in width and direction. Then baste in the altered sleeve, matching notches. The problem is that there will be less ease in the sleeve cap, and the sleeve must be fitted again to see that it looks attractive and that it is comfortable to wear.

Make a note of the fitting correction required. When all fitting has been done, this correction must be transferred to the pattern in the form of a pattern alteration or a correction on a previous alteration. Alter the pattern by folding in a tuck parallel to the grain line; see Figure 7 on page 72 for the proper method.

for heavy arms See Figure 7b. Begin work by ripping the armhole seam for a few inches at the top of the sleeve cap. Slash the sleeve along the lengthwise grain from the shoulder position to the lower edge. Insert a parallel strip of fabric of sufficient width. An absolute minimum of 2 inches of livability is required at the biceps line, and 3 inches for a suit (and as much as 4 inches for some coats) is sometimes required.

The strip of extra fabric must make a parallel addition, as shown, in order to retain proper grain line in the sleeve, but this will undoubtedly be more width than is required in the lower part of the sleeve; excess width can be removed by fitting in the sleeve seams. Be sure that

the sleeve is comfortable when the arm is moved in a natural manner.

This correction should be checked carefully because any change in the sleeve becomes quite involved. Before proceeding, remove the sleeve from the armhole and stitch the extra strip in place, perfecting it in width. Then baste in the altered sleeve, matching notches. The problem is that there will be more ease in the sleeve cap, and the sleeve must be fitted in to be sure that it looks attractive. Reread To Alter Sleeve Width for Heavy Arms on page 88. If the extra ease in the sleeve is unattractive, sew in a dart, as illustrated in Figure 29 on page 91, and refit.

Make a note of the fitting correction required. When all fitting has been done, this correction must be transferred to the pattern in the form of a pattern alteration or a correction on a previous alteration. See page 88 to alter the pattern for this correction.

to correct shoulder width See Figure 8a. If the armhole seam slides off the shoulder, indicating that the shoulder line is too wide for a person with narrow shoulders, pin in a temporary boat-shaped tuck of sufficient width to bring the sleeve into proper position.

This fitting correction should be approached with caution, however. During certain seasons, a slightly dropped armhole seam is fashionable, and unfortunately the pattern may not state that the armhole line has been dropped. And one cannot always tell by the sketch of the design whether the armhole does have a slight drop. However, if it does, the cap of the sleeve has been made correspondingly shorter. So if one should try to shorten the shoulder width, as shown in Figure 8a, on a pattern that was to have a dropped armhole, there would not be sufficient length in the cap of the sleeve;

this would cause a misfit that would be evidenced by diagonal ripples in the sleeve cap leading from the center of the sleeve at the shoulder, diagonally downward toward the underarm.

Therefore, after doing the fitting pictured in Figure 8a, be sure to study the sleeve from the side view on the body to see that it hangs properly and that there is no evidence of diagonal ripples. If the diagonal ripples appear, they indicate that the garment was supposed to be a bit wider than the shoulder line (slightly dropped), and therefore the alteration should not be made. If the sleeve hangs properly after fitting, the total width of the tuck (twice the width as pinned in) is an indication of the correction to be made on the pattern.

Make a note of the fitting correction required. When all fitting has been done, this correction must be transferred to the pattern in the form of a pattern alteration or a correction on a previous alteration. See page 91 to alter the pattern for this correction.

Figure 8b illustrates how to lengthen the shoulder line for wide shoulders. Rip the armhole seam between the notches and repin the sleeve cap, allowing extra width, as shown. If a great amount of extra width is required, add an extra scrap of fabric to the shoulder area (see Figure 6). The width between the original seamline and the new seam position is an indication of the correction to be made on the pattern.

Make a note of the fitting correction required. When all fitting has been done, this correction must be transferred to the pattern in the form of a pattern alteration or a correction on a previous alteration. See page 91 to alter the pattern for this correction.

to fit sloping shoulders If the shoulder of the garment stands away from the shoul-

der or if the garment rests on the shoulder but a diagonal ripple forms from the neckline in the direction of the underarm seam, the lines of the garment are too square for sloping shoulders. Pads can be used to pad out the natural shoulder line, or the following alteration can be made. Figure 9a shows the correction for the garment with a regulation sleeve. Rip the sleeve seam for a few inches on either side of the shoulder seam. Pin in the amount required to fit the slope of the shoulder by beginning at the original line at the neck edge and

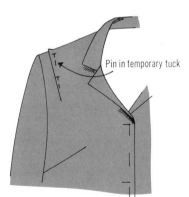

Pin in temporary tuck

(a) To shorten shoulder line for narrow shoulders

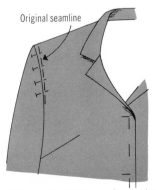

Original seamline

(b) To lengthen shoulder line for wide shoulders

FIGURE 8 To correct shoulder width

gradually increasing the amount at the armhole edge. Reread To Alter Shoulder Height on page 90 and study Figure 30 on page 92. The sketch pictures the correction for square shoulders, but the alteration for sloping shoulders is done in a similar manner.

This correction must be checked carefully because any correction that is in any way involved with the sleeve becomes somewhat complicated. Before proceeding, baste in the corrected shoulder line. Then rip the armhole seam be-

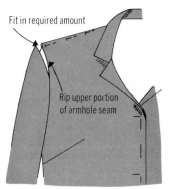

(a) To fit sloping shoulders with regulation sleeve

Fit in required amount

Rip upper portion of armhole seam

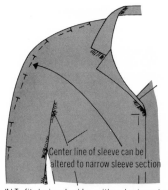

(b) To fit sloping shoulders with raglan-type sleeves

Center line of sleeve can be altered to narrow sleeve section

FIGURE 9 To fit sloping shoulders

tween the notches and sketch in a new seamline, reducing the height of the sleeve cap the same amount the shoulder seam was taken in (see Figure 30 on page 92 for a similar problem). Rebaste the armhole seam, using the original armhole seamline on the jacket or coat and the corrected seamline on the sleeve.

Make a note of the fitting correction required. When all fitting has been done, this correction must be transferred to the sleeve and jacket or coat pattern in the form of a pattern alteration or a correction on a previous alteration.

The correction for sloping shoulders is not as complicated in the design in which the sleeve is cut in one with the body of the garment, as shown in Figure 9b. Pin in the amount required to fit the slope of the shoulder by beginning at the original line at the neck edge and gradually increasing the amount at the shoulder position. The sketch illustrates that the shape of the sleeve seam can be changed and that the sleeve width could be narrowed down at the same fitting.

Make a note to alter the pattern accordingly.

to fit square shoulders If there is a taut look at the outer edge of the shoulder and if diagonal ripples form between the outer end of the shoulder leading toward the bust area, the wearer's shoulders are squarer than average, and the following alteration must be made. Figure 10a shows the correction for the garment with a regulation sleeve. Rip the sleeve seam for a few inches on either side of the shoulder seam. Rip the shoulder seam and bring the cut edges to the outside of the garment, as shown. Pin in a new seamline which will fit the slope of the shoulder by beginning at the original seamline at the neck edge (shown in dotted lines on the sketch) and gradually letting the seam out as required at the armhole edge. Reread To Alter Shoulder Height on page 90 and study Figure 30 on page 92.

This correction must be checked carefully because any correction that is in any way involved with the sleeve becomes somewhat complicated. Before proceeding, baste in the corrected shoulder line. Then rip the armhole seam between the notches and sketch in a new seamline, increasing the height of the sleeve cap the same amount the shoulder seam was let out (see Figure 30 on page 92). Rebaste the armhole seam, using the original seamline on the jacket or coat and the corrected seamline on the sleeve.

Make a note of the fitting correction required. When all fitting has been done, this correction must be transferred to the pattern in the form of a pattern alteration or a correction on a previous alteration. See page 90 to alter the pattern for this correction.

The correction for square shoulders is not as complicated in the design in which the sleeve is cut in one with the body of the garment, as shown in Figure 10b. Rip the seam in the problem area, bringing the cut edges to the outside, and pin in a new seam that will fit the slope of the shoulder line by beginning at the original line at the neck edge and gradually letting out the seam at the shoulder position. The sketch illustrates that the shape of the center sleeve seam can be changed and that extra width could be added to the sleeve at the same fitting.

Make a note to alter the pattern accordingly.

CHANGES IN SHAPE AS WELL AS SIZE

Fitting techniques required to change shape are quite similar to the corresponding pattern alterations. The principles of changing shape are more easily seen in the flat pattern, so it is well to study the corresponding pattern alterations as an aid to applying these principles to the more difficult fitting situation. Therefore, if changes in shape are indicated, study Alterations for Changing Shape as Well as Size on pages 91 to 94 and reread the entire section on jacket alteration beginning on page 97 before attempting to fit the garment.

The need for changes in shape is

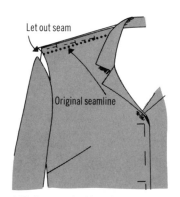

(a) To fit square shoulders with regulation sleeve

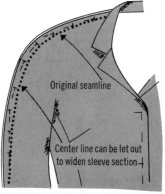

(b) To fit square shoulders with raglan-type sleeves

FIGURE 10 To fit square shoulders

very difficult to recognize and the techniques are more tedious to execute than any other in fitting; yet they are probably the most important fitting techniques to master. The shape of the garment has been created in two different ways: (1) by the use of darts or tucks and (2) by the use of shaped seams. One must learn to study the garment critically, to anticipate that changes in shape will be needed—in other words, to look for trouble. Learning to be discriminating about fit is one of the most difficult tasks in clothing construction, and it is made more difficult by the fact that the person with a figure that is not average has become accustomed to the look and feel of the average-shaped garment. She must now learn that it is possible to attain a much better fit in the garments she makes for herself; she must learn to be dissatisfied with the fit she has been satisfied with in ready-made garments.

Darts play the most important role in creating shape in the garment, and the following changes in darts can be made: (1) Increasing the width of the dart will create more shape for larger-than-average curves; (2) decreasing the width of the dart will create less shape for smaller-than-average curves; (3) changing the position of the dart (position of the tip) will create shape in the area of the tip of the new dart; (4) changing the direction of the dart may create a more becoming line on a particular figure; and (5) lengthening or shortening the dart will create shape in the area of the new tip of the dart. The chart which follows is included here to point out possible problems and to suggest solutions. Bust and shoulder curves will

be discussed, but the principles listed below can be applied to any fitting problem.

problem and indication of poor fit	solution
larger-than-average bust curve	
1 A taut appearance is evident in the bust area, and/or	More size and shape are required in the bust area.
2 Diagonal ripples form in any one of several directions. The ripple always originates at the bust, but it may lead downward toward the side edge, upward toward the neck, outward toward the end of the shoulder, or across to the armhole, and/or	See To Fit Larger-than-average Curves (page 121).
3 The garment may protrude in front, standing away from the body and creating an appearance of maternity wear.	
smaller-than-average bust curve	
1 The garment appears to be too large in the front only and does not lie smoothly over the body.	Less size and shape are required in the bust area.
2 The garment stands away from the body in the bust area, so that one can pinch out excess fabric at the high point of the bust.	See To Fit Smaller-than-average Curves (page 124).
bust in a position that is not average	
1 A taut look is evident at the bust point, while the shaping of the garment is located in another position, and/or	The position, direction, or length of the dart must be changed.
2 The tip of the dart may be	See Check Posi-

too close to the bust point, giving a slightly tight appearance right at the bust point and indicating that the dart is too long, or

3 A little ripple of fabric may form at the end of the dart leading to the high point of the bust, indicating that the dart is too short.

tion of Bust Darts (page 110).

larger-than-average shoulder curve— round shoulders

1 A taut look appears over the shoulder area, and/or

More size and shape are required in the shoulder area.

2 Diagonal ripples form in any one of several directions. The ripple always originates at the high point of the shoulder, but it may lead downward toward the side, upward toward the neck, outward to the end of the shoulder, or across to the armhole, and/or

See To Fit Larger-than-average Curves (page 121).

3 The jacket or coat may jut out in the back, not falling in a plumb line from the shoulders.

smaller-than-average shoulder curve— flat shoulders

1 The garment appears to be too large in the back only and does not lie smoothly on the body.

Less size and shape are required in the shoulder area.

2 The garment stands away from the body in the shoulder area, so that one can pinch out excess fabric at the high point of the shoulder.

See To Fit Smaller-than-average Curves (page 124).

high point of shoulder in a position that is not average

1 A taut look is evident (probably at the shoulder blade), while the shaping of the garment is in a different position, and/or

The position or direction or length of the dart must be changed.

2 The tip of the dart may be too close to the shoulder, giving a slightly tight appearance right at the high point of the curve and indicating that the dart is too long, or

This principle is the same as for bust problems. See Check Position of Bust Darts (page 110).

3 A little ripple of fabric may form at the end of the dart leading to the high point of the shoulder, indicating that the dart is too short.

NOTE If a body curve is larger than average, diagonal ripples form. A diagonal ripple is a ripple of fabric shaped somewhat like a dart, and therefore a diagonal ripple is trying to form a dart. If one thinks of it that way, it is very easy to see that this ripple is an accurate indication that another dart or a larger dart is required for that particular curve.

In every case, the following discussion will concentrate in greater detail on changes of bust curves because the bust curve is the most prominent curve and because bust curves vary more than any others. However, the general principles can be applied to any fitting problem.

to fit larger-than-average curves   Figure 11a shows the fitting involved in horizontal or diagonal bust darts, and Figure 11b shows the same problem in vertical bust

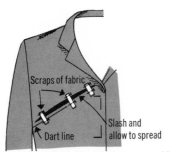

(a) To fit curve larger than average in design with horizontal or diagonal darts

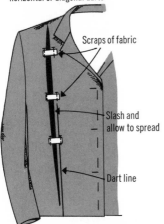

(b) To fit curve larger than average in design with vertical darts

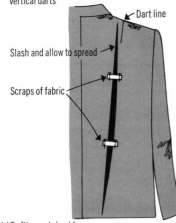

(c) To fit round shoulders

FIGURE 11 To fit larger-than-average curves

darts; the fitting principles are the same for both types of darts. Two similar problems are shown in Figure 12.

Slash through the muslin on a line close to the dart and parallel to it, cutting almost to both finished edges of the garment; note that the slash extends from near the side seam almost to the front edge in Figure 11a and from near the shoulder seam almost to the hemline in Figure 11b. As soon as this slash is made, the garment will spread out as shown, with the greatest amount of spread at the high point of the bust, gradually tapering in near the finished edges. The garment will spread of its own accord to indicate the extra size needed at the bust level. Pin small scraps of fabric to the cut edges to hold them in place temporarily. The amount of spread at the bust level is an accurate indication of the alteration that must be made to the bust dart.

Make a note of the fitting correction required. When all fitting has been done, this correction must be transferred to the pattern in the form of a pattern alteration or a correction on a previous alteration. See page 97 to alter the pattern for this correction.

Figure 11c shows the fitting necessary to fit shoulders that are more rounded than average. Slash through the muslin on a line close to the dart and parallel to it, cutting almost to the shoulder line and hemline, as shown. As soon as the slash is made, the garment will spread out as shown, with the greatest amount of spread at the shoulders, gradually tapering in near the finished edges. Pin small scraps of fabric to the cut edges to hold them in place temporarily. The amount of spread at the shoulder level is an accurate indication of the alteration that must be made to the shoulder dart.

Make a note of the fitting correction

required. When all fitting has been done, this correction must be transferred to the pattern in the form of a pattern alteration or a correction on a previous alteration. See Figure 37 on page 98 for a comparable alteration.

Figure 12 pictures fitting problems for two special designs. Figure 12a shows a popular design with a style line close to the bust point and a short diagonal or horizontal dart leading to the bust point. The garment should be slashed and allowed to spread according to the directions given above. In this case, the spread allows additional length for the larger-than-average curve, but the bust may require additional width as well. If so, rip the seam as shown and pin in the correction, allowing extra width on the jacket-front section, as shown. If a great amount of extra width is needed, a scrap of fabric can be added and used as an extension (see Figure 6). The distance between the original seamline and the new seamline is an indication of the additional width required on the jacket-front piece. Make a note to alter the pattern accordingly.

Figure 12b shows the typical princess-line garment with the style line crossing the high point of the bust. In this case, the change in shape must be made by ripping the seam for several inches above and below the bust level and allowing extra size on the side front, as shown. If a great amount of extra width is needed, a scrap of fabric can be added and used as an extension (see Figure 6). The distance between the original seamline and the corrected seamline is an indication of the additional width required on the jacket-side section. Make a note to alter the pattern accordingly.

NOTE The princess line in the jacket back can be fitted in a similar manner.

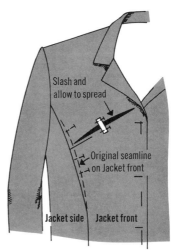

(a) To alter design with style line close to bust point

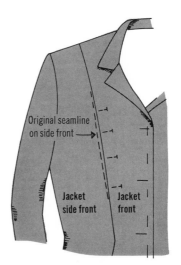

(b) Typical princess line with style line crossing bust point

FIGURE 12 To fit larger-than-average bust curve in two special designs

to fit smaller-than-average curves Figure 13a illustrates the fitting technique for diagonal or horizontal bust darts, and the same principle can be applied to vertical darts, as shown in the jacket back in Figure 13b.

Make a temporary boat-shaped dart, close to the dart line and parallel to it, extending the dart almost to both finished edges. The dart should be widest at the high point of the curve, and the size of the dart is determined by the amount of excess fabric (or shape) at the bust level. The full width of the dart at the bust

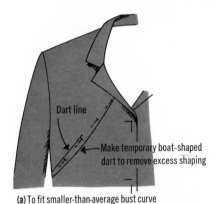

(a) To fit smaller-than-average bust curve

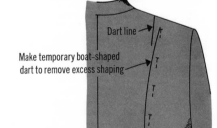

(b) To fit straight back

FIGURE 13 To fit smaller-than-average curves

level (twice the width when it is folded and pinned) is an accurate indication of the alteration that must be made to the bust dart.

Make a note of the fitting correction required. When all fitting has been done, this correction must be transferred to the pattern in the form of a pattern alteration or a correction on a previous alteration. See page 104 to alter the pattern for this correction.

Figure 13b shows the way to fit shoulders that are less rounded than average. Make a temporary boat-shaped dart close to the dart line and parallel to it, extending the dart almost to both finished edges. The dart should be widest at the shoulder level, and the size of the dart is determined by the amount of excess fabric (or shape) at the shoulders. The full width of the dart at the shoulder level (twice the width when folded and pinned) is an accurate indication of the alteration that must be made to the shoulder dart.

Make a note of the fitting correction required. When all fitting has been done, this correction must be transferred to the pattern in the form of a pattern alteration or a correction on a previous alteration. See page 104 to alter the pattern for this correction.

Figure 14 pictures fitting problems for two special designs. Figure 14a shows a popular design with a style line close to the bust point and a short diagonal or horizontal dart leading to the bust point. If the individual's bust curve is very, very small, the fitting shown in Figure 13 may be needed in addition to the correction shown here. Often, however, the correction shown here is all that is needed to solve the problem. The alteration for the typical princess-line garment shown in Figure 14b is done in the same manner. Rip the seam several inches above and below the bust level. Turn under the seam allowance on the jacket front and lap that edge over the side section; retain the ⅝-inch seam allowance at the upper and lower extremities, but lap over more than ⅝ inch on the side-front section at the bust level; note the broken line in the sketch, which indicates the cut edge of the jacket-side section. Mark the new seamline with a pencil. The amount between the original seamline and the corrected seamline is an indication of the alteration required on the jacket-side section. Make a note to alter the pattern accordingly. The princess line in the jacket back can be fitted in a similar manner.

HEM
ALLOWANCES

Hem allowances for tailored garments are quite standard unless some unusual design feature of the garment calls for a special hem width. It is well to work with the hem allowance given on the original pattern. After all adjustments in length have been made, make a note to make any additions and reductions in length so that the hem allowance will be appropriate for the design. The standard hem allowances used in tailored garments are listed below.

1½-inch finished hem width is used for:

fitted or boxy hip-length jacket
  sleeve in a jacket or coat

3-inch finished hem width is used for:

  full-length coat

BUTTON
SIZE
AND
PLACEMENT

This is the time to experiment with button sizes, placement, and effects because any substantial change in size from the

size suggested on the pattern requires a pattern alteration that must be done before the fabric is cut. The size of the button is not stated on the pattern, but

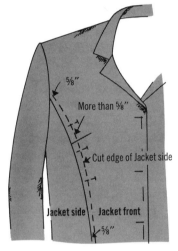

(a) To alter design with style line close to bust point

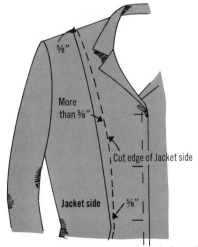

(b) Typical princess line with style line crossing bust point
FIGURE 14 To fit smaller-than-average bust curve in two special designs

one can figure button size by taking a certain measurement on the pattern. See Figure 15. Measure the distance from the center front to the finished front edge (which is a seamline if there is a separate facing and a fold line if the facing is cut in one with the body of the garment). That distance equals the diameter of the button recommended by the designer of the pattern. Figure 15 shows that buttons of the correct size look right and that buttons too small or buttons so large that they almost touch the finished front edge look unattractive.

In general, it is wise to work with a button very similar in size to the button planned by the designer and to use similar placement. However, sometimes an alteration in pattern length makes a change in button placement necessary, and substantial changes in placement will force changes in button size. If the pattern has been lengthened so much that an extra button must be added, the buttons may have to be slightly smaller; likewise, a shortened pattern may require fewer buttons, in which case they may be somewhat larger. Very slight changes (⅛ inch) are quite acceptable.

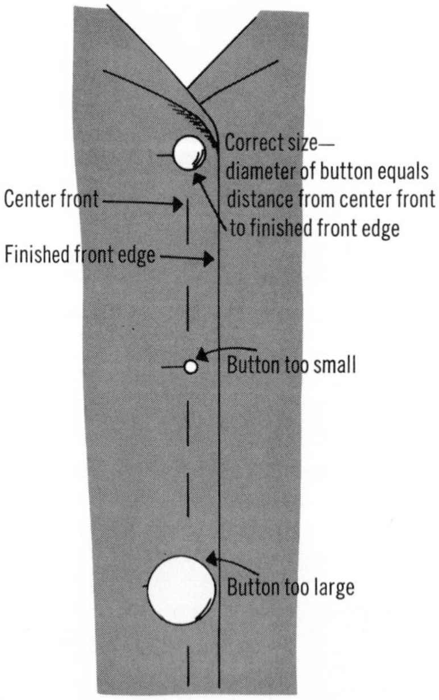

The best way to experiment with button size and placement is to simulate the effect of various buttons. The choice of buttons for the tailored suit or coat is a very important one and deserves a great deal of time and thought. The first decision will be concerned with the choice between purchased decorative buttons and self-covered buttons.

NOTE Refer to Placement on the Garment on page 248 for additional information.

Purchased decorative buttons will attract more attention in the finished costume and may need to be smaller or fewer in number (depending on the degree of design involved) in order to avoid an overdecorated appearance; by contrast, self-covered buttons are "safe" choices because they will harmonize, will become a part of the costume, and will obviously be compatible in color and texture. The above comparison is given as a mere statement of fact and is not intended to discourage the use of purchased buttons; the right decorative, contrasting button can truly enhance the costume.

The selection of the purchased decorative button is a matter of personal choice and of consideration of basic design principles. If there are many buttons, an unusual design will give an overdecorated effect. If, however, there is one large button, its purpose is largely

FIGURE 15 Enlarged view showing general rule for determining appropriate button size

Labels in figure: Correct size— diameter of button equals distance from center front to finished front edge; Center front; Finished front edge; Button too small; Button too large

decorative, and it can be of elaborate design. If purchased contrasting buttons are to be used, it is well to take the fabric (folded to about the size of the jacket or coat) to the department store to test the effect that the buttons will have on the finished garment. If the buttons are sold singly and are not on cards, they can be placed on the scrap of fabric for a very accurate test. Buttons can add dollars in apparent cost to the garment, and by the same token they can cheapen the costume. It is foolish economy to think of button cost as a separate item—to think, for example, that you must spend 10 cents for the button because 75 cents sounds so very expensive. The cost should be compared with the total cost of the garment; for example, a $25 investment in the costume becomes, with three buttons at the prices mentioned, either $25.30 or $27.25. It is false economy to jeopardize the whole costume to save $2.

The button covered with fabric to match the costume is the frequent choice of the designer of ready-made costumes and of the woman who sews. These buttons have great advantages: (1) They are safe choices because one cannot go very far wrong with any of the various types on the market. (2) The button will be appropriate in color and texture; it will harmonize with the garment and will result in a compatible costume. (3) There is little chance of overdecoration. (4) They look professional because the designer of ready-made costumes uses them so frequently. In addition to these advantages, they are not particularly striking and so are a wise choice for a row of several buttons of utilitarian function; yet they are pretty and attractive, and so they do add a nice touch to the design. And they are very much less expensive than a good-quality purchased button.

Metal frames are available at notions counters for covering buttons at home. The alternative is to have them professionally covered by the department store or Singer shop. It is wiser to have these buttons professionally covered because the large commercial machines get a much better grip on the fabric than one can at home, making the buttons more serviceable. Actually, covering the buttons yourself, using a button-covering kit, costs almost as much as having them professionally covered; this fact is surprising to many persons who feel that "doing it yourself" always results in savings. The woman who sews must realize that she is saving little if any money by covering her buttons; she is saving only the few days of time required to have them professionally covered.

Professionally covered buttons are available in a large variety of designs that add subtle interest to the costume. Study Figure 16 to see the infinite variety of effects that can be achieved through the style of the button, the choice of fabric, and perhaps the choice of contrasting thread or decorative trim used. These are all subtle effects and will not overdecorate the costume, even if there are many buttons. The sketches illustrate the wisdom of choosing something with a little bit of interest in preference to the plain round button. The more interesting buttons cost just a few more cents each. Figure 16 shows just one button size; however, all these buttons come in many sizes, and there are other button designs as well. Square designs often enhance the plaid dress, and of course the traditional half-ball

Plain covered button

Combination button with narrow rim and flat center — can be made all in self fabric or one section can be in contrast

Combination button with wide rim and rounded center — can be made all in self fabric or either section can be in contrast

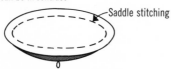

Saddle stitching

Saddle-stitched button — stitches can be in matching or contrasted color

Metallic cord

Usual combination button with gold or silver metallic cord covering the seam

Button with contrasting rim of metal (silver or gold), plastic (in basic contrasting colors), or white or smoke pearl (sometimes available)

FIGURE 16 Button designs

button is the choice for loop-and-button closings.

After having made a tentative decision on the type of button preferred, simulate that button by cutting scraps of paper or fabric (in white to match the muslin for matching buttons or in contrasting paper or fabric for decorative effects) and pinning them to the muslin test copy; several layers of fabric for each button will give a more accurate test by simulating the thickness of the button. Study the effect and experiment with various sizes and placement; do not assume that the size or placement recommended on the pattern is necessarily right for your particular tastes.

If the buttons to be used do not vary more than ⅛ inch in diameter from those suggested by the designer, no pattern alteration is required; if a greater change has been made, make a note to alter the pattern as shown in Figure 17. If the placement must be changed because of an altered pattern or because of personal preference, make a note to respace buttonhole markings before making the buttonholes.

Purchase decorative buttons or order self-covered buttons at this time so that they will be on hand before buttonholes are made. As soon as the buttons are obtained, double-check your choice by pinning them to the garment before making buttonholes. It would be far better to buy a different button now than to use the wrong button in order to save money; to repeat, button choice is important and deserves time, thought, and expense.

Some designs call for button substitutes, which can be tested by similar methods. The decorative frog used on Oriental costumes can be used in place of buttons, but these frogs should be used sparingly on the costume to avoid an overdecorated effect. The corded strip of self-fabric knotted into a ball-like shape makes an attractive, different button. A half bow of self-fabric, to be pulled through the buttonhole like a button, is a nice touch if there is need for just one button.

TO ALTER PATTERN FOR A CHANGE IN BUTTON SIZE

See Figure 17. The sketches illustrate the pattern alteration for buttons larger than those recommended on the pattern; if smaller buttons are used, excess width would be trimmed from the front edge of the front pattern and the front facing, using the principles shown here.

The principle is to alter the pattern so that the distance from the center-front line to the finished front edge equals the diameter of the button to be used. Figure 17a shows the pattern alteration for a jacket or coat with a separate front facing. Make an addition on the front edge of each piece, as shown; the amount of the addition must equal the additional width of the button over and above that planned by the designer. For example,

if the distance from the center front to the finished front edge of the original pattern is ¾ inch and the button chosen is 1¼ inches in diameter, an additional ½ inch must be added to the front edge of the jacket or coat front and the front facing. If there is a separate interfacing pattern, alter it accordingly. No other pattern alterations are necessary. The collar has not been affected, nor has the lining.

Figure 17b illustrates the same principle on the jacket or coat with the facing section cut in one with the body of the garment. Read the directions above because the principle is identical. Cut the pattern apart by cutting along the fold line. Then make the addition to the jacket front and draw in a new fold line. Make an identical addition for the facing section and then Scotch-tape the facing section in place. If there is a separate interfacing pattern, alter it accordingly. No other pattern alterations are necessary. The collar has not been affected, nor has the lining.

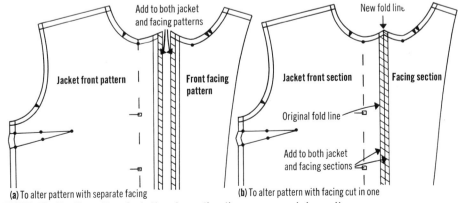

(a) To alter pattern with separate facing   (b) To alter pattern with facing cut in one

FIGURE 17   To alter pattern for buttons larger than those recommended on pattern

MARKING
THE ROLL LINE
OF THE COLLAR
AND LAPELS

Be sure that center-front lines are matching and pin the garment in place very carefully, placing pins at buttonhole markings, as shown in Figure 18. Be sure the garment is settled on the shoulders in the proper position and that the upper collar fits flat over the under collar. Fig-

ure 18a pictures a design with a lapel. The roll line of the lapel begins directly across from the top buttonhole marking and continues around the rolled edge of the collar. Mark the roll line with pins or a pencil line, as shown. Figure 18b pictures a design buttoned up to the neck. The roll line of the collar must be marked along the fold edge of the collar. These markings will be used to establish roll lines on the garment later.

TRANSFERRING
ALTERATIONS
FROM THE MUSLIN COPY
TO THE PATTERN

The statement reading "Make a note to make corresponding pattern alterations" has been made over and over again in this chapter. Now that the fitting is completed, it is important to inspect the garment very carefully and make a

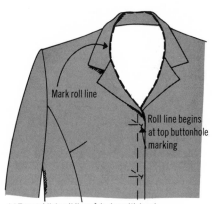

(a) To establish roll line of design with lapel

(b) To establish roll line of design with no lapel

FIGURE 18 To mark roll line of collar and lapels

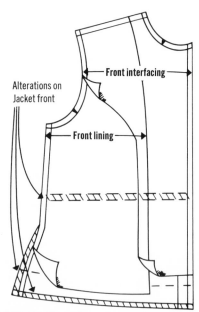

FIGURE 19 To make corresponding alterations

methodical list of every fitting correction that was made so that no correction is overlooked. With a carefully written list, each fitting correction can be checked off as it is transferred to the pattern.

CORRESPONDING ALTERATIONS ON INTERFACING AND LINING PIECES

Before cutting the fabric, do alterations on all corresponding pattern pieces. The safest way to do this is to place the basic pieces on a table and then place all corresponding pieces in the position they will take in relation to each of the basic pieces; the need for alteration will then show up very well, as seen in Figure 19. The illustration shows the jacket-front piece under the front-interfacing piece and the front-lining piece. Note that the jacket front has been lengthened above the waist and at the lower edge and that an addition has been made on the side edge; these alterations must be made to all pieces that will be in a corresponding position in the finished garment. The sketch shows the lining and interfacing pieces as they would appear before the corresponding alterations are made; note that the pieces are shorter than the jacket piece in the sketch.

If extensive alterations have been made, it may be easier and less time-consuming to make new lining patterns from the altered structural pattern pieces. It is a relatively simple matter to make new lining patterns, as explained on page 295.

CUTTING, MARKING, AND STAY STITCHING FABRIC FOR THE TAILORED GARMENT

When making a tailored suit or a coat with an accompanying skirt, the best plan of work involves finishing the skirt before proceeding with the jacket or coat. This order of construction provides two advantages during fittings for the jacket or coat: (1) the extra size which the thickness of the skirt adds to body size can be taken into account, and (2) matters of proportion, particularly skirt length as it affects the length of the jacket or coat, can be studied more accurately. In addition, this order of construction allows one to cut certain fabrics at this time and to delay the cutting of others; for this reason, directions for cutting are interspersed in the book in appropriate chapters.

This chapter includes directions for cutting the fabric of the garment (skirt and jacket or coat) as well as skirt underlinings and linings. Cutting directions for interfacing and/or backing for the jacket or coat are given on page 224, and directions for cutting jacket and coat linings appear on page 298.

Chapter 4, "Special Yardage Requirements," includes a brief discussion on the problems of cutting napped and plaid fabrics. These problems are not discussed in detail in this book, and it is assumed that the reader will look for the necessary information in a general book on clothing construction.

It would be well to review pages 51 to 56 at this time to be sure that the fabric has been properly prepared for cutting.

SUGGESTIONS
FOR CHANGES
IN STRAIGHT-SKIRT
DESIGNS

The experienced person can make any number of changes in her pattern, the number and extent of changes depending entirely on her ability and knowledge. The changes suggested below are simple ones that a novice can execute.

THE SIDE ZIPPER CAN BE CHANGED TO THE CENTER BACK, IF DESIRED

A back zipper has two distinct advantages: (1) It is much easier to insert in most designs because the side edges are curved and therefore can stretch during manipulation, while the back edge is on the straight grain line, and (2) if the finished skirt must be altered (for the person who changes size frequently), the

alteration must be done at both side edges, and a back zipper will not complicate the process.

If there is a back seam in the skirt, this change requires nothing more than marking a point or a notch 7¼ inches down from the seamline at the upper edge. If the back pattern was to be cut on a fold, a seam can be added at the center back, providing it does not detract from the original design. See Figure 1. Add a ⅝-inch extension on the fold line of the pattern and mark a point or a notch on that edge 7¼ inches down from the seamline at the waist.

A change in zipper position will mean that notches on the waistband will not match notches on the skirt. However, the recommended waistband construction (page 201) does not require the use of notches, so this will be no problem.

A CENTER-BACK PLEAT CAN BE ELIMINATED

A pleat appears in the pattern for action purposes, but if the wearer does not take long strides and if short skirts are fashionable, this pleat is unnecessary.

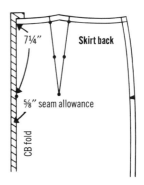

FIGURE 1 To change zipper from the side to the back on a pattern cut on the fold

The most important reason for eliminating a back pleat is to decrease bulk when very heavy fabrics (coatings) are used. If the pleat is not desirable but the wearer does require freedom for walking, a split in the center-back seam can be used. See Figure 2. Trim ⅝ inch beyond the center pleat line to allow for a seam to replace the pleat. The slit opening in a seam requires nothing more than to end stitching of the center-back seam at the desired level. A split of 3 inches in length is generally recommended, but a shorter slit will create better proportion in short skirts. Mark a point on the seamline 2 or 3 inches above the hemline, as shown.

THE WAISTBAND WIDTH CAN BE CHANGED

The recommended waistband construction (page 201) requires a narrower piece of fabric than the usual waistband pattern because the underside of the band is finished with some kind of ribbon; a glance at those directions now

will explain the advantages of that construction. A strip of fabric 1 inch wider than the desired width is all that is required; since a 1-inch waistband is very attractive, a 2-inch strip of fabric is quite sufficient for the waistband. If it becomes necessary to skimp a bit while laying on the pattern, use the directions on page 201 for cutting the waistband and do not cut the wider pattern piece.

A REVIEW
OF
LAYOUT
TECHNIQUES

The person undertaking a tailoring project is probably quite experienced in laying out the pattern, but a brief review of techniques will be valuable:

1 Use a large table and support the weight of any extra length of heavy fabric with chairs. Be sure the fabric takes a rectangular shape on the table. If it is not perfect, it can be straightened again at this time (page 54). Limp fabrics can be Scotch-taped to the table to keep them in position.

2 Use the proper layout from the guide sheet or the special layout made for the garment. There is no reason why the competent, experienced person cannot improvise if she can see a better solution, providing she checks her work carefully to be sure all pattern pieces have been included, that pattern pieces are placed on the proper number of times, and that place-on-fold and straight-of-material lines have been observed.

3 Each pattern piece has been separated on the layout so that it can be easily distinguished; this is a sketching technique used solely for purposes of clarity and does not indicate that there is extra space between the pattern pieces or that

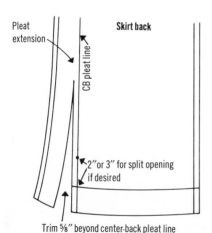

Pleat extension

Skirt back

CB pleat line

2" or 3" for split opening if desired

Trim ⅝" beyond center-back pleat line

FIGURE 2　To eliminate back pleat

the pieces should be separated as they are placed down. Each pattern piece should be placed as close as possible to other pattern pieces on the layout.

4 If an open layout is used for a single thickness of fabric, the pattern is placed right side up on the right side of the fabric unless the layout shows the piece outlined in broken lines or shaded in some way to indicate that it should be reversed.

5 If a combination layout is used, place pieces on the lengthwise section first; then cut the fabric and continue with the crosswise or open section. When making a change to another section of the layout, even off the cut edge before proceeding, as shown in Figure 3; see page 53 for various methods.

6 Place large pieces on the fabric first and fill in with smaller ones later. First rough out the layout by placing pieces on quickly in their approximate positions, as shown in the layout. Then perfect the layout with more careful study.

7 Straight-of-material lines must be parallel to the selvedge edge, and fold lines must be placed accurately on the fold of fabric. See Figure 4 for a quick and accurate way of locating straight-of-material lines properly. Note that a pin at each end of the extended straight-of-material

line will quickly locate the piece in proper position; then additional pins can be added. Pins should be placed close to the cutting line and at approximately right angles to it. The number of pins varies with the contour of the pattern piece and the nature of the fabric. More pins are needed on curved edges, and more are needed on spongy, limp fabrics. In general, pins placed every 3 or 4 inches will prove satisfactory.

CUTTING TECHNIQUES

Do not lift the fabric off the table; keep one blade of the shears resting on the table. Use long slashes with the scissors in preference to short, choppy ones. Never use pinking shears for cutting out a garment because they are too difficult to handle and result in inaccurate cutting lines. Cut exactly along the pattern line

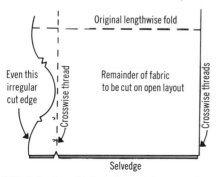

FIGURE 3 Even fabric before cutting second portion of a combination layout

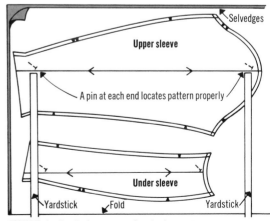

FIGURE 4 Preliminary step in placing pattern on fabric

or the altered pattern line; inaccurate cutting can make the difference between one size and another at some edges on the pattern. Cut curved lines with great care.

See Figure 5. The notches on the pattern must be cut very carefully. In most patterns they will be marked on both sides of the cutting line—into the seam allowance and beyond the cutting edge, as shown. In order to retain the full seam allowance, notches should be cut beyond the cutting line, as shown, and two or three notches can be cut as a unit, as shown.

NOTE If the fabric is very thick and heavy (coating, simulated fur, camel's hair), it may be impossible to cut two layers at one time. Each thickness can be cut separately by slipping the scissors between the two layers of fabric, cutting one thickness on one edge, cutting the second thickness on that edge, and proceeding.

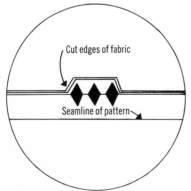

FIGURE 5 Enlarged view showing how to cut groups of notches

NOTE Cutting and construction directions for the interfacing and/or underlining or backing for the jacket or coat are given on page 224.

An underlining (interfacing, backing) is not required in most skirts made of typical suiting-weight fabrics, and most readers will prefer to eliminate this step (and therefore the bulk of the underlining) when using firm, medium-weight fabrics. However, there are circumstances that make the underlining desirable: (1) If the design of the skirt is such that it needs support (the bell silhouette and the A-line skirt), an underlining will give added weight and will, if it has a degree of stiffness, aid in supporting the silhouette; (2) if the figure is more curvaceous than the typical "suit" figure, an underlining, if it is lightweight but slightly crisp, will stiffen the fabric slightly so that it lies more smoothly over rounded contours; (3) if the fabric is of a lighter weight than is desirable for the design (dress woolen used for a dressmaker suit), the addition of an underlining will add apparent weight to make the fabric perform satisfactorily; and (4) if the fabric is too limp or too spongy for the intended purpose, a slightly stiff underlining will improve its character and prevent stretching.

Reread Selection of Supporting Fabrics on pages 45 to 50 and study the chart of appropriate fabrics on page 47. A more detailed discussion of the underlined skirt appears on page 173, and it would be well to read through those directions to see how the underlining will be constructed.

Figure 6 shows a typical straight-skirt pattern; the shaded areas indicate the portions of the pattern to be used for cutting the underlining. This sketch illustrates general rules for cutting. Because the typical underlining is lightweight and will not create great bulk, the underlining can be cut exactly like the original pattern (the pattern companies suggest this method because of its simplicity), but two suggestions illustrated in Figure 6 will aid in decreasing bulk, The underlining should be cut to a level about ⅛ inch (for lightweight fabrics) to ¼ inch (for heavy fabrics) above the hemline; this will prevent the underlining from folding back on itself when the hem is pinned in place. Extra bulk is eliminated from the pleat area by cutting the underlining ⅝ inch beyond the pleat line.

GENERAL RULE Cut underlinings exactly like the pattern, with the following exceptions: cut to a level ⅛ to ¼ inch above hemlines or fold lines (which are really hemlines) and allow a ⅝-inch seam beyond pleat lines.

Pattern lines should be marked with pencil on the underlining pieces. Directions for basting underlining pieces to skirt pieces (the very first step of construction of the underlined skirt) are given on page 173.

CUTTING
THE SKIRT
LINING

The skirt lining has come to be an essential part of the tailored skirt; it is assumed that all readers will line the skirt regardless of the fabric being used. Reread Selection of Lining Fabrics on pages 41 to 45.

Only one method of lining construction is given in this book, and it is recom-

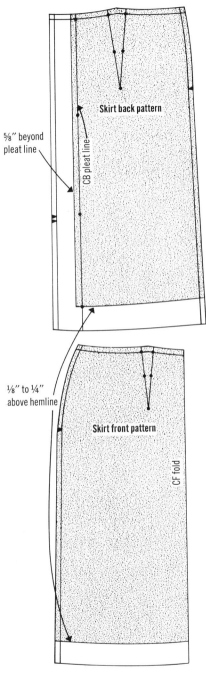

FIGURE 6 To cut skirt underlining (interfacing or backing)

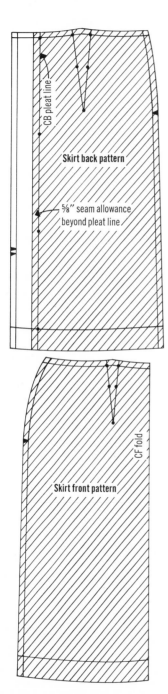

FIGURE 7 To cut lining for basic, straight skirt

mended so highly because it results in a very finished, most elegant effect; from the inside, the skirt lined by this method is as finished as a lined jacket. See pages 199 to 201 for a preview of the construction. Two alternatives are given for finishing the lower edge of the lining. In the simplest method (preferred for most skirts), the lower edge of the lining is secured to the skirt, just as it is in a jacket. In the other method, the lining hangs free from the skirt. The two methods are evaluated in detail on page 171. The method of construction must be chosen at this time because if the free-hanging lining will be used, one can eliminate some of the style fullness in the pattern when cutting the lining; this is the main advantage of this method.

Figure 7 shows a pattern for a typical straight skirt that is very much like most suit skirts; the shaded areas indicate the portions of the pattern to be used for cutting the lining. Note that the lining is cut full length and exactly like the pattern, except that a seam allowance beyond the pleat line replaces the pleat. This lining will be so like the skirt that it can be attached at the lower edge for an attractive finished appearance; see Figures 56 and 57 on pages 214 and 215.

CAUTION Do not confuse Figures 6 and 7. The two are very similar, but the lining (in Figure 7) is cut full length, while the underlining (in Figure 6) is cut to the hemline only.

Probably the pattern has given directions for cutting the lining shorter than the skirt; this is done for reasons of economy only. It is wiser to cut the lining full length, as illustrated in Figure 7.

Figure 8 pictures a skirt-front pattern in a design with style fullness; note the loose pleat at the center front and the greater width of the pattern, which will be gathered to the waistline. If a design has sufficient style fullness not needed for walking action, some of that extra fullness can be eliminated when cutting the lining. This will mean that the lining must be allowed to hang free from the skirt at the lower edge; see Figures 59 and 60 on page 216.

See Figure 8. Extend the loose pleat lines to the lower edge of the pattern. Use the extended pleat lines as a fold line when cutting the lining.

MARKING PATTERN LINES ON FABRIC

The tailored garment can be marked with chalk lines, with tracing wheel and carbon, or with tailor's tacks. Tailor's tacks are recommended because they are very secure in wool fabrics, because they are the only method of marking that marks both the right and the wrong sides of the fabric, and because they can be made in contrasting colors to denote different sizes and shapes of markings. Certainly if one is using a Vogue Paris Original or International Couturier pattern, this method must be used because the complicated design lines and the four sizes and shapes of markings used by Vogue can be very confusing unless they are distinguished by contrasting colors. Center lines, particularly center-front lines in the buttoned-front jacket or coat, must be clearly marked with a marking-basting stitch made with a contrasting color of thread.

The following suggestion for saving time in making tailor's tacks is included for the competent, experienced person only; the novice would be wise to skip over this paragraph. If one understands patterns so well that she can predict the use that each pattern marking will serve before she encounters it in construction,

this suggestion has merit. A study of the comparison of interfacing (underlining or backing) methods given on pages 218 to 223 will reveal that the complete interfacing method is recommended. If this method is to be used, dart lines and seamlines for any construction which will be done from the wrong side of the fabric can be drawn on the interfacing with a pencil. For this reason, there is little value in marking the fabric for the garment with tailor's tacks along those same construction lines. If the reader can understand the various uses each pattern

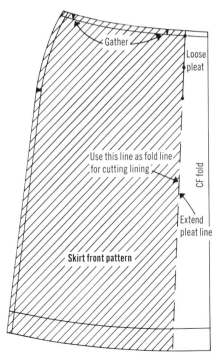

FIGURE 8 To eliminate some style fullness from lining

marking will serve (a marking sometimes serves one purpose on the right side and another purpose on the wrong side), she can save time by tailor tacking only those points which will be needed on the right side or on both sides and marking simple darts with a pencil line on the interfacing only. While this suggestion can indeed save the experienced person a great deal of time, if one is in doubt it is far better to mark all points with tailor's tacks.

STAY
STITCHING

The person experienced enough to undertake a tailoring project has had experience in stay stitching, understands the purposes of staying cut edges of the pattern, knows how to stay-stitch, and understands which edges must be stay-stitched. Directions for stay stitching appear in all basic clothing construction books. This section will be confined to problems that might arise in the tailored garment.

VERY HEAVY COATING FABRICS CREATE UNUSUAL STRETCHING PROBLEMS

Although stay stitching may be strong enough to control vertical seamlines, the extreme weight of some coatings creates a need for greater control on those curved edges which will get great strain during construction and on edges (the same curved edges) that are responsible for size (or width) in the very important shoulder area. Stay stitching will do very little to control the curved neck edge or shoulder line if extremely heavy fabrics are used. See Figure 9. After the fabric has been marked with tailor's tacks and

center lines have been marked, baste ¼-inch-wide cotton-twill tape to neck and front shoulder edges on the right side of the fabric, as shown. This tape is a temporary aid and will be removed as soon as the edge is stitched to another. The tape should be placed about ⅛ inch inside the seamline (in the body of the garment, not in the seam allowance) so that the seam can be basted and stitched without catching in the tape. The ends of the tape should be trimmed off about ⅛ inch from any cross seamline, as illustrated at the back shoulder line. The tape should be pinned first, and the edge should be tested on the corresponding pattern edge to be sure that it has retained the original length. Figure 9 does not picture tape on the back shoulder edge because the dart must be sewn in before tape is used on that edge.

THE TYPE OF INTERFACING AND THE CONSTRUCTION METHOD USED MAY ELIMINATE THE NEED FOR STAY STITCHING JACKET OR COAT PIECES

If a typical suiting-weight fabric is used, and if a firm interfacing is used in the jacket or coat and the complete interfacing method of construction is employed (as recommended in the detailed discussion on page 222), the interfacing prevents stretching and stay stitching is unnecessary.

CARE
OF FABRIC
DURING
CONSTRUCTION

Fabric should be handled in such a way that it is kept in good condition (avoiding wrinkles and creases) from the purchase date to the time the garment is finished. This will cut down on the pressing operations as well as encourage the worker at every stage in construction. Before the pieces are assembled, all but the small pieces should be hung on a hanger between working periods. In the campus situation, a pillowcase bag with open edges pinned on the hanger will offer protection from the weather and prevent loss of pieces.

As soon as the garment is assembled, it should be hung on a padded hanger (skirts on skirt hangers) and should al-

ways be pinned in place carefully at centers. During construction, the worker should learn to keep her work as flat as possible on the table, smoothed out in orderly fashion. She should bring to the worktable only those pieces currently in use.

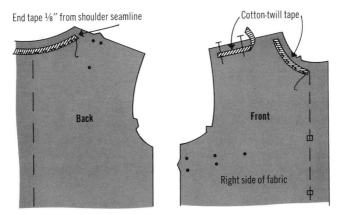

FIGURE 9 To control stretching of heavy fabric temporarily

10

FUNDAMENTALS
OF
CONSTRUCTION
AND
PRESSING

Most of the information in this chapter is a review of clothing construction techniques, probably familiar to the reader. Review these basic principles now because they will be used very frequently during construction of the tailored garment.

BASTING
AND
STITCHING

PREPARATION FOR BASTING

Pins should be placed at right angles to the seamline, and they should catch a very small area of fabric, right at the seamline. For proper control of the edge, first pin the two ends together, with cross lines matching at the seamline, and then match any pattern markings (notches, dots); lastly, pin remaining edges in place. The number of pins is dependent on the fabric and the character (curved or straight) of the seamline; use the number required to hold seam edges together accurately.

Usually the two edges to be joined are so similar in character that there is no problem when pinning them together (side seams of the skirt and shoulder lines are examples). In some cases, however (more often in jackets or coats), the two seam edges are very different. See Figure 1a. Note the character of the two cut edges which must be joined to form the complete front of a princess-line jacket; the side-front edge has an outward curve, while the jacket-front edge has a slight inward curve. The differences in character are more readily seen in Figure 1b, which pictures the side front placed over the front, pinned in one position only. The two cut edges can be forced into position, but it is difficult and may result in inaccurate lines. Figure 1c shows the proper preparation for pinning. Clips (about ⅜ inch long) have been made in the front edge (the inward curve) in the area where it differs in shape from the corresponding edge (the outward curve). Note that the edges can be placed cut edges even very easily because the clips spread out, allowing that shorter cut edge to take the longer cut edge on the side front. This principle can be used on any corresponding edges of different character; an outstanding example is the ruler-straight line of some collars which must be joined to the very curved edge of the neck; clips into the curved neck edge allow it to take a ruler-straight line very easily.

The following explanation should help solve another frequent and puzzling problem. Figure 2 shows simple, basic pattern pieces that offer no problem. Note that in both the skirt and the sleeve pattern pieces, the corresponding corners

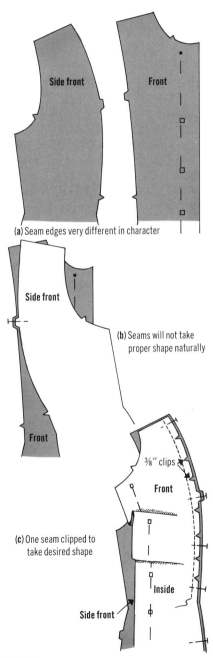

(a) Seam edges very different in character

(b) Seams will not take proper shape naturally

(c) One seam clipped to take desired shape

FIGURE 1

of seamlines form almost identical angles, marked *X* and *Y* on the sketch; the angles are very similar to right angles, as well. When the lengthwise edges are pinned, the angles at the upper edge take the same shape, so that the two pieces meet each other at the seamline and also at the cut edge, as shown. However, a problem arises when the corresponding angles at corners are not identical, as illustrated in Figure 3. There are many such corners, especially in in-

tricately cut designs; the curved design lines of the front pattern pieces pictured are a typical example. Note that corresponding angles *X* and *Y* are very different; angle *Y* is greater than a right angle, and angle *X* is considerably less than a right angle.

The pattern should have a dot at the meeting point of the seamlines, as shown, and the dot should be tailor-tacked for matching when the seam is pinned. Vogue patterns are usually so marked, but many of the other patterns are not. Whenever this type of corner is encountered (whenever the angle formed by cross seamlines is not a right angle), mark the meeting point of cross seamlines with a tailor's tack. See the two enlarged views in Figure 3. Notice that the proper method is to match the dots and that the two cut edges at the upper edge meet each other at the seamline only and do not meet at the cut edge. By contrast, matching the corners at the cut edge only makes for an inaccurate joining, as shown.

PURPOSES OF BASTING AND TYPES OF BASTING STITCHES

Basting stitches are used (1) to hold the garment together for a fitting, (2) to control the edges of the fabric during stitching, (3) as a guideline for topstitching, (4) to mark a line, and (5) as an aid to pressing. It is assumed the reader understands that basting stitches can vary greatly, being entirely dependent on the purpose for which they are used and on the fabric. A few statements will illustrate that general principles must be applied to ever-changing circumstances. Although stitches must be small and secure to hold edges for fitting purposes, they can be longer and less secure on edges that will not get strain during fitting; therefore, they must be short in the fitted hip area of a straight

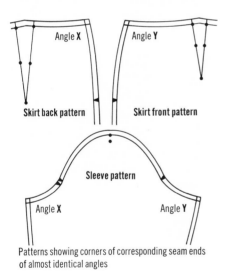

Patterns showing corners of corresponding seam ends of almost identical angles

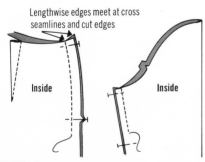

FIGURE 2

skirt and can be longer and less secure below the 10-inch hipline.

The machine has a tendency to push the upper layer of fabric forward. In the most spongy wools, very small basting stitches must be used to prevent this; by contrast, flat and stiff fabrics are not pushed out of line, and a much longer stitch is quite acceptable. The reader should think through her problem, make test samples if necessary, and baste in a way that will be accurate under the existing circumstances.

Hand basting stitches will be the choice of the discriminating person for any work on high-quality garments, and especially on tailored garments. Pin basting is acceptable in utilitarian garments only. Machine basting is acceptable for flat fabrics in which needle marks do not show, but spongy wools will be pushed out of line by machine basting, and delicate lining fabrics will be marred by needle punctures. Short, even basting stitches, reinforced frequently, will be most secure. Uneven basting stitches save time on flat fabrics. Marking basting merely marks a line; it is used to mark center lines. Slip basting is an aid in matching plaids and stripes.

The security of the basting thread is dependent on the frequency of back-stitches or reinforcing stitches; this can be done as often as every inch (when basting a shaped collar seam or when working with very pliable, spongy fabric) or as little as every few inches (when basting straight seams in stiff, flat fabrics). Basting is done with a contrasting color of thread in a single thickness; a double thread is never used.

BASTING AND STITCHING DARTS

The experienced person can further improve her work by employing the proper method of basting and stitching darts. A most common error is shown in Figure

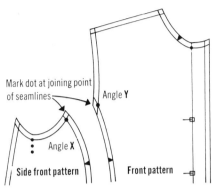

Patterns showing corners of corresponding seam ends of very different angles

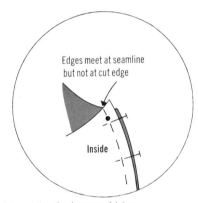

Enlarged view showing proper joining

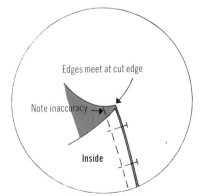

Enlarged view showing inaccurate joining

FIGURE 3

4a. Many darts are composed of ruler-straight lines, as shown, and the most common error is that of basting and stitching in a way that makes the dart too wide at the tip. A good dart line retains the ruler-straight character all the way down to the tip, which results in a smooth fit over body contours. Figure 4b pictures a similar problem. In this case, the dart lines curve, becoming even slimmer at the tip, and a typical mistake is to stitch the curved dart in a ruler-straight line. Figure 4c pictures a subtle technique that can be used on any dart to create a very smooth, molded effect over figure curves. A dart with straight lines is pictured, and it is stitched in straight lines, but note that the stitching is brought to the fold edge about ¼ inch above the dart tip so that the last few stitches are right on the fold edge. This technique is not used in basting because of its intricacy; a bit of practice at the machine will enable one to do this trick very easily on all darts.

GATHERING AND EASING IN FULLNESS

There are three methods of easing in a longer edge to fit a shorter edge:

1 The longer edge can be pinned into position, distributing the fullness evenly. This method is quite acceptable if the fabric is pliable enough to ease well, if the edge involved is relatively short, and if the amount of ease is slight.

2 A long machine stitch (six to eight stitches per inch) can be used on the longer edge in a position just outside the seamline (a scant ⅝ inch from the raw edge). The bobbin thread can be pulled to aid in easing in the edge. This method

is the better choice if fabrics are not entirely pliable and if the length of the edge or the amount of ease is greater.

3 If the amount of ease is great (as in the cap of a sleeve) or if an edge is to be gathered, more help is required. Use two rows of long machine stitches, placed ⅛ inch on each side of the seamline (if needle marks will not show when stitches are removed), or use two rows of stitches placed on the seamline and ¼ inch outside the seamline (if the needle will leave permanent marks on the fabric, as it does in satin). When the bobbin threads are pulled up, the gathers are in good control and can be distributed evenly.

SUGGESTIONS FOR MACHINE STITCHING

It is assumed that the reader has mastered the use of the machine. The following suggestions are limited to those special problems presented by tailoring techniques and typical tailoring fabrics.

Because of its sponginess and thickness, wool tends to push out of line at the machine; the top layer pushes forward. Basting stitches must be firm and reinforced often. If the problem is especially serious, cross bastings will be very helpful (see Figure 8 on page 153). The pressure on the machine foot can be adjusted to compensate for the extra bulk passing beneath it.

If a seam must be stitched across another seam in very thick fabrics, the machine may not move forward or "climb up" to the thicker level at the cross seam; lifting the machine foot, moving the fabric forward slightly, and then releasing the foot will help the machine operate through the thicker area.

Novelty weaves with long floats of exposed yarns or loops create an additional problem. The floats of thread or loops may catch in the machine foot. A strip of tissue paper placed over the seam edge and fed into the machine with the fabric will prevent this problem.

Pile fabrics present similar problems resulting from their thickness, and fur fabrics present all the problems of pile fabrics plus a few additional ones. When basting and stitching seams in fur fabrics, push the pile away from the seam and try to get stitches down to the backing without catching in any of the hairlike fibers. If fibers are caught in the stitching, they can be pulled free by lifting them out with a pin.

Lining fabrics are delicate and easily snagged with a slightly dull needle or pin. A test stiching should be done prior to stitching lining sections; possibly a new needle or one in a smaller size will be required. In the school laboratory situation, the student must test-stitch each time she uses the machine for lining fabrics; another student, using less delicate fabric, may have damaged the needle without being aware of it.

Many lining fabrics are so flat that additional pressure on the machine foot is required. Even so, often the seam will pucker slightly, making it seem that the thread tension is too tight, and yet adjustment of the tension may not help. The problem is simply that the fabric is too thin for the machine to accommodate well. Placing slight pressure on the fabric (in other words, holding the fabric somewhat taut) as it passes through the machine will solve the problem.

Pin basting lining fabrics should be avoided because although the machine will ride over pins, often the needle is damaged slightly in the process and will snag the fabric. If lining fabrics are pinbasted, the pins must be removed before crossing them with the machine.

Most lining fabrics made to add warmth combine the problems created by thick fabrics (like wool) as well as those of delicate lining fabrics.

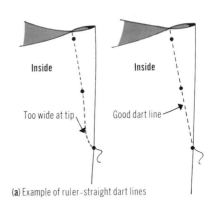

(a) Example of ruler-straight dart lines

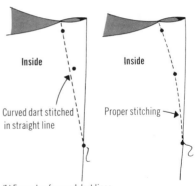

(b) Example of curved dart lines

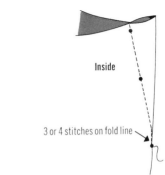

(c) To improve stitching of both straight and curved dart lines

FIGURE 4

SEAM

AND

HEM

FINISHES

As a general rule, seams and hem edges are allowed to remain raw and unfinished in the tailored garment. This book does not include directions for unlined jackets, coats, or skirts, and so there will be little need to discuss seam or hem finishes. There are only three circumstances under which a finish for these edges is required: (1) If the lined skirt has a pleat, the released edges of the pleat will not be lined; therefore, the vertical seam on the inner fold of the pleat and the hem edge in the pleat area will be finished in some way. (2) If some style fullness is removed from the skirt lining, the lining will hang free from the skirt; therefore, the skirt hem and the lining hem will require some kind of finish. Under these circumstances, the skirt seams may need to be finished to prevent raveling. (3) This circumstance is very similar to the preceding one. Although jacket linings are always attached to the lower edge of the jacket, there are some few coat linings that are not attached because style fullness has been removed from the lining. This will occur frequently in seasons when flared coats with a great deal of style fullness are fashionable. Part of the style fullness is removed from the lining because it is a wise economy of fabric. If the coat lining hangs free from the coat, both hems must be finished.

GENERAL RULE If a garment is lined with a

lining attached to the garment at the hemline, no seam or hem finishes are required.

TRADITIONAL SEAM FINISHES

Figure 5 shows three seam finishes that might be used on a tailored garment, although only one of the three will be recommended for high-quality tailored garments; two of the finishes pictured are used in unlined garments. Prior to using any seam finish, seams are pressed open. The sketches on the left in Figure 5 show the seam in position for machine work, while the sketches on the right show the seam as it will appear when finished.

Figure 5a   Raveling can be prevented by using the zigzag feature on the machine. This finish, although not as attractive as some, takes a minimum length of time and adds a minimum of extra bulk. It can be used for seams of the lined garment if the fabric ravels seriously, and it is quite acceptable for the lined skirt in which the lining hangs free from the garment.

The bight of the stitch (from $\frac{1}{4}$ to $\frac{1}{16}$ inch wide) and the closeness of the stitch must be tested on scraps of fabric. The bight should be as narrow as possible and the stitch as long as possible (less thread and therefore less bulk will be created) while providing the necessary protection against raveling. The stitches should be placed $\frac{1}{8}$ to $\frac{1}{16}$ inch in from the raw edge, as shown.

Figure 5b   The traditional bound seam, in which rayon bias seam binding is used, offers excellent protection against raveling. A new, slightly different finish gives a more attractive and less bulky finish and will be recommended as the best of the bound finishes; see The Hong Kong Finish, on page 149. The traditional bound seam requires less time and may be the choice of some readers. A bound finish can be used to prevent raveling of seams in an unlined jacket or coat (the little summer suit-dress or summer sport jackets), for seams in the unlined skirt, and for seams in the lined skirt if the lining hangs free from the skirt. Because of its bulkiness, this finish is used only in cases of serious raveling.

Lap one fold edge of the bias binding ¼ inch over the underside of the raw seam edge and stitch close to the fold. Then turn the binding over the raw edge and stitch close to the fold edge.

Figure 5c The turned-under-and-stitched seam is the least desirable of the three because of its bulk. Its use is limited to finishing seams in unlined garments made of lightweight summer fabrics only. It is done by simply turning under ¼ inch on the raw seam edges and stitching close to the fold edge.

THE HONG KONG FINISH

Travelers to the Orient have been attracted by high-quality workmanship and low prices, and many have returned with beautifully constructed garments. In turn, the enterprising Orientals have entered the mail-order business in America with remarkable success. The Hong Kong finish, coupled with a comparable hem and facing-edge finish, is a distinctive feature of their work, and it is such an attractive effect that it is recommended exclusively for finishing problem seams; in high-quality tailoring, it should replace the traditional bound seam. Actually, this is a simple seam finish which can be extended for use in hems to replace the traditional bound hem and can be used in a rather unique way for a novelty finish on edges of facings of lined jackets and coats (as explained on page 324).

It must be remembered that the aver-

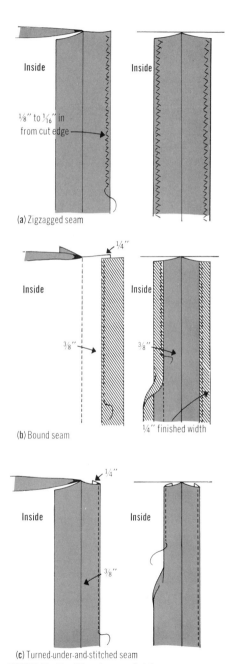

(a) Zigzagged seam

(b) Bound seam

(c) Turned-under-and-stitched seam

FIGURE 5 Traditional seam finishes

age lined jacket or coat will require no seam finish. The lined skirt will not require a seam finish if the lining will be attached to the lower edge of the skirt. But if there is a pleat, parts of it will be exposed, and so that area will need a finish for raw edges. If the lining is to hang free from the skirt and if the fabric ravels, skirt seams may require a finish. For all these circumstances, the Hong Kong finish is highly recommended because it is so attractive and because it is less bulky than the traditional bound seam. The attractive feature is the delicate ⅛-inch finished width; furthermore, because one edge of the binding remains raw, there is one less thickness of binding fabric.

Refer back to Extra Fabric for the Hong Kong Finish on page 44. Ideally, bias strips of lining fabric replace the traditional rayon bias seam binding, although one can use the seam binding by pressing out the fold creases to obtain 1-inch strips. The most attractive effect will be achieved by using lining fabric

(if it is not too heavy) because of the proximity of the bound edges and the lining. An underlining fabric (Si Bonne or Siri) in a harmonizing color can be used. Because the finished width of the binding is so narrow, piecing seams in the bias must be kept to a minimum; strips about 1 yard long will be ideal. The disadvantages of this finish are the greater expense of the yard of lining fabric compared with the cost of bias seam binding and the fact that it does require more construction time.

Figure 6   Cut bias strips of fabric 1 inch wide. See Figure 6a. Stitch the bias strips right sides together on the top side of the seam, as shown. Use an ample ⅛-inch seam allowance and use small machine stitches (about 20 per inch). End the binding at the hemline or slightly above the hemline. To obtain the desired ⅛-inch finish, the seam must be trimmed to slightly less than ⅛ inch; it will be somewhat weakened because it is so narrow, which explains the need for a very short machine stitch. See Figure 6b. Wrap the bias snugly over the seam and secure it in one of two ways. Either machine-stitch directly on the seam joining (which is quicker but less accurate

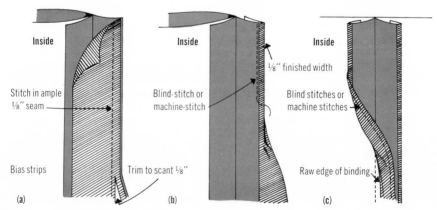

FIGURE 6   The Hong Kong seam finish

and tends to stiffen the seam) or blind-stitch directly in the seam joining (which will ensure greater perfection). The stitches will be quite inconspicuous even if the machine method is used. See Figure 6c. Note that the binding remains raw on the underside of the seam; it will not ravel because it has been cut on the bias. The binding may be too wide; if it is, the raw edge should be trimmed to a scant ¼ inch from the stitches, as shown.

Figure 7 Hem and facing edges are done in an identical manner, as shown in the skirt hem pictured in Figure 7a. A word of caution: If the skirt is flared, gathering stitches must be used to draw up the hem to fit the skirt before this finish is applied, just as is done in the traditional seam-binding method.

See Figure 7b. Hemming stitches are placed down from the finished hem edge and are completely hidden from view. The stitch shown is the tailor's hemming stitch, described in detail and illustrated in working position in Figure 15.

NOTE The catch-stitched hem, used for lined jackets and coats and for skirts in which the lining is attached to the lower edge, is described on page 209. The traditional hem done with rayon bias seam binding is not included in this book, although that method may be used if desired.

TOPSTITCHING

When a design requires topstitched effects, the topstitching becomes part of the design and is extremely important to the ultimate success of the garment. It is well worth the great amount of experimentation that is necessary to obtain the desired result. If directions call for edgestitching, the effect is not intended to be particularly striking, and regular sewing thread may be quite satisfactory.

However, if topstitching is ¼ inch or more from the edge, it is intended as part of the design and should be done in such a way that it is attractively conspicuous.

CHOICE OF THREAD

The pattern usually suggests buttonhole twist for topstitched effects because of its high luster and its thickness. Button-

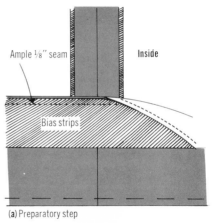

(a) Preparatory step

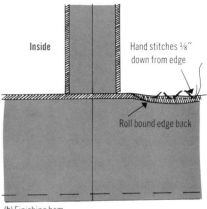

(b) Finishing hem

FIGURE 7 The Hong Kong finish for hems and facing edges

hole twist will be used for the top thread only. It is the ideal choice, but the limited number of colors available makes it necessary to consider alternative solutions. The high luster of silk thread makes it the next logical choice, although the range of colors is somewhat limited in many small stores. If it becomes necessary, mercerized thread must be used because appropriateness of color is more important than luster.

TEST STITCHING

Tests must be done through the proper number of fabric thicknesses. Ideally, several test seams should be stitched to allow experimentation in width from the seam edge and to test the appearance of the stitching itself. In most designs, subtle adjustments in width to please individual tastes are acceptable.

One must be inventive in order to obtain the desired result. The nature, weave, and design of the fabric will demand a variety of solutions. The length of stitch, usually longer than that used for seams, can vary greatly. The tension of the thread may need adjustment because more tension (without drawing up the edge) will make stitches sink into the fabric and create a more conspicuous indentation.

Silk thread and mercerized thread are not as thick and heavy as might be desired, although they are usually quite effective in flat fabrics (wool gabardine, worsteds, etc.). If the fabric is spongy or in a novelty weave, topstitching done with these threads may not be as conspicuous as desired. Another row of stitching can be placed directly on top of the first, providing great care is taken

to stitch directly over the first row; this is so difficult that it is almost impossible to do a perfect job. However, if the fabric has great surface interest, if it is in a fairly dark color, or if it is composed of several colors, as in a tweed, little inaccuracies will not be evident, and this idea may prove to be very effective.

A suggestion of limited applicability is to use a very narrow zigzag stitch with stitches so close together that they give a solid-line effect. This technique is recommended if topstitched effects are an important part of the design and if the fabric is so heavy and tweedlike that more orthodox methods will not give the desired conspicuous effect. The bight of the zigzagged stitch would be very narrow ($\frac{1}{32}$ or $\frac{1}{16}$ inch), and the stitch length should be as fine as is required to give a very slim, solid line. Because such stitches would be difficult to remove if the line were not perfect, it is well to obtain a perfect line of straight topstitching first and then use it for a guide, stitching over it with the zigzag stitch.

CONTROL OF FABRIC

The seam should be carefully pressed in the proper direction before work is begun. Figure 8a pictures the method of basting edges for topstitched details. Because the machine pushes the fabric out of line (more so with more layers of fabric), basting stitches must be very small and firm. The sketch shows two rows of basting, $\frac{1}{16}$ inch on each side of the line to be topstitched. Reinforce with firm backstitches as often as necessary to hold the fabric securely. Firm cross bastings are a further protection against inaccuracy in very spongy fabric. By basting each side of the line desired, excellent control is achieved, and the short, firm stitches can be more easily removed.

Figure 8b shows the use of a small cardboard gauge as a guide for topstitching at the machine. If desired, a basted guideline for stitching can be used.

SPECIAL PROBLEMS

The three thicknesses of fabric which result when a seam is pressed in one direction pad the stitches and help to achieve an attractively conspicuous effect. If topstitching is required in areas where there is no padding or where there is a variation in padding, the resulting stitches will not be consistently conspicuous. Figure 9 illustrates this problem with a topstitched dart. The problem arises because the dart narrows down at the tip, so that stitches in the upper part of the dart are padded with two thicknesses of fabric, but are padded with only one layer in the tip area. The solution is to cut scraps of identical fabric and baste them in a position on the inside to pad the topstitching; be sure that raw edges just meet each other, as shown. As soon as the dart is topstitched, excess fabric can be trimmed close to the stitching.

This idea is applicable to any topstitching problem in which more padding is desired for a greater indentation at the stitched line. A narrow strip of fabric can be basted the full length of any seam to provide extra padding for stitches, and if it is then trimmed close to the stitching, no great amount of bulk results.

TRIMMING
SEAMS
AND REDUCING
BULK

The bulk created by the thickness of seams, cross seams, darts, pleats, hems, and facings is a problem common to all tailored garments. Effective reduction of bulk will do as much for the ultimate success of the garment as any other single construction technique. Study this

entire section thoroughly at this time because it must be understood so well that these ideas are automatically incorporated into action; bulk reduction will be involved with every single step of construction.

TO TRIM CORNERS OF CROSS SEAMS

When a seam, a dart, or a pleat is crossed by another seam (as skirt seams and darts are crossed by the waistband),

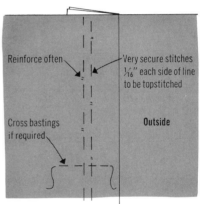

(a) Preparation for stitching

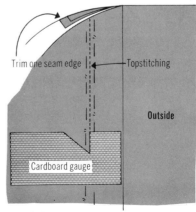

(b) Topstitching

FIGURE 8

some of the bulk of the cross seam can be removed. This bulk is more troublesome when the cross seam will be pressed open. Figure 10a shows how to trim away one thickness of fabric by trimming close to stitching lines of seams; note that the stitching line itself has not been weakened in any way. Figure 10b pictures a more effective method to be used for heavier fabrics in places where the cross seam will be pressed open and in places where the bulk of the cross seams would be apparent as the garment is worn. In this method, the vertical seam pictured is ripped almost down to the cross seamline; if the fabric is heavy, the remaining stitches will not pull out. Now the entire corner of the seam can be trimmed, as shown.

TO REDUCE BULK IN HEM AND FACING AREA

When one seam is turned back on another, as it is when the hem is turned up or when a facing is turned back on the body of the garment (for example, the

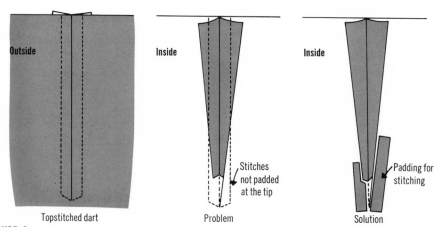

Topstitched dart   Problem   Solution

FIGURE 9

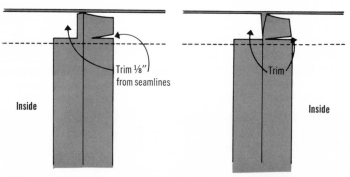

(a) Trim corners of cross seams   **(b)** Effective method for heavier fabrics

FIGURE 10

facing shoulder seam, which falls directly over the shoulder seam in the garment), there will be four thicknesses of fabric at the seam, with a sudden "jump-off" to two thicknesses of fabric. Staggering these seams so that there is a gradual tapering off of thickness will result in a far smoother line. See Figure 11. When the hemline has been established, trim the seam in the hem area down to ⅜ inch so that it will be staggered with the ⅝-inch seam width in the garment. Likewise, as soon as seams in facings are stitched, trim them to a ⅜-inch width before applying the facing.

TO REDUCE BULK IN DARTS

All suggestions in this section must be considered in light of the raveling qualities of the particular fabric being used; bulk must be reduced in darts, but not at the cost of weakening the garment. See Figure 12. The large dart pictured in Figure 12a shows general principles. The fold edge of a dart can be slashed to that level where the fold edge is about ¼ inch from the stitching (⅜ inch in fabrics that ravel seriously). A little clip toward the stitching will allow the dart to press open above that level. If the resulting dart edges are more than ½ or

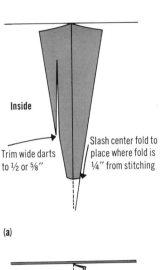

Inside

Trim wide darts to ½ or ⅝"

Slash center fold to place where fold is ¼" from stitching

(a)

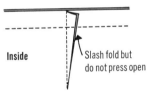

Inside

Slash fold but do not press open

(b)

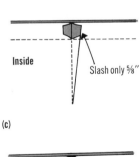

Inside

Slash only ⅝"

(c)

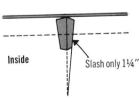

Inside

Slash only 1¼"

(d)

FIGURE 12 To reduce bulk in darts

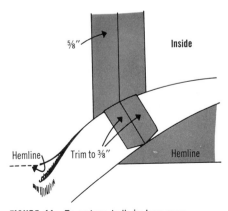

⅝"

Inside

Hemline

Trim to ⅜"

Hemline

FIGURE 11 To reduce bulk in hem area

⅝ inch, the width of the cut edges can be trimmed down, as shown.

Small darts, the size of those shown in Figure 12b to d, are not generally slashed and pressed open. However, in heavy fabrics that do not ravel appreciably and in garments that are completely interfaced and lined, a variety of ideas may be employed. Figure 12b shows a dart that has been slashed on the fold edge for a short distance. This idea can sometimes be used on a dart so small that it cannot be pressed open; the two cut edges are more pliable and apparently less bulky than one fold edge. Figure 12c pictures a method that is quite safe for use in almost any fabric. The fold edge has been slashed only ⅝ inch and then clipped to one side. This allows for pressing the dart open right at the cross seam and has not weakened the dart line in any way. Figure 12d shows the fold edge slashed 1¼ inches so that it might be crossed by a seam which will be pressed open; this method is ideal for small darts, providing the nature of the fabric will allow for its safe use.

NOTE The complete interfacing, which will be recommended for all jackets and coats, is caught in with the stitching of darts and seams, thereby strengthening all stitched edges. For this reason, smaller darts than usual can be slashed.

TO STAGGER SEAM EDGES

Most of the structural seams of the garment remain the full ⅝-inch width for maximum strength, and most of them will be pressed open. However, some structural seams are pressed to one side (for example, those for topstitched ef-

fects, as pictured in Figure 8). If a seam is pressed to one side, one edge should be trimmed down slightly (see Figure 8) for a staggered effect.

Encased seams must be trimmed in total width and must be staggered for a smooth, professional finished appearance. Encased seams are those which will turn back on themselves, creating great bulk; examples are edges of collars, cuffs, pocket flaps, and the entire front edge if a separate facing is used. Because these seams will be entirely protected from friction, they can be trimmed to a narrower width. Figure 13 shows several techniques required for encased edges; all sketches appear in actual size. Three layers of fabric are shown because these edges will be interfaced. See Figure 13a. Begin by trimming the narrowest edge first. Trim the interfacing to ⅛ inch from the stitching. Then trim one seam edge to ¼ inch and lastly trim the remaining edge to a ⅜-inch width. In most cases, it is better to trim the seam which will be directly under the right side of the garment when worn in the widest width. There are exceptions to this rule which will be explained as they occur in the construction process.

Figure 13b shows two corners of encased seams. When corners turn back on themselves, great bulk would result if the corners were not trimmed as shown. After the seams are trimmed and staggered, the corners must be trimmed in such a way that the two angles between the cut edge and the stitched seamline (angle *a* plus angle *b*) equal the angle formed by the stitched seamline (angle *c*).

When the encased seam is turned back on itself, it must be basted properly before it is pressed; these edges cannot be pressed accurately without basting. Do not pin these edges in preparation for basting. The seam should be pulled up with the needle, rolled slightly to the underside (the side that will not be visible when the garment is worn), and then basted in place, as shown in Figure 13c. The seam should be rolled to the inside a very slight amount—from $\frac{1}{32}$ inch (for very flat cottons) to almost $\frac{1}{8}$ inch (for heavier wools). It should be no more than the amount that is necessary to hide the seam from view as the garment is worn.

HAND STITCHES

The tailored garment requires more hand stitching than any other construction project, and yet the secret of success lies in the inventiveness with which a few stitches are used. The worker must think through her own problem and vary her interpretation of basic stitches with each problem. This is especially true when directions call for slip stitching or whipping. The pattern guide sheets frequently say to use these stitches when entirely different solutions are really required. The length of the stitch, the frequency of reinforcing backstitches, the tautness of the thread, and the placement of the stitch in relation to the edges involved —all these factors serve to expand the few basic types into a great variety of stitches. Each problem should be handled in such a way that the edges are held securely enough for the purpose and the stitch remains inconspicuous.

There is no reason why stitches must be called by "textbook" names or why techniques must be described in the most proper manner if other names and descriptions are more effective. The author has discovered that an informal approach and a bit of humor can greatly improve the handwork of students. For example,

ALL SKETCHES IN ACTUAL SIZE

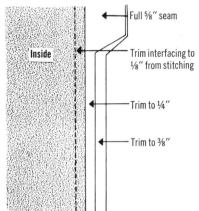

(a) To stagger edges of encased seams

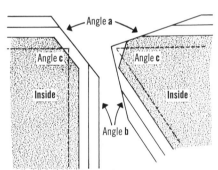

(b) To trim corners of encased seams

(c) To prepare encased seam for pressing
FIGURE 13

hand stitches must be invisible and must not be so tight that one is aware of the construction processes. The expressions "hammered down" or even "bolted down" (if said with good humor) quickly correct the tendency to oversew. Telling a student to be "a little lazier" or to make "lazy" or "easy" stitches is most effective in counteracting slightly taut handwork. If directions state that two fold edges should be slip-stitched, a great variety of stitches will result, most of which will be visible, but if a student is directed to use a "wiggle" stitch, she will slip the needle from one fold edge into the other with almost consistently excellent results.

The directions for doing a particular stitch and the position in which work is held make for convenience of hand position, an economy of time, and effective results. Most readers will quickly discover the advantages of using the accepted methods. On the other hand, if proper methods are tested conscientiously for a period of time without success, the worker can devise her own methods, providing they result in accepted standards of construction and do not require appreciably more time; there is no reason why one must be burdened by being "textbook" right in small issues.

THE CATCH STITCH

Figure 14 pictures the catch stitch interpreted in two ways; both sketches are in actual size. The catch stitch will be used more often than any other hand stitch because it is the best method for securing raw edges; a great percentage of the edges of a tailored garment do remain raw because the garment will be lined. Because this stitch swings back

and forth between the hem and the garment, it allows for a certain amount of shifting of the hem or facing, which results in inconspicuous handwork. The stitch can be varied with each use to allow for more or less shifting and for more or less security.

Figure 14a shows the traditional catch stitch in actual size as it should be done for hemming purposes. Note that stitches are made on imaginary parallel lines ¼ inch above and below the raw edge; the fact that the stitches made in the garment are ¼ inch from the raw edge means that the hem or facing can shift position slightly. An extra reinforcing backstitch, taken in the hem every two or three stitches, will secure the edge without making the stitches conspicuous on the right side of the garment. If these stitches are easy or lazy (not pulled taut to lie flat against the fabric), the hem will be as inconspicuous as possible.

Figure 14b shows the same stitch interpreted for purposes which require more security and for places where the resulting stitches will not be visible when the garment is worn. When an edge is secured to the fold line in a garment, as shown, the stitches will be hidden in the fold edge, and therefore they can be more secure without being conspicuous. Note that the stitches are made on parallel lines. However, the difference is that the stitch taken in the garment is ⅛ inch below the cut edge; the edge cannot shift as much and is therefore more secure. Shorter stitches, reinforced more often, will be firmer, and if the thread is pulled to lie flat against the fabric, this edge will be very secure.

to do the catch stitch Working from left to right, with the needle pointing to the left, take a small stitch in the hem ¼ inch from the raw edge. Move forward for the desired length of stitch and take a very small stitch in the garment the desired distance from the raw edge. Reinforce with backstitches in the hem every few stitches and continue.

THE TAILOR'S HEMMING STITCH

This stitch is used to secure hem edges that have been finished with the Hong Kong finish (as shown in Figure 15) or with rayon bias seam binding. The stitch is made ⅛ inch under the finished edge, with the result that it is invisible and will not catch readily in buckles and heels.

The stitch can be varied in length as the circumstances require, but the typical hemming stitch is about ½ inch long. Reinforcing backstitches, taken every few stitches in the hem only, will aid in making a more secure hem, and allowing the stitch to be slightly lazy (not pulled taut against the fabric) will help to make it inconspicuous.

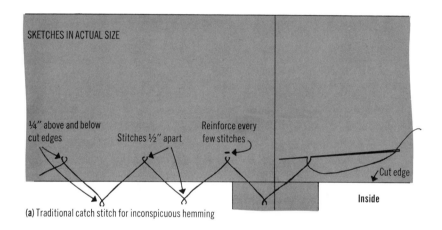

SKETCHES IN ACTUAL SIZE

¼" above and below cut edges

Stitches ½" apart

Reinforce every few stitches

Cut edge

Inside

(a) Traditional catch stitch for inconspicuous hemming

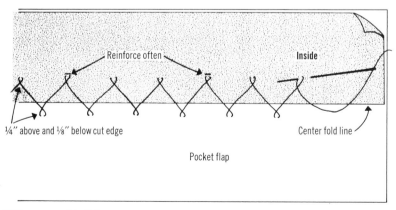

Reinforce often

Inside

¼" above and ⅛" below cut edge

Center fold line

Pocket flap

(b) More secure catch stitches

FIGURE 14 To catch-stitch cut or unfinished hem edges

to do the hemming stitch See Figure 15. Baste the hem in place with stitches a scant ¼ inch from the upper edge of the hem. Fold the hem back to the right side of the garment along the basting line; note that about ⅛ inch of the bound edge extends beyond the fold edge of the garment. Do the hemming stitch by taking a very small stitch in the garment and then moving forward for the desired length of stitch and taking a small stitch ⅛ inch in from the edge of the binding. Reinforce with backstitches in the binding every few stitches and continue.

THE SLIP STITCH

It must be remembered that this stitch suffers from overuse and is sometimes incorrectly recommended on instruction sheets and in textbooks. For example, if directions read to slip-stitch the hem in place, the hemming stitch is used. The true slip stitch should slide into the fold and out to the other edge and continue. It runs parallel to the edge and is done from the right side of the fabric.

It cannot be truly secure because if it were, it would be too conspicuous. Consequently, the traditional slip stitch should be reserved for those uses which require a minimum of security.

a special problem See Figure 16. Very often design details (pockets, flaps, and trimming details) are applied by hand because a topstitched effect is not desired for the particular design, and almost invariably directions will recommend the slip stitch. If the detail is a pocket that must withstand strain during wearing, the slip stitch will not be secure enough, especially at the upper corners of the pocket; a stitch parallel to the edge will pull out very easily. The suggestion given in Figure 16 results in invisible stitches that are as strong as machine stitches and can be made even stronger.

Pin and then baste the detail firmly in the proper position with stitches a scant ¼ inch from the finished edge; examine the result to be sure it is in perfect position. Work from the inside. The edge of the pocket extends ¼ inch from the visible basting stitches, and so stitches taken in the area just ⅛ inch outside the basted guideline will fall just inside the finished edge of the pocket and will be

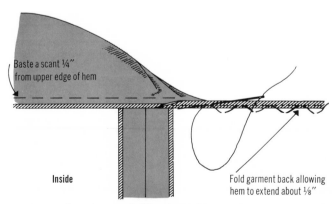

Baste a scant ¼"
from upper edge of hem

Inside

Fold garment back allowing
hem to extend about ⅛"

FIGURE 15 Tailor's hemming stitch for finished hem edges

invisible from the outside. Care must be taken that the stitches go through only one layer of the pocket or detail. Take small hand stitches at right angles to the edge for maximum security, as shown; the stitches can be very small and firm at the upper corners and less firm in areas of less strain, as shown.

In most cases the result will be excellent, and the detail will look as if it "just grew," but in heavy fabrics the finished edge may need additional slip stitches made from the outside to hold the heavy edge to the garment; in this case the slip stitch can be inconspicuous because it is not required for strength.

NOTE Padding stitches (another type of hand stitch) will be used for shaping the collar and lapel areas of the jacket or coat. They will be described in detail as they are required during construction.

REINFORCING CORNERS

If directions read to clip to a corner or slash directly to a point before the edge is stitched to another edge, the point must be reinforced to prevent raveling during construction. See Figure 17 for two examples. Although these points appear infrequently in skirt designs, they appear often in jacket and coat designs and very frequently in Vogue Paris Original and International Couturier designs.

Either of two methods of reinforcement can be used, the choice being dependent on the raveling qualities of the fabric and the strain the point will receive as the garment is worn. For example, there is a corner comparable to the one pictured in Figure 17a at the meeting point of the neck and shoulder edges if a collar is cut in one with the

garment. The corner will lie under the finished collar, and there will be little strain on the point. Even if fabric ravels somewhat, the simple method would serve this purpose. By contrast, the tip of a gusset opening, as shown in Figure 17b, receives great strain, and the point must be securely reinforced even if the fabric does not ravel appreciably.

NOTE Figure 17 pictures points reinforced and clipped or slashed. As work is done, the corners or points are not slashed directly following reinforcement; the cuts are included in these

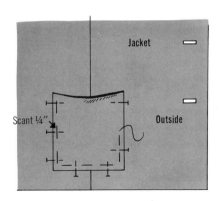

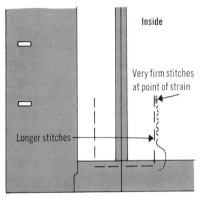

FIGURE 16

The scrap must be placed on the outside (on the right side of the garment pieces as the garment will be worn).

sketches to aid in the complete understanding of the two methods. The cuts are made just prior to the time they are required in construction; this step will be included in the pattern directions at the appropriate place.

SIMPLE REINFORCEMENT

See Figure 17a. Using a short machine stitch (18 to 22 stitches per inch), stitch through the marking at the corner, extending the stitches along the seamlines for about 1 inch on each side of the corner.

SECURE REINFORCEMENT

See Figure 17b. Slashed openings will be marked on the pattern with lines converging at a point; the lines may be curved or straight. The area between these lines will become seam allowance, and near the tip the seam allowance narrows down until there is none at all. As an aid to providing something to serve as a seam allowance at the tip, an extra scrap of fabric is included in the machine stitches which reinforce the tip. The scrap of fabric must not be bulky, and it need not match the color of the garment because it will not be visible after the slashed opening is finished; silk organza, voile, batiste, one of the sheer underlining fabrics, and thin, firm lining fabrics are all excellent choices.

Cut scraps of fabric about 1½ inches square. Place the scrap on the outside of the garment, covering the point in such a way that about ½ or ⅝ inch extends beyond the seamlines, as shown in step 1.

NOTE There is a tendency to place this scrap on the inside of the garment to hide it from view.

Using a short machine stitch (18 to 22 stitches per inch), stitch along the seamlines, as shown, being careful to make a distinct point and to avoid retracing stitches at the point.

Step 2 is not done at this time; it will be done just prior to the time it is needed in construction. But this step illustrates that the scrap of fabric will eventually turn to the inside of the garment and will serve as a seam allowance when these slashed edges are joined to corresponding edges.

REINFORCING SEAMS WITH TAPE

Preshrunk cotton-twill tape (¼- to ⅜-inch wide) will be used to prevent edges from stretching and to stiffen certain edges in the tailored garment. The tape can be applied in a variety of ways, depending on the particular problem.

The tape will reinforce the seam or edge, but it will also stiffen the seam. Because skirt seams are usually more attractive if they are pliable and lie smoothly over body contours, the use of reinforcing tape in the skirt will be confined in general to utilitarian garments. However, the seams involved with a pleat, particularly in heavy or spongy fabric, should be strengthened. By contrast, a firm, somewhat stiff edge is more desirable and appropriate in jackets and coats, and many seams in jackets and coats will be reinforced with tape. Directions for using tape will appear throughout the book.

PRESSING
TECHNIQUES

Pressing is as important as quality construction to the ultimate beauty of the tailored garment. There are three common mistakes even the more experienced persons make. One is to iron (sliding the iron across the fabric in back-and-forth movements) rather than press (an up-and-down movement of placing the iron on the fabric and lifting it up before proceeding). The ironing process tends to slick down surface fibers in the fabric, causing it to look flat and slick, possibly resulting in a shiny appearance. The worker must concentrate on pressing (not ironing) the fabric during the construction processes and throughout the lifetime of the tailored garment.

Overpressing (too often, with too hot an iron or too little moisture, or with unnecessary pressure on the iron) is another common problem. Review Care of Fabric during Construction on page 141; careful attention to the way fabric is handled during work and the condition of the fabric as it is put away between work periods will prevent unnecessary pressing. Following a procedure indicated by test pressing will solve problems of temperature, pressure, and moisture requirements.

The third common mistake is to sew an entire garment together and then attempt to press the finished garment. This mistake is a most fatal one and must be avoided. There is no more important pressing rule than "press as you go," carefully pressing each seam, dart, or edge before it is crossed by another.

VARIATION IN PROCEDURE

Each new fabric must be tested to determine the pressing methods that will be most effective with it. Because of the

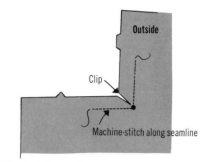

(a) Simple reinforcement

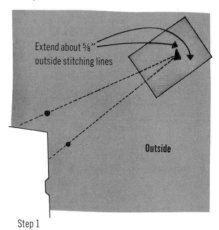

Step 1

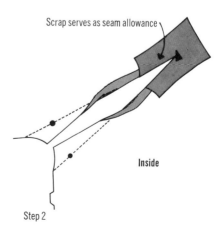

Step 2

(b) Secure reinforcement

FIGURE 17 To reinforce corners before clipping

great variety of fabrics on the market, because new fibers and fabrics are introduced each season, and because many of the new fabrics are made of a combination of two or more fibers, it is impossible to predict how any given fabric will react during pressing. Tests must be made on the fabric as it will be handled during construction; seams, pleats, darts, and the even heavier encased seams will require different techniques to produce a flat effect without harming the fabric. Figure 18 shows samples of fabric prepared in the various ways it will be handled during construction. The encased seam, composed of two layers of fabric and one layer of interfacing, must be stitched and the seam edges staggered and basted in preparation for testing. If the garment will be underlined or interfaced, the test sample should be handled in an identical manner.

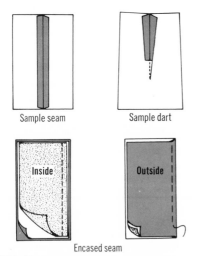

Sample seam   Sample dart

Inside   Outside

Encased seam

FIGURE 18   Tests for effective pressing

TESTS FOR PRESSURE AND MOISTURE

The pressure on the iron can vary from a slight tap to maximum pressure, with the worker leaning heavily on the iron and using a great amount of body weight. Some heavy, wiry wools will require tremendous pressure to force seams and darts to lie flat, while lightweight dress woolens will require little pressure. Examine the pressed seam or dart on the right side; it must be consistently flat and inconspicuous.

The amount of moisture required will vary greatly; there must be sufficient moisture to press the seam open without shrinking the fabric. For some fabrics, the degree of moisture from the steam iron will be too great and must be reduced by the use of a dry press cloth. Heavy and wiry fabrics may require more moisture than can be obtained with the steam iron; in that case, a dampened press cloth must be used with the iron.

Despite the advertising claims that a press cloth is not required with a steam iron, the surface of the fabric will be somewhat flattened by the slick iron; a press cloth is required for high-quality tailoring. It may be entirely dry for some purposes or truly wet for others. Dampen the press cloth by soaking the entire cloth and then wringing it out. Then press over the entire area of the cloth (for consistent moisture) until the proper degree of moisture remains.

More pressure and moisture will be required to press darts and seams flat than to press wrinkles from fabric; even more pressure and moisture will be required to press a firm edge on heavier encased seams and folded edges.

Examine the test samples in a strong light to determine whether the surface of the fabric has been adversely affected by pressing. Fibers may be flat, and seam ridges may appear somewhat shiny. This is an indication that the pressure was probably too great, but if these flaws appear even if less pressure is applied, correct them with a "touch-up" on the right side of the fabric. First hold the steam iron about ⅛ inch above the fabric, allowing steam to escape; the flattened fibers may be loosened and picked up by the released steam. For more serious problems, use the same technique with a press cloth (almost wet) over the fabric.

The heavy edges of encased seams must be basted prior to pressing; see Figure 13c on page 157. Later when basting threads are removed, marks of the thread may be imprinted in the fabric. Touching up on the right side of the fabric (with the steam iron held slightly above the fabric and with or without a dampened press cloth, depending on the degree of the imprint) will remove thread marks.

CONDITION OF THE IRON

Prior to pressing, the condition of the iron must be tested, a step that is more necessary in the school laboratory, where many persons use one iron. Be sure the steam iron is adjusted to the steam setting, and if there might be water in the iron, be sure the iron is plugged in and that the water has turned to steam. Leakage of water from the iron, with subsequent spotting of the fabric, is almost always the result of careless working habits. A small amount of water replenished as needed will serve the purpose; use about ¼ cup of water when filling the iron.

If the iron does not slide easily over the ironing surface, check the condition of the plate. If it has been used for a fabric that has a great amount of sizing or if it has been used at too high a temperature on some synthetic fabrics, a crust of burned matter will have formed and must be removed.

GENERAL SUGGESTIONS

The initial pressing of the garment (as soon as the seams are stitched) should take a considerable length of time; about half an hour may be required to do an excellent job on a skirt. By contrast, final pressing of the skirt may take only a matter of minutes. Press each seam or construction line before it is crossed with another; press small units of work before they are joined to larger units.

Always press on the wrong side of the fabric and do only touching up from the right side. Allow some moisture to remain in the fabric after it is pressed; one should be able to see steam escape as the press cloth is removed. Because the fabric will wrinkle readily when it is slightly moist, work should be planned in such a way that each pressed unit can be allowed time to dry by natural means before being handled again.

seams See Figure 19. Cut edges of seams (or darts or pleats) should be pressed flat, in the condition they were stitched. This will flatten the stitching line and make it much easier to press the seam open.

In most cases, seams can be pressed open flat on the surface of the board. However, some fabrics (brushed woolens are an example) will show unattractive ridges at seam and pleat edges, and extra precautions are required during pressing. Two solutions are shown in Figure 19; either method, or both, may be used. A rolled magazine, covered with scraps of wool or any unsized cotton fabric, is an excellent pressing aid; the rounded surface will allow for heavy pressure on the seamline itself without pressure on the cut edges of seams. Strips of paper inserted under the seam or pleat edges will cushion the seam from the garment.

Ruler-straight seams should be pressed in a ruler-straight position on the board. Curved seams (such as side seams in the skirt above the 7-inch hipline) should be pressed over the tailor's cushion, as seen in Figure 20.

darts and tucks To press a dart out to the tip while avoiding unattractive creases in the surrounding area, place the tip of the dart right at the end of the board and smooth out the garment in the dart area, as shown in Figure 20. Curved darts should be pressed over a comparable curve on a tailor's cushion; even ruler-straight darts will be improved by pressing them over the tailor's cushion because this will help to mold the area to fit body contours.

Figure 21 pictures similar problems. The fold edges of tucks can be pressed flat by placing the end of the stitched line at the end of the board, as shown. A

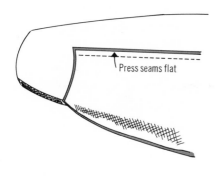

Press seams flat

To press tips of darts

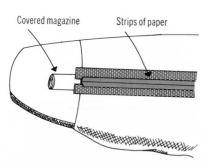

Covered magazine   Strips of paper

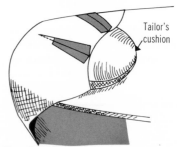

Tailor's cushion

To mold darts and seams to body contours

FIGURE 19 To prevent ridges at seams and pleat edges

FIGURE 20

gathered edge can be pressed in a similar position, allowing the gathered line to shape around the end of the board, smoothing out the fabric, and pressing the area with the tip of the iron point toward the gathered edge.

pleats Pleat edges are pressed like other seams, although the greater bulk of a pleat will require taking more precaution against unattractive ridges. Baste the pleat along the fold edge, as shown in Figure 22. Press pleat seams to a level of about 5 or 6 inches from the lower edge; this will give an advantage when finishing the hem. The remainder of the seams are pressed after the hem is finished.

shrinking out fullness Shrinking out fullness is shown in Figure 23. When an eased-in edge has been drawn up, minute puckers may be evident. These can be removed with steam. Place the rippled, eased area over the tailor's cushion and smooth out the fabric as much as possible. Using a very damp (perhaps very wet) press cloth, hold the iron about ⅛ inch above the fabric, allowing steam to penetrate the area. Lift the press cloth frequently to see whether the area has flattened; the process can be repeated and more moisture added if necessary. When the ripples have flattened, press the area using pressure on the iron and a dry press cloth.

This technique can be used to solve many other problems with fabrics which, like wool, respond well to shrinking. For example, the unattractive bowed-out appearance of a skirt stretched from hours of sitting can be improved by shrinking. Place the skirt flat on the board; allow the stretched area to ripple up on the board as it did on the figure. Using a very wet press cloth, go through the shrinking process; it may have to be re-

To press tucks

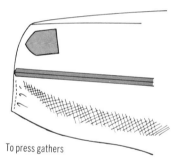

To press gathers

FIGURE 21

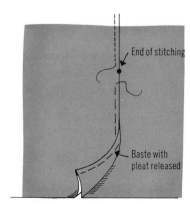

End of stitching

Baste with
pleat released

FIGURE 22

peated often, but gradually the ripples will settle down to the board, and the skirt can be pressed flat.

hems The fullness in the eased-in hem shown in Figure 23 must be shrunk out without shrinking the area of the garment directly beneath it. A piece of cardboard, shaped in a curve similar to the curve of the lower edge and slipped between the hem and the skirt, will prevent moisture from passing through to the body of the skirt.

The first step of hem construction is to baste ⅛ inch from the finished edge. This basting should remain until the hem is pressed. Then after the bastings

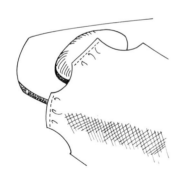

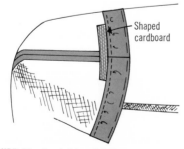
Shaped cardboard

FIGURE 23 To shrink out fullness

are removed, do touch-up pressing on the right side to remove thread imprints.

problems of pressing various fabrics Pressing fabrics with great surface interest (pile and fur fabrics and brushed wools) will require careful testing and additional care. The needle board is ideal for use as a pressing surface for these fabrics, but its cost is prohibitive for many home sewers. A layer of the same pile fabric, placed right side up on the board, will be of some help.

The importance of test pressing cannot be overemphasized. This is especially true of lining fabrics because of the great variety of fabrics that might be chosen. The problem of water spotting from a steam iron must be avoided by carefully testing the iron prior to every use; it may well be that a dampened press cloth cannot be used and that the usual press cloth will leave weave marks on delicate fabrics. Tissue paper can substitute for a dry press cloth.

THE FINAL PRESSING

Because all seams, darts, and edges—and actually all portions of the garment—have been pressed well during construction, there is little to do at the final pressing. The main purpose of a final pressing is to remove those folds and wrinkles caused by working with the garment. Many of them will fall out if the garment is allowed to hang for a few hours after work is finished. If the final pressing is done at home, the general suggestions given earlier in this chapter should be followed.

Professional pressing of costumes that will play leading roles in the wardrobe is well worth the cost. The large-area irons and the pressure and steam control available at the professional establishment result in a more finished appearance. The cost is relatively nominal.

11

FITTING
AND
TAILORING
THE
SKIRT

A review of certain sections of this book just prior to beginning construction will be helpful. Reread Suggestions for Changes in Straight-skirt Designs (page 133), Selection of Supporting Fabrics (page 45), Cutting the Skirt Underlining (page 136), Cutting the Skirt Lining (page 137), and the entire contents of Chapter 10.

Most skirts are very simply designed, while more interesting details are reserved for the jacket. This is unfortunate if much of the time the jacket will be worn open or the skirt and blouse will be worn without the jacket. The suit should be a distinctive, important costume, with or without the jacket. Little details can create desirable interest if they do not dominate the details of the jacket or give a cluttered look. In general, these details should be confined to the area under the jacket. The details must be compatible with the "feeling" created by the jacket and also the blouse.

Several ideas are pictured in Figure 1; note that each has a different character, from the tailored plaid blouse with matching belt to the elegant velvet and rhinestone combination. Both visible and concealed waistbands are shown; either waistband may be used in any skirt design. Fabric combinations should be used imaginatively. For example, the cummerbunds pictured may match the skirt fabric or the blouse fabric or contrast in color and texture to both; the plastic-leather belt section suggested may create interest through mere contrast in texture, or it may be more striking in a contrasting color. A nice idea, which is not pictured, is simply to make the skirt waistband of the blouse fabric; this has a tendency to make the skirt and blouse look somewhat more like a dress. A purchased leather belt is a very simple way to add a finished touch to the skirt.

CHOICES OF CONSTRUCTION METHODS FOR THE SKIRT

The directions in this chapter would have been extremely simple to read (and to write) if it had been possible to say "this is the one way to do it." But each fabric and each design makes demands on construction methods, and in addition, each person has her preferences, which must be taken into account. Alternative construction methods are given for several details of the skirt. The choices of methods and an evaluation of each appear in several sections of this chapter. It is important to read this section and glance through other parts of the chapter before work is begun as an aid to making all decisions of construction methods at this time.

The skirt can be completely underlined or not, as desired. Most skirts that are made of fairly firm, medium-weight, typical suiting fabric do not require an underlining. However, a skirt in a very spongy fabric or one that is really too lightweight for the skirt (dress woolens) will need the extra body the underlining provides. The underlining is the very first step of construction, and so this decision must be made before the skirt is basted together. See The Underlined Skirt, on page 173, for directions. All construction techniques involved with the underlining are discussed in that section, so the person making an underlined skirt must refer back to it at various stages in the construction process. The underlining is not pictured or discussed in the remainder of the chapter.

The zipper may be in the side position or in the center-back position. The construction involved with the zipper is essentially the same regardless of the position of the zipper. Each sketch is marked "front (or left back)" and "back (or right back)" so that they are applicable to either zipper position. Two methods of zipper construction are included; read Evaluation of Zipper Methods on page 193.

Although there are many ways a waistband can be applied and constructed, only two choices are given; read Evaluation of Methods on page 201. Separate directions for the two methods are included.

Two hem finishes are given: the Hong Kong finish conceals raw edges, and the catch-stitched hem leaves raw edges exposed. The choice between the two hems is entirely dependent on the way the lining will be finished at the lower edge. The choice of finished or unfinished seams is also involved with the lining treatment.

Therefore, the decision concerning lining finishes is especially important. Two choices of finishes for the lower edge of the lining are included. The lining attached to the skirt (like the lining in a jacket or coat) is shown in Figures 56, 57, and 58, and the free-hanging lining is shown in Figures 59 and 60. It is important to study those sketches now as an aid to making a decision; the decision must be made by the time seams are stitched because it is then that the seam finish should be done, if one will be required.

Each method of finishing the lower edge of the lining has certain advantages. The lining attached to the skirt is favored by most persons who delight in a certain illusive elegance; it is very attractive. It is far less time-consuming than the alternative method because seams and hem edges are never exposed to friction and therefore can remain raw.

Welt pocket

Belt to match blouse

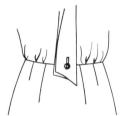

Tie ends of blouse buttoned to skirt

Bound pocket with loop and button closing

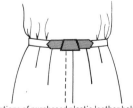

Velvet cummerbund with rhinestone pins and chain

Sections of purchased plastic leather belt stitched to waistband

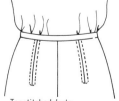

Topstitched darts

Contrasting cummerbund worn with bolero blouse

FIGURE 1 Details for the skirt

Unfinished seams and raw hem edges have another advantage in that they allow the edges to be less stiff and less bulky, with the result that the skirt is much more attractive. Even though the construction around the pleat area is more difficult (compare Figures 57 and 60), the entire operation at the lower edge requires less time.

There are disadvantages of the attached lining that are important to some persons. The first is that pressing of the finished skirt is slightly more difficult because the lining and skirt must be pressed in one operation. This is no disadvantage when the skirt is dry-cleaned; it will be returned in excellent condition. However, the person who needs to press clothing after each wearing and the person who purchases low-quality fabric (which will wrinkle and require frequent pressing) will probably prefer the free-hanging lining. The second disadvantage has to do with possible alterations in size on the finished skirt. The attached lining will have to be removed and replaced for fittings, while the free-hanging lining will allow for easier alteration. This is no great disadvantage to most persons, but the person who changes size frequently or who anticipates a change in size might prefer the free-hanging lining. The third disadvantage has to do with the inevitable stretching in bias areas of very flared (circular or nearly circular) skirts. Because both the skirt and the lining fabric will stretch and because very probably they will not stretch an identical amount, it would be a mistake to attach the lining to the skirt; the free-hanging lining, which would allow for corrections in hem length on the skirt

and lining separately, would be the better choice.

The free-hanging lining has the advantages mentioned above—the skirt can be more easily altered in size, it can be more easily pressed by an inexperienced presser, and if it is flared, corrections in hem length can be more easily made. There is one other advantage that is of more value; it was discussed under Cutting the Lining on page 137. If the skirt has a great deal of style fullness (loose pleats or gathers), some of the fullness can be eliminated from the lining to reduce bulk and to save lining fabric; an example appears in Figure 8 on page 139. If style fullness is removed, the lining will not be the same width as the skirt at the lower edge and therefore must hang free from the skirt.

One disadvantage of the free-hanging lining is that it is not as attractive from the inside because the stitches in the lining hem are conspicuous; it does not look as elegant. The other disadvantage is that it requires a great deal more time, especially if seams must be finished. A recent test made by the author revealed a surprising difference in time required for the two methods. Two identical slightly flared six-gore skirts were tested. One was done by the free-hanging method in a way that would make it as elegant as the attached lining—with care to make the finished seams even and with the second step of the seam finish done by hand rather than machine. The skirt was hemmed with the Hong Kong finish, and the lining was turned under and hemmed. This skirt required a total of six additional hours more than the identical skirt with raw seam and hem edges and with the lining attached to the skirt at the lower edge.

With the above factors taken into account and assuming that the fabric being used is of fairly high quality and that the wearer is reasonably careful to avoid wrinkles as she wears the skirt, the following general statement will be an aid in making the choice: *Use the attached lining for a more attractive appearance and as an economy of time, and use the free-hanging lining if style fullness has been removed from the lining or if the skirt is very flared.*

THE UNDERLINED SKIRT

Most suit skirts will not be underlined, and therefore the skirt underlining will not be pictured in the remaining sections of this chapter. The underlining is included for those few skirts made of dress-weight or very spongy fabric which might need additional body and for those skirts (like the A-line) which require an underlining for silhouette support.

NOTE All problems of construction related to the underlining are discussed in this section. Refer back to this section while following directions in the remainder of this chapter.

PINNING AND BASTING DIRECTIONS

See Figure 2. Smooth all skirt sections out on a table with the wrong sides uppermost; if there is a prominent center fold in the fabric, it should be pressed flat before the skirt and underlining sections are combined. Place the underlining sections on the inside of the skirt pieces, cut edges even, as shown in Figure 2a. Remember that the underlining was cut to a level about $\frac{1}{8}$ to $\frac{1}{4}$ inch above the hemlines and $\frac{5}{8}$ inch over from any pleat line; place the underlin-

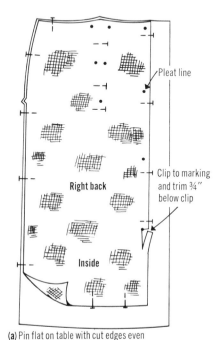

(a) Pin flat on table with cut edges even

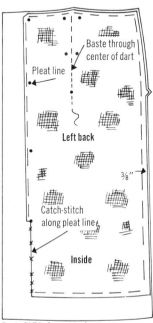

(b) Baste 3⁄8″ in from cut edges

FIGURE 2 The underlined skirt

ing in proper position. Smooth the two together flat on the table and pin all edges of the underlining in place; pin along the center of dart lines.

If there is a released pleat, study the pattern to discover where the stitching of the pleat seam will end. Then make a ¾-inch clip at that point, as shown, and trim ¾ inch from the edge of the underlining below that point; the underlining, trimmed in this way, will be ⅛ inch inside the pleat line and will not create bulk in the pleat.

Figure 2b shows the underlining properly affixed to the skirt pieces. Baste about ⅜ inch in from the cut edges of the underlining; the basting stitches must be done by hand and must be firm enough to hold the fabric in accurate position, but they need not be perfectly even. The ⅜-inch measurement stated is simply one that gives control near the seamline, where it is needed, while avoiding the seamline itself.

The two fabrics must act as one when the darts are stitched, so baste down the

center of the dart lines, with stitches small and very secure right at the tip of the dart; extend the basting stitches for a short distance beyond the tip of the dart. With firm stitches, catch-stitch the underlining to the skirt in the lower pleat area.

The skirt and underlining pieces have been combined in such a way that they can be handled as one during construction. The skirt should be basted for a fitting in the usual manner, but one precaution should be taken: Because each seam or dart edge is composed of four layers of fabric, basting stitches must be firmer and reinforced more often to control the spongy character of each edge. The skirt will be fitted in the usual manner.

STITCHING PRECAUTIONS

The four layers of fabric through which machine stitching will be made will make a thicker seam with a spongy character, and there will be a tendency for the various layers of fabric to push out of line at the machine. Very secure bastings and cross bastings when necessary (see Figure 8 on page 153), as well as less pressure on the machine foot, will prevent seam distortion.

Even though basting stitches were placed at the center of the dart lines in order to make the two fabrics act as one, a problem will be encountered at the tips of the darts. See Figure 3. If the stitching ends directly on the fold edge at the tip of the dart, in the usual manner, the stitches will have slipped off the wool fabric (catching in only the underlining) before the tip is reached, simply because of the thickness of fabric. The enlarged view in Figure 3 shows the solution. Note that the stitches end not right at the fold at the tip but ¹⁄₃₂ or ¹⁄₁₆ inch (sometimes as much as ⅛ inch in very thick fabrics) from the fold. Set up a

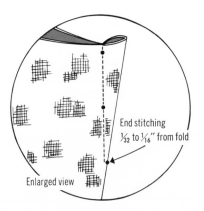

End stitching
¹⁄₃₂ to ¹⁄₁₆″ from fold

Enlarged view

FIGURE 3 To stitch darts in the underlined skirt

test dart and stitch the dart, ending the stitches about $\frac{1}{16}$ inch from the fold. Examine the effect on the right side. The stitching should end properly at the tip on the outside layer. Make corrections until the proper effect is achieved and then stitch all darts in the same manner.

TRIMMING SEAMS

The seams and darts of underlined garments must be staggered to decrease unnecessary bulk; this is done after stitching and prior to pressing or crossing with another seam. The underlining fabric must be trimmed to a narrower width, while the structural seams of the garment remain the full $\frac{5}{8}$-inch width, as shown in Figure 4. Trim both layers of underlining down to about $\frac{1}{4}$ or $\frac{3}{8}$ inch from the stitching line; the wider width is advisable if the underlining fabric ravels appreciably.

NOTE The underlining or interfacing is trimmed from encased seams in a somewhat similar manner; the difference is that encased seams will not get strain while the garment is worn, and so the underlining or interfacing is trimmed to a narrower width (see Figure 13 on page 157) if an encased seam is involved.

PROBLEMS AT THE HEMLINE

The underlining was cut to the hemline level of the pattern and was basted in place in a preliminary step. Prior to measuring the hem, it is well to remove these bastings to allow the underlining to hang "as it will" on the figure. Additional steps are required when measuring and finishing the hem. See Figure 5a. The assistant who hangs the hem should place one hand inside the skirt and pin the underlining pieces to the skirt, allowing the underlining to hang in a natural manner; pins should be a few inches apart and about 5 inches up from the desired hemline. This pin line will control the under-

lining while the hem is being measured. The hem is measured in the usual manner with pins caught through both layers of fabric.

Very often the lower edge of the underlining will not be the desired length ($\frac{1}{8}$ to $\frac{1}{4}$ inch above the established hemline), and adjustments in length are necessary. See Figure 5b if the underlining is too long. Mark a pencil line $\frac{1}{8}$ to $\frac{1}{4}$ inch above the measured hemline. Then slip the pins from the underlining layer, being sure to replace them in proper position in the garment. Now

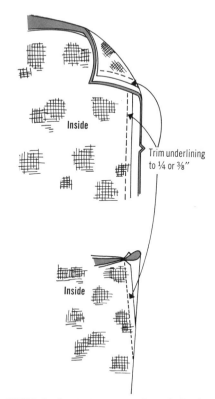

Inside

Trim underlining to $\frac{1}{4}$ or $\frac{3}{8}$"

Inside

FIGURE 4 To stagger seams in underlined garments

carefully trim the excess underlining along the pencil line, being very careful not to cut into the skirt; as a precaution,

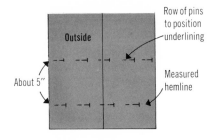

(a) Extra step when measuring hem

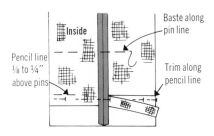

(b) To trim off excess length

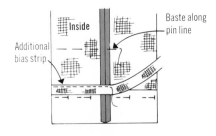

(c) To add extra length

FIGURE 5 Additional steps for finishing hem of underlined skirt

have the rounded blade of the scissors next to the garment.

If the underlining does not reach the hemline, the problem is not serious in most fabrics, providing the amount is not great. However, if the fabric of the garment is so light in weight that a color difference is noticeable where the underlining ends, an extension must be added to the underlining. See Figure 5c. Cut a bias strip of underlining fabric in the required width. Lap the strip over the lower edge of the underlining, slip one hand under the underlining layer, and hand-sew the two edges together. Trim the bias strip to a level about $\frac{1}{8}$ to $\frac{1}{4}$ inch above the measured hemline. The lower edge of the underlining strip will not be secured to the garment. See Hemming Stitches, below.

HEMMING STITCHES

Hemming stitches (either catch stitches or tailor's hemming stitches) must catch into the underlining and also the layer of skirt fabric because the underlining alone will not support the weight of the hem. See the special note on page 228. Hem directions will be given in detail later in this chapter.

NOTE The underlining will not be pictured in the remaining sketches in this chapter, nor will these special problems of underlining be mentioned as they occur in the construction process. Refer back to this section frequently while constructing the underlined skirt.

PREPARATION FOR FITTING

BASTING SKIRT SECTIONS

The skirt sections will be basted together according to directions on the instruction sheet. See Figure 6. Prepare the zipper opening by turning under the seam allowance on the front (for side-opening skirts) or on the left back (for back-opening skirts) and basting, as shown. Run a marking-basting line along the seamline of the remaining edge.

Turn under the hem allowance (see the pattern for the proper amount) and pin the hem in place.

PREPARATION OF WAISTBAND STIFFENING

Regardless of the type of waistband construction to be used, a temporary waistband is required for fitting. The waistband which is shown in Figures 7 and 8 and which appears in subsequent sketches in the section on fitting is a temporary band that will be used for fitting, will be corrected if necessary, and will then be used as a guide for the permanent waistband. The width of the band and the shaping of the end of the band will be discussed later.

Cut a strip of Pellon 1 inch wide and about 5 inches longer than waist measurement. See Figure 7. Wrap the strip around the body (over a blouse if one will be worn with the skirt) and pin it in a comfortable position. Keep in mind that the waistband will be worn for hours at a time and must be comfortable; avoid the tendency to' wrap it as tightly as a tape measure. Then let it slip about ¼ inch to allow extra length required for bulk of the skirt, lining, waistband finish, etc. Mark the position where one end laps over the strip; this indicates the desired finished length of the waistband. Trim off excess length, allowing a 1½-inch extension beyond the desired finished length.

Figure 8 shows how to establish center-front, center-back, and side positions on the band. This step is much simpler to do than the sketches indicate. The problem is complicated by the fact that the average figure measures 1 inch

larger in the front than in the back (½ inch larger on each half of the body). Keep this fact in mind as you proceed. In each case, the steps must be done in the order stated.

for the side-opening skirt

1 Label the two left side positions.
2 Fold over the strip with the two left side positions together and mark the midpoint with a dotted line. Locate the right side position ½ inch in back of the mid-

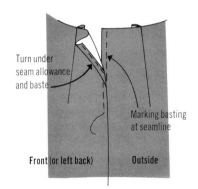

Turn under seam allowance and baste

Marking basting at seamline

Front (or left back) Outside

FIGURE 6

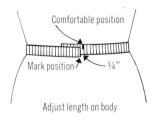

Comfortable position

Mark position ¼"

Adjust length on body

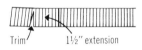

Trim 1½" extension

FIGURE 7 Preparation of waistband stiffening

point. By moving the right side position ½ inch in back of the midpoint, ½ inch has been added to the front and ½ inch removed from the back, thereby making the front a total of 1 inch longer than the back.

3 Now fold the left side markings over to the right side marking and mark the midpoints, which are the center-front and center-back positions.

for the back-opening skirt

1 Label the two back positions. Fold the strip over with the two center-back lines together and mark the center front at the midpoint.

2 Fold each center-back line over to the center-front line and mark the midpoint with a dotted line. Establish the side positions ¼ inch in back of the midpoint lines. By moving two side lines ¼ inch toward the back, a total of ½ inch has been added to the front (¼ inch on each side) and ½ inch removed from the back, thereby making the front a total of 1 inch longer than the back.

See Figure 9. Lap the raw edge of the skirt ⅝ inch over the lower edge of the stiffening, matching centers and sides; place one end of the band at the turned-under edge of the skirt and the remaining end marking at the seamline of the remaining opening edge. Pin in place, easing in fullness between matching points. It is possible that there may be a great deal of fullness in some areas and that it will not look attractive eased in; nonetheless, pin it in for the time being, and during the fitting it can be corrected for the particular figure.

DRESSING FOR THE FITTING

Wear the foundation garment that will be worn with the skirt and a blouse of the proper weight. Posture (and consequently shape) is affected by the height of heels, so shoes should be similar in height to those which will be worn with the garment. It is always encouraging to look attractive (makeup, hairstyle) while the garment is being fitted.

FITTING THE SKIRT

If the skirt is too large, do not be concerned at this time. Taking in excess size is a very simple matter, but it is better

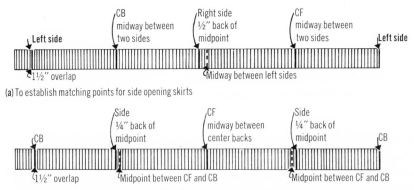

(a) To establish matching points for side opening skirts

(b) To establish matching points for back opening skirt

FIGURE 8

done after several other less obvious flaws in fit are corrected. However, if the skirt is too small, as evidenced by the fact that it will ride up and thereby form horizontal ripples below the waist, it is well to rebaste it, letting out seams as much as possible before attempting to do any fitting. Although a mistake in overall size is the one thing that concerns the wearer most, it is not the most serious fitting problem. Approach the fitting in the order presented below.

DIRECTIONS OF SEAMLINES

Center-front and center-back lines should fall as plumb lines at the center of the figure. Side seamlines should fall as plumb lines and should divide the body in attractive proportions.

placement of waistband The average figure is 1 inch larger in the front than in the back. The markings on the temporary waistband (or on a waistband included with the pattern) are in a position to control the skirt for the average figure. Figure 10 pictures a flaw in side-seam direction at the waist and for a few inches beneath the waist. This kind of short curve in the seam indicates that the figure is not average (is not exactly 1 inch larger in front than in back). The problem shown is that of the person who has a larger front measurement and a smaller back measurement than average, as indicated by the seam pulled toward the front.

GENERAL RULE The seam will pull to the direction of the curve that is larger than average, so a curve toward the back indicates larger-than-average back measurements.

Correct the misfit by removing pins from the waistband and distributing the ease in the skirt in such a way that the side-seam direction is corrected. This

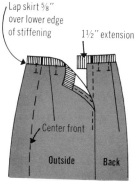

FIGURE 9 Pin stiffening to skirt, matching centers and sides

FIGURE 10 Distortion of side seams on figure that is not average

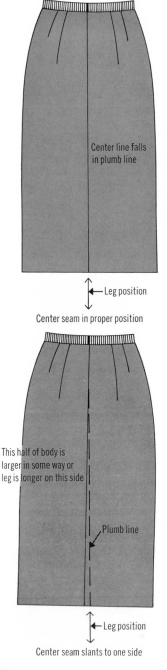

Center line falls
in plumb line

←Leg position

Center seam in proper position

This half of body is
larger in some way or
leg is longer on this side

Plumb line

←Leg position

Center seam slants to one side

FIGURE 11   Center-seam direction

will mean that every marking on the waistband will be incorrect for this figure. Pin the waistband in place and mark the new side-seam positions. Then cut a new strip of Pellon and mark the corrected side positions and, from them, the new center lines. Use the corrected waistband for all subsequent fittings.

center-seam direction The upper sketch in Figure 11 illustrates the center line (front or back) in proper plumb-like position; note that the line divides the body in half and that it ends, as it should, between the legs. The other sketch illustrates a very common problem; note that the center line slants toward one side and is not centered with the leg position. This error is easily recognized on the figure because the skirt hugs closer to one leg and stands away from the other. The problem is quite common because many people have one leg slightly longer than the other, which forces one hip to curve more at the side than the other. In addition, one hip may have more curve (more flesh) than another.

GENERAL RULE   The seam will slant in the direction of the side that is larger or the side with the longer leg.

Figure 12 shows one step required to correct center-seam direction; this step is done on the figure by lifting the skirt on the side that is smaller until the center line falls properly and then pinning the waistband to the corrected level at the waistline. A word of caution: The sketch pictures the skirt as if it were not on the figure, and the waistband is not pictured in order that the fitting techniques can be shown more clearly. Note that the skirt is lifted on the smaller side (or the side with the shorter leg) so that the seam allowance becomes greater (1¼ inches used as an example) on that side, while the original ⅝-inch seam remains on the larger side. The new seamline will be gradually tapered between the two side edges so that its width is about halfway between the two extremes as it crosses the center-front and center-back lines. This step is done on the figure by lifting the skirt up and pinning the waistband to the desired level. Do not be concerned at this time with the size at the waist; there will be excess size on the lifted side. Ease extra fullness to the waistband for the time being.

NOTE Place a marking-basting line along the corrected seamline. If a change in seam width has been made at the opening edge (either left side or center back), the opening for the zipper must be lengthened an equal amount, and when the zipper is inserted, the tab end must be placed ⅛ inch below this corrected seamline.

Lifting the skirt on one side has possibly forced it to stand away from the hipline on the side of the smaller hip. The side seam on the side of the smaller hip will possibly have to be taken in a small amount; in this case, one must fit the two sides of the body differently.

side-seam direction The center sketch in Figure 13 shows the side seamline in a plumb line, dividing the body beautifully. The other two sketches show mistakes in seam direction, with the side seam slanting either to the front or to the back. Note that the lower edge of the skirt is not level and that the skirt "sticks out" from the body in one area; for example, if the seam slants toward the front, the skirt tips upward and projects toward the front.

Corrections of side-seam directions are difficult and complicated because there are several figure irregularities which might cause each misfit. Two of

the most common have been indicated on the sketches. The fitter and the wearer should consider the particular figure and determine which of several figure irregularities is present. Start by going through the procedure to correct that flaw, and if there is still a misfit, try another, and so on.

Three figure irregularities may cause improper side-seam direction:

1 The seam may slant away from the part of the figure in which the waistline dips lower than average—toward the front if the waistline on the figure dips lower than average in back or toward the back if the waistline dips lower than average in front.
2 The seam may slant away from the part of the body that is smaller than average —toward the front if the back hips are very flat or toward the back if the front of the figure is unusually flat.
3 The seam may slant toward the part of the body that is larger than average—toward the front if the thighs or stomach is larger than average or toward the back if the hip curves are larger than average.

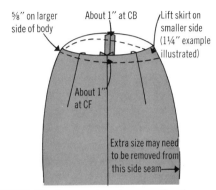

FIGURE 12 To correct center-seam direction

The problem is further complicated by the fact that more than one irregularity may be present; in fact, an unusual posture may result in all three problems on the same figure. For example, if the wearer stands in a position similar to the "debutante slouch," her hips will project forward, her back hips will be flatter than average, and her waistline will tend to dip downward in the back—the side seam will certainly slant forward because all three figure irregularities are present.

Try to correct the problem by adjustments on the waistline level first because they are relatively simple; proceed if necessary to the more difficult solu-

tions. Figure 14 illustrates how to adjust the waist level to lift the skirt up in one area; the example pictures the back skirt lifted to correct a side seam which slants forward. The same technique can be used to lift the front skirt if the seam slants toward the back. A word of caution: The sketch pictures the skirt as if it were not on the figure, and the waistband is not pictured in order that the fitting techniques can be shown more clearly. Note that the skirt is lifted up in the back so that the seam allowance is greater (1 inch used in the example) in the back, while the original ⅝-inch seam allowance remains at the center front. The new seamline should gradually taper between the two centers so that its width is about halfway between the two extremes as it crosses side seamlines. This step is done on the figure by lifting the skirt up and pinning the waistline to the

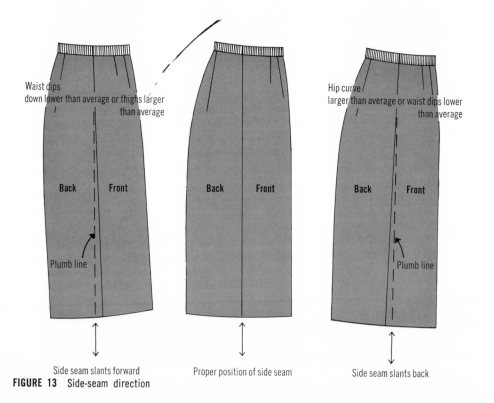

Waist dips down lower than average or thighs larger than average

Back Front

Plumb line

Side seam slants forward

Back Front

Proper position of side seam

Hip curve larger than average or waist dips lower than average

Back Front

Plumb line

Side seam slants back

FIGURE 13 Side-seam direction

desired level. Do not be concerned at this time with the size in the skirt waist; there will be extra size in the section that was lifted. Ease in any extra fullness for the time being.

NOTE Place a marking-basting line along the corrected seamline. If a change of seam width has been made at the opening edges (either left side or center back), the opening for the zipper must be lengthened an equal amount, and when the zipper is inserted, the tab end must be placed ⅛ inch below this corrected seamline.

If the figure indicates that the problem is that of one area of the body being flatter than average, excess width across the smaller area can be removed by increasing the width of the seam allowance or creating a seam at the center-fold line. But this is only one simple part of the problem. Flatter-than-average curves require less shape and therefore less dart fitting. Study carefully Changes in Shape as Well as Size on pages 186 to 190. The dart which fits the flatter-than-average area (whether it is front or back) must be decreased in width (see Figure 20 on page 189). The waistline will probably be too large, and the excess size must be removed from one seam edge only, as shown in Figure 21 on page 189.

If the seam distortion is caused by one area of the body being larger than average, the problem is more serious because unless the skirt is too large in overall size, there may not be sufficient fabric to make the required adjustments. This problem, perhaps more than any other, indicates the need of a muslin test copy for the skirt.

Two solutions are given in Figure 15. The examples shown are for larger-than-average thighs (the side seam slants toward the front); the principles can be applied to the side seam that slants toward the back. Figure 15a illustrates

what can be done if the skirt is already cut in the fabric of the garment; this solution may not solve the problem entirely, but it is all that can be done. Figure 15b shows a solution which will solve the problem entirely but which is possible only if the fitting is being done on a muslin test copy so that additions can be made on the pattern prior to cutting in good fabric.

Larger-than-average curves require more width and more dart shaping. Study carefully Changes in Shape as Well as Size on pages 186 to 190.

See Figure 15a. If the skirt has already been cut and if there is no extra overall size, there is little opportunity to obtain more width in the front and, in particular, more width at the front waistline to increase the existing dart or to add a new dart. If there is some extra width at the waist (or if some can be stolen from the side-seam allowances), the problem can be partly solved, although there will be less length in one section of the skirt. Rip the side seam-

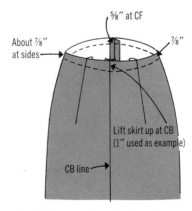

FIGURE 14 To lift skirt back at waist

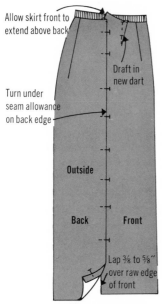

Allow skirt front to
extend above back

Draft in
new dart

Turn under
seam allowance
on back edge

Outside

Back   Front

Lap ⅜ to ⅝"
over raw edge
of front

(a) If skirt is cut in fabric

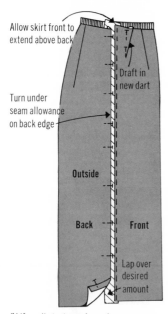

Allow skirt front to
extend above back

Draft in
new dart

Turn under
seam allowance
on back edge

Outside

Back   Front

Lap over
desired
amount

(b) If muslin test copy is used

FIGURE 15 To correct side seam slanting toward front

line. Pin under the seam allowance on the back edge; this turned-under edge will be lapped over the remaining raw edge during fitting. Create more dart fitting in the front skirt by increasing the width of the existing dart or pinning in a new dart (see Figure 23 on page 190); the increase should be whatever is required by the curve of the figure, but it must be limited necessarily by the amount of fabric available. Work on both sides as you do each step. The extra dart fitting has caused the side edge to curve upward, as shown; allow it to move upward and pin it to the waistband. Now lap the turned-under back edge ⅜ to ⅝ inch over the raw front edge, allowing the skirt sections to fit together at different levels, as shown. The differences in the horizontal levels of the two sections should be identical at the waistline and the lower edge, as shown. Use a marking-basting line to mark all corrected seamlines.

See Figure 15b if the skirt is being fitted with a muslin test copy. Rip the side seams. Sew a strip of muslin to each side edge of the front, using directions accompanying Figure 6 on page 115. Pin under the side-seam allowance on the back skirt sections and pin the back sections to the waistband for support. Pin the front sections to the waistband for support. Work on both side edges as you proceed with each step. Create more dart fitting in the front skirt by increasing the width of the existing dart or pinning in a new dart (see Figure 23 on page 190); the increase should be whatever amount is necessary to fit the body curves smoothly. The extra dart fitting has caused the side edge to curve upward, as shown; allow it to move upward and pin it to the waistband. Now lap the turned-under back edge over the raw edge of the extension strip, using as much of the extra width as is required by the figure and allowing the skirt sections to fit together at different levels, as shown. The differences in the horizontal levels of the two sections should be identical at the waistline and the lower edge, as shown. Use a marking-basting line to mark all corrected seamlines. Use the muslin copy as a guide for making identical alterations on the pattern prior to cutting the skirt.

distortion in one portion of a seam If there is irregularity in only one portion of a seam, it is an indication that the figure is larger than average in a somewhat confined area.

GENERAL RULE The seam will curve toward that part of the body which is larger than average.

Common examples are shown in Figure 16. In each case, extra width or size is required for the larger-than-average area, and if it is possible, extra dart fitting is required. Figure 17 pictures an example of the fitting correction that is required. If the garment is already cut, it may not be possible to correct this misfit entirely (seams can be let out little more than ¼ inch in some fabrics). Depending on the amount of distortion, this is a figure irregularity which might require a muslin copy.

One way of gaining some extra width over the pad of fat which causes this seam distortion is to rip out the dart, which is probably about 7 inches long, and pin in a new, shorter dart, as shown; this will allow some extra width at the pad of fat, and the shorter dart will fit the body better because it will create shape higher on the figure, where the larger-than-average curve is located (see Figure 23 on page 190).

NOTE If the skirt is being fitted with a muslin test copy, an extension strip can be used in much the same way illustrated in Figure 15.

CORRECTIONS IN LENGTH

Subtle changes in skirt length are better decided just prior to hanging the hem. Changes at this time should be confined

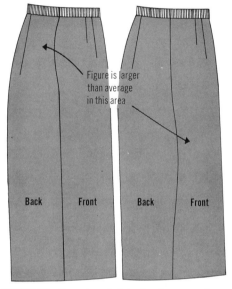

Figure is larger than average in this area

Back   Front   Back   Front

FIGURE 16 Examples of distortion in one portion of a seam

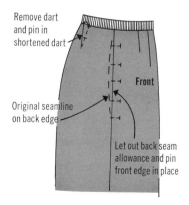

Remove dart and pin in shortened dart

Front

Original seamline on back edge

Let out back seam allowance and pin front edge in place

FIGURE 17 To correct distortion in one portion of a seam

to establishing a length that is approximately correct; the skirt must be reasonably correct in length so that proportions in relation to other design features can be studied. If the skirt is several inches too long, it would be well to trim some excess from the lower edge at this time.

The wearer can test various widths of waistbands by folding a strip of fabric and studying the effect on her figure. The position, size, and shape of pockets or trimming features can be modified to create more interest or a better division of space on the figure.

If the skirt is shortened a considerable amount, check to see that the released edge of any pleat is sufficiently long to give walking comfort and attractive proportions. In general, the released edge of a pleat should be about 6 to 8 inches long, depending on the total length of the skirt and on personal preferences. The stitching line of the pleat can end at any point which will allow the desired length on the released edge.

CORRECTIONS IN SIZE AND WIDTH

The person who aspires to couturier levels in her sewing must also be alert to acceptable standards of fit. Unfortunately, the person with a problem figure has become so accustomed to the way ready-made clothing fits that she has come to accept it; she must learn new standards.

The skirt should hang from the waist, rest easily on the hips (not "hug" the hips), and fall freely below the hips without revealing body contours below the hips (should not "cup in" below the hips). The amounts of livability recommended in the measurement charts result

in proper fit; those amounts are 1 inch of livability at the 3-inch hip level and 2 inches of livability at the 7- and 10-inch hip levels. Test the amount of livability present by pinching out the excess ease at the three hip levels, pulling the skirt snugly against the figure. Then the skirt can be nipped in or let out at the side seams as desired; work on both sides of the figure at once. Remember that fitting is very much like pattern alteration; it will help to review this same problem handled as a pattern alteration (see page 82). For example, if the skirt has 3 inches of livability at the 7- and 10-inch hiplines, the extra 1 inch can be removed by nipping in each side seam one-quarter of that amount ($\frac{1}{4}$ inch). Work for proper fit at the hiplines at this time; the fit of the waistline will be perfected later.

CHANGES IN SHAPE AS WELL AS SIZE

The need for changes in shape is very difficult to recognize, and the techniques are more tedious to execute than any other in fitting. The shape of the skirt has been created by darts (tucks or gathers) and by shaped seams. One must learn to study the garment critically and to anticipate that changes will possibly and probably be required. The order of fitting as presented in these directions has taken care of seam direction and size of the skirt in general. It is the area above the 7-inch hipline (where body contours are curved and where great differences in figures occur) that must be properly shaped as well as properly sized.

Darts play the most important role in creating shape in the skirt. They may be increased in width to create more shape or decreased for less shape; new darts can be drafted into the desired position; existing darts can be removed; and the position and length of the dart can be altered as the figure requires. The following table is included to point out possible problems and to suggest solutions.

problem and indication of poor fit	solution
larger-than-average front curves	
1 There is evidence of diagonal ripples leading downward from the stomach or hipbone area toward the side seam.	More shape, and possibly more size, is required in this area.
2 The garment may protrude in front, standing too far from the body and not hanging in a plumb line below the hip level.	See To Fit Larger-than-average Curves (page 188).
prominent hipbones	
1 A taut, tight appearance is evident at the high point of the hipbone.	A new dart must be created, or the position, direction, or length of the existing dart must be changed. See To Draft in New Darts (page 188) and To Change Dart Position (page 190).
smaller-than-average front curves	
1 Ripples of fabric will form at the tips of darts, and the skirt will not rest smoothly on the body.	Less shape, and possibly less size, is required in this area. See To Fit Smaller-than-average Curves (page 188) and To Remove Existing Darts (page 190).
larger-than-average back hip curve— protruding hips	
1 There is evidence of diagonal ripples leading downward from the hips toward the side seam.	More shape, and possibly more size, is required in the back hip
2 The garment may protrude in the back, standing too far away from the body and not hanging in a plumb line below the hip level.	area. See To Fit Larger-than-average Curves (page 188).
smaller-than-average back hip curve— flat hips	
1 Ripples of fabric will form at the tips of darts, and the skirt will not rest smoothly on the body.	Less shape, and possibly less size, is required in this area. See To Fit Smaller-than-average Curves (page 188) and To Remove Existing Darts (page 190).
body more curvaceous than average between waist and 3″ hip level	
1 A tight, taut look appears at the high hip level, but the skirt is too large (too much ease) at the waist.	More shape, and possibly more size, is required in the trouble area. This type of figure should be fitted with several small, short darts.
2 Horizontal ripples of fabric form between the high hip level and the waist; the skirt tends to "ride up" on the figure.	See To Draft in New Darts (page 188) and To Change Dart Position and Length (page 190).

SPECIAL NOTE The fitting techniques given below are those involved with fit at the waist. When fitting the waist, fit it somewhat loosely (allow perhaps a total of ½ to 1 inch of extra size) so that it will ease to the waistband when the band is permanently attached. A slight amount of ease (more for curvaceous figures and more for fabrics that ease well) in the skirt gives the skirt a molded look over body curves directly below the waist, while allowing the waistband to fit snugly.

to fit larger-than-average curves Figure 18 illustrates how to increase dart width to create more shape for larger-than-average curves. Rip out the existing dart. Crease on the original dart line nearest the center line and bring that dart line to the desired position beyond the remaining original dart line. Pin in position, allowing the new dart to fall "as it will" to fit body curves. Lap the dart over at the waistline and allow it to fall in place; it will tend to fall into proper position, forming a tip at the high point of the curve.

If the skirt was the proper size at the waistline before the dart was altered, the increase in the dart must necessarily be confined to the amount that can be compensated for by letting out the side seam, as shown in Figure 19. Note that the

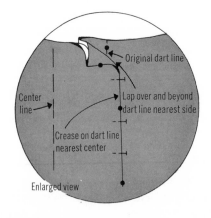

FIGURE 18 To increase dart width for more shape

seam has been let out on only one edge (the section with the widened dart). If the waistline was too large as this fitting began (if extra size had been eased in temporarily), the extra ease will allow for an increase in dart width. If the waist is too large after the dart has been properly fitted, the excess size should be removed from the side seamline.

NOTE Fit both sides of the body, but follow directions accompanying Figure 22 to mark new darts in identical positions on the right and left sides of the skirt.

to fit smaller-than-average curves Figure 20 illustrates how to decrease dart width to create less shape for smaller-than-average curves. Rip out the existing dart. Crease on the original dart line nearest the center line and bring that dart line to the desired position, letting out some of the original dart width. Pin into position, allowing the new dart to fall "as it will" to fit body curves. Lap the dart over at the waistline and allow it to fall in place; it will tend to fall into proper position, forming a tip at the high point of the curve.

If the skirt was the proper size at the waistline before the dart was altered, the extra dart width which was let out will make the waist too large. Excess size must be removed from one edge of the side seam (the section with the narrowed dart), as shown in Figure 21.

NOTE Fit both sides of the body, but follow directions accompanying Figure 22 to mark new darts in identical positions on the right and left sides of the skirt.

to draft in new darts Any curve must have a dart to create shape at the high point of the curve. A taut, tight look at a certain area (at hipbones, for example) is an indication that a dart must be drafted into position in that area. Figure 22 shows the steps for drafting in new darts. First mark the high point of the curve with a pin. Then pinch in a new dart, allowing the dart to fall "as it will" to fit body curves. It will tend to fall in proper position, forming a tip at the high point of the curve. Fit both sides of the figure with a dart of approximate position and character, as shown in step 2, of Figure 22. The two darts will not be identical in width, length, or position and must be corrected before basting. Step 3 shows the dart released on one side and marked

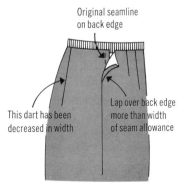

Original seamline on back edge

This dart has been decreased in width

Lap over back edge more than width of seam allowance

FIGURE 21 Additional fitting may be needed if darts are narrowed

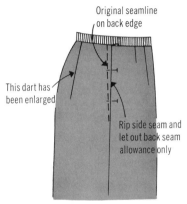

Original seamline on back edge

This dart has been enlarged

Rip side seam and let out back seam allowance only

FIGURE 19 Additional fitting may be required if darts are widened

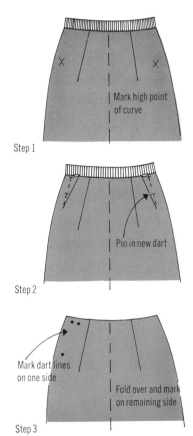

×   ×

Mark high point of curve

Step 1

Pin in new dart

Step 2

Mark dart lines on one side

Fold over and mark on remaining side

Step 3

FIGURE 22 To draft in new darts

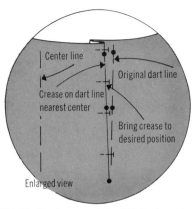

Center line

Original dart line

Crease on dart line nearest center

Bring crease to desired position

Enlarged view

FIGURE 20 To decrease dart width for less shape

with tailor's tacks to establish position and size. Then fold the garment in half lengthwise, matching side seams, and mark an identical dart on the remaining side of the garment. Now the two darts can be basted for refitting.

If the skirt was the proper size at the waistline before the dart was altered, the width of the dart must necessarily be confined to the amount that can be compensated for by letting out the seam, as shown in Figure 19. If the waistline was too large as this fitting began (if extra size had been eased in temporarily), the extra ease will allow for an additional dart. If the waist is too large after the dart is properly fitted, excess size should be removed from the side edge, as shown in Figure 21.

to change dart position and length Figure 23 pictures a fitting which involves changing dart position and length and then drafting in new darts. This fitting is frequently required for the small-waisted figure which is very curvaceous directly below the waist and in which the high

point of the hips is closer to the 3-inch hip level than to the 7- or 10-inch hip level (as in the average figure). Rip out the existing darts, which are longer and create shape lower on the body than this figure requires. Pin in several new, smaller darts (perhaps only 1/4 inch wide), allowing them to fall as they will, creating shape where the body is most curvaceous; several smaller darts fit the curvaceous contours better than one large dart because they distribute shape over an entire area.

NOTE Fit both sides of the body, but follow directions accompanying Figure 22 to mark the new darts in identical positions on the right and left sides of the skirt.

to remove existing darts If the darts create more shape than the figure with flatter-than-average curves requires, one of the darts can simply be ripped out. Very often the skirt front and back have two darts on either side of the center, and either dart (but preferably the dart nearest the side edge) can be entirely removed, if desired. If the waist of the skirt was the proper size before this fitting, the excess width must be removed from the side seam, as shown in Figure 21.

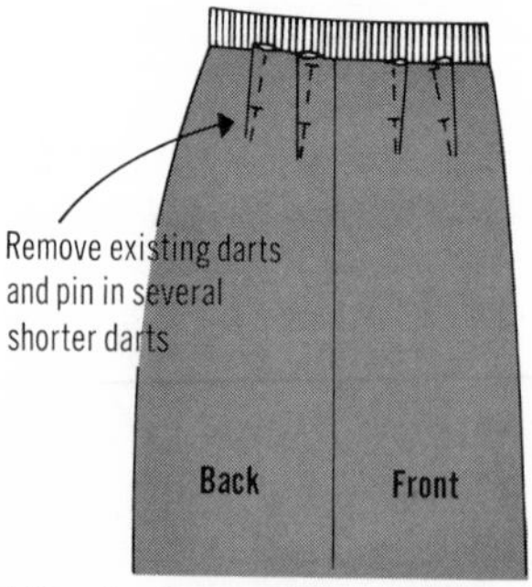

FIGURE 23 To fit the figure that is very curvaceous between the waist and the 3-inch hip level

Remove existing darts and pin in several shorter darts

Back Front

THE SECOND FITTING

Carefully baste all fitting corrections, being sure that corrected darts and seamlines are identical on both sides of the body. The fitter will not have been able to fit both sides identically as she pinned in corrections, and now her pinned lines must be corrected with measured accuracy. In some cases, different fittings on the two sides of the figure will be required (for example, if one leg is longer or one hip is larger), but in general most corrections should be the same on both sides.

Refit the skirt, with the temporary waistband pinned in position. Check the fit of the skirt and make any other corrections that might be necessary. Always refit every new correction to check it for accuracy.

FITTING
CORRECTIONS
TRANSFERRED
TO LINING SECTIONS

When the skirt fits properly, it is wise to sketch the altered seamlines and dart lines on the skirt pattern pieces, as a record for future use. If the pattern is used again, the skirt can be basted for the first fitting on these corrected lines, and although one would not assume that it would be perfect in fit, there should be little fitting to do.

This is the time (when fitting corrections are basted and before the skirt is stitched) to baste lining sections together, following the corrected lines on the skirt as a guide for basting.

BASTING AND FITTING THE LINING

The skirt lining will be worn with the right side next to the body; therefore, if there is a side opening in the skirt, leave the opposite side (what is apparently the right side as the skirt is basted) open for the zipper.

Be very sure that the lining is basted like the skirt—that the opening edge for the zipper (either back or side) is exactly the same length as the opening in the skirt and that the basting for pleat or split openings at the lower edge ends at exactly the same level as the opening on the skirt itself.

Do not assume that the lining will

fit properly, even though it has been basted exactly like the skirt itself, using the same corrected lines. There is a danger that the spongier fabric from which the skirt is made stretched somewhat on the figure, whereas the firmly woven lining fabric will not stretch on the figure; therefore, it is possible that the lining will appear to be smaller than the skirt, especially at the waist and upper hip level, where the skirt fits the body quite snugly. Baste the lining and then pin the temporary waistband in place on the lining prior to fitting.

Put the skirt lining on the figure wrong side out, with the right side of the lining next to the body. Pin the opening edges together and fit the skirt. The lining will probably fit exactly as the skirt did below the hiplines, but it may need a slight adjustment above the hiplines (1) because it does not stretch as the skirt fabric might have and (2) because there are many seams and darts in that area, and a slight difference made in basting each one may cause a considerable difference in overall size. Make necessary corrections, even though this may mean that darts and seam allowances will be slightly different from those in the skirt.

If a limp, flat lining fabric has been used, allow the lining to be eased slightly to the waistband—do not fit it tight to the figure right at the waistline. A slight amount of ease in a limp lining will not be noticeable in the finished skirt, and it will make the skirt much more comfortable.

NOTE Refer back to Chapter 10 for fundamentals of construction. See directions for basting

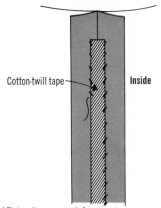

Cotton-twill tape

Inside

(a) Flat, quite secure reinforcement

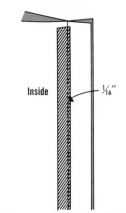

Inside

⅟₁₆″

(b) Bulkier but more secure method for utilitarian garments

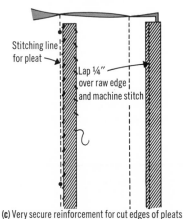

Stitching line
for pleat

Lap ¼″
over raw edge
and machine stitch

(c) Very secure reinforcement for cut edges of pleats

FIGURE 24 Methods of reinforcing skirt seams with tape

and stitching techniques on page 142. If there is to be topstitching, see page 151. Study the entire section on pressing techniques on page 163. If extra details (pockets, etc.) are desired, see page 161 for ideas. If the skirt is underlined, reread The Underlined Skirt on page 173.

REINFORCING
SEAMS
WITH
TAPE

Reread Reinforcing Seams with Tape on page 162. Keep in mind that most skirt seams will not be reinforced with tape because a molded, free-flowing line is desired and that tape will be used mainly for strengthening the seams of a pleat when the weight of fabric is excessive.

Figure 24 pictures several methods of using tape for skirt seams. Method a will be used most frequently in high-quality tailored garments. After the seam is stitched and pressed (and a seam finish applied if necessary), pin and baste narrow cotton-twill tape (preshrunk) over the seamline. Do not strech the tape in applying it but simply place it over the seam, patting and smoothing it in place, and pin and baste in place. Hand-whip both edges of the tape in place, being sure that the stitches catch through the seam only and do not pass through to the right side of the garment. This method results in a very flat seam that is sufficiently secure for most purposes.

Method b will not be used in high-quality tailoring, but it is a stronger reinforcement and would be favored for utilitarian garments and for the crotch seam in slacks and shorts. The fact that the tape is caught in with the stitching of the seam makes for great strength, but also creates a seam that will not be as flat when pressed open. Note that the tape is not centered over the seamline;

by placing it 1/16 inch over the seamline, the two edges of tape will not fall in the same position and will therefore be staggered when the seam is pressed open.

Method c is another way of applying tape as well as an application of method a. The two cut edges of a pleat seam are not pressed open, but will remain in the position shown. Because great strength may be desired on these edges, the tape can be lapped 1/4 inch over the two raw edges and machine-stitched in place. The stitching line for the pleat itself will get strain during wearing, and it can be reinforced as shown, using method a; note that the tape is placed just inside the stitching line, in the pleat area, so that the hand stitches will not show as the garment is worn.

See Figure 25 for a view of the reinforced pleat edges when finished. Tape should end about 1 inch above the point where the stitching for the pleat ends, as shown. The released edges of the pleat will be exposed when the lining is inserted, and the cotton-twill tape (either white or black) would give an unattractive appearance.

Remembering that tape will stiffen as well as strengthen, it can be used to solve unique problems that might occur. Figure 26 shows an unusual use of tape. If there is a hollow in the figure between two hip levels (frequently just below the 7-inch hipline), cotton-twill tape can be hand-sewn in the area to stiffen that portion of the seam and give the skirt a smoother line over the hollow.

ZIPPER CONSTRUCTION

GENERAL INFORMATION

Figure 27 pictures the two most common zipper construction methods. Either method is quite acceptable for basic skirt

openings, although there are seasons when one is slightly more fashionable than the other.

evaluation of zipper methods In general, the regulation zipper is a better choice than the slot-seam construction because it completely hides the zipper teeth,

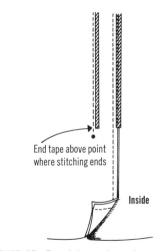

End tape above point where stitching ends

Inside

FIGURE 25 To reinforce pleat edges

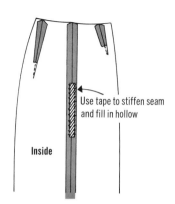

Use tape to stiffen seam and fill in hollow

Inside

FIGURE 26 Tape used to stiffen a portion of a seam

while the slot-seam method reveals a suggestion of the metal and color of the zipper. The regulation zipper, although more difficult to construct than the slot-seam, will probably result in a better appearance because slight variations in width of topstitching are less noticeable when the stitching is about ½ inch from a fold edge; the slightest flaw in stitching the slot-seam zipper is magnified because the rows of stitching are so close to the fold. The one disadvantage of the regulation construction is that it is slightly more bulky.

methods of construction Although methods of achieving the pictured effect vary,

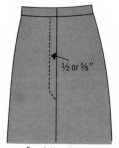

Regulation zipper

Slot seam zipper

FIGURE 27

only one method for each zipper will be recommended. The slot-seam zipper construction on page 197 is the same method suggested on the direction folder in the zipper package. The regulation method, which appears below, is different from that on the direction folder; it is recommended in this book because it offers the advantage of basting and testing the zipper before stitching is done.

check length of opening edges Measure the opening edges of the skirt to be sure that the opening is the proper length for the zipper. See Figure 28. The tab end of the zipper will be placed about ⅛ inch below the seamline at the waist, so the opening should be the length of the metal part, plus ⅛ inch, plus a seam allowance of ⅝ inch: 7¾ inches for a 7-inch zipper. If the seamline at the waist was raised or lowered during fitting, a marking-basting line was used to record the new seamline; in that case, the opening should be the length of the metal part of the zipper, plus ⅛ inch, plus the width of the corrected seam.

THE REGULATION SKIRT ZIPPER

NOTE In all sketches, the back and front of the skirt are labeled for the side-opening zipper. Underneath each label, the words "right back" and "left back" appear for use with a back-opening zipper.

Read General Information on page 193. The zipper should be put in when the vertical seams have been finished and pressed and before the waistband is applied.

See Figure 28. Cut a piece of seam binding ½ inch longer than the opening. Lap it ¼ inch over the raw front edge and stitch it in place with stitches very close to the edge of the binding. The purpose of this binding is to extend the seam allowance of the front edge; if there is an ample ⅝-inch seam on the front edge, the seam binding is not needed.

NOTE The garment should be turned right side out while the zipper is put in. Because the opening edges are often bias, handle the garment carefully to avoid stretching the fabric.

See Figure 29. Turn the front opening edge to the inside along the seamline and baste in place. Run a marking-basting line along the seamline of the back.

See Figure 30. Turn under the back opening edge ⅛ inch (or ³⁄₁₆ to ¼ inch in spongy or heavy fabrics) beyond, or outside, the seamline and baste in place. Press. Hold work in the position shown in the sketch, being sure it looks just like the sketch.

See Figure 31. Pin the zipper on the inside of the skirt with the metal tab ⅛ inch below the seamline, thereby leaving an ample allowance for stitching the waistline seam. Lap the back opening edge over the zipper with the fold edge about ⅛ inch from the zipper teeth. This is a helpful hint for side-opening zippers: Hold the zipper and the skirt in the position they will take on the body. From

the waist down, the body curves outward, and the zipper and skirt must fit that curve. Study the particular curve of the body and then hold the zipper in that curve and pin the back edge in place. Because the side edges of the skirt are often bias, there is a great danger of stretching the opening edges during construction. Avoid this—in fact, it is a good

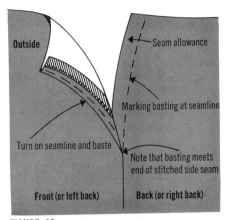

FIGURE 29

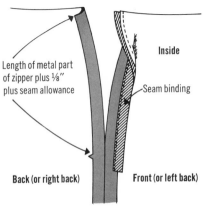

FIGURE 28

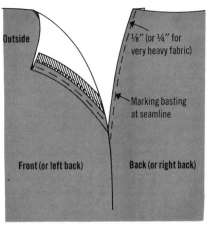

FIGURE 30

idea to ease the skirt slightly (perhaps ⅛ inch) while pinning it to counteract the almost inevitable stretching. Baste the edge with small, firm stitches. Trim off the excess tape even with the waist-line edge of the skirt.

If, when the garment is fitted, there is a ripple directly below the zipper, return to this step and rebaste, easing up the fabric even more as it is pinned to the zipper.

See Figure 32. Lap the front edge over the zipper so that the fold edge (which is the seamline) meets the marking-basting line on the back (which is the seamline). Notice that the front laps over the back and hides the zipper completely. Hold the skirt and the zipper in the position they will take on the body (an outward curve if it is a side-opening zipper) and pin the front edge in place. Note the position of pins in the sketch. Insert the pin on the fold edge of the front, pass it underneath the zipper, and bring the end up about ½ inch

over from the fold edge; this gives excellent control for basting.

Baste with firm, small stitches about ½ inch from the fold edge. Have the stitches take a diagonal direction at the lower end, with stitches slightly below the metal part of the zipper.

Fit the skirt. See that the zipper lies flat on the body. The most common defect of zipper construction is the formation of a ripple at the lower end. This means that the opening edges have been stretched. If this occurs, see directions with Figure 31; rebaste the zipper, easing the skirt as needed.

Figure 33 pictures the opening edges with directions for machine stitching the zipper in place. The zipper can be sewn in with machine stitches as shown or with secure hand stitches. Hand stitches might be the choice of the person who does not handle the machine well; hand stitching is a less conspicuous method. The stitches should be small and firm and done with a tiny backstitch so that mere dots or indentations appear at ¼-inch intervals on the right side. Hand stitches would be positioned exactly like the machine stitches in the sketch.

For machine stitching, an adjustable

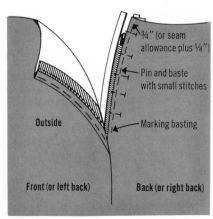

FIGURE 31

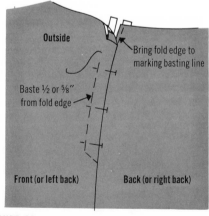

FIGURE 32

zipper foot, which can be moved from one side of the needle to the other, is an essential. Notice that the foot is on the left side of the needle as the back edge is stitched and on the right side as the front edge is stitched. The foot of the zipper must be away from the metal part of the zipper.

Test-stitch to check length of stitch and tension of thread. Be sure there is sufficient thread on the spool and bobbin before proceeding.

Both edges must be stitched from the bottom up, as shown. The zipper must be stitched from the outside, but by turning the garment wrong side out, the stitching can be done more easily on the top side. There is no sketch to illustrate this position, but turn the skirt wrong side out, and it will be apparent how this aids machine stitching on the top side. The zipper should be closed while machine work is done because this keeps the whole area in better control.

Notice that a cardboard gauge is used to ensure even topstitching. The gauge must be held firmly in position before stitching; it cannot be moved at the same time the machine is moving. It is well to practice stitching with the gauge;

remove the top thread from the needle and practice on the garment for best results.

Notice in Figure 33 that the front edge of the skirt is flipped up so that stitching can be placed right along the fold of fabric on the back edge, just $\frac{1}{16}$ inch from the fold. Notice that this machine stitching falls inside the marking-basting line; thus this stitching will not show when the garment is worn.

THE SLOT-SEAM ZIPPER

See Figure 34. Read General Information on page 193. Turn the garment inside out and pin the opening edges together. Check to see that the length of the opening is $\frac{3}{4}$ inch longer than the metal part of the zipper. Baste the opening edges along the seamline with small, firm hand stitches or, better still, with a long machine stitch. Press the seam open.

See Figure 35. Place the zipper on the inside of the garment with the right side of the zipper to the wrong side of

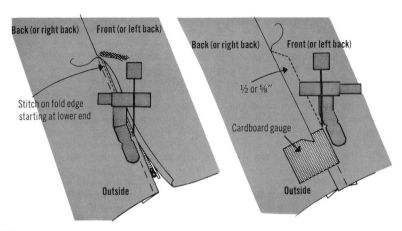

FIGURE 33

the garment. Place the tab end of the zipper ⅛ inch below the seamline, thereby leaving sufficient allowance for that edge to be finished later. Note the position of pins in the sketch. Insert one pin on one side of the center, pass it underneath the zipper, and bring the end up on the other side of the center; this gives excellent control for basting. Be very sure to keep the seam centered over the center of the zipper teeth.

From the outside, baste the zipper in place with stitches ¼ inch from the seamline. Use small, firm stitches, being sure that the stitches are slightly below the metal part of the zipper at the end.

Figure 36 pictures the opening edges with directions for machine stitching the zipper in place. The zipper can be sewn in with machine stitches, as shown, or with secure hand stitches. Hand stitches might be the choice of the person who does not handle the machine well; hand stitching is a less conspicuous method. The stitches should be small and firm and done with a tiny backstitch so that mere dots or indentations appear at ¼-inch intervals on the right side. Hand stitches would be positioned exactly like the machine stitches shown in the sketch.

For machine stitching, an adjustable zipper foot, which can be moved from one side of the needle to the other, is an essential. Test-stitch to check length of stitch and tension of thread. Be sure there is sufficient thread on the spool and bobbin before proceeding.

Both edges must be stitched from the bottom up, and stitching must be done from the outside. By turning the garment wrong side out, the stitching can be done more readily on the top side. There is no sketch to illustrate this position, but turn the skirt wrong side out, and it will be apparent how this aids machine stitching on the top side.

Notice that a cardboard gauge is used to ensure even topstitching. The gauge must be held firmly in position before stitching; it cannot be moved at the same time the machine is moving. It is well to practice stitching with the gauge to become accustomed to using it; remove the top thread from the needle and practice directly on the garment for best results.

After one side is stitched, pull the

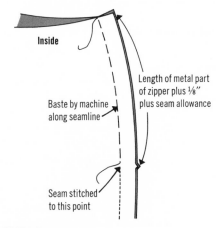

FIGURE 34

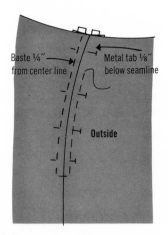

FIGURE 35

threads at the end to the wrong side and tie them before stitching the other side.

INSERTING
THE SKIRT LINING
(INCLUDING FINISHING
ZIPPER EDGES)

WAISTLINE EDGES

See Figure 37. Slip the lining inside the skirt, wrong sides together, and pin the waistline edges together. Match center and side positions. For the time being, turn under the seam allowance on the opening edges and pin to the seamline of the skirt, following directions in the note below.

NOTE Seamlines must match. If the slot-seam zipper construction was used, the turned-under edges of the lining will be placed even with the finished fold edge of the skirt, temporarily covering the zipper teeth. If the regulation zipper construction was used, the turned-under edge of the lining will be placed even with the stitching line on the back skirt (or right back for the back-opening skirt). The turned-under edge of the lining will be placed even with the fold edge on the front skirt (or left back for the back-opening

skirt), temporarily covering the zipper teeth, as shown in Figure 37.

Dart lines in the lining and the skirt should match each other, but a small amount of variation (which is almost inevitable if there are many darts) is acceptable as long as centers and sides match. Baste waistline edges, cut edges even, easing in the lining to fit the skirt.

See Figure 38 for additional directions if the skirt has gathers or loose pleats at the waistline. Remove basting

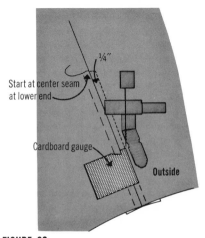

FIGURE 36

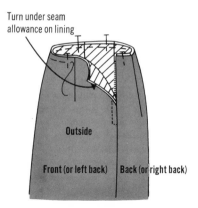

FIGURE 37   To insert lining in skirt

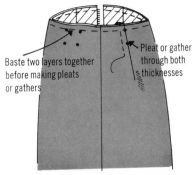

FIGURE 38   For skirt with gathers or loose pleats at the waistline

or gathering stitches in the skirt. Baste the waistline edges together with the pleated or gathered edge flat and free, as shown in the left half of Figure 38. Then fold in the pleats or put in gathering stitches through both the lining and the skirt in one operation, as shown in the right half.

ZIPPER EDGES

Zipper edges are handled differently for the regulation and slot-seam zipper con-

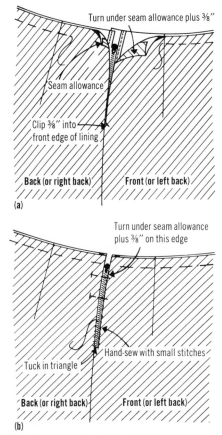

FIGURE 39 To finish lining for regulation zipper

structions. See Figure 39 for directions for the regulation zipper and Figure 40 for directions for the slot-seam zipper.

regulation zipper See Figure 39a. The turned-under edge of the lining should be pinned into position with the fold edge along the line of stitching on the back edge (or right back for the back-opening skirt). In order that the zipper teeth can be exposed, a clip must be made into the lining at the lower end of the front edge (or left back for the back-opening skirt); make a clip into the lining to a point ⅜ inch from, and directly across from, the end of the stitching of the seam, as shown. This clip will allow a turn-under the width of the seam allowance plus ⅜ inch (1 inch if the lining has a traditional ⅝-inch seam allowance). See Figure 39b. Turn under the seam allowance plus ⅜ inch on the edge of the lining on the front edge (or left back for the back-opening skirt) and pin it in place with the fold edge about ⅛ inch over from the zipper teeth. Baste in place. Tuck under the triangle of fabric at the end.

NOTE Be sure that the opening edges of the lining were not stretched as they were pinned in place. If the edges are stretched, a ripple of lining will form at the end of the zipper, indicating that the lining "wants" to move upward. If this happens, repin, easing the lining edges upward.

Hand-sew all edges of the lining to the zipper teeth. Use small stitches and be sure that long floats of thread are not exposed to catch in the zipper teeth.

slot-seam zipper See Figure 40a. In order that the zipper can be exposed, two clips must be made into the lining at the lower end of both opening edges. Clip into the lining on both sides of the seam

¼ inch from, and directly across from, the end of the stitching of the seam, as shown. This will allow for a turn-under on each edge of the width of the seam plus ¼ inch (⅞ inch if the lining has a traditional ⅝-inch seam allowance). Turn under each edge the width of the seam plus ¼ inch and baste the fold edge along the stitching lines for the zipper. Tuck under the triangle of fabric at the end.

NOTE Be sure that the opening edges of the lining were not stretched as they were pinned in place. If the edges are stretched, a ripple of lining will form at the end, indicating that the lining "wants" to move upward. If this happens, repin, easing the lining edges upward.

Hand-sew all edges of the lining to the zipper teeth. Use small stitches and be sure that long floats of thread are not exposed to catch in the zipper teeth.

WAISTBAND CONSTRUCTION

EVALUATION OF METHODS

The stiffened waistband construction is different from the regulation waistband construction that was probably suggested in the pattern. It is the only visible waistband construction included in this book because it has the great advantage of being very firm and flat and because it will always keep its shape; the grosgrain or decorative ribbon used to finish the underside of the band is much less bulky than the fabric of the garment, which finishes the underside in the traditional waistband construction.

The visible waistband will be the choice of most readers for most skirts, but there are circumstances under which the concealed, or inner, waistband is pre-

ferred. If the waistband is not visible, the skirt will tend to look less tailored; if the fabric is unusually heavy (a coating), the concealed waistband will be less bulky.

THE STIFFENED WAISTBAND

The very best stiffening material is heavy Pellon. A lighter-weight Pellon, folded to double thickness, can be used. The waistband can be any width the wearer desires. Usually the pattern is made for a

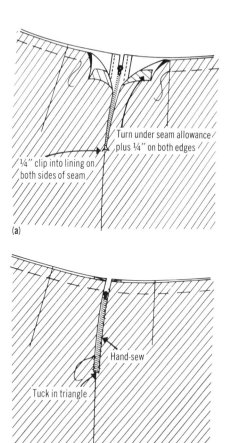

(a)
Turn under seam allowance plus ¼" on both edges
¼" clip into lining on both sides of seam

(b)
Hand-sew
Tuck in triangle

FIGURE 40 To finish lining for slot-seam zipper

band of about 1¼ to 1½ inches in width, but this width tends to make the garment look somewhat utilitarian and tailored. A narrower width of 1 inch to as narrow as ¾ inch (for very delicate and dressy effects) will be much more attractive. The end of the band which will be visible when the garment is worn can be shaped as desired. Figure 41 shows four possible choices, all of which are attractive with compatible designs. Note that in every case the true end of the band is a straight line, as indicated by a broken line, and that the extensions are simply for design purposes.

Before making a definite choice of width, it is well to select the grosgrain ribbon or decorative ribbon which will be used to finish the underside of the band (see directions accompanying Figure 43c). The ribbon should be the same width as the waistband, so it is wise to decide on an approximate width of band desired, then select the ribbon to be used, and then make the definite decision on waistband width. Grosgrain ribbon (matching the skirt or the lining or contrasting to both if desired) is excellent for finishing the underside of the band. Satin ribbon will give a more elegant

effect, but will be less durable and slightly limper. The decorative ribbons with woven designs are very attractive and offer the opportunity to combine the colors of the lining and the garment in interesting ways. If the fabric color offers a particular problem because it cannot be matched to a compatible color in ribbon, a strip of lining fabric (cut 1 inch wider than the desired width of the band) can be used, or velvet ribbon can be used, if desired. Although it is somewhat more bulky, the velvet gives an elegant appearance and its sticky surface is an aid in keeping blouses in place.

Rule off parallel lines on Pellon to mark the desired width. Using the temporary waistband (which has been marked off for center and side positions and perfected during fitting) as a guide, cut the strip of Pellon in the proper length. Be sure that fitting corrections on the temporary band have been completed and that any changes have been recorded and new center and side positions indicated. Then mark off center and side positions, as indicated on the temporary band; see Figure 8 on page 178 for a review.

See Figure 42. Cut a strip of fabric 1 inch longer and 1 inch wider than the strip of Pellon. Wrap the strip firmly around the Pellon, turning under ½ inch on all edges, and baste with secure stitches. Mark center and side positions

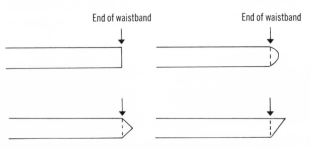

FIGURE 41 To shape end of stiffening for visible waistband

with tailor's tacks on the outside of the band, as shown.

See Figure 43. Lap the waistband over the upper edge of the skirt, with the lower edge of the band along the seamline of the skirt. Match centers and sides and pin in place, as shown in Figure 43a. Note that the extension for the overlap is on the back edge for side-opening zippers and on the right back for back-opening zippers. Baste with firm stitches. Refit the skirt, making corrections if necessary.

Topstitch all edges of the band, as shown in Figure 43b, being sure that the stitches are about $\frac{1}{8}$ inch from the edges of the band. The stitches must not be placed closer to the edge, especially in thick fabrics, or they will not catch into the Pellon; in very heavy fabrics, these stitches must be an ample $\frac{1}{8}$ inch from the edge.

Figure 43c pictures the skirt turned wrong side out as an aid to showing the construction details, but as work is done, the skirt should be right side out and held in the type of curve it will take on the body. To finish the underside of the band, pin the ribbon $\frac{1}{8}$ inch below the upper edge of the waistband, turning in the ends of the ribbon at the ends of the waistband. Whip all edges in place with small, secure hand stitches.

TO FASTEN WAISTBAND

Figures 44 and 45 show the techniques of using the traditional type of hook and

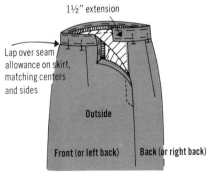

Lap over seam allowance on skirt, matching centers and sides

1½" extension

Outside

Front (or left back)   Back (or right back)

(a) Pin and baste

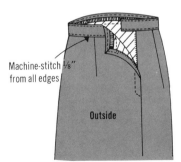

Machine-stitch ⅛" from all edges

Outside

(b) Topstitch

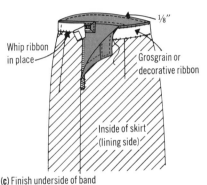

Whip ribbon in place

⅛"

Grosgrain or decorative ribbon

Inside of skirt (lining side)

(c) Finish underside of band
FIGURE 43 The stiffened waistband

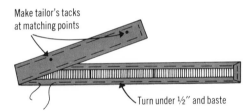

Make tailor's tacks at matching points

Turn under ½" and baste

FIGURE 42 To cover stiffening

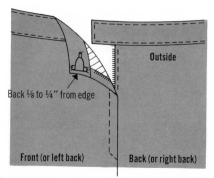

Step 1 Sew hook in place

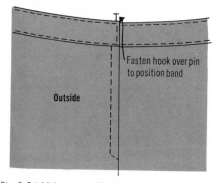

Step 2 Establish proper position for straight eye or band

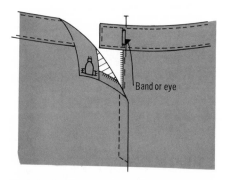

Step 3 Sew band in place

FIGURE 44 To sew on hook and band or eye

eye or the special skirt hook and band-like eye. The special hook-and-eye sets, like those used by manufacturers, make a flat and extremely secure closure, and although they were originally associated with sportswear, they are so superior that it is wise to use them for all skirts.

Figure 44 shows three steps of construction. First sew the hook in place, centering it on the underside of the front end of the waistband and setting it back about ⅛ to ¼ inch from the edge. Use firm, secure stitches. Then close the zipper and lap the waistband into proper position; see that the front end laps over the back end of the band, making a clean, straight line, as shown. Using a pin to simulate the band or eye, fasten the pin into the back waistband in such a way that the hook can slip over it. When the pin is in proper position to hold the waistband in place, see the sketch in step 3. Sew the band or eye firmly in place, using the position of the pin as a guide for placement. One set of these special hooks and eyes will fasten the waistband very securely.

Figure 45 shows traditional hooks and straight eyes. The enlarged view is included to show that the hook must be fastened down at the hook end as well as at the curved, looped ends and that the slight curve in the straight eye must be placed so that it is curving toward the hook, in the direction of the pressure of the hook as the skirt is worn.

If the waistband is 1 inch or more in width, four sets of hooks and eyes should be used, as shown. Follow the directions accompanying Figure 45 for details. First sew the hooks on the underside of the front end, setting them back ⅛ to ¼ inch from the front end of the band. Then sew the hooks to the back end of the band on the outside, as shown. Establish the proper position for straight eyes as shown in step 2 in Figure 44, using one additional technique: Hold the skirt and the band in the kind of curved position they will take on the body while positioning the pins. Holding the skirt and the band in this position will place the greatest pull on the hooks on the overlap at the back end of the band; with this greatest pull occurring about 1½ inches from the visible end of the band, there will not be a strained, taut look at the visible end as the skirt is worn. Sew the eyes in place, using the testing pins as a guide for placement.

THE CONCEALED OR INNER WAISTBAND

The inner waistband will be stitched to the upper edge of the skirt and then turned to the inside; this construction forces the skirt to ride up on the body because the waistline edge of the skirt rides up the width of the waistband. To understand the problem created, turn under a fairly wide waistband on a skirt and notice the effect. The wider the waistband, the greater the amount the skirt will rise. For this reason, the inner waistband should be no more than ½ inch in width.

The waistband must be somewhat stiff, but because of its narrow width, it need not be as stiff as a traditional waistband. Two thicknesses of ribbon will be used, and for most fabrics, these two thicknesses alone will be sufficient. However, if the skirt fabric is very heavy or if the wearer enjoys the feeling of a very stiff waistband, an extra layer of Pellon can be used. The Pellon is shown in the sketches, and directions for inserting it accompany Figure 46. The reader can eliminate that step if she prefers a firm but somewhat limp waistband.

Figure 46 pictures the preparation of an inner waistband that will be very attractive. Narrow grosgrain ribbon, satin ribbon, or decorative ribbon (in a color matching the lining or the skirt or con-

trasting to both) will be used to encase the waistline edges of the skirt. Twice the usual length of ribbon will be required. One strip may be stitched to Pel-

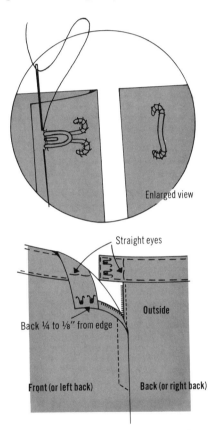

Enlarged view

Straight eyes

Back ¼ to ⅛" from edge

Outside

Front (or left back)

Back (or right back)

FIGURE 45 Traditional hooks and straight eyes

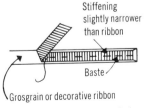

Stiffening slightly narrower than ribbon

Baste

Grosgrain or decorative ribbon

FIGURE 46 Preparation of concealed or inner waistband

lon (if extra stiffness is desired), and this strip will be applied to the skirt as the first step of construction, while the remaining strip will be used later to encase raw edges.

Using the temporary waistband (which has been marked off for center and side positions and perfected during fitting) as a guide, cut two strips of ribbon; the ribbon should be 1 inch longer than the finished length of the waistband. If extra stiffness is desired, cut a strip of Pellon 1 inch shorter and ⅛ inch narrower than the ribbon. Mark off center and side positions, as indicated on the temporary band; see Figure 8 on page 178 for a review.

See Figure 46. Baste one strip of ribbon to the strip of Pellon, turning under the ends of the ribbon, as shown; allow ¹⁄₁₆ inch of ribbon to extend beyond the long edges of the Pellon. This step can be eliminated if the extra stiffness of a layer of Pellon is not desired.

A clip must be made into the front (or left back for back-opening skirts), as shown in the enlarged views in Figure 47. The clip is made parallel to and just outside the stitching line and extends down to the seamline at the waistline (⅝ inch). Tuck the two layers of fabric inside, concealing all raw edges, as shown (very tedious work), and whip the upper edges together; if these edges are trimmed down to a seam width of ¼ inch before they are tucked inside, the work will be less tedious.

See Figure 48. Lap the waistband ½ inch over the upper edge of the skirt with the ribbon side outside, as shown in Figure 48a. Match centers and sides and pin in place. Note that the extension for the overlap is on the back edge for side-opening zippers and on the right back for back-opening zippers. Note that the end of the band is even with the front (or left-back) opening edge of the skirt, but is not attached to the little finished extension on the skirt. Baste with firm stitches. Refit the skirt, making corrections if necessary.

Figure 48b pictures the skirt turned wrong side out as an aid to showing construction details, but as this step is done, the skirt should be right side out and held in the kind of curve it will take on the body. To finish the underside of the band, pin a second strip of ribbon, edges even, over the first, turning in the ends,

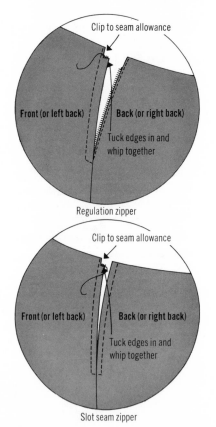

FIGURE 47 Preparation of skirt for concealed waistband

as shown. Baste. Then machine-stitch close to all edges of the ribbon through all thicknesses.

Turn the waistband to the inside, allowing the upper edge of the band to roll ⅛ inch in from the skirt edge. Baste the band in place and press. If it is necessary, the lower edge of the band can be tacked to darts and seams, as shown.

See To Fasten Waistband on page 203. The little free extension on the front (or left-back) edge may lie in place very nicely, but if it does not, use a hook and straight eye to fasten it in position.

HEM
FINISHES

GENERAL INFORMATION

Study this entire section before having the hem measured. The width of the hem and the hem construction, although seemingly small details, are of great importance to the ultimate success of the garment.

factors influencing hem width The hem must be as inconspicuous as possible, but a slight ridge does show, thus creating an issue of proportion. The hem must make attractive proportions with the length of the skirt, and so it can be slightly narrower when skirts are short and likewise can be slightly wider when the total skirt length is considerably greater.

The type of fabric makes certain demands. One purpose of the hem is to add weight, and therefore a wider hem can be used in lighter-weight fabrics.

The design of the garment is a factor. The hem of a skirt should be (in very general terms) about 2½ inches wide. Perhaps that is the ideal width and yet that ideal width is not always the wise choice. Any skirt based on a rectangle

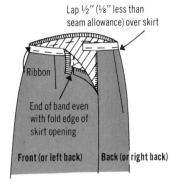

(a) Pin and baste

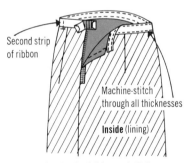

(b) Add additional strip of ribbon and stitch

(c) Turn to inside

FIGURE 48 The concealed or inner waistband

(the straight skirt, all-around pleated skirts, etc.) can have a hem width of about 2½ inches. But a flared skirt (the A-line skirt, circular skirt) cannot have such a wide hem because of the problem of easing in extra fullness.

The size and height of the wearer are considerations. If the hem is to create attractive proportions with the total length of the garment, the tall girl will require a wider hem than the short girl. Follow the general rules below but make the hem about ½ inch narrower than average if your height is under 5 feet and add about ½ inch if your height is 5 feet, 9 or 10 inches.

general rules for hem width   The following estimates are based on the figure of average height (5 feet, 6 inches), and are mere guidelines because each prob-

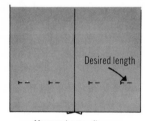

Measure hem on figure

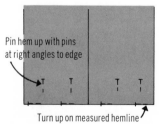

Turn up on measured hemline

FIGURE 49   Pin hem in place for testing

lem must be given individual consideration.

1½-inch finished hem width is used for:
hems in very flared and circular skirts
hems in hip-length jackets
three-quarter- and full-length sleeves in jackets and coats

2½-inch finished hem width is used for:
straight skirts
any skirt (gathered or pleated) which is based on a rectangle
three-quarter- and full-length coats

preparation for hanging the hem   Be sure to wear the undergarments and shoes that will be worn with the costume. The hem of the lining will not be done at this time, so pin up the lining so that it will be well out of the way (about 3 or 4 inches shorter than the skirt will be).

Before putting on the garment, turn up the hem at approximately the desired level. This length will probably not be correct, but it will be a starting point for deciding on the most attractive length. Study the effect in a mirror; this is the time to be critical and to experiment with various lengths by turning up slightly more or less hem in the front area (do not measure—this is just an estimate). When the wearer is satisfied, an assistant can measure the hem.

measuring the hem   Figure 49 pictures the row of pins, measured with an L square or pin marker. After the hem is measured, it must be tested and criticized for effect. The assistant should pin the hem in position along the row of measured pins. Note in the sketch that the pins which hold the hem in place are placed at right angles to the lower edge; this allows the hem to hang more naturally.

Examine the skirt before a full-length mirror. The length which seemed attractive when only a portion of the skirt was tested may not be as attractive in the total skirt. The skirt must appear to be parallel to the floor, and the fact that it was measured parallel to the floor is no assurance that it will look even. Sometimes (for illusive reasons of figure or posture or design) the measured skirt will look uneven, and the optical illusion must be corrected. Whenever a garment has concentrated style fullness (pleats, gathers, a flared area), it tends to look longer in that area. Quite often a garment will tend to look longer in the back, beginning perhaps at the side seam or perhaps at a point a few inches in front of the side seam; this is often a result of posture irregularities or visible horizontal design lines in the fabric. A garment may look longer on one side than the other if the wearer has one hip larger than the other or one leg longer than the other. The important point to remember is that these optical illusions may appear in a variety of guises, and the wearer and her assistant should look for them and be critical. No matter what the illusion, correct it by using the measured pin line as a guide. Do not remove the original pin line, but make adjustments as required, gradually returning to the original pin line in the area that appears to be parallel to the floor and always testing the result before a mirror.

THE CATCH-STITCHED HEM WITH RAW EDGES (FOR USE WITH THE LINING ATTACHED TO THE SKIRT)

NOTE Study General Information on page 207. If there is a seam on the inside fold of a pleat, see page 211. If there is a split opening, see page 212.

See Figure 50.

step 1 Perfect the measured pin line by putting in pins at right angles to the fold.

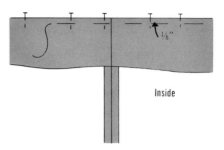

Inside

Step 1

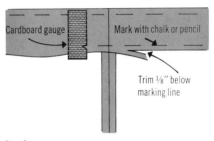

Cardboard gauge   Mark with chalk or pencil

Trim ⅛" below marking line

Step 2

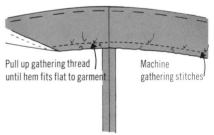

Pull up gathering thread until hem fits flat to garment   Machine gathering stitches

Step 3 (for flared or circular skirts only)

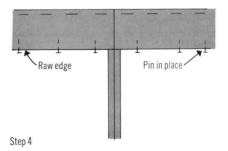

Raw edge   Pin in place

Step 4

FIGURE 50 The catch-stitched hem

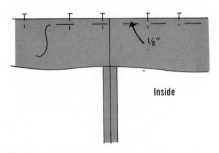

Inside

Step 1

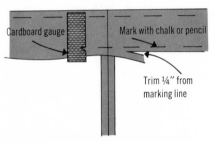

Cardboard gauge

Mark with chalk or pencil

Trim ¼" from marking line

Step 2

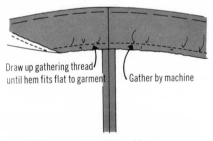

Draw up gathering thread until hem fits flat to garment

Gather by machine

Step 3 (for flared or circular skirts only)

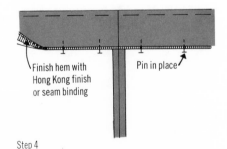

Finish hem with Hong Kong finish or seam binding

Pin in place

Step 4

FIGURE 51 The Hong Kong hem finish

Baste ⅛ inch from the fold edges with stitches small enough (about ½ inch) to hold the hem in a secure position.

step 2 Make a cardboard gauge the desired width of the hem. With chalk or pencil, mark a line on the hem parallel to the fold edge. Trim ⅛ inch from this marking line, as shown.

step 3 (for flared or circular skirts only) Put a row of gathering stitches ⅛ inch from the cut edge, as shown. Put a pin through one of the bobbin stitches every few inches and draw up the edge slightly by pulling out loops of thread. Adjust the ease and pull up the thread until the hem fits flat to the garment. If there is considerable ease and rippling in the hem (very flared skirts), shrink out the fullness before proceeding; see Figure 23 and the accompanying directions on page 168. This gathering line should not be removed, but should remain to control the finished hem.

step 4 Pin the upper edge of the hem flat to the garment. Catch-stitch the hem in place; see Figure 14a on page 159 and the accompanying directions. Press, remove bastings, and do touch-up pressing if necessary.

THE TAILOR'S HEM FINISHED WITH THE HONG KONG FINISH (FOR USE WITH THE FREE-HANGING LINING)

NOTE Study General Information on page 207. If there is a seam on the inside fold of a pleat, see page 211. If there is a split opening, see page 212.

See Figure 51.

step 1 Perfect the measured pin line by putting in pins at right angles to the fold edge. Baste ⅛ inch from the fold edge with stitches small enough (½ inch) to hold the hem in a secure position.

step 2 Make a cardboard gauge the desired width of the hem. With chalk or pencil, put a marking line on the hem parallel to the fold edge. Trim ¼ inch from the marking line, as shown.

step 3 (for flared or circular skirts only) Put a row of gathering stitches ¼ inch from the cut edge, as shown. Put a pin through one of the bobbin stitches every few inches and draw up the edge slightly by pulling out loops of thread. Adjust the ease and pull up the thread until the hem fits flat against the garment. If there is considerable ease and rippling in the hem (very flared skirts), shrink out the fullness before proceeding; see Figure 23 and the accompanying directions on page 168.

step 4 See Figure 15 on page 160 and the accompanying directions for finishing the hem with the Hong Kong finish and the tailor's hemming stitch. If desired, traditional seam binding (rayon bias) can be used.

HEM TREATMENT FOR A PLEAT SEAM

Very often a seam will fall at the inner fold of a pleat, as shown in step 1 of Figure 52. This seam has not been pressed open because it must extend and lie flat, as shown. However, the bulk of this seam in the hem area is a problem, and the problem is greater if the seam is turned in one direction only. This construction method decreases the bulk and ensures a pleat that will be as flat as possible and will remain in proper position for the lifetime of the garment.

The seam treatments pictured in Figure 52 are for the skirt which will have a lining attached to the lower edge, as jacket and coat linings are handled. Notice in the sketch in step 4 that the hem is left raw and is catch-stitched but that the pleat seam and the area of the

hem in the pleat area have been finished with the Hong Kong finish (or traditional seam binding). When the lining is at-

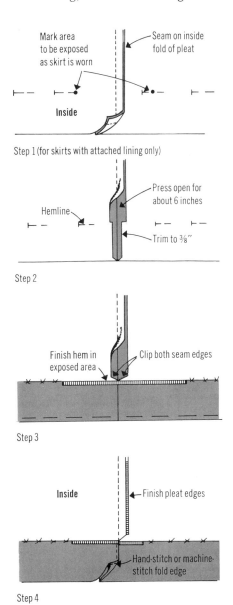

FIGURE 52 Treatment of pleat seam

tached, these pleat edges will be exposed, and therefore they must be finished. If, however, a free-hanging lining is to be used, the entire hem edge will be finished with the Hong Kong finish (or traditional seam binding).

step 1 (for skirts with attached linings only) Put a tailor's tack about 1 inch outside the area of the folded-in pleat. This is the area that will be finished, while the remaining edge will remain raw.

step 2 Press the pleat seam open for about 6 inches from the lower edge. Trim both edges of the seam allowance down to ⅜ inch in the area below the measured hemline.

step 3 Return to the hem directions (catch-stitched or tailor's hem) and fin-

ish the hem, treating this seam exactly as any pressed-open seam is treated. If the attached lining is to be used, finish the area between the tailor's tacks, as shown in the sketch. If the free-hanging lining is to be used, finish the entire edge.

When the entire hem is finished, clip into both edges of the seam directly above the finished hem, as shown.

step 4 Fold the pleat into position. This seam is necessarily bulky. As an aid to holding these very thick edges flat and secure during the lifetime of the garment, sew by hand or machine about ¼ inch from the inner folded edge.

As a last step, finish the pleat seam from the clip to a point about 1 inch above the released edge of the pleat.

HEM TREATMENT FOR SPLIT OPENING
See Figure 53.

step 1 Turn under the opening edges, beginning with the seam allowance at the upper edge and gradually increasing the seam allowance to ⅞ inch at the lower cut edge, as shown. Baste.

step 2 Return to hem directions being used (catch-stitched or tailor's hem). Notice that the fold edges of the split opening are not even with the fold edge of the skirt, but gradually separate until each fold edge is ¼ inch from the seamline at the upper edge. Blind-stitch the opening edges in place.

FINISHING
THE LOWER
EDGE
OF THE LINING

This step can be done with the skirt well supported on a skirt hanger or, preferably, with the help of an assistant. Allow

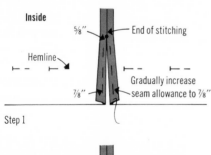

Step 1

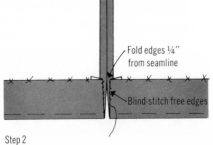

Step 2

FIGURE 53 Treatment of edges of split opening

the lining to hang down free. Do not pull or tug at it, but allow it to hang as it will. Seams in the lining must match seams in the skirt and should be shifted into position. With one hand inside the skirt and lining, place a row of pins about 5 inches from the finished edge of the skirt, matching seamlines, as shown in Figure 54a. If there is a pleat or split opening, carefully position the center seam of the lining over the stitching line of the pleat and put in a rectangle of pins, as shown in Figure 54b; place the pin line close to (about 1½ inches outside) the pleat or split area.

Baste along the pinned lines, catching through the skirt and lining layers. Figure 55 shows how to even off the lining hem. With the skirt right side out and a magazine or notebook slipped between the layers of the skirt, trim off the excess width of the lining. The lining should be about 1 inch longer than the finished skirt if the skirt is flared and about 1½ inches longer than the finished skirt if the skirt is straight. Measure this line carefully, especially if a light weight-lining in a light color is used.

The lower edge of the lining can be handled in two very different ways. The attached lining is shown in Figures 56, 57, and 58, and the free-hanging lining is shown in Figures 59 and 60.

THE LINING ATTACHED TO THE SKIRT
See Figure 56 for the basic construction and incorporate the directions for pleat and split edges accompanying Figures 57 and 58.

step 1 The sketch shows a magazine or notebook slipped between the skirt layers; it will not be pictured in the remaining sketches, but it is very convenient to use while pinning the lining in position and when preparing pleat edges.

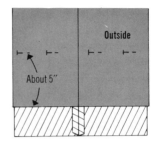

(a) To position lining

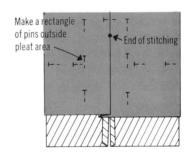

(b) To position lining for pleat or split opening

FIGURE 54   Hanging lower edge of lining

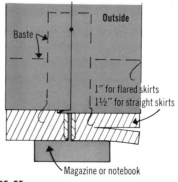

FIGURE 55

With the skirt turned lining side out, turn under the lining with the fold edge about ½ inch from the finished edge of the skirt. Pin the lining in place, matching seamlines. Baste the lining to the skirt hem with stitches 1 inch from the fold edge of the lining. Do not press at this time.

step 2 Fold the lining back ¼ inch from the basted line and slip-stitch one layer of lining to the hem; be sure the stitches do not pass through both layers of lining. When all work is finished, let the lining

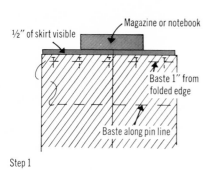

Step 1

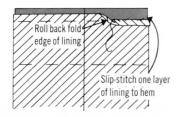

Step 2

FIGURE 56 To finish lower edge of lining attached to skirt

down into position and press a sharp crease at the fold edge of the lining. When bastings are removed, the lining can shift position somewhat without disturbing the lines of the skirt.

TO FINISH PLEAT EDGES

See Figure 57 and study the finished sketch in step 4 as an aid to understanding what is to be done. The purpose of this construction is to finish the pleat edges in such a way that the pleat area is exposed for movement. A knife pleat, which folds in one direction only, is shown in the sketches; if the skirt has a box pleat, the techniques required would be the same, but both sides of the skirt lining would be slashed to expose the pleat on both sides of the center line.

step 1 One turned-under edge of the lining can be basted directly to the skirt because the pleat folds in one direction only (shown on the left side of the sketch).

To expose the pleat, a slash must be made into the lining; it is made to a point on a level with the end of the stitching of the pleat seam, and it must extend to a point just outside the pleat edges. See the finished sketch in step 4 to understand the reason for the position of the slash—the slash must be made to the point that will be the corner of the exposed pleat.

step 2 Trim off the tip of the triangle of lining fabric, as shown, leaving a ⅝-inch allowance below the end of the stitching. Fold the slashed extension of the lining to the outside, as shown, folding it along a straight line, just outside the finished pleat edges. Pin in place temporarily and trim off the excess lining, leaving a ⅝-inch seam beyond the folded edge.

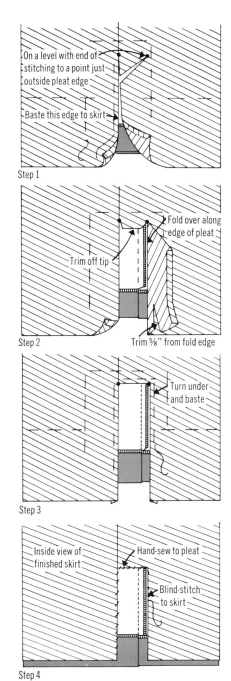

Step 1

Step 2

Step 3

Step 4

FIGURE 57 To finish pleat edges of lining attached to skirt

step 3 Turn under the remaining raw edges, making a corner at the slashed point, and baste the lining to the skirt. Finish the lower edge of the skirt according to the directions accompanying Figure 56.

step 4 Blind-stitch the lining edges to the skirt, taking great care to make the stitches very inconspicuous on the right side of the garment. These stitches will catch into the skirt fabric, but they need not be strong or secure; catch in just a thread or a portion of a thread of the skirt fabric. Do not use firmer or tighter stitches at the corner.

TO FINISH EDGES OF SPLIT OPENING
See Figure 58.

step 1 Turn under the seam allowance on both opening edges, beginning with a ⅝-inch seam at the upper end and gradually increasing the seam allowance to ⅞ inch at the lower edge, as shown. Baste.

step 2 Finish the lower edge of the skirt according to the directions accompanying Figure 56. Baste the opening edges of the lining to the skirt. Notice that the lining edges are not even with the fold edges of the skirt, but are ¼ inch from the finished edge of the skirt at the lower end; thus the lining will not be visible as the skirt is worn.

THE FREE-HANGING LINING
See Figure 59 for the basic construction and incorporate the directions for pleat or split openings in Figure 60.

step 1 The hem in the skirt will have been finished with the Hong Kong finish or by using traditional rayon bias seam binding. The sketch shows a magazine or notebook slipped between the skirt layers; it is very convenient to use while pinning the lining in position.

With the skirt turned lining side out, turn under the lining with the fold edge about ½ inch from the finished edge of the skirt. Pin the lining hem up with pins through layers of lining only, as shown.

step 2 Hem the lining just as if it were a separate skirt. The sketch shows the raw edge turned under and hemmed, which is a most acceptable method if the usual lightweight fabric is used. If for

some reason a very heavy lining fabric is used, it would be better to finish the hem with rayon bias seam binding.

to finish pleat or split edges See Figure 60. Make a narrow hem (using the seam allowance) on both opening edges. Finish the lower edge of the skirt according to the directions above.

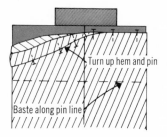

Step 1

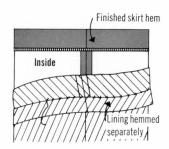

Step 2

FIGURE 59 To finish lower edge of free-hanging lining

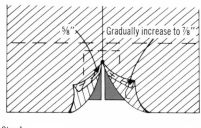

Step 1

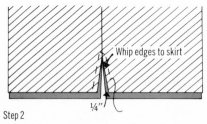

Step 2

FIGURE 58 To finish edges of split opening of lining attached to skirt

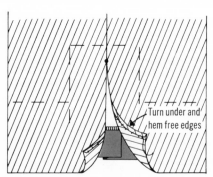

FIGURE 60 To finish pleat or split edges for free-hanging lining

12

CONSTRUCTION METHODS FOR INTERFACING AND UNDERLINING (OR BACKING)

The new supporting fabrics available on the market, coupled with innovations in the methods of using these fabrics, are responsible for many changes in construction techniques. Unfortunately, the variety of supporting fabrics and the variety of uses for them have resulted in a great deal of customer confusion. Reread Selection of Supporting Fabrics on page 45. In review, the following brief definitions will be helpful.

underlining Underlining is a lightweight fabric (offered in two grades—soft or somewhat crisp) which is used to add a small amount of body to the fabric. Because its purpose is to add weight to the fabric, it is cut very much like the structural pieces for the garment and will be combined with each piece of fabric to give support and body to the entire garment. The yardage amount stated on the envelope will be great (greater than the amount stated for interfacing).

backing This term is used interchangeably with "underlining." There are not even subtle differences in the meanings of the two words.

interfacing Interfacing is a heavier fabric which is used to add a greater amount of body and stiffness to certain portions of the garment. The yardage amount stated on the pattern will be small because usually only portions are stiffened with interfacing.

Figure 1 pictures three ways of using interfacing and underlining. The sketches are unfinished and simply show the interfacings in place; they will aid in evaluating the three methods. Compare the sketches while studying the following section.

EVALUATION
OF
CONSTRUCTION
METHODS

NOTE Collars, cuffs, pocket flaps, etc., are not pictured because they are always interfaced in the same way in every method of construction.

Methods 1 and 2 are those used most frequently by the pattern companies at the present time; in general, the pattern companies which cater to the mass mar-

ket (Simplicity, Butterick, McCall's) use method 1 most frequently, and Vogue uses method 2 quite consistently. The great advantages of method 2 over method 1 should result in a wider acceptance of this method in the future. Method 3 is the method recommended in this book for reasons which will be explained. It is, in reality, quite like method 2 with certain improvements; it is not more difficult, but it is different from the method that will be suggested on the pattern guide sheet.

THE PARTIAL INTERFACING

See method 1 in Figure 1. This is the traditional method of interfacing used almost exclusively until the late 1950s. It is still used for fairly simple patterns that are planned for the beginner, although it is not really very much simpler to do than the other methods. The front interfacing may be cut from the facing pattern piece (in which case it is the shape indicated by the broken line on the sketch), or a separate front-interfacing pattern is included (the shaded area) which allows the interfacing to extend over the front shoulder area, as shown. The back interfacing pictured is usually not included in the pattern directions, but it has obvious advantages and can be added, if desired. The bias strip of interfacing extending above the hemline may or may not be included in the pattern directions, and it may be placed in this position or in a slightly different position in relation to the hemline. A similar strip of interfacing is used at the hemline of the sleeve.

purpose The purpose of the partial interfacing is to stiffen the front portion of the jacket or coat and to strengthen the shoulder areas to prevent stretching in the area that gets great strain as the garment is worn. The bias strip above hemlines stiffens the hem area for a firm, well-defined edge, and if it is cut ½ inch wider than the hem and placed in the position shown, it cushions the hem and makes it inconspicuous as the garment is worn.

fabric used The fabric for a partial interfacing is a typical interfacing fabric (muslin or hair canvas, etc.) in a variety of weights to complement various weights of fabric.

advantages and disadvantages The partial interfacing requires less fabric, of course, and judging by the fact that it is often suggested in easy-to-make patterns, there may be some feeling that it is simpler to construct; this is doubtful, however.

The great disadvantage of this method has to do with the consistency of effect and thickness of the total jacket or coat. See the basic construction of this method in Figure 5. Note that in the front area, faced and interfaced, there are two thicknesses of fabric and one thickness of interfacing and that the same amount of thickness is present in the hem area. By sudden contrast, there is just one thickness of fabric in the remaining body of the garment. This results in a great difference in thickness, body, and weight within the areas of the garment—a difference which is often obvious because the area that is not faced and interfaced looks very limp compared with the stiffer areas. The other methods do not have this disadvantage, which will probably result in their increasing popularity.

suggested uses The great disadvantage of this method limits its use for tailored garments; its one advantage, the fact that less fabric is required, is relatively insignificant because the saving is so slight compared with the total cost of a tailored garment. It seems best to reserve this

method for use in little dresses and blouses in which additional body throughout the total garment is not desirable. Brief cutting directions are included on page 224; certain suggestions given there (that do not appear on the pattern) will help somewhat to make a transition between the thick and thin areas, thereby improving this method.

THE COMBINATION INTERFACING AND UNDERLINING (BACKING)

See method 2 in Figure 1. This is the newer method of construction which was introduced to the American sewing public first in the late 1950s, when Vogue presented its first Dior design in the Paris Original collection. This method is used in all Vogue Paris Original and International Couturier designs at the present time. Note that the structural pieces of the entire jacket or coat have been cut of underlining fabric and that it is caught into seams and darts so that the underlining and the fabric of the garment act as one during construction. The pattern includes a separate interfacing piece for the front, extending over the front shoulder area; note that it is exactly like the front interfacing used in the partial interfacing. The sketches shown here and the sketches on the pattern guide sheet show the underlining and interfacing shaded or marked differently so that they can be distinguished. The worker should study the sketches on her instruction sheet to see the plan of shading or marking for that particular pattern. The entire sleeve can be underlined, or it can be handled like the sleeve in the partial interfacing method by using a strip of interfacing at the hemline.

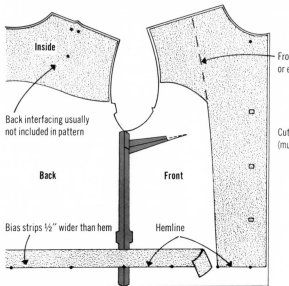

Inside

Back interfacing usually
not included in pattern

Front may extend to this line
or entirely across shoulder

Cut of typical interfacing fabric
(muslin, hair canvas, etc.)

Back

Front

Bias strips ½″ wider than hem

Hemline

Method 1 The partial interfacing

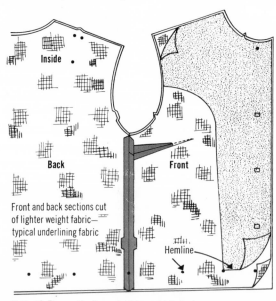

Inside

Cut of typical interfacing fabric
(muslin, hair canvas, etc.)

Back

Front

Front and back sections cut
of lighter weight fabric—
typical underlining fabric

Hemline

Method 2 The combination underlining and interfacing

FIGURE 1 Methods of interfacing or underlining

purpose The purpose of the lightweight underlining is to add a small amount of body to the fabric; it gives the fabric a firmer and perhaps crisper hand, enhancing its appearance and making it more durable. The purpose of the (partial) interfacing of heavier fabric is to stiffen the front portion of the jacket or coat and strengthen the shoulder area for the strain it will receive during wearing.

fabric used The underlining is cut from a lightweight, typical underlining fabric (Siri, Undercurrent, etc.) in a limp or crisp grade to achieve the desired effect. The fabric for the partial interfacing is a typical interfacing fabric (muslin or hair canvas, etc.) in a variety of weights to complement various weights of fabric.

advantages and disadvantages The great advantage of this method is that it adds weight, body, and/or stiffness to the

fabric of the garment. It does not entirely correct the disadvantage (inconsistency of effect and thickness of the total garment) of the partial interfacing. See the basic construction of this method in Figure 6. Note that the front edge is composed of two layers of fabric, one layer of interfacing, and one layer of underlining—a total of four layers; the hem area is also composed of four layers, but is slightly less bulky because it is composed of two layers of fabric and two layers of underlining. By contrast, there are two layers (one of fabric and the other of lightweight underlining) in the remaining body of the garment. This results in a great difference in thickness, body, and weight within the areas of the

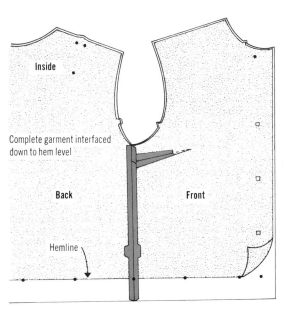

Inside

Complete garment interfaced down to hem level

Back

Front

Hemline

Cut of typical interfacing fabric
(slightly lighter in weight than
usually used, if desired)

Method 3 The complete interfacing
FIGURE 1 continued

garment—a difference which is often obvious as the garment is worn, although less obvious, perhaps, than it would be if the partial interfacing method were used.

suggested uses   The circumstances under which this method is recommended cannot be fully understood until method 3 is discussed. Uses for this method appear in a special note on page 223.

THE COMPLETE INTERFACING

See method 3 in Figure 1. This method has been tested by the author for several years in her personal sewing and in classes with all kinds and weights of fabric and with a great variety of patterns— a total of hundreds of garments. The results are so very satisfying that this method is recommended (with but few exceptions, which appear in a special note on page 223) very highly for high-quality tailored garments. Note that the interfacing is caught in the stitching of darts and seams. Although brief directions for cutting and constructing all three methods appear in this chapter, the discussion of this method will be more detailed (because directions for it do not appear on the instruction sheet), and the sketches throughout Chapter 13, "Tailoring the Jacket or Coat," will show this method. The entire sleeve can be interfaced, it can be supported with an underlining fabric for more freedom of movement, or it can be handled like the sleeve in the partial interfacing method by using a strip of interfacing at the hemline.

purpose   The purpose of the complete in-terfacing is to add body (a greater amount than the underlining provides) to the entire jacket or coat, while at the same time adding body to the areas that are ordinarily stiffened with a partial interfacing. Note that the interfacing is cut to the hemline so that when the hem turns up, it will give a well-defined edge; cutting the interfacing to the hemline means that only one layer of interfacing will be present to add bulk at the hemline.

fabric used   The fabric used will be very comparable to a typical interfacing fabric that would be used in a partial interfacing (muslin or hair canvas, etc.) in a variety of weights to complement various fabrics. Because the complete interfacing serves the dual purposes of an underlining and an interfacing, the fabric can be slightly lighter in weight than a typical interfacing but definitely heavier in weight than a typical underlining fabric. Surprisingly, many persons who have tested this method find that a typical interfacing fabric is not too heavy.

advantages and disadvantages   This method has proved to be so very effective that it is difficult to state any great disadvantage other than the fact that it is different from the methods shown on the pattern guide sheet. There are some circumstances under which the combination method (method 2) will be preferred, and they are stated in a special note on page 223.

The very great advantage of this method is in the consistency of thickness, body, and weight of the total garment. See the basic construction of this method in Figure 7. Note that the front and hem areas are composed of two thicknesses of fabric and one thickness of interfacing, three in all. By contrast, the difference in thickness in the remaining area is a subtle one because the remainder of the garment is composed of only one less thickness of fabric. When the lining is in place, it will cover this thinner area, and the resulting garment will have a very consistent hand and appearance. The other two methods allow for greater differences in feel and appearance in various areas of the garment, and it is because this method does not result in these differences that tests of it have been so very successful. A comparison of the three methods of construction pictured in Figures 5, 6, and 7 reveals that the complete interfacing is actually the simplest method and that it requires less time because of the small amount of handwork required.

suggested uses This method is recommended for all high-quality tailored garments with only a few exceptions, stated in the special note below. In addition to being excellent for a typical suiting-weight garment, it has great advantages for use with cotton and silk suitings because it gives them enough body to be tailored with the excellent results formerly found in wool only. Two bonus advantages are these: (1) If an all-wool hair canvas is used, the interfacing serves the purpose of adding warmth to the entire garment, and (2) because the interfacing is heavier than the underlining used in the combination method, it will hide a lining of a dark color or a gay and even splashy print used with a light-colored garment. This method is more costly than the paritial interfacing method, but it is usually less costly than the combination method. If wool hair canvas is used, the cost would be considerably greater. The cost can be kept very low; muslin is inexpensive and is a most excellent interfacing fabric.

SPECIAL NOTE (USES OF COMBINATION METHOD) In some cases, the combination method will be preferred over this method; however, if the combination method is used, the worker would be wise to cut the underlining to hem level rather than full length, thereby gaining one advantage of the complete interfacing method.

There are persons who require great freedom of movement and who might find the slightly heavier completely interfaced garment too restraining; however, many such active persons report that the completely interfaced garment is most comfortable.

The interfacing must be subordinate to the fabric of the garment, and the little dressmaker suit, possibly made in a dress-weight crepe, would require a lightweight interfacing fabric very comparable to an underlining fabric. If this is the case, an adaptation of the combination method might be a wise choice of construction because limp fabric and a lightweight interfacing might not support the weight of buttons on the front. The two supporting fabrics used in the combination method need not be different—one could use a lightweight backing or underlining fabric for the underlining and the very same fabric for the partial interfacing.

A full-length straight-line coat may not be comfortable to some persons if it is completely interfaced by method 3, especially if it will be worn frequently while sitting down. This coat can be handled with the combination method if desired, using a lightweight underlining and a typical interfacing fabric.

CUTTING
THE JACKET
OR COAT INTERFACING
OR UNDERLINING

The instructions on the pattern must be brief to conserve space and must be simple and uncomplicated so that they can be easily understood by the average woman who sews; pattern instructions cannot include too many subtleties. The directions for cutting the partial and combination interfacings (the two methods which will appear on patterns) given below are essentially like those on the pattern, but there are slight differences and improvements which have been included here because there is not the same need to conserve space in a book.

NOTE Collars, cuffs, pocket flaps, etc., are not pictured. They are cut in the same manner for all three methods; directions will be included on the pattern instruction sheet.

PARTIAL INTERFACING

See Figure 2. The pattern may include a special front-interfacing pattern piece, and if so, it will be the shape of the shaded section illustrated. However, it may not be ½ inch wider than the facing, and this is a desirable subtlety because it allows for staggered edges. Place the facing pattern over the interfacing pattern, as shown, and if the interfacing is not wider, an extension strip can be added to the pattern to gain the effect pictured.

If an interfacing pattern is not included, the pattern directions will state that the interfacing piece should be cut from the facing pattern. Rather than use the facing pattern piece, it is simple to make an interfacing pattern and thereby gain the advantage of staggered edges and greater firmness in the front shoulder area. To make the interfacing pattern, place the facing pattern, cut edges even, over the jacket or coat pattern and pin.

NOTE If the pattern has a facing cut in one with the body of the garment, fold the facing section back along the fold line and make the pattern in the same way shown in Figure 2.

Copy from the jacket or coat pattern as indicated by the shaded section in the sketch; note that the interfacing pattern is exactly like the pattern on the front and upper edges (curving off to a level just above the notch position at the armhole) and that it is made ½ inch wider than the facing pattern and cut to a level ⅛ to ¼ inch inside or above the hemline. Cutting the interfacing slightly above the hemline will allow the hem to fold up smoothly. If the fabric is unusually heavy, use the ¼-inch measurement; for most suiting-weight fabrics, use the ⅛-inch measurement.

The pattern does not usually include a pattern for the back shoulder interfacing illustrated, even though extra firmness and strength are as desirable in the back shoulder as they are in the front. Copy from the back pattern as indicated by the shaded section in the sketch; note that the interfacing is exactly like the garment at the cut edges and that it is cut to a level of about 3 or 4 inches from the neck edge at the center back, curving off to a level just about the notch position on the armhole edge.

The bias strips for strengthening hemlines should be cut from scraps of fabric. These strips should be ½ inch wider than the hem allowance so that they cushion the hem and stagger the raw edges for an inconspicuous hemline. The bias strips will be used at the hemline of the jacket or coat and also at the hemline of sleeves.

COMBINATION UNDERLINING AND INTERFACING

There is no sketch to illustrate this method. Since it is essentially a combination of a partial interfacing and a complete interfacing, read the suggestions for both of the other methods and incorporate the advantages of each into this method.

The pattern will probably give directions for cutting the underlining exactly like the structural pieces of the garment. As explained earlier, this will create the thickness of two layers of underlining in hem areas. The person using this method can improve her garment by cutting the underlining like the complete interfacing pictured in Figures 3 and 4; cut the underlining to hemlines and fold lines as an aid to decreasing bulk in these areas.

The sleeve can be completely underlined to the hem level, or if the wearer wants less stiffness and body in the sleeve, bias strips at the hemline like those used in the partial interfacing can be used.

The front-interfacing pattern piece included with the pattern may or may not be ½ inch wider than the facing. If it is not, see Figure 2 and the accompanying directions before cutting.

THE COMPLETE INTERFACING

See Figures 3 and 4. Figure 3 illustrates general cutting rules for the complete interfacing, rules which can be applied to any design with all shapes of pattern pieces:

1 Use the structural pieces of the pattern only. Do not cut pattern pieces for facings, etc.

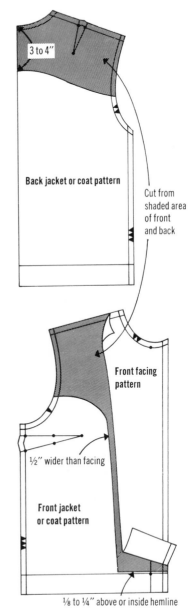

3 to 4″

Back jacket or coat pattern

Cut from shaded area of front and back

Front facing pattern

½″ wider than facing

Front jacket or coat pattern

⅛ to ¼″ above or inside hemline

FIGURE 2 To cut partial interfacing (method 1)

2 Cut the interfacing exactly like the pattern on all edges that have seam allowances—in other words, on all edges that will be seamed.

3 This point is concerned with treatment at hemlines and fold lines. In general, the rule stated here serves most purposes best, but an alternative method (recommended for lightweight or dress-weight fabrics) is shown in Figure 4. Cut the interfacing to a level ⅛ to ¼ inch inside or above the hemlines and fold lines. Cutting the interfacing slightly inside the hemlines and fold lines will make these edges fold back smoothly. If the fabric is heavy, use the ¼-inch measurement; for most suiting-weight fabrics, use the ⅛-inch measurement.

Because the fabric used for the complete interfacing is somewhat heavy (a typical interfacing fabric) it will create more body than an underlining, and the issue of additional body and stiffness in the sleeve becomes an important consideration. The sleeve can be treated in three different ways: it can be completely interfaced by cutting the interfacing to the hemline, according to the general rules given above; it can be underlined (with a lighter-weight fabric than the interfacing in the garment) and cut in the same manner; or it can be treated like the sleeve in the partial interfacing method, by using a bias strip at the hem edge only. All three methods will give an excellent effect; because the armhole seam separates the sleeve from the body of the garment, there is no discernible difference in effect between an interfaced garment and a sleeve that is not interfaced. The choice is an individual one, dependent on the preferences and comfort requirements of the wearer. The interfaced sleeve will feel somewhat

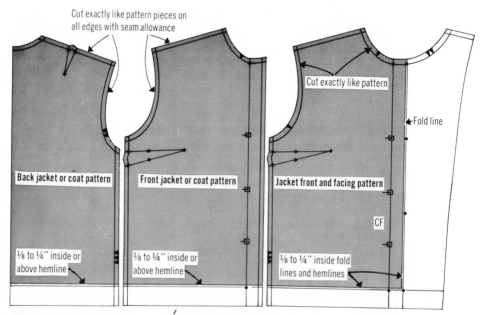

FIGURE 3 General cutting rules for complete interfacing (method 3)

confining to some active persons; the underlined sleeve will feel less confining; and the sleeve interfaced only at the hem edge will give the greatest amount of freedom.

APPLICATIONS OF GENERAL RULES

The rules stated above can be applied to any pattern shape or design. Most persons have no difficulty understanding the purpose of cutting to a level above or inside a hemline, but many are confused by self-facings and the accompanying fold lines. It will be helpful to think of self-facings as if they were hems and to keep in mind that no matter where a facing and its fold line appear (at the front edge, as shown, or at a pocket edge or at the lower edge of the yoke, etc.), the facing will fold back exactly like a hem.

The garment with a sleeve cut in one with the garment can be interfaced by the general rules; the principles are the same, the only difference being that the sleeve hem and the garment hem appear in the same pattern piece.

Alter and adapt general rules to solve special problems. General rules are mere guidelines that best serve most purposes and most persons, but rules are to be used and followed and (under some circumstances) to be broken. Figure 4 illustrates an exception to the general cutting rules to serve a specific purpose. Note that the interfacing is shown extending ½ inch beyond or outside the hemlines and fold lines, rather than being cut inside those lines. If the interfacing is cut this way, a ½-inch edge will fold back on itself, creating a double thickness at those edges. This may be very desirable if the fabric is a dress-weight woolen or a silk suiting and the interfacing is correspondingly light in weight; two light-weight fabrics combined will be im-

proved by a crisper, firmer effect at the finished edges.

Although the general rule states that all structural pieces should be interfaced, adaptations are often wise. For example, a gusset is a very small piece, and because of its position in the garment, there is no advantage in giving it additional stiffness; the gusset is a structural piece, but it need not be interfaced if the wearer would like less stiffness under the arm. The sleeve can be handled in three different ways, as mentioned above; it is a structural piece, but it need not always be cut by the general rules.

Usually the entire garment is interfaced with the same fabric and yet several different interfacings can be combined in the very same garment to achieve the desired effect. As mentioned

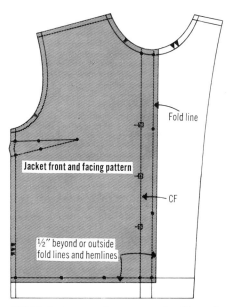

FIGURE 4 An exception to general cutting rules

above, the sleeve interfacing might be lighter in weight than the interfacing used for the garment. Some other portion of the garment might be improved with a different weight; for example, a dressmaker suit with fullness gathered into a waist seam and a stand-out peplum calls for two interfacing fabrics—a lightweight interfacing in the softly draped areas and a stiffer weight to support the peplum silhouette.

BASIC
CONSTRUCTION
METHODS

Figures 5, 6, and 7 picture an inside view of a jacket or coat constructed by the three methods of interfacing. The

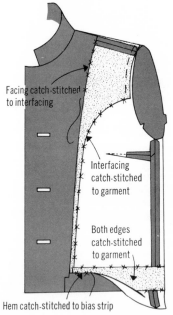

Facing catch-stitched to interfacing

Interfacing catch-stitched to garment

Both edges catch-stitched to garment

Hem catch-stitched to bias strip

FIGURE 5 Basic construction of partial interfacing (method 1)

sketches are included as an aid to understanding the three methods before work is begun. Directions for the partial interfacing and the combination underlining and interfacing are brief because these two methods will probably be described on the instruction sheet. Directions are more complete for the complete interfacing, which is the method recommended in this book. Many of the construction details included for this method are applicable to both of the other methods.

PARTIAL INTERFACING

See Figure 5. Seamed edges of the interfacing are caught in with the stitching of seams (front, neck, shoulder, and armhole edges). The inner edge of the interfacing is catch-stitched to the garment. Both edges of the bias strip are catch-stitched in a position $\frac{1}{8}$ to $\frac{1}{4}$ inch above the hemline. The fact that the front interfacing and the bias strips were cut $\frac{1}{2}$ inch wider than the facing and hem makes it possible to catch-stitch those edges to the interfacing only, without catching the stitches through to the garment. Note that there is a great deal of handwork involved in this method.

COMBINATION UNDERLINING AND INTERFACING

See Figure 6. The underlining is basted to the pieces of the garment before any stitching is done so that it is caught in with the stitching of seams on all edges. The inner edge of the interfacing is catch-stitched to the underlining, without catching the stitches through to the garment. The inner edge of the facing is catch-stitched to the interfacing only. The hem is catch-stitched through the underlining to the underside of the garment fabric.

SPECIAL NOTE There is disagreement about hemming stitches in the underlined or interfaced garment. The stitches will be less conspicuous if they do not pass through the underlining—in other words, if they are handled like the inner edge of the facing, which is secured to underlining or interfacing only. However, all too often the weight of the hem is too great to be supported by stitches through the underlining only, especially on long expanses between seams. If there are several vertical seams in the garment (every 4 or 5 inches), the stitches can be caught in the underlining only, and tacking the hem at the seams will be sufficient to support the weight of the hem. However, if the expanses are great (for example, an entire back cut on the fold), the hemming stitches must catch through the underlining to the underside of the garment fabric.

COMPLETE INTERFACING

The basic construction is pictured in Figure 7, and more detailed directions accompany Figures 8 to 10. The interfacing

is basted to the pieces of the garment before any basting or stitching is done so that it is caught in with the stitching of seams on all edges. The inner edge of the facing is catch-stitched to the interfacing only. The hem is catch-stitched through the interfacing to the underside of the garment fabric (or use the alternative idea in the special note above). Note that this method, which is being recommended in this book, requires the minimum amount of handwork. This method has great advantages, among them the fact that most persons consider it to be the simplest and least time-consuming method.

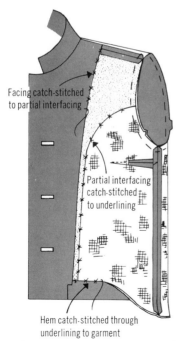

Facing catch-stitched to partial interfacing

Partial interfacing catch-stitched to underlining

Hem catch-stitched through underlining to garment

FIGURE 6 Basic construction of combination underlining and interfacing (method 2)

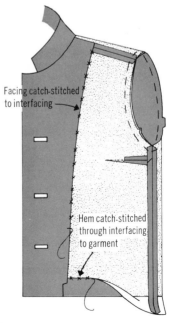

Facing catch-stitched to interfacing

Hem catch-stitched through interfacing to garment

FIGURE 7 Basic construction of complete interfacing

APPLICATION
OF INTERFACING
OR
UNDERLINING

The first step in constructing any interfaced or underlined garment is to combine the interfacing and garment sections so that they act as one fabric while the seams are basted and stitched. The sketches picture the complete interfacing, but this step is done in the same manner for the underlining of method 2. This section is concerned with the main structural pieces of the garment (the body of the garment and the sleeve) and with those sections which might be basted together for a first fitting. Collar sections are combined in a quite different manner that will be described later.

PINNING AND BASTING DIRECTIONS
FOR STRUCTURAL PIECES

See Figure 8. Smooth the body sections of the jacket or coat on a table with the wrong side uppermost; if there is a prominent center fold in either fabric, it should be pressed flat before the garment and interfacing sections are combined. Place the interfacing sections on the inside (wrong side) of the garment pieces, cut edges even. Remember that the interfacing was cut to a level $\frac{1}{8}$ or $\frac{1}{4}$ inch inside hemlines and fold lines; place it down in the proper position. Smooth and pat the two together flat on the table. Although seamed edges were cut in such a way that they should fall cut edges even, little inaccuracies in cutting will result in very slight differences in the cut edges. Do not force the edges together in perfect cut-edges-even position if it seems obvious that there are slight cutting irregularities. Pin all edges in place. Pin along the center fold lines and along the center of darts, as shown in Figure 8a.

Figure 8b shows the interfacing prop-

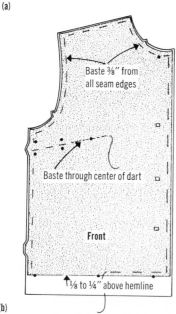

Pin at center fold lines and dart lines

Inside

Back

$\frac{1}{8}$ to $\frac{1}{4}$" above hemline

(a)

Baste $\frac{3}{8}$" from all seam edges

Baste through center of dart

Front

$\frac{1}{8}$ to $\frac{1}{4}$" above hemline

(b)

FIGURE 8   To apply complete interfacing

erly affixed to the garment. Baste about ⅜ inch in from the cut edges of the interfacing; the basting stitches must be done by hand and must be firm enough to hold the fabric in accurate position, but they need not be perfectly even. The ⅜-inch measurement stated is simply one that gives control near the seamline, where it is needed, while avoiding the seamline itself.

The combined fabrics must act as one when darts are stitched, so baste through the center of dart (or tuck) lines with stitches very secure right at the tip of the dart; extend the basting stitches for a short distance beyond the tip of the dart, as shown.

NOTE If the design has a lapel, certain shaping must be done in the lapel area, and the basting stitches in that area are temporary; they will be removed later and replaced after the lapel has been shaped.

TREATMENT AT FOLD LINES

The interfacing was cut in one of two different ways in relation to the fold lines. Figure 9a pictures the method of securing the interfacing that was cut ⅛ to ¼ inch inside the fold line. Although this edge should be basted at this time, eventually it should be catch-stitched, as shown, with stitches catching into the underside of the garment fabric along the fold line. Figure 9b shows the alternative construction for the interfacing cut ½ inch beyond the fold line. Use a running blind stitch right along the fold line, catching tiny stitches into the underside of the garment fabric. In either method, the stitches will be completely hidden by the creased edge of the fold line.

NOTE If the design has a lapel, it is important to baste these edges at this time and to wait

until the lapel has been shaped before securing them permanently.

TREATMENT OF SLEEVES

See Figure 10. If the sleeve is interfaced (or underlined), special handling is required when combining sections. Sleeve sections cannot be smoothed out flat on the table because the sleeve takes such a sharp curve on the body. Pieces combined while they are flat on a table are identical in size, and if the sleeve sections were handled this way, the inter-

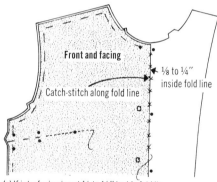

Front and facing

⅛ to ¼"
inside fold line

Catch-stitch along fold line

(a) If interfacing is cut ⅛ to ¼" inside fold line

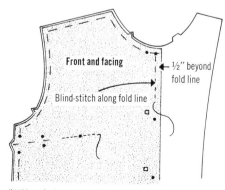

Front and facing

½" beyond
fold line

Blind-stitch along fold line

(b) If interfacing is cut ½" beyond fold line

FIGURE 9 To secure interfacing at fold lines

facing (which must take a sharp inside curve on the arm) would be too wide and would ripple or buckle on the inside of the sleeve. To prevent this, sleeve sections must be handled in such a way that the interfacing is narrower than the garment section.

Use a magazine rolled into a tube approximately the size of the sleeve—about 6 inches in diameter; fasten it with string or rubber bands. Place the interfacing piece on the magazine and then place the garment sections over the interfacing with the outside (right side) uppermost, as shown in Figure 10. First match the pattern markings at the cap of the sleeve (and at the underarm position in the under sleeve) and then secure those matching points with the first pin.

Continuing to work over the curved surface, smooth and pat the two fabrics together, and pin the remaining edges in place. This takes care and thought be-

cause the edges will not fit cut edges even. The interfacing edges will extend slightly beyond the vertical edges of the sleeve, as illustrated in the sketch; the interfacing will extend a greater amount if the fabric is heavy. The worker must balance the two sides of each sleeve section—if the interfacing extends ⅛ inch beyond one vertical seam, it should extend about the same amount beyond the other vertical seam. If the two vertical edges are not the same, it means that the two sections were not properly centered before work was begun. After the edges are properly pinned, baste in the usual manner and then trim the interfacing even with the cut edge of the garment sections.

The directions in this section are to be used for the structural pieces of the garment only. The collar and lapel area requires special treatment—see Principles of Shaping the Tailored Garment on page 234. A suggestion for interfacing belts, welts, and other striplike, small units of design appears under Adaptations of the Shaping Principle on page 242.

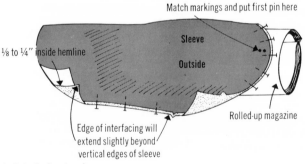

FIGURE 10 To apply interfacing to sleeve

13

TAILORING
THE JACKET
OR
COAT

Each jacket or coat design presents individual problems which have been carefully worked out by the writer of the
instructions. The fact that techniques
included in great detail in a book do not
appear in such detail on the instruction
sheet is in no way a reflection on the
quality of the instructions included with
the pattern. Pattern directions must necessarily be brief, but there is no substitute for those directions; a tailoring book
is merely a supplement to the instruction
sheet. The worker should follow both—
the instruction sheet for specific problems
and proper order of construction and the
more detailed directions in a book as an
aid to understanding principles which
can be applied to the individual pattern.

CAUTION   The order of construction in this chapter is based on the assumption that a muslin test
copy was made; if a test copy was not made, a
different order of work must be followed.

The muslin test copy served many purposes: fitting was done, and so the garment need not be basted together before work is begun; the roll line was established on the collar and lapel area, and so one can proceed with the intricate work in these areas without basting the entire garment together; the position and size of buttons were established, and so buttonholes can be made before the entire garment is assembled; and proportions of details were studied and corrected, and so they need not be basted for testing. Consequently, many intricate details can be done when the garment is still in relatively small pieces; for example, the collar and lapel are shaped, pad-stitched, and taped as one of the first steps of construction, and buttonholes are made before the right front is joined to any other section.

IF A TEST COPY WAS NOT MADE
The worker must baste the entire garment together, including the structural pieces, the under collar, and the sleeve sections. She must refer back to Chapter 8 and go through the steps in that chapter, paying particular attention to the material on pages 109 to 125. After this has been done, it will be advantageous to take out the bastings in order to separate the front sections, the under collar, and the sleeve. In other words, after recording the changes made, she can separate pieces so that the order of construction presented here can be followed; that is, she can regain the advantage of working on small sections.

REVIEW FUNDAMENTAL CONSTRUCTION DETAILS
Chapter 10 (page 142) was concerned with the fundamentals of construction

and pressing that will be used throughout the construction of the garment. These techniques will not be explained in great detail in this chapter. It is important for the worker to know the fundamentals so well that she can use them automatically and unconsciously because she will need to give her conscious thought to the more difficult tailoring principles presented in this chapter.

SPECIAL NOTE The novelty method of finishing the facing edges and inserting the lining (the Hong Kong finish) requires a different order of construction and different techniques from those given on the commercial pattern or in a tailoring book. The order of construction and directions for this method of finishing are given on page 324; study that section now if the novelty method will be used. The difference in construction of the jacket involves finishing the facing and neck edges and inserting the lining before securing those edges; the difference, then, is in the last steps of construction.

PRINCIPLES OF SHAPING THE TAILORED GARMENT

The one thing, more than any other, that separates tailoring from sewing is the shaping and molding that is an integral part of tailoring. And one of the advantages of knowing tailoring is that these shaping principles can be carried back to sewing, thereby improving the quality of all home-sewn garments. The shaping and molding is difficult to achieve, and for this reason it is not usually considered a part of sewing; the average woman who "just sews" would not want to spend the time and effort in shaping, nor would the average woman, making her first or second garment, be capable of understanding the principles involved.

A simple question will aid in understanding the principle of shaping: Can three wooden boxes, identical in size, be stacked into the area required for one box? This is very obviously impossible unless the boxes are graded in size. Keep this example in mind and consider the identical problem in sewing. In sewing, the "boxes" are fabric rather than wood, and they fit around curved edges rather than square corners, but the problem is identical. Two or more "objects" (wood, paper, or fabric), identical in size, cannot be contained in the same area—the one on the inside must be smaller, or it must "give" in some way to decrease its size.

Consider the typical blouse collar, which is composed of two identical layers of fabric and one of interfacing—three boxes identical in size. These three are sewn to the garment and then curve in two ways because the collar rolls over, and it also bends around the neck. The three layers cannot be contained in the same area, and so something has to give a little; usually the interfacing ripples up and a tiny crease is formed, and often the layer which is on the inside curve (the under-collar section) creeps out, allowing the facing seam to show on the right side. The problem would not be present if the three layers differed slightly in size, with the one on the outside curve (the top section) being slightly larger than the one in the middle (the interfacing section) and both being slightly larger than the piece on the inside curve (the under-collar section).

The wooden boxes and the typical blouse collar illustrate the problem. It is a greater problem in the tailored garment because of the thickness of fabric used for tailoring. Again the example of the boxes will be helpful: If the boxes were made of wood $\frac{1}{4}$ inch thick (like very heavy fabric), they would have to

differ greatly in size in order to be contained in the same space, whereas if they were paper-thin (like lightweight fabric), the size differences would not be as great. The very nature of tailoring fabrics demands careful attention to this problem.

The commercial pattern for a tailored garment takes care of this problem to some extent. This is why the typical suit or coat pattern includes two collar patterns—the under-collar pattern is smaller than the upper-collar pattern, so that it can take the inside curve on the figure. However, it is impossible for the pattern company to solve every problem of size gradations. The worker must solve most of these problems because many of them could not be taken care of by the commercial pattern; likewise, the worker must consider the weight of her own fabric because the pattern company must make the pattern for "average" fabric (usually medium-weight fabric).

The problem of shaping is solved by the position in which each edge and each segment of work is held as construction proceeds. Work must be held in the position it will take when the garment is worn—in other words, in wearing position. The reader has met this problem several times, although the issue has not been discussed in detail. It will be helpful to review certain construction details at this time. Refer back to the directions accompanying Figures 31 and 32 on page 196. Note that the skirt with a side opening was held in an outside curve like the body curve; this allowed the skirt to take the outside curve over the zipper. An example that is very easy to understand is mentioned in the directions accompanying Figure 43c on page 203. Although the sketch shows the skirt turned wrong side out, so that the construction is visible, the directions state that the skirt should be held in wearing position as the underside of the waistband is finished; this allows the waistband to take the outside curve, while the ribbon is shaped to the inside curve. If the ribbon were stretched out flat it would not be as long, by actual measurement, as the waistband stretched out flat, but holding them in this position makes the two the same length.

An example which is comparable to the problems that will be encountered in tailoring appears in the directions accompanying Figure 10 on page 232. Because the sleeve takes such a sharp curve on the arm, the interfacing for the sleeve must be narrower than the sleeve. By shaping the sleeve section over the interfacing on a curved surface comparable to the curve of the arm, the work was held in the proper wearing position.

This principle is greatly involved with work on the collar and lapel areas because these areas take sharp curves when the garment is worn and because they are such prominent features of the finished costume.

SHAPING THE COLLAR

Figure 1a shows the typical collar composed of two pattern pieces. Place the upper-collar pattern over the under-collar pattern with neck edges (notched edges) and center-back lines matching. Note that the upper-collar pattern is slightly wider and perhaps slightly longer because the upper collar must take the outside curve on the figure. The amount is about $\frac{1}{8}$ to $\frac{1}{4}$ inch for a suit pattern and about $\frac{1}{4}$ inch or perhaps slightly more for a typical "winter" coat pattern; the pattern company has estimated the size difference based on the fabric that will be used by most persons. Note that the under collar will be cut on the bias as a further aid to folding over and shaping to the inside curve on the figure.

Figure 1b pictures the one-piece collar pattern in which the upper and under collar are combined in one piece. Usually this pattern is cut on the bias, as shown. When this pattern is folded along the fold line, there may be no size differences between the two halves; this is because the bias cut allows one half, which will become the under collar, to ease slightly to shape to the inside curve, while the other half, which will become the upper collar, stretches slightly to take the outside curve.

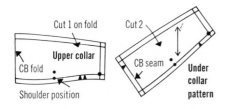

(a) Typical pattern includes two collar patterns

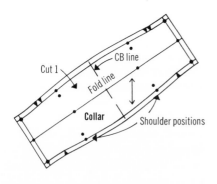

(b) Upper and under collars combined in one piece

FIGURE 1 Examples of collar patterns

shaping the two-piece collar   See Figure 2. Join the center-back seam of the under-collar sections. Trim the seam to ⅜ inch and press open, as shown in Figure 2a. Join the center-back seam in the inter-facing sections, as shown in Figure 2b. In order to reduce bulk, this must be a lapped seam. Lap one raw edge of inter-facing 1¼ inches over the other (in other words, lap seamlines) and machine-stitch. Trim each seam edge to ¼ inch. Then pin the interfacing to the under collar, neck edges (notched edges) even, as shown in Figure 2c, and baste the neck edge only.

See Figure 3. The roll line which was established on the muslin copy must be established on the collar. No two roll lines are alike, although they all take a boat-shaped line, as shown in both sketches. Corresponding measurements must be taken.

CAUTION Remember that seams have been stitched in the muslin copy but not in the collar, so measurements must be taken to seamlines (not to cut edges).

The measurement between the roll line and the corner marking of the collar must correspond, as shown in Figure 3a. The distance from the seamline at the neck edge to the roll line at the center back must correspond. If there is no lapel, the distance from the seamline to the roll line at the center back and at the end of the collar must correspond, as shown in Figure 3b. With a pencil, sketch in the roll line on the interfacing.

See Figure 4. To shape the collar, hold it in a curve similar to wearing posi-tion, with the interfacing taking the out-side curve over the under collar. Smooth the two together and baste along the roll line. With the collar in wearing position, pin the remaining edges in place, allow-ing the under-collar edge to extend as it

will beyond the interfacing; because both layers were cut from the same pat-tern, the one taking the outside curve must have more width. The difference will not be great. Trim off the corner of the interfacing to a point about 1/16 inch inside the seamlines, as shown. Baste the remaining collar edges together with basting stitches ⅝ inch in from the cut edge of the under collar. Then pin the collar ends together and keep the collar in this position at all times.

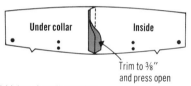

(a) Join under collar sections

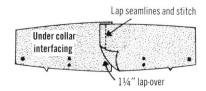

(b) Join interfacing sections with lapped seam

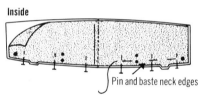

(c) Baste interfacing to under collar
FIGURE 2

shaping the one-piece collar See Figure 5. The one-piece collar is interfaced to within ⅛ or ¼ inch from the roll line. The interfacing should be basted to the half which will become the under collar; determine which half will be the under collar by comparing notches on the collar and neck edge of the garment. The under half of the collar will be sewn to the garment and will be notched like the garment pieces; the upper half will be sewn to the neck edges of the facing pieces. In these sketches a single notch has been used for the garment and the under collar, and a double notch for the upper collar and facing edges; be sure to check each pattern to see the notch system used for that particular pattern.

The one-piece collar is shaped in exactly the same manner as the two-piece collar; see the detailed directions above. The principles are the same, and the extra width of the collar is of no concern in this step of construction.

SHAPING THE LAPEL AREA

The principles of shaping the lapel area are exactly the same as those for the col-

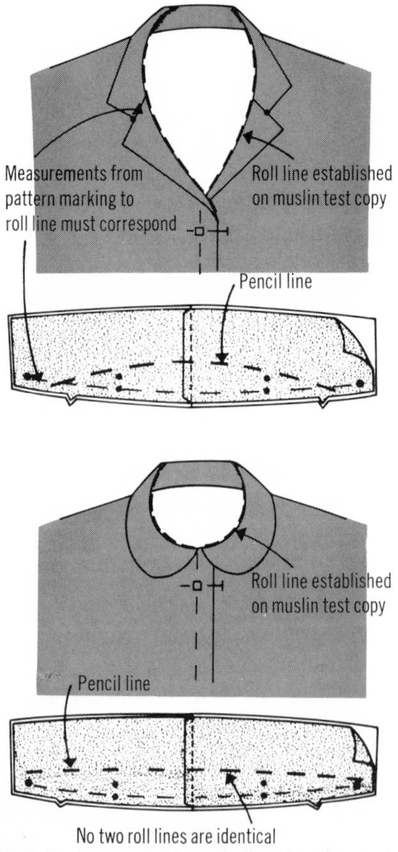

Measurements from pattern marking to roll line must correspond

Roll line established on muslin test copy

Pencil line

Roll line established on muslin test copy

Pencil line

No two roll lines are identical

FIGURE 3 To establish roll line in the under collar

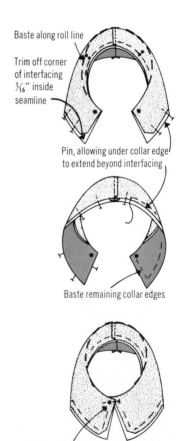

Baste along roll line

Trim off corner of interfacing ¹⁄₁₆″ inside seamline

Pin, allowing under collar edge to extend beyond interfacing

Baste remaining collar edges

Pin ends together and keep collar in this position

FIGURE 4 To shape under collar and interfacing

lar. Remove any bastings in the lapel area. See Figure 6. Establish the roll line of the lapel by taking corresponding measurements from the muslin copy, just as with the collar. The roll line on the lapel is a ruler-straight line which ends at the level of the top buttonhole marking, as shown. The roll line is established in the same manner for the garment with a separate facing or a self-facing, as shown.

See Figure 7. To shape the lapel, hold it in a position similar to wearing position, folding the lapel to the outside along the roll line. Garments with separate facings and those with self-facings are shaped in the same manner, as shown. With the lapel in wearing position, pin the remaining edges in place, allowing the interfacing to fall into place as it will. The interfacing will not appear to be as wide as it was originally (will not reach to the cut edge or the fold line) because some of the width was required to bend around the curve. In the garment with a separate facing, trim off the corner of the interfacing, as shown. Baste the interfacing in place. Pin the lapel to the garment to keep it folded to the outside at all times.

SHAPING THE COLLAR CUT IN ONE WITH THE GARMENT

Figure 8 illustrates that the collar cut in one with the garment presents shaping problems that are identical to those of a collar and a lapel combined in one piece. The principles are the same, and the detailed directions given above can be adapted to this design.

PADDING STITCHES AID IN SHAPING THE GARMENT

Padding stitches are small running stitches made from the interfacing side and caught through the layer of interfacing to the underside of the garment fabric. The stitches are done in such a

way that they take a slightly diagonal line, which allows for a certain amount of movement or freedom in the area.

The purposes of padding stitches are (1) to hold two layers of fabric together so that they truly act as one fabric, (2) to aid in shaping the garment by molding the shaped areas together in wearing position, (3) to ensure that the shaped area will retain its shape throughout years of wear, and (4) to stiffen the area for the desired effect. The collar and lapel areas of the garment, where a molded, shaped effect is especially important, must be pad-stitched. The stitches will aid in shaping the garment if they are done while holding the garment in the position it will take when worn. A stiffening effect is required to

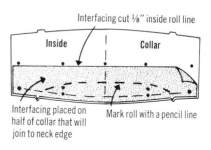

Interfacing cut ⅛" inside roll line

Inside Collar

Interfacing placed on half of collar that will join to neck edge

Mark roll with a pencil line

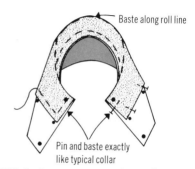

Baste along roll line

Pin and baste exactly like typical collar

FIGURE 5 To shape the one-piece collar

support the stand of the collar and is often an advantage at corners where a limp fabric might tend to curl.

The length of the stitch, the frequency of rows, and the kind of thread used allow for great differences in re-

sults. See Figure 9, which pictures a portion of a collar to illustrate the placement of stitches and their purposes. The sketch pictures the collar in a flat position, but the collar should be kept in a shaped position when work is in progress. Note that no stitches are placed in the seam allowances so that the interfacing can be trimmed later for a staggered seam. The area between the neck edge and the roll line is the portion of the collar that will

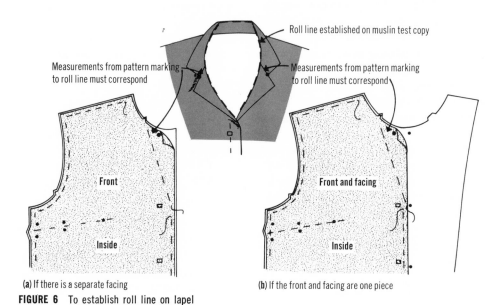

Roll line established on muslin test copy

Measurements from pattern marking to roll line must correspond

Measurements from pattern marking to roll line must correspond

Front

Front and facing

Inside

Inside

(a) If there is a separate facing

(b) If the front and facing are one piece

FIGURE 6   To establish roll line on lapel

Outside

Trim off corner of interfacing

Fold to outside along roll line

Pin and baste, allowing garment to extend beyond interfacing

Outside

Fold to outside along roll line

Pin and baste, allowing interfacing to fall naturally in place

(a) If there is a separate facing

(b) If the front and facing are one piece

FIGURE 7   To shape the lapel area

stand at the neckline, and so smaller stitches spaced in narrow rows are used for extra stiffness and body. The portion of the collar that is visible as the garment is worn can have a somewhat softer effect, which is achieved by larger stitches, spaced less frequently. The small area at the corner, which might have a tendency to curl, is stiffened with small stitches. Note that rows of stitches are placed parallel to the roll line as an aid to more effective shaping.

The tautness of the stitch used has an effect on the result. A firm, taut stitch, pulled flat against the fabric, will create more stiffness than a loose, "lazy" stitch. Therefore, the stitch can be held flat in the lower part of the collar and can have greater freedom in the remaining part if a soft, somewhat limp effect is desired.

The padding stitches will make a noticeable change in the hand or character of the fabric—the entire collar will feel much firmer, and the areas with smaller stitches will be definitely stiffer. The kind of thread used also influences the firmness and stiffness of the collar. Silk thread will create less bulk and stiffness than mercerized thread in a utilitarian weight.

to do padding stitches See Figure 10 for general directions; the sketch is in actual size. The two lengths pictured are used most frequently, but there is no reason why stitches must be a certain length; they can be longer for a softer effect or

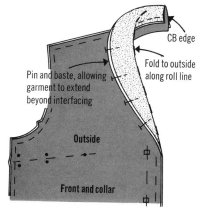

FIGURE 8 To establish roll line and shape the collar cut in one with the garment

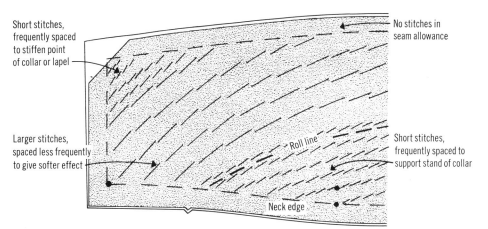

FIGURE 9 Placement and purposes of padding stitches

as small as ⅛ inch if a great deal of body and stiffness is desired.

A single thread is used, and it should never be knotted but merely fastened with a few short stitches. The position in which work is held can vary with individual preferences, but the position shown, with rows in a vertical position, allows for a very comfortable hand position because the stitch is made at right angles to the row; note that the needle can be held in a comfortable right-to-left position. The fact that the stitch into the fabric is made at right angles to the direction of the row results in the diagonal stitch that is visible from the interfacing side. The stitch that passes through the interfacing to the underside of the fabric should be as small as possible (never larger than ⅛ inch), and this stitch does not vary in size, no matter what length of visible stitch is used. The longer visible stitch is merely a result of taking fewer stitches and spacing rows a greater distance apart.

NOTE Work must be held in wearing position. Refer to the drawings in Figures 4 to 8 and hold the work in the same position while doing padding stitches. The entire collar and the lapel area (between the roll line of the lapel and the finished front edge) should be pad-stitched.

PRESSING AS AN AID TO SHAPING

Figure 11 shows a typical under-collar and lapel area, shaped and pad-stitched. The faint lines (parallel to the fold lines of the collar and lapel) indicate rows of padding stitches.

NOTE The rows of padding stitches will not appear in the remaining sketches in this chapter.

The shaped areas should be pressed over a curved surface similar to the curve these areas will take on the body. A rolled turkish towel is excellent as a pressing surface for the collar; tip the iron as required to press over the curve, pressing only very small segments at a time. The tailor's cushion should be used for pressing lapel areas.

ADAPTATIONS OF THE SHAPING PRINCIPLE

Figures 12, 13, and 14 show various bandlike design features. The way inter-

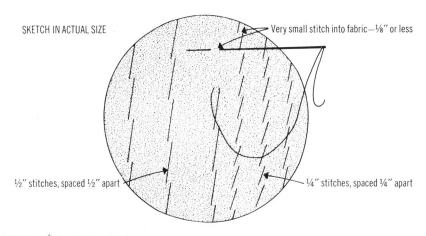

SKETCH IN ACTUAL SIZE

Very small stitch into fabric—⅛" or less

½" stitches, spaced ½" apart

¼" stitches, spaced ¼" apart

FIGURE 10 To do padding stitches

facing is applied and the manner of construction of these striplike details can incorporate the shaping principles discussed on page 234. The traditional method of construction is pictured in Figures 12a and 13a. Note that the interfacing is caught in with the seams and that it will be turned to the inside, forcing it to occupy less space; since it cannot occupy less space, the interfacing will buckle and form a tiny crease or ripple. The recommended construction shown in Figures 12b and 13b allows for shaping and will result in flat bands. Note that the interfacing is cut to the finished size and that it is not caught in with the end seams. The garment fabric is folded over the interfacing, and finishing is done by hand.

Figure 14 pictures this recommended construction adapted to belts. The traditional construction of the belt is very similar to that of the welt or pocket flap pictured in Figure 12, with the interfacing caught in with the stitching of the belt seam. By cutting the belt interfacing to the desired width and length, the fabric can be worked over the interfacing for a very flat and attractive effect.

Rolled turkish towel   Rows of padding stitches, parallel to roll lines

Outside

Tailor's cushion

FIGURE 11 Pressing aids in shaping collar and lapel areas

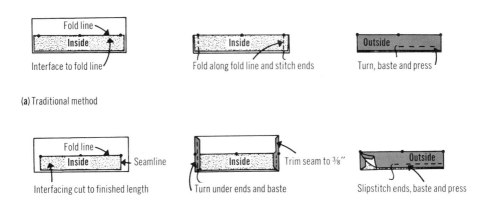

Fold line

Inside

Interface to fold line

(a) Traditional method

Inside

Fold along fold line and stitch ends

Outside

Turn, baste and press

Fold line

Inside ← Seamline

Interfacing cut to finished length

Inside   Trim seam to ⅜"

Turn under ends and baste

Outside

Slipstitch ends, baste and press

(b) Recommended method which allows for shaping

FIGURE 12 To interface welts, flaps, etc.

NOTE Pellon is an excellent interfacing fabric for any belt, welt, or other striplike design feature. The heavier weights are ideal for belts, and lighter weights can be used if desired for softer effects in welts or pockets.

TAPING THE FRONT AND LAPEL AREAS

Narrow cotton-twill tape, available in white or black, is used for several purposes in the tailored garment. The tape must be preshrunk because it shrinks considerably in dry cleaning. It is available in a variety of widths; widths recommended for tailoring purposes are ¼ or ⅜ inch.

The tape serves the following purposes: (1) It strengthens those edges which will get constant strain as the garment is worn (front edges), (2) it strengthens bias lines that will be subject to strain and subsequent stretching (the lapel line), (3) it strengthens slightly bias seams to prevent stretching (shoulder and armhole edges in all garments and the waistline in fitted garments), and (4) it stiffens those edges where a flat, hard line is desirable. The fourth purpose requires some explanation. A flat, hard line is desirable at the finished front edge of the garment (seamline or a fold line); the front edge should look flat and sharply creased, and the addition of twill tape will be helpful. In general, this is the only place where tape is used for this particular purpose in women's tailoring. It is used at many more edges in men's tailoring; for example, it is used at all edges of the collar in men's suits and coats to achieve the very flat, hard-pressed appearance that is desirable in menswear.

NOTE The taping of shoulder, armhole, and waistline edges (of fitted garments) will be done after the garment has been assembled; directions appear on page 258.

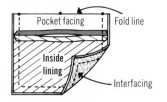

(a) Popular method of handling interfaced and lined pocket

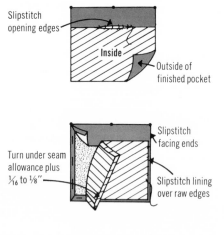

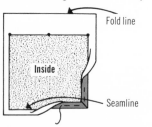

(b) Recommended method which allows for shaping

FIGURE 13 To interface and line patch pockets

The general rules appear in Figure 15, and adaptations are shown in Figure 16. The general rules are:

1 Place the tape ⅛ inch inside the finished front edge (⅛ inch inside the seamline if there is a separate facing or ⅛ inch inside the fold line if there is a self-facing), with the tape placed in the body of the garment, not in the seam allowance.

2 End the tape about ⅜ inch from seamlines (at the neck edge, for example) and from the hemline, as shown. This will allow for seam allowances to turn back with a minimum of bulk created.

3 Do not lap over the ends of the tape as the tape of the roll line of the lapel meets the tape at the front edge; the garment must bend over at this point and will need freedom. The tape should be trimmed so that the end just touches the tape at the front edge, as shown.

4 Center the tape over the roll line of the lapel.

NOTE In the typical garment pictured, the stitches which will secure the tape will catch into the interfacing layer only.

ADAPTATION OF GENERAL RULES

Figure 16 pictures several circumstances that might be encountered. Figures 16a and b are concerned with the garment with a self-facing, which might have been interfaced in the two ways pictured. The rules for placement of the

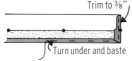

(a) Belt with seam at one edge—one fold line

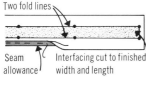

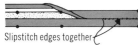

(b) Belt with center seam—two fold lines

FIGURE 14 Suggestions for interfacing belts

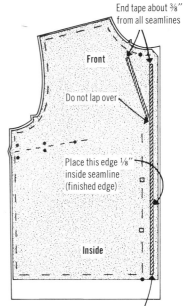

FIGURE 15 General rules for placement of twill tape

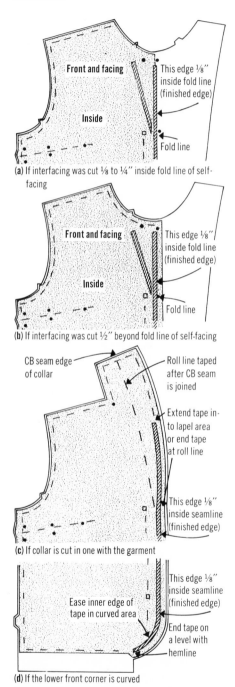

(a) If interfacing was cut ⅛ to ¼″ inside fold line of self-facing

(b) If interfacing was cut ½″ beyond fold line of self-facing

(c) If collar is cut in one with the garment

(d) If the lower front corner is curved

FIGURE 16 Adaptations of general rules for placement of twill tape

tape are exactly the same: the tape is placed ⅛ inch inside the finished front edge, which is, in these examples, a fold line. The only difference is that the stitches which secure the tape will not be exactly the same. In Figure 16a, one edge of the tape will be hand-stitched to the interfacing layer, and the other edge will be secured with stitches placed right along the roll line into the underside of the garment fabric. In Figure 16b, one row of stitches (at the inner edge) will be secured to the interfacing only, while the stitches along the fold line should pass through the interfacing and catch into the underside of the garment fabric right along the roll line.

Figure 16c pictures the collar cut in one with the garment. The tape is placed ⅛ inch inside the seamline at the front edge according to the general rules. It can extend into the collar area to achieve the effect desired. It can stop at the roll-line level if a very soft effect is desired on the collar edge. It can continue into the lapel area or even extend entirely to the center-back line if a hard-creased edge is desired. The roll line for the collar and lapel should not be taped at this time; it should be taped after the center-back seam is joined so that it can pass across the center-back seam in one continuous strip.

Figure 16d pictures a curved front edge. The tape is placed ⅛ inch inside the seamline at the front and curved edge according to the general rules; it should end ⅛ inch above the hemline, as shown. The tape must be flat to the garment at the outer curved edge and therefore must be eased in slightly at the inner curve.

TO APPLY TWILL TAPE

See Figure 17. The garment must be held in wearing position as the tape is applied. Pin the tape to the garment between the hemline and the roll line, with the garment flat on a table. Do not pull and tug at the tape, but simply pat it in place along a ruler-straight line. A pencil line at the seamline will be an aid to proper placement. Pin it in place with pins spaced frequently to obtain a perfectly straight line. Then working from the outside with the lapel area held in wearing position, pin the tape over the curve and into proper position. Baste along the center of the tape. The enlarged view shows the tape in proper position along a seamed edge. Both edges must be whipped in place with small (⅛-inch) stitches, as shown.

BUTTONHOLES

NOTE Buttonholes are made before the garment is assembled to gain the advantage of working with smaller sections of the garment. This order of construction is possible only if the number, size, and placement of buttons have been tested either on a muslin test copy or on the garment itself (basted for fitting).

GENERAL INFORMATION

There are two types of buttonholes recommended for tailored garments. One of various types of bound buttonholes is most suitable for the softly tailored effects desired in women's tailoring, and the handworked tailor's buttonhole is reserved for menswear and women's garments that are obviously planned for a man-tailored look. The machine-worked buttonhole, rather than the tailor's buttonhole, could be used for man-tailored effects, but is not recommended for high-quality tailoring.

The bound buttonhole that is appropriate for most designs can be constructed in a great variety of ways. The one construction that is superior to all

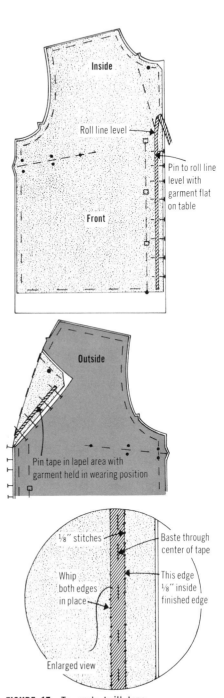

FIGURE 17 To apply twill tape

others is the two-piece corded button-hole; this is the construction used by talented professionals on all high-quality ready-to-wear. The rounded lips of this buttonhole are much more attractive than the flat lips of the buttonholes made by all other construction methods. In addition, the stiffer, firmer edge results in a more serviceable buttonhole. However, the construction of a two-piece corded buttonhole is very difficult and requires great finger dexterity; results are somewhat unpredictable, and a mistake early in the construction process cannot be corrected later. Many persons who can make one beautiful two-piece corded buttonhole find that making a row of beautiful ones is almost impossible. Because consistently excellent results are so difficult for most people to achieve by that method, the only construction included in this book is one which requires less finger dexterity and in which slight mistakes can be corrected. The construction includes a corded feature that results in a buttonhole so very like the two-piece one in appearance and serviceability that there is no need to attempt a method that is less predictable.

placement on the garment Buttonholes are placed on the right front of women's garments for a right-over-left button closing; they are placed on the left front of men's garments. The buttonhole is usually made at right angles to the front edge because this placement will hold the button more securely. If there is a band-type design feature at the front edge, buttonholes must be made on the center-front line and parallel to the de-

sign feature. Special consideration must be given to the buttonhole placement on tailored garments:

1 If there is a lapel, the upper buttonhole controls the roll line of the lapel—the lapel will fold back at the level of the upper buttonhole. If the lapel line was changed during fitting to allow for a longer or shorter lapel than that planned on the pattern, the buttonhole marking must be moved to the corrected level, and all buttonhole markings must be respaced.

2 If the garment is fitted snuggly at the waist, there will be great strain at that level, and a button and buttonhole will be required at the waistline; a fastening that is a mere ½ inch above or below the waist will not control garment lines well. If the pattern marking is not exactly on the waistline of the figure, it must be moved to the corrected waist level, and all buttonhole markings must be respaced.

3 If the garment is snuggly fitted (the typical figure-hugging fitted suit or coat), there will be a buttonhole marking very near the bust level because of the strain at that level as the garment is worn. However, if the design is semifitted or boxy, it will have been made with more freedom, and there may not be a buttonhole marking at the bust level. However, if the wearer is large-busted and if she chooses to fit a boxy garment very snuggly, there will be strain at the bust level; in this case, a buttonhole must be placed at that level, and all buttonhole markings may have to be respaced.

4 If the jacket or coat has been lengthened or shortened, some adjustment of buttonhole markings may be required. If the garment is a full-length coat, marking an additional buttonhole or removing one marking may solve the problem. A change

in jacket length requires more subtle changes, and probably all buttonhole markings will have to be respaced.

the double-breasted garment   Many persons are confused about the placement of buttonholes on double-breasted designs. This confusion is a result of feeling that every button should have a buttonhole and of finding that most directions do not suggest buttonholes for one of the two rows of buttons. The illustration in Figure 18 pictures a jacket front; the broken line indicates the center-front line. The worker will proceed with more confidence if she understands why most designers use only one row of buttonholes. Buttons must be an equal distance from the center-front line, as they are pictured. However, both the button and the buttonhole are a part of the total design effect and must be balanced (as balanced as possible) on each side of the center front; the button and the buttonhole make up the design unit.

Buttons pinned in place can be perfectly balanced, as shown at level 1.

A unit of buttons and buttonholes can be perfectly balanced if the buttonholes are made in the position illustrated at level 2. However, a buttonhole is functional only if it extends from the button position toward the right half of the figure; if it extends toward the left of the button (as shown in the left half of the sketch), it looks wrong to the eye and will not be functional. Therefore, although a perfectly balanced effect has been achieved, this placement is not acceptable. The unit shown at level 3 is composed of functional buttonholes, but notice the resulting off-center effect. Although this placement is sometimes suggested (infrequently), it is not a wise choice. The effect at level 4 is the one most favored by designers; although the unit is not as perfectly centered as the units at levels 1 and 2, it is more nearly centered than the unit at level 3. In other words, level

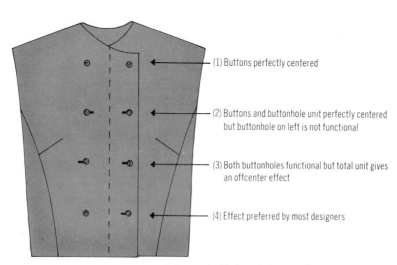

(1) Buttons perfectly centered

(2) Buttons and buttonhole unit perfectly centered but buttonhole on left is not functional

(3) Both buttonholes functional but total unit gives an offcenter effect

(4) Effect preferred by most designers

FIGURE 18   Placement of buttons and buttonholes on double-breasted garment

4 pictures the best placement to combine attractiveness and usefulness.

NOTE The left front will need the support that buttonholes would give it; it will be supported with large snaps, placed in position directly under the decorative row of buttons.

standards of appearance for bound buttonholes
See Figure 19, which shows a section of the finished garment in actual size. The finished front edge is a seamline (if there is a separate facing) or a fold line (if there is a self-facing); the sketch shows the facing turned to the inside, as it will be when the garment is finished. The measurement from the finished front

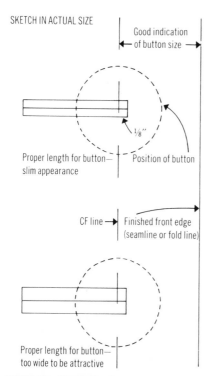

SKETCH IN ACTUAL SIZE

Good indication of button size

1/8''

Proper length for button— slim appearance

Position of button

CF line → Finished front edge (seamline or fold line)

Proper length for button— too wide to be attractive

FIGURE 19 Standards of appearance

edge to the center-front line is an indication of the button size recommended by the designer; buttons should not vary greatly from that recommended size. Note that one end of the buttonhole is about 1/8 inch beyond the center-front line; therefore, a button placed on the center line of the left front will fasten in such a way that center-front lines will match.

The buttonhole should be slim in order to give an attractive appearance; a wide buttonhole is too conspicuous. Buttonholes have a tendency to look slightly smaller (in length and width) when finished, and because they should appear to be a scant 1/4 inch wide when finished, a good general width for stitching is 1/4 inch. Very short buttonholes should be slightly narrower to create similar proportions.

The length of the buttonhole is determined by the button to be used. The line on the pattern is not necessarily the proper length. The pattern will have only one marking which is close to the center-front line (see the pattern in Figure 20) with a straight line extending from it; the fact that there is no definite pattern marking at the other end is an indication that the length must be decided by button size.

The minimum length of the buttonhole is the diameter plus the height of the button to be used.

Because buttonholes have a tendency to look shorter when finished, it is possible that more than minimum length may be required. After a test buttonhole is made, place a button in position and study the effect; the buttonhole may look too short even though the button will pass through the opening. The buttonhole can be lengthened to give attractive proportions.

Buttonholes must be even in four

different ways: they must be an equal distance from the finished front edge, they must be an identical width, they must be an identical length, and they must be spaced evenly.

BOUND BUTTONHOLES WITH A CORDED FEATURE

CAUTION A test buttonhole, perhaps more than one, must be made to determine proper width and length and to discover problems that will arise as a result of the nature of the fabric. Raveling and weak corners are serious problems, and one must know what to expect before work is begun on the garment.

1 Read General Information on pages 247 to 251. Buttonholes must be slim-looking to give a professional appearance. Figure 19 illustrates good and poor proportions. To our fashion-conscious eyes, the too wide ones look unattractive, too big for their purpose, and unsightly. In order to keep the important slim look, short buttonholes must be narrower than longer ones.

2 To ensure accurate measurements in the four ways in which the buttonholes must be even, a paper pattern will be made with the necessary lines drawn on it. This pattern will then be pinned in the proper position on the garment, the machine stitching will be done through the paper, and the paper will be torn away. Ticker tape is ideal for this purpose, but any strip of paper 3 or 4 inches wide can be used. Short pieces can be stitched together on the machine or pinned together to obtain sufficient length. Cut a piece of paper 3 or 4 inches wide and long enough to cover all buttonhole markings on the pattern.

3 To make the paper pattern, use the pattern as a guide and transfer the measurements of the buttonhole markings to the strip of paper, as shown in Figure 20. Use a ruler, be sure all lines are parallel,

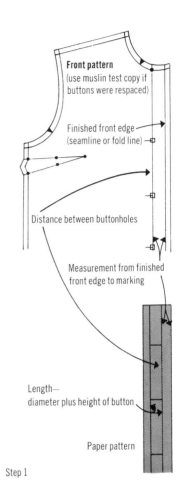

Front pattern (use muslin test copy if buttons were respaced)

Finished front edge (seamline or fold line)

Distance between buttonholes

Measurement from finished front edge to marking

Length— diameter plus height of button

Paper pattern

Step 1

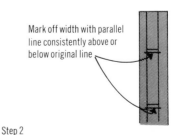

Mark off width with parallel line consistently above or below original line

Step 2

FIGURE 20 A pattern for bound buttonholes

measure accurately, and use a fine pencil for best results. Drawing the lines shown in step 1 will ensure that the buttonholes are even in three of the four ways: an equal distance from the finished front

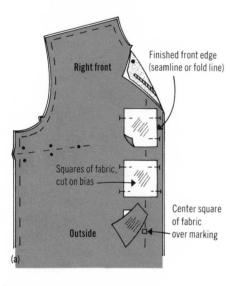

Right front

Finished front edge (seamline or fold line)

Squares of fabric, cut on bias

Center square of fabric over marking

Outside

(a)

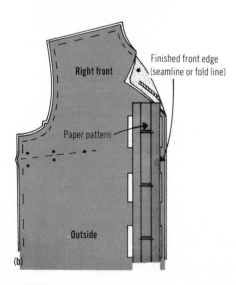

Right front

Finished front edge (seamline or fold line)

Paper pattern

Outside

(b)

FIGURE 21

edge, an equal distance apart, and equal in length.

Draw another horizontal line about ¼ inch beneath the first line shown in step 2 to make the buttonhole even in width. Draw this last line so that the buttonhole is in beautiful proportion (see Figure 19).

4 Cut 3-inch squares of fabric on the bias to be used as the binding for the buttonholes. Usually the binding squares are of self-fabric, but they can be of a compatible fabric in a contrasting color for special effects if desired. See Figure 21a. Center the squares over each buttonhole marking, having one edge of the square along the finished edge (the seamline or fold line) of the garment, as shown. Pin in place.

Place the paper pattern over the squares of fabric; have the long cut edge of the pattern along the finished front edge of the garment; see that the top and lower buttonhole markings on the pattern fall in the same position as the top and lower markings on the garment, as shown in Figure 21b. Pin in place.

5 See Figure 22. Test the machine for tension, etc. Use matching thread and set the machine to sew about 17 to 22 stitches per inch. Begin stitching the small rectangles at one corner. Count the stitches at the ends so that all buttonholes for a garment will have exactly the same number of stitches in width since a difference of one stitch can make a great difference in the resulting size; leave the needle down in the fabric to pivot around the corners. Double-stitch for a few stitches so that knots will be unnecessary.

6 Carefully tear the paper pattern away from the stitches. See Figure 23. Using small, sharp scissors, cut down the center of the buttonhole to within ⅛ inch of the ends. Then cut diagonally to each corner, cutting directly to the machine

threads. Cut only one buttonhole and finish it before cutting the others.

Now turn the binding through the slash to the wrong side of the garment. It should lie flat with no puckers at the corners. If it does not lie flat, forming a perfect rectangle, turn the binding back to the right side again and clip into the puckered corner; it puckers only if it has not been cut to the machine stitches.

7 See Figure 24. Turn the garment to the wrong side. Flip up one edge of the binding and notice the small seam. That seam has a tendency to lie toward the buttonhole, but it must be forced to lie away from it, as shown. To hold the seam in the correct position, catch it down to the interfacing with small hand stitches.

NOTE In some fabrics that ravel badly, these hand stitches tend to ravel the seam even more. If so, press this seam in the correct position.

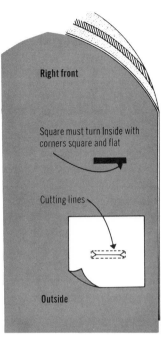

Right front

Square must turn Inside with corners square and flat

Cutting lines

Outside

FIGURE 23

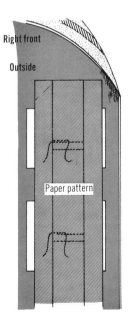

Right front

Outside

Paper pattern

FIGURE 22

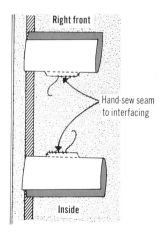

Right front

Hand-sew seam to interfacing

Inside

FIGURE 24

8 Figure 25 illustrates the common flaws in buttonhole appearance and the reason that testing is absolutely necessary. In this method with a corded feature, the width of the lips of the buttonhole will be controlled by the size of the cord. The desired effect is a buttonhole with edges almost meeting at the center, as shown in the upper sketch. If the rectangle is too narrow for the size of cord and the thickness of fabric used, the edges will bow out, and the resulting buttonhole will be fat and heavy-looking; a thinner cord must be used, or the original rectangle must be made wider. If the edges do not meet each other (see the lower sketch), the cord must be thicker, or the original rectangle must be narrower. Study the test buttonhole, make corrections, and retest before proceeding.

9 The advantage of a corded buttonhole is that the lips will be rounded instead of flat and the buttonhole will feel firm and be more serviceable. The two-piece corded buttonhole is the most professional buttonhole, but it is far more difficult to do than this method, and results are less predictable. However, a corded feature included in these directions results in a buttonhole so nearly like the true corded one that there is no need to consider a more difficult and less predictable construction. The cord used for this purpose should be pliable and of a diameter slightly less than ⅛ inch. Cut the cord in 3-inch lengths.

See Figure 26. Pin one edge of the binding flat against the garment and work with only one lip of the buttonhole at a time. Lay the cord inside the stitching line, as shown; do not attempt to pin it—it must be held in position with the fingers.

10 See Figure 27. Working from the right side of the garment, wrap the binding snugly around the cord and, using no pins, blind-stitch along the seam of the buttonhole, encasing the cord; blind stitches should be a scant ¼ inch long and should be firm but not tight. This step is easier to do than it sounds because the cord is a great aid in keeping the lip of the buttonhole even in width. When one edge is finished, place a length of cord in the remaining edge and repeat the process. From the wrong side, fasten the ends very securely, passing the

The desired effect

Lips too wide for
size of rectangle

Lips too narrow for
size of rectangle

FIGURE 25

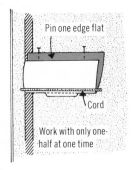

Pin one edge flat

Cord

Work with only one-
half at one time

FIGURE 26

stitches through both cords and as many thicknesses of fabric as possible without allowing the stitches to show on the outside.

Hold the lips of the buttonhole together with diagonal basting stitches; pull them only tightly enough to hold the buttonhole in a perfect rectangle, as shown. These stitches should remain until the garment is finished and should be taken out only when it is time to mark the position of the buttons.

11 Trim the binding strips to ½ inch from the stitching on the long edges and ¼ inch on the ends (Figure 28). Whip the edges of the binding strip to the interfacing.

THE TAILOR'S BUTTONHOLE

This construction is done after the garment is entirely finished. These buttonholes can be made just before the garment is lined or as the very last step of construction. Read General Information on page 247 before beginning work.

Figure 29 pictures the finished jacket or coat. The position of the buttonholes should be marked with basting lines; this step is quite similar to the making of the paper pattern for bound buttonholes (see Figure 20 and the accompanying directions).

Figure 30 pictures the right front edge of the finished garment with a row of buttonholes in various stages of completion.

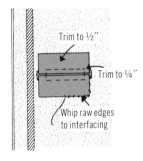

FIGURE 28

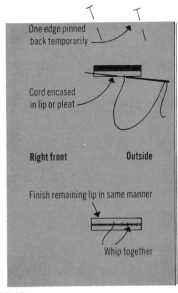

FIGURE 27

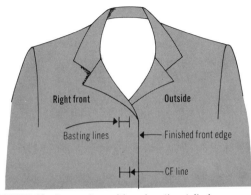

FIGURE 29 To mark position for the tailor's buttonhole

step 1   Mark the position of the button-holes with basting lines.

step 2   Machine-stitch with short stitches (about 20 per inch) $\frac{1}{16}$ inch on each side of the marked line and continue stitching around a small circle ($\frac{1}{4}$ inch in diameter) at the center front, as shown. The circle will allow for a larger opening to accommodate the shank of the button and will also allow for radiating stitches, which will better withstand strain during wearing.

step 3   Slash down the center line with small, sharp scissors. Make several clips to the stitching at the circle, as shown.

step 4   The thread used for buttonhole stitches should be buttonhole twist. The stitches should be worked over a very small cord as an aid to stiffening and strengthening the opening edges. The cord can be a very heavy cotton thread, similar to a tiny cord, or one or two strands of matching buttonhole twist can be used to serve the purpose.

Thread the cord on a heavy needle, knot one end, and secure the knot a short distance away from the buttonhole (it will be trimmed off later). Stretch the cord across the cutting line for the buttonhole and fasten it in place by wrapping it around the needle, as shown. Using another needle, work buttonhole stitches along one cut edge, encasing the cord in the stitches, as shown.

step 5   Release the cord and carry it along with the stitches at the end. Radiate the stitches around the circular end, as shown. Stretch the cord flat again and proceed.

step 6   Trim off the ends of the cord. The sketch shows the finished button-hole.

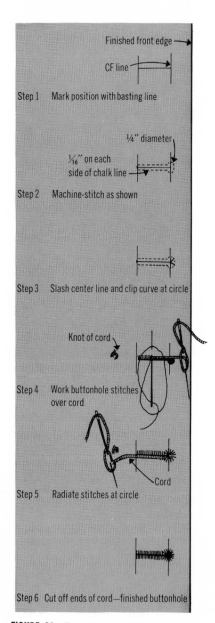

Finished front edge →

CF line

Step 1   Mark position with basting line

$\frac{1}{4}$" diameter
$\frac{1}{16}$" on each side of chalk line

Step 2   Machine-stitch as shown

Step 3   Slash center line and clip curve at circle

Knot of cord

Step 4   Work buttonhole stitches over cord

Cord

Step 5   Radiate stitches at circle

Step 6   Cut off ends of cord—finished buttonhole

FIGURE 30   The tailor's buttonhole

ASSEMBLING
THE MAIN
BODY
OF THE GARMENT

Under normal circumstances if a muslin test copy was made and if all fitting problems were solved at that time, there is no need to baste the entire garment together again for a second fitting. However, in some cases, basting and a careful second fitting at this time will be required. A snugly fitted, body-hugging garment should be refitted. The thickness of the fabric (which could only be estimated in the fitting of the muslin copy) makes a great deal of difference in any snugly fitted design; if unusually thick fabric is used for such a garment, a fitting in the actual fabric is absolutely essential. If the fitting of the muslin test copy was not completely perfected (if certain little issues were not taken care of), another fitting at this time is required. If many problems were encountered in fitting the muslin copy (and there were many pattern alternations), it would be wise to fit the garment again.

Although the darts and seams need not be basted for fitting purposes, it is very important to baste all seams before stitching. Review Basting and Stitching on page 142. The spongy fabric used in tailoring and the additional thicknesses of the complete interfacing require small, firm stitches for control of the fabric as it passes through the machine.

STITCHING DARTS IN THE INTERFACED GARMENT

See Figure 31. Even though basting stitches were placed at the center of dart lines to force the two layers of fabric to act as one, a problem will be encountered at the tips of darts. If the stitching ends directly on the fold edge at the tip of the dart in the usual manner, the

stitches will slip off the garment fabric (catching in only the interfacing) before the tip was reached (because of the thickness of the fabric). The sketch in Figure 31 shows the solution. Note that the stitches end not right at the fold at the tip but $\frac{1}{16}$ to $\frac{1}{8}$ inch from the fold. Make up a test dart using a layer of fabric and interfacing; end the stitches about $\frac{1}{16}$ inch from the fold and examine the effect on the right side. The stitching should end properly at the tip on the outside layer. Make corrections until the proper effect is achieved and then stitch all darts in the same manner.

TREATMENT OF STRUCTURAL SEAMS AND DARTS IN THE INTERFACED GARMENT

The structural seams and darts in interfaced garments must be staggered to decrease unnecessary bulk; this is done as soon as they are stitched and before they are pressed and crossed with another seam. The interfacing should be trimmed to a narrower width, while the structural seam remains the full $\frac{5}{8}$-inch width, as shown in Figure 32. Note that both

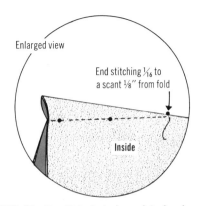

Enlarged view

End stitching $\frac{1}{16}$ to a scant $\frac{1}{8}$" from fold

Inside

FIGURE 31   To stitch darts in an interfaced garment

layers of interfacing are trimmed down to about ¼ or ⅜ inch from the stitching line; the wider width is advisable if the interfacing fabric ravels appreciably. The interfacing is trimmed from a dart in the same manner, as shown.

Darts should be slashed and pressed open. See the directions accompanying Figure 12 on page 155.

TREATMENT OF ENCASED SEAMS

The interfacing is trimmed from encased seams in a somewhat different manner; because these seams will not be subject to strain when the garment is worn, the interfacing can be trimmed to a narrower width (⅛ inch). See the directions accompanying Figure 13 on page 000.

TAPING SEAMS
AND EDGES
OF THE ASSEMBLED
GARMENT

Figure 33 shows additional uses for cotton-twill tape. Seamlines which are slightly bias and which will get strain as the garment is worn should be strengthened with tape. After a seam is stitched and pressed open, tape is centered along the seamline, as shown at the shoulder seam in Figure 33a. Reread General Rules for Placement on page 245. Whip both edges in place, catching in the seam thickness only.

The neck edge of a collarless garment will get considerable strain in wearing and will stretch unless it is strengthened with twill tape, as shown in Figure 33a. Tape the neck edge between the center-front lines by easing the tape to fit around the curve (see the directions accompanying Figure 16d on page 246) and placing the tape ⅛ inch inside the seamline. Whip both edges of the tape in place, catching in the interfacing only.

The slightly bias, curving lines at armhole edges should be taped, as shown in Figure 33a. Tape the armhole edge between the notches, as shown, placing the tape ⅛ inch inside the seamline. The armhole edge has a slight curve, so the tape must be shaped and eased to the curve. Whip both edges of the tape in place, catching in the interfacing only.

If the sleeve is cut in one with the garment, tape a portion of the shoulder seam, as shown in Figure 33b. The aver-

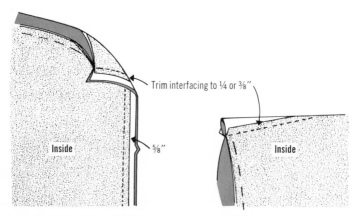

Trim interfacing to ¼ or ⅜″

Inside

⅝″

Inside

FIGURE 32 To stagger seams in an interfaced garment

age length of the shoulder line is about 5 inches, and it is this portion of the seam that will get strain as the garment is worn.

If the garment is snugly fitted at the waist, there will be a great deal of strain at that level when it is worn. Figure 33c shows how tape can be used to strengthen the garment. Hold the garment in the curve it will take on the figure and pin the tape along the waist level; this position will ensure that the strain will fall on the tape, rather than on the garment. Tack the tape to vertical seams and fasten one end to the end of the buttonhole scrap, as shown. On the left front, where there is no buttonhole, the tape can extend to the front edge and be tacked to the tape along the front edge.

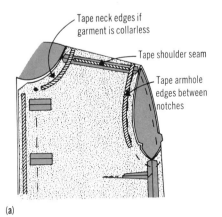

Tape neck edges if garment is collarless

Tape shoulder seam

Tape armhole edges between notches

(a)

CONSTRUCTION OF GUSSETS

A gusset is a piece set into the underarm area of a garment with the sleeve cut in one with the body of the garment. Its purpose is to make the garment fit well and look trim, while at the same time providing extra spread for arm movements. A garment with a gusset can be fitted more snugly to the body than a similar design without a gusset. Because of its aid to smart fit, the gusset (in one of many guises) is used frequently, and especially often in highly styled Vogue patterns. Gussets can vary so much that their only common characteristic is that they have at least one square or almost square point that must be set into a slash in the garment. Figure 34 pictures four examples of the most common gusset patterns. The diamond-shaped piece is the traditional gusset and is the most difficult to do because it has four corners, two of which are set into slashes in the

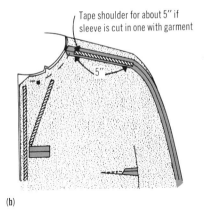

Tape shoulder for about 5″ if sleeve is cut in one with garment

5″

(b)

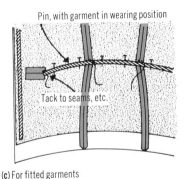

Pin, with garment in wearing position

Tack to seams, etc.

(c) For fitted garments

FIGURE 33

garment. The half gusset is the simplest to do and appears in easy-to-make designs only; two halves are cut for each side, and the resulting gusset is very much like the traditional gusset (with just the addition of a seam down the center). The half gusset is much easier to do because each half is set in separately before the center seam is joined.

A gusset can be combined with a portion of the body of the garment, in which case the name of the pattern piece will probably not include the word "gusset." The two examples of combination gussets pictured are most frequently used, and the name of the pattern piece usually describes the portion of the body of the garment (jacket side, under

sleeve). Although the pattern piece for a combination gusset may appear in a great variety of sizes and shapes, it will usually have one pointed end and will extend in boxlike fashion to become the underarm section of the garment or the sleeve. This gusset is easier than the traditional gusset simply because it has one less corner.

Regardless of the shape of the pattern piece, there are certain general principles which must be understood before work is begun. In all gussets, there are always certain corners that are set into slashes in the body of the garment and other corners that are set into points formed by the joining of two seams; the most difficult corners to do are those set into slashes in the garment. There will be matching pattern markings at all corner points. The illustrations picture a system of four different markings (as used by Vogue patterns), but other patterns may use only two different markings; before beginning work, study the marking system on the pattern being used. In these illustrations, the difficult points or corners which will set into slashes in the body of the garment are marked with squares (□) and triangles (△), and the simpler points are marked with small and large circles.

NOTE The diamond-shaped gusset, which is more difficult because there are more corners, will be described in detail. The most difficult step, that of basting and stitching in the gusset piece, is shown in Figure 39. As an aid to constructing the half gusset and combination gusset, the same step is illustrated in Figures 41 and 42. The principles described in detail for the diamond-shaped gusset should be applied to all gusset problems.

See Figure 35, which pictures a jacket or coat pattern with typical lines for gusset construction.

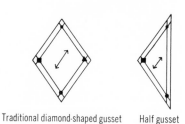

Traditional diamond-shaped gusset   Half gusset

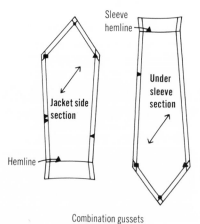

Combination gussets

FIGURE 34 Types of gussets

The main principle to understand is this: The pattern piece for the gusset has a ⅝-inch seam allowance on all edges (see Figure 34), whereas the stitching lines on the garment converge, and therefore there are varying seam allowances on the garment.

When the slash is made down the center of the stitching lines, the seam allowance on the garment varies from perhaps ½ or ⅜ inch at the widest point to no allowance at all at the point. When two edges with different seam allowances are sewn together, they must be sewn with seamlines matching, rather than with cut edges even, as one usually sews.

This is the most important principle: Gussets are constructed with seamlines matching, not cut edges even.

THE DIAMOND-SHAPED GUSSET

See Figure 36. The very first step of construction (before seams are basted) is to reinforce the points that will be slashed. This is done by placing a scrap of fabric on the outside of the garment, allowing it to extend ⅝ inch outside the stitching lines, as shown. Lining fabric or a lightweight interfacing fabric is a good choice; the fabric will not show when the garment is finished. Machine-stitch with short stitches (15 to 20 stitches per inch) and with matching thread along the stitching lines, as shown, catching in the scrap of fabric; make a sharp, distinct point—do not retrace stitches at the point because a slash must be made directly to the point.

The pattern directions state that the slash should be made at this time. It is wiser to slash to a point about 1 inch from the tip at this time; seams in the garment will be stitched and pressed before gusset construction continues. Then slash to the tip just prior to joining the

gusset seam; this will prevent unnecessary strain at the point.

See Figure 37. This sketch shows another very important principle. As the underarm seams of the garment and sleeve are stitched, the stitching must end directly at the marking and must not extend all the way up to the cut edges. Note that the stitches extend to the large

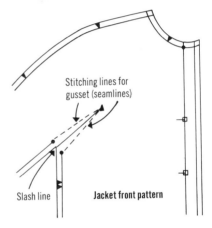

Stitching lines for gusset (seamlines)

Slash line   **Jacket front pattern**

FIGURE 35

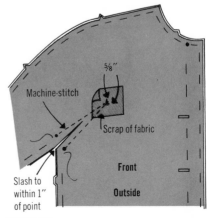

Machine-stitch   ⅝"

Scrap of fabric

Slash to within 1" of point

Front

Outside

FIGURE 36

O's and small o's and are secured with backstitching. This is a very common trouble point; the instruction sheet will read, "Join underarm seam below large O"—the word "below" is very important, and it is easily overlooked in brief, "telegram English" terminology.

See Figure 38. All the remaining sketches show the opening as it would look if the arm were held at shoulder level and the body viewed from the side. Notice that the scrap of fabric turns to the inside and acts as "seam allowance" at the point, which otherwise would have no seam allowance at all. Note the little opening at the end of the two underarm seams; these openings will act as "clips" as the gusset is set in, and without them, setting in a gusset would be all but impossible.

See Figure 39. The sketch shows the gusset basted in place. The little scrap of fabric, which is a great aid in sewing,

covers up some important points of construction, and so it is pictured on the left side of the sketch only, to illustrate how it would look in place, and does not appear on the right side in order that the construction can be shown more clearly; do understand that a scrap of fabric is needed at each slashed point.

This drawing illustrates the principle of seamlines matching, rather than the usual cut-edges-even construction. Study the sketch carefully (particularly the right half) and see that the gusset edge, with its ⅝-inch seam allowance, extends beyond the slashed edge, with its varying seam allowance. Pull the scrap of fabric to the inside and use it like seam allowance. With right sides together and all markings matching, pin the gusset to the slashed edges, having seamlines matching (not cut edges even). Pin and baste very securely, especially at all corners. Stitch just inside the reinforcing lines with the garment seam uppermost,

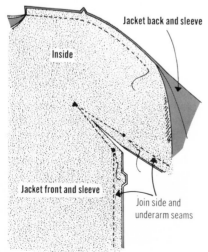

Jacket back and sleeve

Inside

Jacket front and sleeve

Join side and underarm seams

FIGURE 37

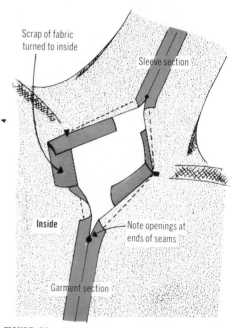

Scrap of fabric turned to inside

Sleeve section

Inside

Note openings at ends of seams

Garment section

FIGURE 38

leaving the needle of the machine down to pivot around each corner; all edges can be done in one continuous stitching if the unit is pivoted around the needle.

See Figure 40. Trim the edges of the scrap of fabric down to about ¼ inch. Press the seam toward the garment, as shown. The gusset is finished and will wear well for most special-occasion clothing. However, even though the slashed points are reinforced and very secure, the points are necessarily weak. To strengthen those points on utilitarian garments, the gusset seam can be top-stitched ¹⁄₁₆ inch from the seamline. This will strengthen the points considerably, but the stitching line will make the seam more prominent and therefore less attractive.

THE HALF GUSSET

Figure 41 shows the basting and stitching of the half gusset and compares with

Figure 39. The point is constructed in the same manner, but the half-gusset piece is set in before the side seams are basted or stitched. When the two halves have been inserted, the entire underarm of the garment, gusset, and sleeve is sewn in one easy operation.

COMBINATION GUSSETS

Figure 42 pictures a gusset combined with a portion of the garment; a gusset combined with a portion of the sleeve is constructed in the same manner. This sketch compares with Figure 39; note how much easier and simpler this construction is, and yet the only difference is that it has one less corner than the traditional diamond-shaped gusset.

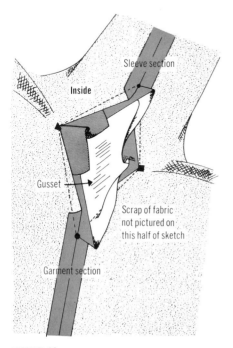

FIGURE 39

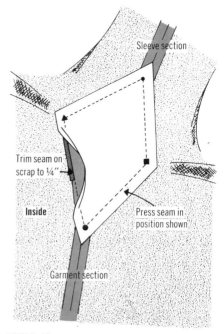

FIGURE 40

THE TYPICAL
TAILORED
COLLAR

The collar of a suit or coat is constructed very differently from a similar collar on a blouse or dress; it is so different that this is probably the most confusing construction detail encountered in tailoring. Actually, all the steps in the process are simple, but each one must be done with great care and accuracy before proceeding to the next. The collar is attached in a different manner, which makes it possible to press the neck seams open,

thus distributing the great bulk of that seam over a larger area. The directions on the instruction sheet will be essentially like these, but they will be necessarily brief.

TESTS FOR FABRIC WEIGHT

The section entitled Principles of Shaping the Tailored Garment on page 234 includes an explanation of the differences between the upper-collar and under-collar patterns for the typical two-piece collar. The upper-collar pattern is wider than the under-collar pattern so that the upper collar can take the outside curve (over the under collar) as the garment is worn. The average difference in width between the two collars is about ¼ inch (usually varies from a scant ¼ inch to an ample ¼ inch); the patternmaker es-

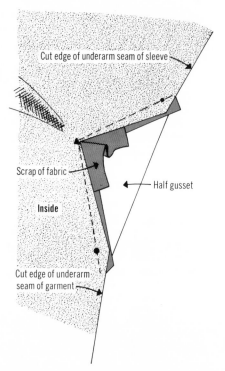

FIGURE 41 Basic construction of the half gusset

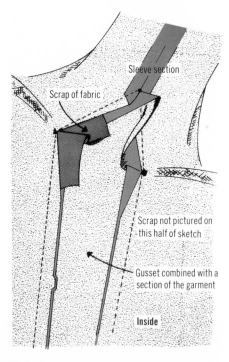

FIGURE 42 Basic construction of the combination gusset

timates how much extra width is required for the average weight of fabric that most customers will use. If the customer uses fabric in a lighter or heavier weight than average, the width difference will not be correct for her particular fabric. The issue of fabric weight can be tested prior to construction, and the collars can be corrected at this time. See Figure 43. The sketches show the upper-collar piece placed over the under collar (which has been shaped and pad-stitched), pinned with neck edges even, and with the collars held in wearing position. Figure 43a shows the collars in the proper width, and so this fabric is average in weight. The upper collar should be about ⅛ inch wider than the under collar (when held in wearing position) because after the collar seam is joined and turned to the inside, the seam will be rolled slightly back from the edge.

Figure 43b pictures a collar cut in fabric that is heavier than average in weight. Note that the upper collar is not wide enough to take the outside curve over the under collar, thus allowing the under-collar edge to extend. Correct this problem by trimming off the excess width on the under collar so that the trimmed edge will be ¼ inch narrower than the upper collar. To do this, pin the edges together carefully and then trim the under collar even with the upper collar; then, as a last step, trim an additional ¼ inch from the edge of the under collar.

Figure 43c pictures a collar cut in fabric that is lighter than average in weight. Note that the upper collar extends more than ⅛ inch beyond the under collar. Correct this problem by trimming off the excess width from the upper collar so that the trimmed edge will extend only ⅛ inch beyond the under collar. Pin the edge carefully before trimming.

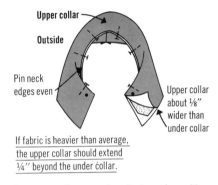

If fabric is heavier than average, the upper collar should extend ¼″ beyond the under collar.

(a) Place upper collar over under collar in wearing position

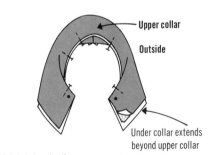

(b) If fabric is heavier than average

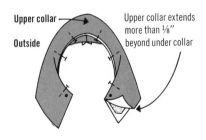

(c) If fabric is lighter than average

FIGURE 43 Test collar for fabric weight

PROBLEMS OF COLLAR CONSTRUCTION

See Figure 44. The finished collar must fit into the neck edge of the garment, forming a corner that will look smooth and "easy." Note that the curving neckline edge and the extension beyond the collar are on the same level, thereby creating one continuous line.

The most common flaw of construction results in a corner that looks tight and puckered, as shown in the center sketch. This problem is especially troublesome because a very tiny mistake in

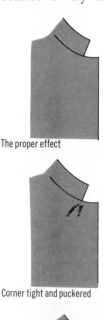

The proper effect

Corner tight and puckered

Extension seam not stitched at proper level

FIGURE 44

stitching can produce a very prominent puckered effect. The following directions are very detailed because of the intricacy involved at this corner; pay careful attention to the enlarged views in Figures 50 and 51 to eliminate this problem entirely.

Another common flaw is shown in the lower sketch in Figure 44. If the curved neck edge and the extension do not appear as a continuous line, the effect is very unattractive. The enlarged view in Figure 51 shows the stitching of the extension edge and illustrates that it must be on a level with the stitching of the neck seam.

The tailored collar construction is different and more difficult because the under collar will be joined to the neck edge of the garment, while the upper collar will be joined to the facing; then the upper collar and facing are joined to the under collar and garment. One problem that is often encountered results from the brevity of pattern directions; the necessarily brief directions for this last step (joining the upper collar and facing to the under collar and garment) sometimes give the impression that this step is done in one operation. This step must be done in three separate operations: the collar portion in one operation, and then the two facing portions in two separate operations.

PATTERN DIFFERENCES

The most typical tailored garment is one with a two-piece collar and a separate front facing. The garment may or may not have a back facing; the greater percentage of garments will not have a back facing, and the lining will finish off the back neck area. However, the reader will encounter many garments that are not as typical: the garment with a one-piece collar, the garment with a front facing cut in one with the garment front, and the garment with a back facing. It is important to remember that general principles, explained in connection with the typical garment, can be applied to any design.

The following directions are given in great detail for the typical garment. At crucial points in construction, sketches are included to illustrate how the same construction can be applied to garments of a slightly different cut. Garments that are not typical (combined-section garments) are somewhat more difficult to handle simply because work cannot be done on small units; but regardless of the shape of the pattern pieces, the construction principles remain the same.

STEPS
OF CONSTRUCTION
OF THE TAILORED
COLLAR

See Figure 45. The neck edges of the garment and the facing should be reinforced with machine stitches and then clipped. This step is not usually included in the instruction sheet, but it is an aid to easier construction. The stitches reinforce the neck edge for clipping, and the clips release the seam allowance so that it can "give" and shape to the lines of the collar.

Machine-stitch ½ inch from the neck edge of the garment between the tailor's tacks which mark the position for the end of the collar; use about 15 to 18 stitches per inch and see that the row of stitches is exactly ½ inch from the raw edge, as shown in Figure 45a. Clip to the stitching line. Reinforce and clip the neck edges of the facing sections in the same manner. The separate facing is shown in Figure 45b. If the garment has a back facing, the shoulder edges of the facing should be joined before reinforcing and clipping the neck edge, as shown in Figure 45c.

See Figure 46 for the basic method of joining collar sections to corresponding garment and facing sections for the typical tailored collar. Figures 47 and 48 show the same step applied to less typical garments.

See Figure 46a. Baste the under collar to the garment, right sides together and cut edges even, with center backs, notches, shoulder markings, and large O's matching. This seam is so thick that very secure basting stitches are required to hold the under collar in place accurately. Notice how the clips at the neck

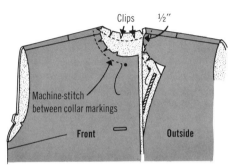
(a) Machine-stitch neck edge of garment

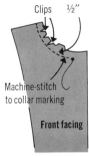
(b) If there is no back facing

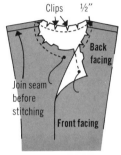
(c) If there is a back facing

FIGURE 45 Reinforce and clip neck edges

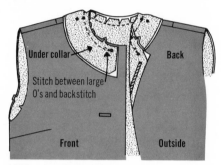

(a) Join under collar to garment

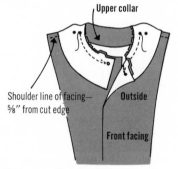

(b) Join upper collar to front facing

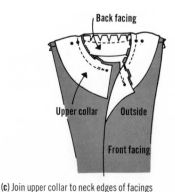

(c) Join upper collar to neck edges of facings

FIGURE 46 Typical two-piece tailored collar

edge of the garment spread out to take the shape of the under collar.

Baste the upper collar to the facing sections in the same manner. If there is no back facing, see Figure 46b. Notches, large ○'s, and shoulder lines must match; the shoulder marking on the collar should match the seamline at the shoulder edge of the facing. If there is a back facing, see Figure 46c. Baste the upper collar to the entire neck edge, with notches, large ○'s, and shoulder lines matching.

Check work very carefully before stitching. The measurements from the large ○ to the front edge at the four corners involved should be equal. If these measurements vary as much as ⅛ inch, correct them at this time. They will eventually become the important lapel extensions, and since they will be so near to one another as the garment is worn, any slight variation will be noticeable.

Stitch these seams as basted, taking the following precaution: the machine stitches must end at the large ○ and must be secure; backstitch exactly to the large ○ and then proceed around the neck edge to the other large ○ and backstitch.

Figure 47 shows this same step of construction on a garment with a two-piece collar and a self-facing instead of the typical separate facing. The construction is done in the same manner, and the difference is in the position in which work must be held. Figure 47a shows the under collar joined to the neck edge of the garment. Note that neck edges are reinforced and clipped before work is begun. Figure 47b shows the position in which work must be held to join the upper collar to the neck edge of the self-facing. Note that the under collar has been pulled up so that it stands up at the neck edge. Fold the self-facing to the outside (right sides together) along the fold line. In this position, join the upper collar to the neck edge of the facing, with right sides together and notches and pattern markings matching.

Figure 48 shows the same step of construction on a garment with a one-piece collar and self-facings. The construction is done in the same manner, and the difference is in the position in which work is held. Figure 48a shows one collar edge (on the half of the collar that has been interfaced) joined to the neck edge of the garment. Note that neck edges are reinforced and clipped before work is begun. Figure 48b shows the position in which work must be held to join the remaining edge of the collar to the neck edge of the self-facing. Note that the collar has been folded in half

(with right sides together) so that it stands up at the neck edge. Fold the self-facing to the outside (right sides together) along the fold line. In this position, join the remaining edge of the collar to the neck edge of the self-facings, with right sides together and notches and pattern markings matching.

The neck seams are the bulkiest seams in the garment; all unnecessary bulk must be removed from them. After trimming the interfacing and the bulk from cross seams, trim the neck

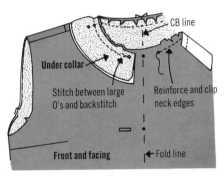

(a) Join under collar to garment

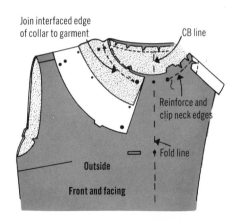

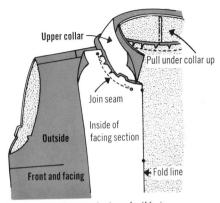

(b) Join upper collar to neck edges of self-facings

FIGURE 47 Two-piece collar on garment with self-facing

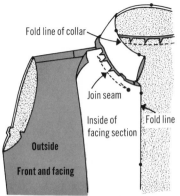

FIGURE 48 One-piece collar on garment with self-facing

seam of the under collar and garment to about ⅜ inch. Trim the seam of the upper collar and facings to about ½ inch; these two seams, which will eventually lie on each other, are thus staggered to reduce bulk.

These seams must be pressed open, and because they are so curved, this is difficult to do. It is wise to baste them open first. See that they lie flat; if they do not, clip wherever necessary. See Figure 49. Because the garment and under collar are interfaced, that seam can be whipped in place with stitches catching into the interfacing only; this will ensure a seam that will always remain flat.

Press the seams very well, for this is the last opportunity to do so. Use a tailor's cushion that is the correct shape for a particular segment of the seam and

press small segments of the seam at one time.

See Figure 50. Pin the upper collar and facings over the under collar and garment, with right sides together and cut edges even, matching notches, large O's, and center lines. All these raw edges must now be basted and stitched, but do this step in three operations—the collar stitching first and then the two front and extension edges.

Before stitching the collar seam, examine the enlarged view very carefully. The collar should be stitched on the seamline, and the stitches should end at the large O, but if they are placed just

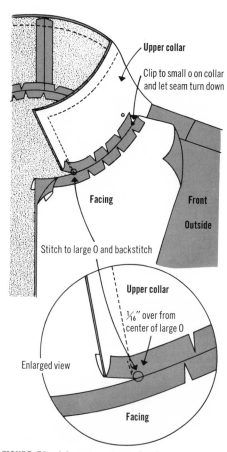

Upper collar

Clip to small o on collar and let seam turn down

Facing

Front

Outside

Stitch to large O and backstitch

Upper collar

1/16" over from center of large O

Enlarged view

Facing

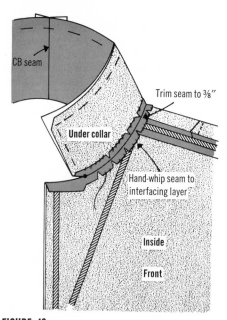

CB seam

Trim seam to ⅜"

Under collar

Hand-whip seam to interfacing layer

Inside

Front

FIGURE 49

FIGURE 50 Join outer edges of collar

⅟₁₆ inch outside the large ○, as shown (note that the stitching line is not centered in the large ○), the corner will turn very much better. Notice that the neckline seams are pressed up and are caught in with the stitching of the collar seams. Stitch the entire collar seam, backstitching at the large ○'s, as shown. Clip the neck edge of the upper collar to the seamline at the shoulder edge, as shown.

See Figure 51. Flip up the seam of the extension edge in preparation for stitching the front and extension edges. Before stitching, examine the enlarged view very carefully. The stitching, as it approaches the large ○, must be on a level with the stitching of the neck seam, but should not extend all the way to the end of the stitching of the neck edge. Stitch the front edge, turn the corner and stop stitching, and backstitch about ⅟₁₆ inch from the end of the neckline stitching (note that the stitches do not extend to the center of the large ○). This will allow the corner to turn easily and lie flat.

Turn the collar and facing to the inside to see whether the corner of the collar and lapel will turn into a flat, square corner. If it puckers and appears tight, one of the stitchings (the collar or the front and lapel) went a stitch or so too far; a stitch or so must be removed. If the lapel does not make a smooth, even line with the collar seam, the stitching of the lapel was not on a level with the stitching line of the neck seam and must be ripped and moved to the proper seamline.

NOTE The seams on all stitched edges will become encased seams and must be trimmed before the collar and facings are turned to the inside. Special treatment is required on the front edge and is described below. The construction of the collar will be continued later.

Figure 52 shows this same intricate step of construction applied to a one-piece collar and a garment with a self-facing. The principles of construction are almost identical. Note that the collar of the garment shown in Figure 52a is identical to that of the typical garment shown in Figure 50, with the one exception that there is no seam at the outer edge. Note that the collar of the garment shown in Figure 52b is identical to

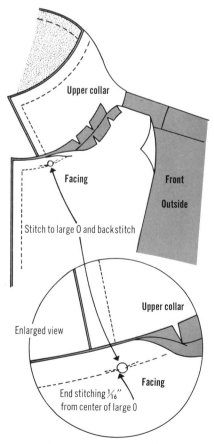

FIGURE 51 Join front and extension edge

that of the typical garment shown in Figure 51, with the one exception that there is no seam at the front edge. Follow all directions included with the typi-

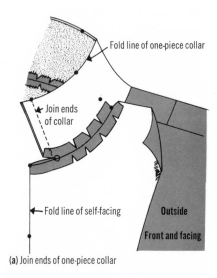

(a) Join ends of one-piece collar

Fold line of one-piece collar

Join ends of collar

Fold line of self-facing

Outside

Front and facing

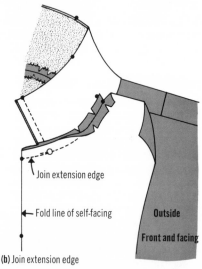

(b) Join extension edge

Join extension edge

Fold line of self-facing

Outside

Front and facing

FIGURE 52 General principles applied to one-piece collar and self-facing

cal collar, making only these slight changes.

TREATMENT OF FRONT ENCASED SEAM FOR GARMENTS WITH A SEPARATE FACING

The front edge is one of the most prominent lines on the garment, and it is especially important that the front seam be invisible as the garment is worn. The seam will be rolled slightly to the inside before it is pressed, but often after much wear and many dry cleanings, this seam has a tendency to creep out to the edge, creating an unattractive line. The suggestion illustrated in Figure 53 will prevent the seam from slipping *to the outside*. The words "to the outside" are very important because this suggestion can be used only on a seam (that will be rolled to the inside) to prevent it from slipping *to the outside*. The typical garment pictured in Figure 54 illustrates that the front edge rolls to the inside from the roll line of the lapel to the lower edge. From that level upward, the seam is rolled to the outside. Therefore, the construction pictured in Figure 53 is done on the front edge only, from the lapel level downward.

All encased seams must be trimmed in a staggered manner, and ordinarily it does not make a great deal of difference which edge is trimmed to the wider width, although a good general rule is to have the wider seam next to the side that will be uppermost as the garment is worn. The front edge of a tailored garment is an exception to that general rule. The interfacing should be trimmed to ⅛ inch, as usual. Then the seam edge of the garment should be trimmed to ¼ inch from the stitching line, and the seam edge of the facing should be trimmed to

½ inch from the seamline, as shown in Figure 53a.

See Figure 53b. Turn the seam toward the garment (covering the twill tape) and baste it in place from the lapel level down to the hemline. Do not pull the seam tightly against the stitching line, but allow it to fold over easily and naturally; an "easy" roll will force the seam to lie slightly back from the edge (the effect pictured in Figure 54). The seam should roll $\frac{1}{16}$ inch from the edge in lightweight fabrics to as much as $\frac{1}{8}$ inch from the edge in very heavy fabrics. Baste a small section of the seam and then turn the facing to the inside to study the effect; if the seam falls too far away from the edge, it must be held more snugly against the stitching line, etc.

See Figure 53c. Whip the seam in place, being very careful that the stitches do not pass through to the garment fabric. The stitches can be caught into the interfacing or into the twill tape. End the stitches about 2 inches from the hemline, as shown. The stitches should begin at the roll line if there is a lapel (or at the neck edge if there is no lapel) and should end about 2 inches above the hemline, as shown.

NOTE All seam edges on the outer edge of the collar and lapel are encased seams and should be trimmed in a staggered manner.

See Figure 54. Turn the facing and the collar to the inside and baste the finished edges in preparation for pressing. The seams must be rolled slightly in one direction or another so that they will be invisible as the garment is worn. Note that the seam at the front edge must be rolled to the inside (the facing side) from the lapel line downward but that the seam in the collar and lapel area must be rolled slightly to the outside

(the garment side). The seam should be rolled away from the edge just enough to hide it from view; avoid rolling it so far to one side that it shows an unattractive line on the side that will not be as readily visible.

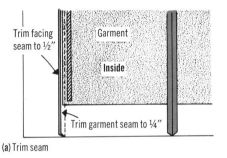

(a) Trim seam

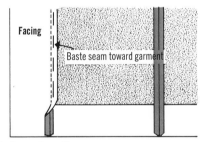

(b) Baste seam in position

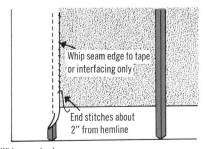

(c) Whip seam in place

FIGURE 53 Treatment of front encased seam

SECURING
THE ROLL LINE
OF THE COLLAR
AND LAPELS

Refer to Figure 18 and the accompanying directions on page 130. The upper-collar and lapel area must be smoothed into place over the under collar, as shown in that sketch. Be sure to hold the garment in wearing position while pinning along the roll line.

See Figure 55. The sketch shows the garment in a position that reveals construction details, but this step should be done with the garment in wearing position. Fold the facing and upper collar back along the roll line, as shown, and secure the upper layer to the under layer along the roll line with invisible hand stitches that catch into the underside of the collar and facing fabric; this is a further aid to molding and shaping the collar. In certain lightweight fabrics, especially those in plain, light colors, this step must be eliminated because the stitches are noticeable as the garment is worn.

This technique can be used to secure the roll line of cuffs or of sleeve facings that roll back to give a cuff effect.

FINISHING
COLLAR
AND SHOULDER
EDGES

NOTE If the novelty Hong Kong method of finishing facings and lining is to be used, see page 324 at this time. Facings and neck edges will be handled in a manner different from the traditional method given below.

See Figure 56a. The seam of the collar and facing should lay into place directly over the seam of the under collar

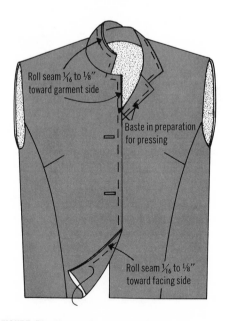

Roll seam 1/16 to 1/8"
toward garment side

Baste in preparation
for pressing

Roll seam 1/16 to 1/8"
toward facing side

FIGURE 54 Preparation for pressing

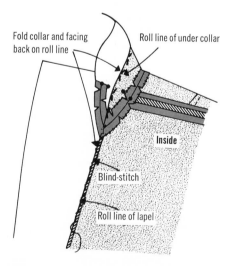

Fold collar and facing
back on roll line

Roll line of under collar

Inside

Blind-stitch

Roll line of lapel

FIGURE 55 To secure roll line of collar and lapel

and garment, with shoulder lines matching. If they miss slightly (this is possible if the width of the upper collar was not exactly correct for the weight of fabric used), it is better to allow them to miss than to force them to match and thereby destroy the smooth lines of the collar. At-

tach the lower half of the collar and facing seam to the lower half of the corresponding seam. By hand sewing the lower edge of the collar seam to the corresponding seam with stitches close to the seamline, these stitches can be made to serve a double purpose; they will mold the two seams together and at the same time will aid in keeping the collar-and-facing seam in a pressed-open position.

NOTE Figure 56 shows a garment without a back facing. If there is a back facing, the entire neck seam (both front and back) is handled in the same manner. Be sure shoulder positions match.

See Figure 56b. If there is no back facing, hand-sew the raw edge of the collar into position over the back neck seam, with stitches about $\frac{1}{16}$ inch below the seamline. The back lining will hide the raw edge and the stitches eventually.

If there is no back facing, pin the raw shoulder edge of the front facing to the garment, matching shoulder seamlines, as shown in Figure 56b. Hand-sew the shoulder edge in place with stitches about $\frac{1}{16}$ inch back of the shoulder seamline. The shoulder edge of the lining will hide these stitches eventually.

Baste the inner edge of facings in place with stitches through the interfacing layer only. If there is a lapel, the garment should be held in wearing position with the lapel area folded to the outside as the inner edge of the facing is pinned into position. These edges will eventually be catch-stitched to the interfacing, but it is well to wait until the hem is completed to do this hand finishing.

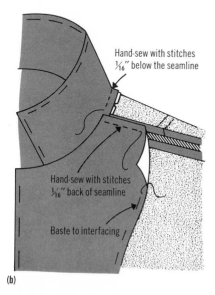

(a)

(b)

FIGURE 56 To finish neck and shoulder edges

The set of the sleeve plays an important role in the ultimate success of the garment. Perhaps no other step in construction can add so much to, or detract so much from, the final professional appearance of the costume. The directions on the instruction sheet must necessarily be brief, and perhaps this is why setting in sleeves is such a great problem to so many women who sew. Actually it is not difficult if several very simple little tricks are employed. The following directions are written in great detail and should be followed step by step as the construction proceeds.

DIFFERENCES IN SLEEVE PATTERNS

Figure 57 shows the three most commonly used sleeve patterns. The two-piece sleeve will appear quite frequently in patterns for tailored garments because its more intricate cut results in a better-fitting sleeve. The curving lines of the sleeve and the fact that there is ease on one edge of the upper sleeve, as shown, are responsible for the shaping usually created by the elbow dart. Note that neither seam is at the underarm position; the underarm position falls within the under sleeve and is marked with small o's, as shown.

The familiar one-piece sleeve may be either fitted or boxy. The boxy sleeve will not have an elbow dart, and the fitted sleeve may have a dart, or the back edge may have ease to allow for shaping at the elbow.

The biceps line of the sleeve is a line at the base of the armhole curve, as seen most clearly in the one-piece sleeve. The biceps line is in an identical position in the two-piece sleeve. It is a line at right angles to the straight-of-material line,

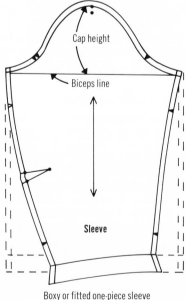

Cap height

Underarm position

Biceps line

Biceps line

Ease

Upper sleeve

Under sleeve

Two-piece sleeve

Cap height

Biceps line

Sleeve

Boxy or fitted one-piece sleeve

FIGURE 57

beginning at the base of the armhole curve in the under sleeve and extending into the upper sleeve at the same level, as shown. The area above the biceps line is the sleeve cap, and the measurement from the biceps line to the seamline at the shoulder indicates the cap height. The illustrations show a regulation sleeve which has the greatest cap height; this sleeve is used most often because it gives maximum wearing comfort. A sleeve which has a shorter cap height with a somewhat flatter curve in the cap is used for dropped-shoulder effects.

The greater the cap height, the more difficult construction is because the sleeve with greater height has more ease that must be worked into the armhole. The regulation sleeve pictured has about 2 inches of ease between the notches, whereas the sleeve for a dropped shoulder line with a shorter cap height may have as little as 1 inch of ease.

Many persons are confused by the less familiar two-piece sleeve and have difficulty setting it in. It is not surprising that many women who have made simple, basic garments in the past, with the usual underarm seam in the sleeve that matches the usual underarm seam in the garment, have an unconscious habit of matching seams. However, more intricately cut designs, and particularly designs with the two-piece sleeve, frequently have seams that do not match; in these designs there are matching points that may not be seamlines. Figure 58 explains why seams do not necessarily match each other when the two-piece sleeve is used. Some seams are purely functional, while others are purely decorative or serve both a decorative and a functional purpose. The seams of a two-piece sleeve are functional seams to aid in fitting the sleeve and are placed in a position to hide them from view as much as possible. By contrast, a seam that

serves a decorative purpose is placed in a prominent position to give the desired effect. Because of these conflicting reasons for placement, a functional seam need not match a decorative seam. The worker is often confused by a decorative seam, as shown in the lower curve of Figure 58, that is very close to the functional seam of the two-piece sleeve, and she tends to think that if the seams are in almost the same position, they should match. It is important to remember that a decorative seam may match the functional seam but that the two may miss each other by as little as ¼ inch or as much as several inches (as in the upper curved line in Figure 58).

In all sleeves, notches control the basic position. The underarm positions are another control, but the underarm position may not be a seam. The shoulder position is yet another control, but

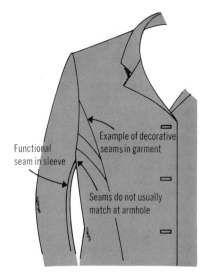

Functional
seam in sleeve

Example of decorative
seams in garment

Seams do not usually
match at armhole

FIGURE 58

the shoulder position on the garment may not be a seam.

NOTE In the following directions, the illustrations will picture a garment with the usual shoulder and underarm seams, used with a two-piece sleeve. The principles of setting in the sleeve are exactly the same regardless of the lines of the garment. To repeat: Shoulder positions, underarm positions, and notches should be matched, and seams may or may not match.

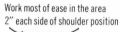

Work most of ease in the area 2″ each side of shoulder position

Gather ⅛″ each side of seamline

(a) Draw up ease

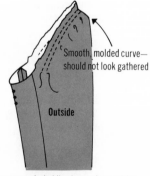

Smooth, molded curve— should not look gathered

Outside

(b) Test for appearance by holding in wearing position

FIGURE 59

BASIC PRINCIPLES OF SETTING IN THE SLEEVE

See Figure 59a. Put two rows of machine gathering stitches in the cap of the sleeve between the notches; place the rows of stitches ⅛ inch on each side of the seamline. Pull up the bobbin threads and attempt to estimate the proper amount of ease; it will never exceed 2 inches (as a total amount) between the notches. Work most of the ease in the upper portion of the sleeve cap (in the 2 inches on either side of the shoulder marking).

Test the effect by holding your fingers under the sleeve cap (to simulate a shoulder), as shown in Figure 59b, and see that the sleeve looks smooth and molded. It should not look gathered, and if it does, it has been drawn up too much. Be sure that it is not drawn up too tightly because if it is, the remaining steps of construction will be more difficult. Do not fasten threads, for this is a temporary estimate; the exact amount of ease will be determined when the sleeve is pinned in the armhole of the garment. It is helpful if this guess is quite accurate, and with experience it is possible to judge the right amount of ease with great accuracy. When making this estimate, keep in mind that too much ease will make construction more difficult than too little ease; when the sleeve is set in, it is simpler to draw the bobbin threads up more than to have to release them.

NOTE Some directions suggest drawing up the ease and then removing the sleeve to shrink out fullness in the sleeve cap. This should be avoided if possible because of the great danger of creating a series of flat surfaces rather than the desired rounded and molded line. Careful attention to the directions accompanying Figure 60b will result in a sleeve that will not require shrinking.

See Figure 60a. Work with the garment turned wrong side out. With right sides together and cut edges even, locate the sleeve in the armhole at four matching points: the underarm position, the two notch positions, and the shoulder position. First pin the area between and below the notches. The sleeve may be larger than the garment in that area because there is often about ¼ inch of ease between each notch position and the underarm position of the sleeve; it is so slight and so easy to work in that the instruction sheet directions seldom mention it, and the worker may well be unaware of it.

See Figure 60b. This sketch pictures a technique that makes setting in sleeves very much easier. The technique has to do with the way the work is held. Hold the garment and the sleeve in such a position that the sleeve takes the outside curve over your fingers; note that the seam is turned toward the garment for this step. Held in this position, the ease works in so magically that it almost seems to disappear. Adjust the ease, pulling up or releasing the gathering threads as required, being very careful not to draw the sleeve up too tightly. Pin in place, cut edges even. Baste with small stitches that are firm but not so tight that they draw up the garment. Test the seam for tightness by putting your hands into the armhole and gently pulling the sleeve against your hands. If you are aware of stitches "cutting in," the basting stitches are too tight, and the thread should be clipped at several points to release it.

Turn the garment right side out and examine the sleeve. Be sure the garment has not been drawn up and that it does not pucker at the seamline. The upper edge of the sleeve should not look gathered; the eased-in fullness should not be obvious. Fit the garment to test the hang of the sleeve and the width of the shoulder line. Make necessary adjustments and refit.

Machine-stitch the seam with the sleeve side uppermost for better handling of the eased edge. Stitch over the bast-

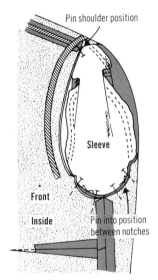

(a) Match corresponding positions

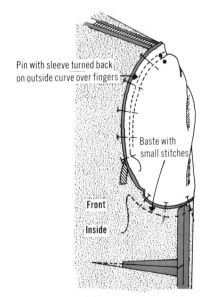

(b) Baste sleeve in armhole

FIGURE 60

ings very slowly and carefully; at this time, careless stitching can create tiny tucks in the sleeve cap. Remove bastings and gathering threads.

See Figure 61. Most structural seams of the garment are not trimmed down in width, but the armhole seam is an exception. It should be trimmed down to a $\frac{3}{8}$-inch width so that the sleeve can fall naturally over the shoulder (a $\frac{5}{8}$-inch seam allowance would force the sleeve to stand out that far beyond the armhole seam and would make shoulders look too wide). The ripples formed in the cap of the sleeve as the seam is turned toward the sleeve make the sleeve cap bulky; to prevent this, notch out the ripples until the seam lies flat and smooth, as shown in the sketch. The seam must be clipped almost to the stitching in the underarm area, as shown; clip about every $\frac{1}{2}$ inch.

The sleeve seam turns toward the sleeve. Avoid pressing the seam if it lies in that direction without pressing. If the seam must be pressed, press just the seamline, allowing the iron to extend only about $\frac{1}{8}$ inch over the seamline into the sleeve; this will avoid a series of flat surfaces the iron would otherwise create and allows the sleeve to retain a natural roll.

NOTE Refer to the instruction sheet for special pressing directions. The sleeve seam in a garment with a dropped armhole is often pressed open.

SETTING IN SHOULDER PADS

Review Shoulder Pads on page 16. The sketches in this section show both round and square pads with one squared-off corner like the typical coat pad. The squared half of the pad must be placed in the front section of the garment, as shown in the sketches. If the pad is triangular in shape, the two halves are identical, and it will make no difference which edge is located in the front.

In general, the square pad is used if there is an armhole seam and a regulation sleeve. However, if the armhole seam is a dropped line (deliberately planned to drop below the shoulder line), the round pad should be used.

SQUARE PADS FOR REGULATION ARMHOLES

See Figure 62. Because the pad is thick and probably stiff as well, it is espe-

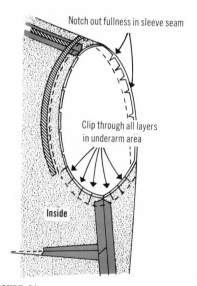

Notch out fullness in sleeve seam

Clip through all layers in underarm area

Inside

FIGURE 61

cially important to hold the garment in wearing position as the pad is pinned into place; that position is shown in Figures 62b and c.

Figure 62a is included as an aid to understanding construction details. The pad may extend almost to the neck edge, in which case stitches at the shoulder edge of the facing must be removed so the pad can be placed under the facing. The center line of the pad, a line from the point at the neck edge to about midway between the two ends at the outer edge, should be located at the shoulder line of the garment. Note that the square portion of the pad is placed in the front of the garment. The pad extends ⅜ inch beyond the stitching line into the sleeve. This will give the natural shoulder line that is favored for most fashions. However, the pad can extend any distance into the sleeve to achieve the desired effect; for example, in the middle 1940s, pads extended an inch into the sleeve to give the exaggerated wide-shouldered effect that was fashionable at the time.

NOTE The pad may extend beyond the neck seam in some garments with wide necklines; if it does, the tip or point of the pad must be trimmed off.

See Figure 62b. Working from the outside, locate the center line of the pad over the shoulder line, with the pad extending the desired distance into the sleeve, and place the first pin at the shoulder end of the pad; do not catch through the entire pad thickness with the pin, but simply catch through to the top layer. Again checking to be sure the center line is located on the shoulder line, place the second pin at the neck edge of the pad.

The broken lines indicate the position of the pad and illustrate that the armhole edge of the pad does not follow

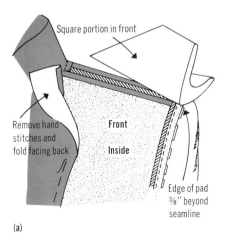

Square portion in front

Remove hand stitches and fold facing back

Front

Inside

Edge of pad ⅜" beyond seamline

(a)

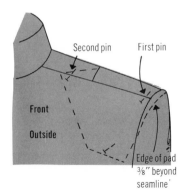

Second pin   First pin

Front

Outside

Edge of pad ⅜" beyond seamline

(b)

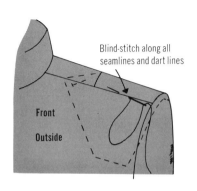

Blind-stitch along all seamlines and dart lines

Front

Outside

(c)

FIGURE 62 To set in square pads (for regulation armholes)

along the armhole seam in the garment; the edge of the pad will cross the armhole seam in both front and back, as shown. Holding the garment in wearing position, smooth it over the pad and place a pin at each remaining corner, as shown.

Fit the garment to test the effect. See that the pad extends the desired amount into the sleeve; a person with narrow shoulders may want to broaden her shoulder line by allowing the pad to extend a greater distance into the sleeve. See that the garment fits smoothly over the pad; sometimes the corner pins are not in perfect position, causing a little ripple or pucker in the garment. Make all necessary corrections.

See Figure 62c. Working from the outside, blind-stitch the pad in place with stitches about ½ inch long; do not pull stitches tightly enough to make a prominent stitch indentation. Blind-stitch through any seam or dart line that crossed the pad (the shoulder seam, a portion of the armhole seam, and possibly a portion of the back shoulder dart). Stitches need not pass through the entire pad thickness; catch them through the garment to the top layer of the pad.

Reposition the shoulder edge of the facing over the pad and hand-sew the shoulder edge to the inside of the pad.

ROUND PADS FOR MOLDED SHOULDER LINES

See Figure 63. Because the pad is thick and probably somewhat stiff as well, it is especially important to hold the garment in wearing position as the pad is pinned in place; that position is shown in Figures 63b and c.

Figure 63a is included as an aid to understanding construction details. The pad may extend almost to the neck edge, in which case stitches at the shoulder edge of the facing must be removed so the pad can be placed under the facing. The center line of the pad, a line from the point at the neck edge to about midway between the two ends at the outer edge, should be located at the shoulder line of the garment. Note that the square portion of the pad is placed in the front of the garment. The pad must extend into the sleeve section to give the desired effect; it is well to estimate the position and pin the pad in and then make adjustments on the figure until the proper effect is achieved.

NOTE The pad may extend beyond the neck seam in some garments with wide necklines; if it does, the tip or point of the pad must be trimmed off.

See Figure 63b. Working from the outside, locate the center line of the pad over the shoulder line, with the pad extending the desired distance into the sleeve portion of the garment, and place the first pin at the shoulder end of the pad; do not catch through the entire pad thickness with the pin, but simply catch through the top layer. Again checking to be sure the center line is located on the shoulder line, place the second pin at the neck edge of the pad.

Fit the garment to test the effect. See that the pad position results in the shoulder effect desired; a person with narrow shoulders may want to broaden her shoulder line by allowing the pad to extend a greater distance into the sleeve section. Make all necessary corrections.

See Figure 63c. Working from the outside, blind-stitch the pad in place with stitches about ½ inch long; do not pull stitches tightly enough to make a prominent stitch indentation. Blind-stitch through any seam or dart line that crosses the pad (the shoulder seam and a portion of the back shoulder dart). Stitches need not pass through the entire pad thickness; catch them through the garment to the top layer of the pad.

Reposition the shoulder edge of the facing over the pad and hand-sew the shoulder edge to the inside of the pad.

FINISHING THE HEM

GENERAL INFORMATION

Two hem finishes are used in tailored garments. The catch-stitched hem, with edges left raw, is used most frequently because it is appropriate for use with the lining that will be attached to the garment. The attached lining is used in all jackets, boleros, and short coats unless some unusual feature of the design requires a free-hanging lining. This finish is used exclusively for sleeve hems. The alternative method finishes the raw edge with seam binding or the Hong Kong finish in those few garments (usually coats) which will have a free-hanging lining.

hem width Patterns for sleeves and jackets give a hem width that is appropriate for the particular garment. The favored hem width for traditional jackets and sleeves is 1½ inches unless some unusual feature of the design calls for an especially wide hem. The hem allowance given on a full-length coat pattern is approximately (but not exactly) the recommended width. The pattern will probably have a 3-inch hem to allow for some adjustment when the hem is measured. But a 3-inch finished hem is too wide to be attractive; the finished hem width of a coat should be about 2½ inches. Several factors influence the width of the finished hem of any full-length garment; see page 207.

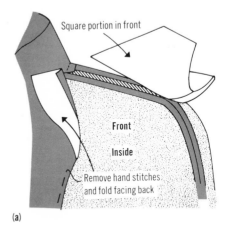

(a)

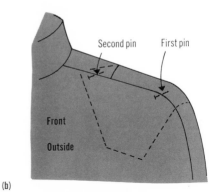

(b)

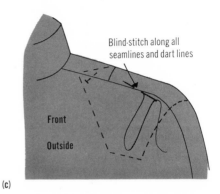

(c)

FIGURE 63 To set in round pads

to establish the desired hemline The hemline of three-quarter- or full-length coats is measured in the same manner as any other full-length garment, with a line measured parallel to the floor. Above-hip-level jackets are not measured parallel to the floor. They should be turned up along the hemline as indicated on the pattern and corrected on the figure to give the desired effect. These jackets are very often cut somewhat longer in the back for a slightly dipped effect that is very attractive on most figures. Likewise, sleeve length is established by eye rather than by measurement.

The full-length coat should be tried on over a skirt or dress that is the length of the typical garment over which it will

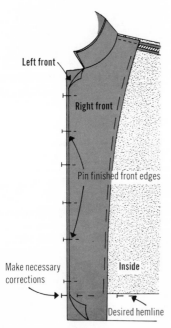

FIGURE 64 A test for accuracy

be worn. The coat must be at least ½ inch longer than other garments and can be as much as 1 inch or more longer. It should be measured and then pinned into place for testing; follow the directions accompanying Figure 49 on page 208.

The jacket should be tried on over its accompanying skirt. The hem should be pinned up along the hemline indicated by the pattern. Experiment with jacket length and make corrections, if necessary, to obtain the line that is most flattering for the individual figure.

In many cases, sleeve length, like jacket length, is a matter of personal preference. Three-quarter-length sleeves (or any sleeve that is not full length) should be a length that is most flattering to the whole figure and to the arms and hands. Experiment with sleeve length to obtain flattering proportions. The full-length sleeve allows for less personal choice. A good test is to bend the elbow and bring the arm to about waist level against the body. In this position, the finished edge of the sleeve should be at the bend of the wrist. With this length as a guide, a slight ⅛-inch variation can be made to please individual tastes.

See Figure 64. Because of the thickness of fabric at the front corner, it is difficult to measure a tailored garment with absolute accuracy. After the desired hemline has been established, the length of corresponding front edges must be tested for accuracy. Pin the right and left front edges together with corners meeting at the neck edge, as shown. Make sure the two edges are the same length by correcting the position of pins at the hemline.

See Figure 65. The illustrations show a problem that may require a slight adjustment in length, especially on jackets. The right front must lap over the left front, hiding the lower edge of the left front. If the two front edges are exactly the same length, the left front may be visible to the eye (at jacket levels, but probably not at full-length-coat levels). The right front of jackets may need to be from a scant ⅛ inch (in lightweight fabrics) to an ample ⅛ inch (in heavier fabrics) longer than the left front. Make this adjustment by lengthening the right front one-half the amount of the desired correction and shortening the left front by a similar amount, gradually tapering back to the desired hemline a few inches from the front edge.

NOTE A similar correction may be required on any edge that laps over another edge—vent closings, sleeve closings, etc.

BASIC CONSTRUCTION DETAILS FOR THE HEM

See Figure 66. Very often the lower edge of the interfacing will not be the proper

length (⅛ to ¼ inch above the established hemline), and adjustments in length are necessary. Figure 66a shows the interfacing the proper length. Figure 66b pictures trimming off the interfacing

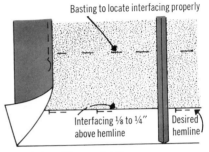

(a) Interfacing cut to proper length

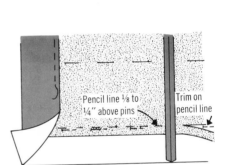

(b) Interfacing cut too long

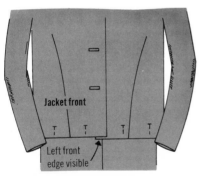

Unattractive effect

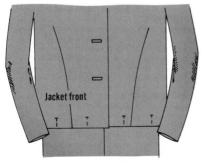

The desired effect

FIGURE 65

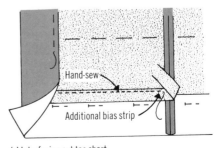

(c) Interfacing cut too short

FIGURE 66

if it is too long. Mark a pencil line ⅛ to ¼ inch above the measured hemline. Then slip the pins from the interfacing layer, being sure to replace them in the proper position in the garment. Now carefully trim the excess interfacing along the pencil line, being very careful not to cut into the garment; as a precaution, have the rounded edge of the scissors next to the garment.

If the interfacing does not reach the hemline, the problem is not serious in most fabrics, providing the amount is not great. However, if the fabric of the garment is so light in weight that a color difference is noticeable where the interfacing ends, an extension strip must be added, as shown in Figure 66c. Cut a bias strip of interfacing fabric in the re-

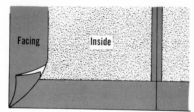

(a) Garment can be lengthened but front corners will be very bulky

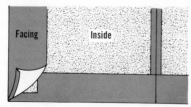

(b) Garment can not be lengthened but front corner will be flat and smooth

FIGURE 67 Methods of handling front corner

quired width. Lap the strip over the lower edge of the interfacing, slip one hand underneath the interfacing layer, and hand-sew the two edges together.

treatment of the front corner See Figure 67. Note that the hem is always turned up before the facing is turned back. The thickness of the hem and facing in the front corner creates a problem of excessive bulk in a very prominent area. Figure 67a shows one method of handling the front corner; it results in four thicknesses of fabric and one thickness of interfacing that will necessarily be very bulky. This method is used in most ready-to-wear simply because these garments are often altered in length before purchase. The one advantage of this method over the alternative method is that the garment can be lengthened at a later date. However, this is a questionable advantage except for children's clothing and strictly utilitarian garments. The tremendous amount of work involved in changing the length of the garment and the lining discourages most persons from undertaking the job. Furthermore, results are unpredictable because of the crease that may not press out, because of dust lodged in the hemline that leaves an unattractive line, and because of possible fading of color in the exposed area. So the advantage of this method is limited.

The method shown in Figure 67b is recommended for high-quality tailoring and for most purposes and under most circumstances; all subsequent sketches will picture this method. Note that bulk has been trimmed away and that the two edges have been trimmed to different widths for a flat, staggered effect. The effect is much more attractive, but the garment can never be lengthened.

Figure 68 shows details for the garment with a separate facing; see Figure

69 for the garment with self-facing. See Figure 68a. Make a clip into the hem allowance 1 inch over from the inner edge of the facing. Put a marking-basting line in the facing layer at the desired hemline as shown. See Figure 68b. Trim away the portion indicated by the shaded area in the sketch (in front of the clip), trimming ¾ inch below the desired hemline of the garment and ½ inch below the hemline of the facing section.

See Figure 68c. Turn up the entire lower edge of the garment along the measured hemline and baste ⅛ inch from the lower edge, as shown; note that the seam at the front edge is pressed open for a short distance. There will still be a great deal of bulk as the pressed-open seam is turned back on itself. Clip the seam open and cut out a little wedge-shaped notch of the seam, as shown. Whip the ¾-inch seam allowance in the garment to the interfacing, as shown.

NOTE Finish the entire hem before proceeding to the next step. Hem finishes are shown in Figure 70. If the novelty Hong Kong method of finishing facing edges and lining is to be used, see page 324 before proceeding to the step shown in Figure 68d.

Figure 69 shows the construction details explained above applied to the garment with a self-facing. The same area shown in Figure 68b should be trimmed away, as shown. Figure 69b shows the same details pictured in Figure 68c, but made somewhat simpler because there is no seam. It is helpful to cut out a little wedge-shaped notch of the seam right at the fold line, as shown. Read the note above before proceeding.

Figure 70 shows the steps in finishing the hem by catch-stitched or bound methods. This step is done just as it is in any hem; if more detailed directions are desired, see the text accompanying

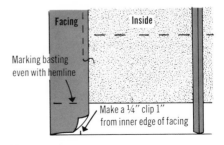

(a)

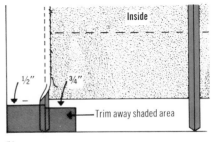

(b)

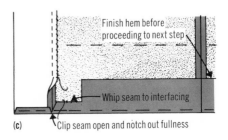

(c)

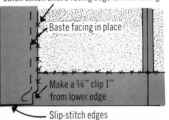

(d)

FIGURE 68 Treatment of front corner for garment with separate facing

Figures 50 and 51 on pages 209 and 210. Before doing hand stitches, read the special note on page 228; the hand hemming stitches may need to pass through the interfacing layer to the underside of the garment fabric, as explained in that note.

FINISHING FACING EDGES

Return to Figure 68d. Turn the facing to the inside over the hem. Make a ¼-inch clip into the inner edge of the facing about 1 inch from the lower edge, as shown. Baste all edges of the facing in place, turning under ¼ inch below the

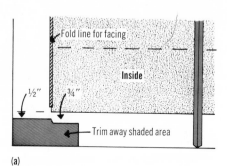

(a)

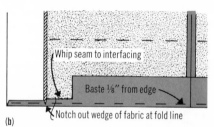

(b)

FIGURE 69 Treatment of front corner (or vent opening) for garment with self-facing

clip, as shown; this provides a finished edge for that portion of the facing that will be exposed beneath the lining. Slip-stitch (a wiggle-in-and-out stitch) the

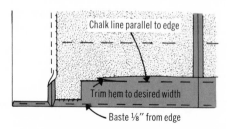

(a) Trim to desired width

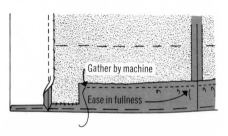

(b) For flared garments only

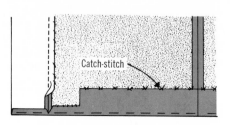

(c) The catchstitch hem

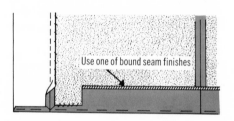

(d) The Hong Kong finish

FIGURE 70 Hem finishes

lower edge of the facing in place, extending the stitches to the clip.

Catch-stitch the entire facing edge (from shoulder to hemline) in place, with stitches catching into the interfacing only; be sure the stitches do not catch through the interfacing into the garment fabric.

FINISHING
THE UNDERSIDE
OF
BUTTONHOLES

See step 1 in Figure 71. Baste about ½ inch from the buttonhole rectangles, as shown, to be sure the facing is held securely to the garment in proper position. Then from the outside of the garment, stick a pin directly down through the center of the ends of the buttonhole, as shown. These pins will designate the length of the buttonhole marking.

The buttonhole should be the same length and width on the facing side and on the right side; keep in mind the slim proportions of the original buttonhole when doing all steps of construction.

Glance through steps 2 and 3, but do not do them before reading this entire paragraph. As the sketches show, fabric will be cut and must be turned under with very little seam allowance. Raveling is a serious problem, and this step should be tested on scraps of fabric, using the test buttonhole, before work is begun on the garment. To prevent raveling and to make the remaining steps very much easier, clear fingernail polish can be used; it is applied very carefully to just that area underneath the rectangle of the buttonhole. It must be applied lightly so that it does not penetrate through all thicknesses of the fabric. It is easier to do than it sounds, and although it discolors some fabric slightly, if it is applied

only under the buttonhole, the stained area will be turned to the inside and will not show. There are no resulting bad effects after washing or dry cleaning, although one should be wary of using this idea with light-colored silks and similar fabrics without pretesting. Apply the polish and allow it to harden before proceeding to step 2.

See step 2. Cut to within ¼ inch of the pin (through the facing only) and then diagonally to the corners, thus making cuts exactly like those made previously as the buttonhole was made.

See step 3. Turn under the raw edges with the needle and carefully hem the turned-under edges to the binding; pins

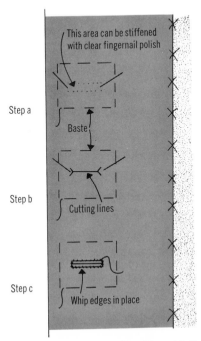

FIGURE 71 To finish underside of bound buttonholes

will not be helpful. Handle this work most carefully because the seam is so small and there are no protective stitches to prevent raveling.

Ideally, these stitches should be inconspicuous, but they must also be sturdy. The edges will be more secure if each stitch is pulled firmly and tightly into the fabric, and the weak corners will be more secure if they are strengthened by one or two diagonal stitches. The stitches must be very small for maximum control of the very small seam and clipped corners. Test this step with scraps of fabric on the test buttonhole to determine how the stitches should be done to allow for the most attractive appearance while serving the necessary utilitarian purpose. Press.

THE TAILOR'S
BUTTONHOLE

If handworked buttonholes are to be used, they are done at this time; see page 255 for directions.

The garment should be finally pressed just prior to inserting the lining. Because all seams, darts, and edges (actually all portions of the garment) have been pressed well during construction, there should be little to do at the final pressing. The main purpose of the final pressing is to remove folds and wrinkles that may have formed while the garment was in the final stages of construction. Depending on the nature of the fabric (some fabrics hold a press so well that a final pressing is unnecessary) and the quality of pressing as work was in progress, the final pressing may be a very simple and quick operation.

However, the heavy weight of many fabrics used in tailoring presents additional problems of bulk, and even the most talented and experienced worker may want to have the finished garment professionally pressed. The large-area ironing surfaces and the greater pressure and steam control available in the professional establishment will result in an appearance that is more attractively finished.

THE FINISHING
TOUCHES

SEWING ON BUTTONS

Figures 72 and 73 give general directions for placement, and Figures 74 to 76 give directions for various types of buttons. Buttons can be sewn in place at this time, or for easier handling while lining the garment, they can be done as the very last step of construction. See Figure 72. Remember that the center-front line of the garment is about ⅛ inch over the end of the buttonhole nearest the front edge and that it is the same distance

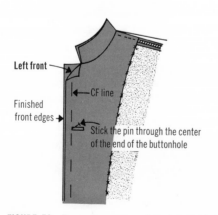

Left front

CF line

Finished front edges

Stick the pin through the center of the end of the buttonhole

FIGURE 72 To mark position of first buttonhole

from the left front edge. As an aid to getting the first button in the proper position, hold the two front edges together, with finished edges even and upper and lower edges even. Then mark the position for the first buttonhole at either the upper or the lower edge by placing a pin through the end of the buttonhole on the center-front line, sticking the pin directly down to the left front of the garment.

Figure 73 illustrates how to mark the position for the remaining buttons. Center-front lines must be matched and all buttons placed along the center-front line so that when the garment is worn, the button is at one end of the buttonhole. (A word of caution: Many persons think the button should be centered between the two ends of the buttonhole. This is not correct because under the strain of wearing, the button would pull to the end of the buttonhole, and the center fronts would not be in a matching position.)

NOTE In double-breasted designs, buttons are not placed along the center-front line. Button

positions for the two rows of buttons will appear on the pattern. The two rows of buttons are placed an equal distance from the center-front line.

Do not mark the position for all buttons at once because if there is a slight error of placement on one button, many would have to be changed. Mark one position, sew on that button, button it, and then mark the next position and proceed. After sewing on each button, button up the garment and see that each button is properly placed before proceeding to the next.

Figure 74 shows buttons with four eyes, which can be sewn on in a variety of ways for subtle changes in effect. This type of button is frequently used for tailored garments, in which case the eyes are relatively small. Some large novelty buttons of this type are available with eyes of an exaggerated size. If the button is highly styled with very large eyes, it becomes an important part of the design, and heavier thread will be required. Buttonhole twist will make the stitches more prominent. Sometimes additional stitches made from raveling yarns of the fabric will be needed to create better proportions with the size of the eye. If the but-

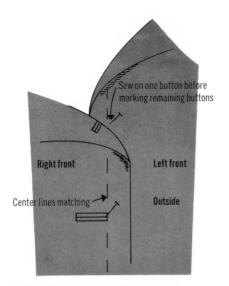

FIGURE 73 To mark position for buttons

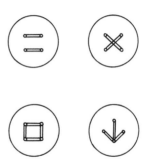

FIGURE 74 Buttons with four eyes

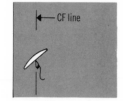

Button with metal shank

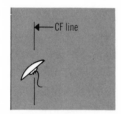

Button with padded fabric shank

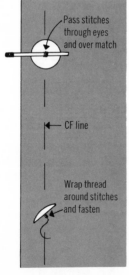

Button with thread shank

FIGURE 75 Buttons with thread shank

tons are large and the eyes are exaggerated in size (more than ⅛ inch in diameter), a strip of garment fabric with raw edges concealed can be used in place of thread.

All buttons for tailored garments must have some type of shank that keeps the button a certain distance from the garment. The purpose of the shank is to allow for the thickness of the right front when the garment is buttoned, and so heavier fabrics require longer shanks, etc. Most purchased buttons will have a metal shank, and fabric-covered buttons may have a metal or a padded shank; buttons with eyes will require a shank made of thread.

Figure 75 illustrates how to sew on buttons with the three types of shanks. In each case, the stitches should pass through the outer layer of garment fabric and the layer of interfacing, but should not be prominent on the facing side. One or two tiny stitches made through all thicknesses (including the facing) will make the button more secure, but most of the stitches should not pass through to the facing side.

When using medium-weight fabrics, the length of the metal shank is such that the shank can be sewn tight to the garment, as shown. However, if very heavy fabric is used, the shank may not be long enough to accommodate the thickness of the right front, and additional length must be obtained with thread, rather like the thread shank shown in the lower sketch. A padded shank offers the same problem because it may or may not be sufficiently long, depending on the thickness of the fabric; it too can be extended with stitches.

For buttons with eyes, hand stitches provide the extra length for the shank. Some method of obtaining extra length must be devised, and several toothpicks or a match will be helpful. Place the match in such a position that stitches must pass over it. Then remove the match and wrap the thread around the stitches, pulling the stitches firmly against the button, as shown in the lower sketch.

For garments made of sturdy fabrics for utilitarian purposes, see Figure 76. A flat button placed on the facing side and held in place with the same stitches used to secure the decorative button will protect the fabric from heavy strain.

SUPPORT FOR DOUBLE-BREASTED CLOSINGS

The left front edge of the garment with a double-breasted front must be fastened in place to support the weight of the left front and to keep the garment in smooth condition. This is done by sewing snaps directly underneath the row of decorative buttons on the right front; this position will require that snaps be sewn either to the right front facing or to the lining of the right front. Sturdy, large snaps (about ½ inch in diameter) are available on the market. They can be covered with matching fabric (explained below) for a more attractive effect. Sew the flat side of the snap underneath the decorative button on the right front. Before sewing the corresponding snap section to the left front edge, button the garment for its entire length, being sure the left front is in proper position. Mark the placement for one snap, snap that snap, and reposition the two front edges again before proceeding to the next.

SEWING ON SNAPS

Snaps are used infrequently on jackets and coats because they are distracting when the garment is unbuttoned. However, there are circumstances of design that make a snap necessary. Snaps for tailored garments should be covered with a lightweight (lining) fabric in a matching color. Cut little circles of fabric that will extend ⅛ inch beyond the edge of

Pass stitches over match and through eyes of both buttons

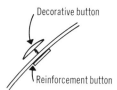

Decorative button

Reinforcement button

FIGURE 76 To reinforce buttons for utilitarian garments

the snap. Hold the circle of fabric over the snap and tuck in the raw edges, holding them in place with hand stitches as the snap is sewn in place. As the snap is fastened, it will make the center holes in the fabric; the little hole is left raw. If the covering frays with extended use, the snaps can be recovered.

HOOKS AND EYES

Hooks and eyes are used infrequently on tailored garments because they are difficult to fasten hurriedly in public and because they are somewhat distracting as the garment is unbuttoned. If this kind of fastening is required, a crocheted thread loop should be used to replace the eye. The hook will be in a less prominent position as the garment is worn, and depending on the fabric, a silver or black hook may not be too prominent. If the fabric is such that either silver or black will be prominent, the hook can be covered with buttonhole stitches made with matching thread.

14

LINING
THE TAILORED
GARMENT

The commercial pattern will give directions for cutting the lining in one of several different ways, depending on company policy and on the nature of the design:

1 The pattern may include separate lining pattern pieces for the front and back sections because these sections are cut very differently from the pattern for the garment. Vogue patterns always include separate lining patterns (one reason for their higher cost), and the other companies frequently do. However, even if lining pieces are included, certain pieces (such as sleeve and side sections, etc.) that are cut exactly like garment pieces will not be included. Therefore, the separate lining pieces plus any other pattern pieces pictured in the lining layouts must be used when cutting the lining.

2 There may be no pattern pieces for the lining, and cutoff lines on certain pattern pieces will indicate the cutting line for the lining. Simplicity patterns usually employ this method. There will be a cutoff line on the front pattern, and there

may be a cutoff line near the back neck edge if there is a back facing; note the position of the dotted lines in Figure 1. Not all pieces will have cutoff lines because some pieces should be cut exactly like the garment pieces. Directions for cutting linings appear at two places: on some pattern pieces and in notes and illustrations on the lining layouts. Cutoff lines will be shown in dotted lines on the layouts, and a pleat allowance for the back will be obtained by the way the back pattern is placed on the fabric; layout techniques of this method are pictured in Figure 6.

3 Directions on the pattern may combine the two methods described above. There may be some separate lining pieces, some garment pieces may be used exactly as they are, and other pattern pieces may have cutoff lines. It is important to study the cutting layout carefully, looking for brief notes of instruction and being aware that cutoff lines are shown as dotted lines on the layout.

TO
MAKE
LINING
PATTERNS

It is a very simple matter to make lining patterns by constructing cutoff lines as the professional patternmaker does. Although this is not ordinarily necessary, there are two circumstances under which one might wish to make a lining pattern. In the very simple pattern planned especially for the beginner, there may be no directions for a lining, and yet a lining would be required if this pattern were used for a tailored garment. Another circumstance will be encountered more frequently. If there are very complicated pattern alterations on the original pat-

tern, it is often easier to use a cutoff line on the altered pattern than to repeat intricate alterations on another pattern piece. Making the pattern is a simpler process, and sometimes it is the only way that truly accurate results can be obtained. For example, if a lining pattern piece is a "combination" piece (if one lining pattern covers a seam in the garment, thereby serving as the lining for two sections of the garment) and if intricate fitting has been done on the seam that does not appear in the lining, it is absolutely necessary to make lining patterns in order to have seams identical to those in the garment. Likewise, if intricate alteration has been made on a dart and if that dart does not appear in the lining pattern (if a separate lining piece is given, dart positions are not always identical to those in the garment), it is essential to make a new lining pattern.

See Figure 1. The lining pattern is different from the garment pattern in the front area because of the front facing and in the back section because a pleat must be added; the back-lining pattern may be different at the neck edge if there is a back facing. A basic two-piece garment is shown, but the principles illustrated in the sketch can be applied to any design. If there are additional sections in the body of the garment, they are cut from the original pattern piece; sleeve linings are cut from the original pattern pieces.

TO ESTABLISH THE CUTTING LINE ON THE FRONT
This step is shown in Figure 1 for the pattern with a separate facing; it is done in the same manner for the pattern with a self-facing, as shown in Figure 2. Place the front-facing pattern under the front

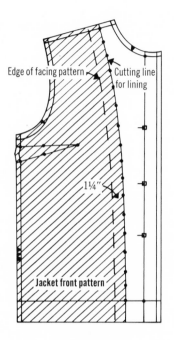

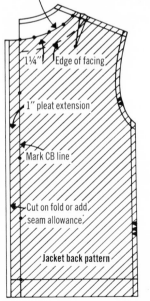

FIGURE 1 To make lining patterns for front and back

pattern, front and neck edges even; the inner edge of the facing is shown by a broken line in the sketch. Construct the cutting line for the lining 1¼ inches over (closer to the front edge) from the inner edge of the facing; this allows for a ⅝-inch turn-under on the front edge of the lining and a ⅝-inch lap-over on the inner edge of the facing. This is the way the professional patternmaker establishes the cutting line that appears on some commercial patterns.

TO ESTABLISH THE CUTTING LINE ON THE BACK NECK EDGE

This is done only if there is a back facing on the garment; usually this step is not necessary because the greater percentage of tailored garments do not have a back facing. Place the back-facing pattern under the back pattern, shoulder and neck edges even; the inner edge of the facing is shown by a broken line in the sketch. Construct the cutting line for the lining 1¼ inches above (closer to the neck edge) the inner edge of the facing; this allows for a ⅝-inch turn-under on the lining and a ⅝-inch lap-over on the inner edge of the facing.

GENERAL RULE FOR ESTABLISHING CUTTING LINES FOR THE LINING The cutting line for the lining is located 1¼ inches over the inner edge of the facing.

TO MAKE A PLEAT ALLOWANCE AT THE CENTER BACK

Scotch-tape a strip of paper to the center back of the pattern. Draw a line 1 inch over from the center-back line for the pleat extension. This edge may be cut on the fold if the layout permits, or by adding an additional seam allowance, as shown in the sketch, this edge can be seamed. Mark dots along the center-back line; this line should be tailor-tacked just like any other marked line on the pattern.

LINING
PIECES
INCLUDED
WITH THE PATTERN

The lining cut from the original pattern by use of cutting lines is identical to the garment in seam and dart location. However, a separate lining pattern made by a professional may be different in shape, and it may have dart lines that are not identical to those in the garment. Figure 3 pictures an example of the front-lining pattern included with the pattern for a princess-line garment. Figure 3a shows the pattern pieces for the garment, and a broken line indicates the inner edge of the facing. The lining-front pattern shown in Figure 3b is a combination piece because it is cut in sufficient width to cover the side front piece and to extend far enough over the front to cover the inner edge of the facing. A dartlike fitting in the lining front provides essentially the same shaping that the shaped seam provides in the garment.

The cut of this lining is superior to

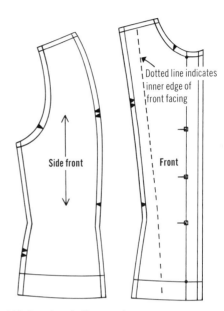

(a) Pattern pieces for the garment

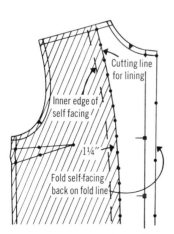

FIGURE 2 Principles of making lining patterns applied to garment with self-facing

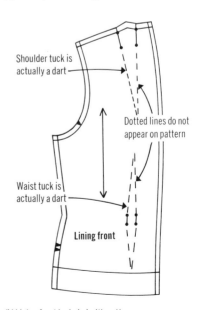

(b) Lining front included with pattern
FIGURE 3

should understand that the alternative cutoff-line method is entirely acceptable.

that of the lining made by the method shown in Figures 1 and 2, but it is not a method that should be undertaken by one who is not trained in patternmaking. One advantage is that the lining will be more attractive because a seam as close to the front edge as the princess-line seam will result in a very narrow strip. However, if intricate fitting has been done in this seam (very probable in this type of design), making identical alterations on a very different pattern piece is most difficult and often impossible; under these circumstances, it is wiser to make the lining pattern according to the directions accompanying Figures 1 and 2. The proper fit of the lining is more important than the attractiveness of a seam that is not prominent as the garment is worn.

Note that the lining made by the professional patternmaker has tucks at the shoulder edge (and at the waistline in some fitted designs). The shoulder tuck is actually a dart that is stitched for a short distance only; the tuck lines (which do not appear on the pattern itself) are extended in the sketch to illustrate that they converge at a point at approximately bust level. The tucks are really released darts, and although they fall in place as darts as the garment is worn, they can release with body movements to give a slight amount of freedom in the lining. This small advantage is not present if the lining is cut by using cutting lines on the pattern (as shown in Figures 1 and 2). This explanation is included as an aid to understanding the lining pattern that might be included with the commercial pattern. The advantages listed do have merit, but the reader

SUGGESTIONS FOR CUTTING THE LINING

Before cutting the lining, it is well to give careful thought to pattern alterations. Corresponding alterations on lining pieces should have been done after the muslin copy was fitted (see Corresponding Alterations on Interfacing and Lining Pieces on page 130); if they were not done at that time, they must be finished now. If any additional fitting alterations were made in the garment after it was cut in the fabric, these alterations should be incorporated in the pattern before the lining is cut; for example, if a seam was let out in the garment, the lining pattern can be altered so that there will be a full seam allowance in the lining.

NOTE The suggestions given below differ from the directions included with some patterns. Each suggestion has great advantages, but the reader should understand that her pattern directions are accurate and scientifically correct. The merit of these suggestions lies in their value for individual problems of figure, etc., and in the fact that they are a precaution against mistakes. Read all suggestions before cutting.

TESTS FOR LENGTH OF LINING PIECES

The lining of a sleeve or a jacket need not be as long as the corresponding pieces of the garment because smaller hem allowances are used and because the finished lower edge of the lining is at least ½ inch shorter than the garment. The hem allowance in the lining of a full-length coat is approximately the same as that in the coat itself, and so coat linings are usually cut as long as the corresponding pieces for the garment. In an effort to save yardage for the customer, commercial pattern companies sometimes (but not always) give directions for cutting the lining pieces for jackets and sleeves in a shorter length. See Figure 4. This is done in two different ways. Figure 4a illustrates how a cutoff line might be used. A note on the pattern may indicate that the cutting line for the lining is at the hemline of the original pattern, or a new cutoff line may be indicated slightly below the hemline. Figure 4b shows a separate lining pattern cut in a shorter length than the garment pattern. These lengths indicated by the pattern company are correct, providing all work done on the garment is scientific (all seam and hem allowances are accurate) and providing the garment has not been lengthened by even a slight amount.

Insufficient length in the lining results in much more difficulty of construction. The best and safest rule for the nonprofessional worker is to cut the lining as long as the original pattern for the garment. If this is not possible because of yardage restrictions, it is well to cut the lining pieces as long as possible. See Figure 4a. Cut the lining at least ½ inch below the hemline of the garment, and if possible cut it ¾ or 1 inch below the hemline. If there is sufficient yardage, cut the lining the full length of the original pattern; some of this length will be trimmed off later, but the extra length will allow for possible mistakes that have been made or slight additions in the length of the garment.

See Figure 4b. Place any lining pieces included with the pattern over the corresponding pattern pieces for the garment, corresponding edges even. The sketch shows a quite typical pattern in which the lining pattern extends about ½ inch below the hemline of the gar-

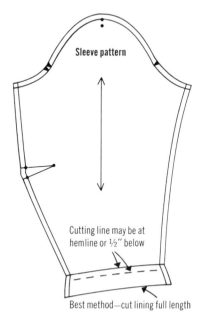

Sleeve pattern

Cutting line may be at hemline or ½″ below

Best method—cut lining full length

(a) Examples of cut off lines on pattern

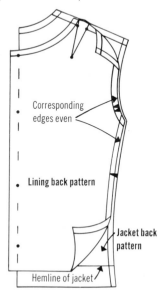

Corresponding edges even

Lining back pattern

Jacket back pattern

Hemline of jacket

(b) Example of separate lining pattern cut shorter than garment

FIGURE 4 Test for length of lining pieces

ment. Add an extension strip on the lining pattern to make it full length (if there is sufficient yardage) or to extend it to a level at least 1 inch below the hemline.

CUTTING THE LINING FOR A VENT OPENING

Figure 5 pictures the lining-back pattern for a garment with a vent opening. Note that two pieces are to be cut by the pattern piece. However, in the vent area, one layer of fabric is cut very differently from the other layer, as indicated by a cutoff line and a note which usually reads "cutoff line for left side." A glance at the sketches which show how to line the vent opening (Figures 27 to 30 on pages 321 to 324) will illustrate that cutting the wrong layer of lining would be a serious mistake. Because it is difficult at this time to determine exactly what "left side" means (does it mean left back of the lining or the side that will line the left back of the garment?), it is not wise to cut one layer of the fabric at this time.

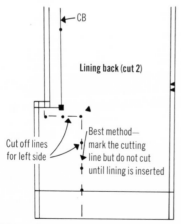

CB

Lining back (cut 2)

Cut off lines
for left side

Best method—
mark the cutting
line but do not cut
until lining is inserted

FIGURE 5 Cutting lining for a vent opening

Instead, cut both layers the same and tailor-tack the cutting line, as shown. After the lining is positioned in the garment and certain tests are made that will correct little inaccuracies of construction, the proper layer will be cut.

ADDING A PLEAT ALLOWANCE

See Figure 6. Pattern companies that do not include pattern pieces for linings and use the cutoff technique make allowance for the back pleat as the pattern is cut from the fabric, with directions on the lining layout, as shown in the two sketches. Figure 6a shows a method that results in a wedge-shaped or dart-shaped pleat; this pleat serves the purpose for which it was intended (freedom in the shoulder area), but it is more difficult to baste and press, and this method does force the grain line of the lining into a different position from that of the garment. Figure 6b shows a parallel pleat like the pleat used by those companies which provide a separate lining-back pattern; a slight change in the placement of the pattern on the fabric will transform the wedge-shaped pleat into the parallel pleat pictured.

NOTE The sketch shows broken lines at the back neck edges; these lines indicate that there is a cutoff line on the pattern.

SUGGESTIONS FOR CUTTING AND HANDLING LININGS OF HEAVY FABRIC

Sun Bac satin, simulated fur, and quilted lining fabrics are so heavy that they frequently tend to dominate the garment fabric; every effort must be made to reduce this bulk. It is wise to eliminate the back pleat (it serves a good purpose, but it is not entirely necessary) and if possible to eliminate a seam at the back. This can be done by cutting the lining back with the center-back line of the pattern placed on a fold of fabric. If there is a shoulder tuck (see Figure 3), it is wise to extend the tuck lines, as shown, and sew the entire dart by machine; a dart is less bulky than the released tuck and can be slashed and pressed open to distribute the bulk. Darts are not usually slashed in lining fabrics, but darts of sufficient width should be slashed and pressed open in these very heavy fabrics.

DRESSMAKER
TOUCHES
TO ADD
DESIGN INTEREST

There are many little touches that can be added to the lining for design interest, and the person with a great appreciation for detail will enjoy this subtle method of adding distinction to her costume. Most of the suggestions given below are ideas for finishing the front and neck edges of the lining. The reader should be aware of the emphasis being placed on linings as a source of design interest and should always study the lining techniques used in exclusive ready-to-wear. One of the best sources of lining ideas is the fur coat; the great expense of a fur coat warrants a truly custom-made lining that so often includes wonderful details that look

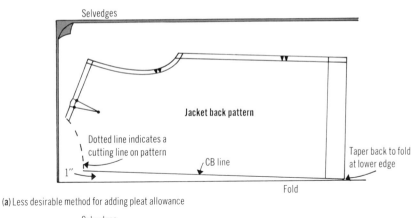

(a) Less desirable method for adding pleat allowance

(b) Preferred method for adding pleat allowance

FIGURE 6

very expensive but (for the woman who sews) require nothing more than time and ambition.

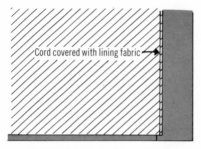

(a) Front edge of lining corded with matching or contrasting fabric

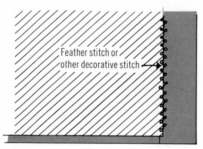

(b) Front edge of lining secured with decorative hand stitches

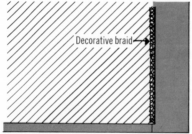

(c) Decorative braid applied over finished front edge of lining

FIGURE 7 Ideas for finishing front edge of lining to add design interest

Dressmaker details are interesting touches only if they are compatible with the design and the fabric and only if they are not overdone. As in all matters of design, good taste and judgment are required. Design interest is desirable on a garment with uncomplicated lines in a solid color with a solid-colored lining; it is less desirable when the fabric or the design is very active and interesting. Certain touches lend themselves to a theater suit and would be inappropriate used on a tailored reefer; in general, the suggestions given are more appropriate for dressmaker suits and coats than for man-tailored garments. Detailed instructions are not given, but each suggestion is relatively simple to do.

Figure 7 pictures methods of finishing the front and neck edges of the lining. The method shown in Figure 7a is probably the most popular, and it does give a subtle but very attractive effect. This idea was copied from fur-coat linings and is suitable only for fairly heavy garments. The cord (which should be limp and fine) does create a certain amount of stiffness and bulk, and therefore it can be used only on those fabrics which are heavy enough to dominate the stiffness of the cord. The fabric used to cover the cord should be limp and lightweight for a minimum of bulk and stiffness. Cord covered with matching lining fabric gives a subtle and very delicate effect. The fabric for the cord may be in a contrasting color (black coat with a black lining, corded in bright red). The effect will always be subtle, for the width of covered cord should not exceed ⅛ inch.

The cord should be covered with bias strips of fabric; then, instead of basting under the front and neck edges, the cord is stitched right sides together to those edges. Then the corded edge is basted under and lapped over the facing edges. The hand stitches which secure the finished edges of the lining should be placed along the stitching line in the cord; see the enlarged view in Figure 21. If the finished edge is not corded, stitches are placed $\frac{1}{16}$ inch under the edge of the lining, as shown; when cord is used, stitches should be placed $\frac{1}{8}$ inch under the corded edge, falling in the stitching line.

Figure 7b shows a decorative stitch used to secure the finished edge of the lining. Because of the very delicate effect, this suggestion lends itself to very feminine and softly tailored garments. The feather stitch is an effective stitch, and it can be placed so that it is more prominent on either the lining or the garment or so that it is equally prominent on both, as shown in the sketch. The thread can match the lining or the garment fabric, or it can contrast to both (gray coat with a white lining, hand-stitched in chartreuse thread).

Figure 7c shows decorative braid (another idea copied from fur-coat linings), which is necessarily stiff and somewhat bulky; the comments concerning the corded effect shown in Figure 7a are true of this suggestion as well. To be truly effective, the braid must be very decorative with a great deal of openwork; a bandlike braid will not give an attractive effect. There is a simple metallic cord available that is a mere $\frac{1}{8}$ inch in diameter and is most effective on some costumes (gray coat with a lighter gray satin lining and silver metallic cord). The braid or decorative cord is applied after the lining is completely finished and is secured to the front and neck edges with the usual hand stitches. Then the braid is whipped in place in the desired position. It can be placed over the lining only, as shown in the sketch, or it can cover the front edge of the lining. The braid can match the lining or the garment fabric; because of the

decorative nature of the braid, it should not contrast to both fabrics, but should match one or the other.

Some imported garments have truly exciting linings which involve the use of padding and quilting, or trapunto work. Some of them have a band of quilting, or trapunto, along the entire front edge that is several inches wide, and others have the decoration extending over the front shoulder area or around the lower front corners as well. It is a very decorative and elegant effect, but it must be used only with heavy fabrics that will not be dominated by its extra bulk, and it must be done by a person who is talented in handwork.

Figure 8a pictures a bound pocket in the lining. A welt pocket or an interesting patch pocket can be used. Welt or bound pockets can be in the horizontal position shown, and they are equally attractive in a vertical position. Even though the pocket should not be used (at least for nothing more than emergency bus fare), it should be placed in a position that would be convenient. Right-handed persons should have the pocket on the lining on the left front, and it should be at a convenient level between the waist and the hipline. The initials shown in Figure 8b should be placed in a comparable position.

METHODS OF LINING

There are two methods of lining the tailored garment, and a third, which is a combination of the two, is included in these directions. The two basic methods are the machine and the hand methods. The discussion below will aid in selecting the best method for the particular fabric and design.

In both methods of construction, certain work is done by machine, and certain work is done by hand. Darts, tucks, the center-back seam of a pleat, and vertical sleeve seams are done by ma-

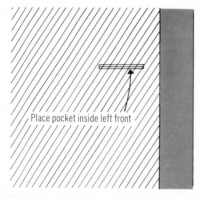

(a) A bound or welt pocket or an interesting patch pocket is attractive

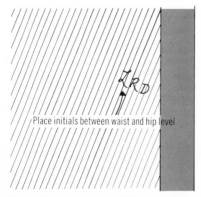

(b) Hand embroidered or purchased initials give a personalized touch

FIGURE 8 Ideas to add interest to the lining

chine in both methods. The front and neck edges are done by hand, and the sleeve is attached by hand in both methods. If the lining is attached to the garment at the lower edge, it is done by hand in both methods.

MACHINE METHOD

In this method, the structural seams of the lining are stitched by machine, so that the body of the lining is assembled before the lining is inserted into the garment. As mentioned above, the sleeve is not sewn in by machine, but will be attached by hand after the body of the garment has been lined.

advantages and disadvantages This method appears in the pattern directions with all makes of commercial patterns. It is the method used in all ready-to-wear in all price ranges, up to the most exclusive bracket. This method requires much less time than the alternative method and should be favored over the hand method in most garments. Seams can be pressed open (they must be lapped in the alternative method), and so they create a minimum of bulk.

The disadvantage of this method will be better understood after the advantages of the hand method are discussed. One disadvantage has to do with intricate fitting and is a disadvantage only in those fitted garments which are composed of intricate, shaped seams and in garments that have many vertical seams.

Another disadvantage of this method has to do with inaccurate construction. The person who has carelessly stitched the garment in $\frac{1}{2}$-inch seams and has stitched seams in the lining in the proper $\frac{5}{8}$-inch width will find that the lining will not fit properly, and the greater the number of seams, the greater the misfit. Careless work is more easily corrected in the alternative method.

Because the body of the lining is assembled before it is inserted, it is more difficult to discover the cause of trouble, should it arise. In the alternate method, problems are more easily discovered and solved.

uses of the machine method All the disadvantages listed above are not great problems in boxy and semifitted designs. Therefore, this method should be used for full-length coats and jackets that are relatively straight-lined. This method should be used for all linings that are heavy (heavy-weight satins, simulated fur, or fabrics with thickness added for warmth) to avoid the bulkier lapped seam that must be used in the alternative method. This method can be used for fitted designs (as an economy of time), but results will not be excellent if the worker has been careless and inaccurate.

HAND METHOD
In this method, the structural vertical seams are done by hand, so that each section of the lining is inserted into the garment as a separate piece. Darts, tucks, the center-back seam of the pleat, and vertical sleeve seams are done by machine, as in the machine method of lining.

advantages and disadvantages Because a great deal more time is required for this method and because it does not lend itself to the alterations necessary for all ready-to-wear, this method is never used in manufactured garments. However, there are great advantages, not the least of which is the "I cared" pride of the wearer.

The great advantage of this method lies in the fact that each section is inserted as a separate piece. This means that intricate fitting can be done at each seamline, that inaccuracies can be cor-

rected, and that trouble points can be detected easily in each piece before proceeding to the next. The advantage is of obvious importance in all fitted garments that have more intricate seams and a greater number of seams.

The additional time this method requires will be considered a disadvantage by some readers, but by the many readers who sew for the delight of it, the extra time will mean that much more pleasure and so will be considered an advantage.

The fact that seams done by hand must be lapped seams is a disadvantage because of the problem of bulk. Lapped seams create no problems in typical limp and lightweight lining fabrics, but problems would be encountered with heavy brocades and satin or lining fabrics with extra thickness for warmth; the bulk problem with these fabrics is so great that the machine method should be used for all heavy linings.

uses of the hand method This method should be used for fitted, body-hugging designs (the typical princess-line garment), providing the lining fabric is not unusually heavy and thick. This method can be used in straight, boxy garments if the worker enjoys handwork or if she tends to be inaccurate and anticipates fitting problems.

COMBINATION METHOD
The two methods can be combined in any number of ways to solve individual problems on garments with conflicting demands. For example, vertical sleeve seams are not done by hand, and therefore the garment with a sleeve combined with the body of the garment should be

done by the machine method; certainly gussets must be machine-stitched. But a garment with a gusset and with a sleeve combined with the body of the garment might have very frequent and intricately fitted seams in the waist and hip area. This garment could be done by the machine method in the shoulder and sleeve areas to a point an inch or so below the gusset, and the remainder of the garment could be done by the hand method.

NOTE The novelty Hong Kong finish for facing edges (explained on page 324) does not influence the basic method of lining; the lining can be done by any one of the three methods discussed above.

EXPLANATION
OF
ILLUSTRATIONS

Almost all the illustrations in this chapter picture a jacket rather than a coat simply to conserve space. The two garments are lined in an identical manner.

It would be well to review Principles of Shaping the Tailored Garment on page 234 before beginning work. As work is done on the lining, the garment should be held in wearing position so that the lining pieces are fitted to take an inside curve under the garment. However, all illustrations (in books and on instruction sheets) must necessarily picture the garment turned wrong side out in order that the construction details can be shown. The worker should study the sketches for the details, but she should hold her own work in wearing position whenever possible.

NOTE In order to simplify the sketches, the cotton-twill tape at the armholes is not shown.

SPECIAL NOTE If the lining fabric looks essentially the same on both sides, the right side will be folded to the inside. Manufacturers fold the right side outside on only those fabrics which are either unattractive on the wrong side or so different on the wrong side that the true nature of the fabric would not be evident on display counters. If a lining fabric does look almost identical on the two sides, special care must be taken to be sure that pieces are assembled for a right and a left side; for example, be very sure to baste sections together for a right and a left sleeve.

THE MACHINE
METHOD
OF
LINING

PREPARATION OF LINING SECTIONS

See Figure 9a. Baste along the center-back line to hold the pleat in place for pressing. This should be done when working with all fabrics except satin or similar fabrics which might be permanently marked by pressing over a basting thread; when working with satin, it is better to hold the pleat in place for pressing. If there is a seam at the back edge, stitch the seam. Stitch darts, etc.

See Figure 9b. The pleat must be pressed in one direction, and although it can be pressed in either direction, it is usually pressed in the direction illustrated.

CAUTION The direction of the pleat is very important if there is a vent-back closing, and the direction should be tested before the pleat is pressed. See Figure 27, which pictures the lining placed in the coat for testing purposes.

The basting stitches for the pleat will be removed later, and the pleat must be controlled at two points. The instruction sheet will recommend a bar tack or catch stitches; the bar tack is more serviceable.

The position of the tack is shown in Figure 9b, and a sketch in actual size appears in Figure 10. The tacks should be placed about 3 inches down from the neck edge if there is no back facing and about 1½ inches down from the neck edge if there is a back facing. One is placed at approximately waist level. They are placed about ⅜ inch over from the fold edge of the pleat.

See Figure 10. Working from the outside and using a single strand of matching thread, take two or three horizontal stitches in the proper position, making the stitches ¼ inch long and confining them to a ¹⁄₁₆-inch area, as shown. Then encase these stitches with vertical stitches ¹⁄₁₆ inch long, spaced evenly. The resulting effect should be a delicate line that is hardly discernible.

See Figure 11. Stitch darts or tucks in the front-lining sections. Figure 11a shows an assembled lining for the garment that has no back facing; note that the shoulder edge of the back extends a

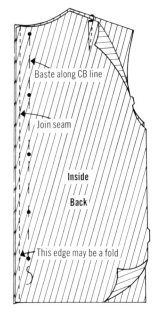

(a)

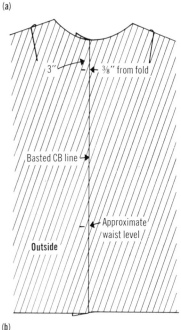

(b)

FIGURE 9 Preparation of back lining for machine method

SKETCH IN ACTUAL SIZE

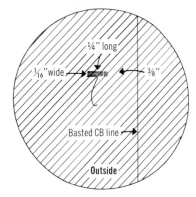

FIGURE 10 The bar tack

distance beyond the front edge. Baste under ⅝ inch on the front edge of the lining, but do not press. Join all seams; note that the turned-under edge of the front is caught in the seam at the shoulder edge. Clip the curve at the back neck edge and baste under ⅝ inch on that edge. The shoulder seam should be pressed toward the back, and the remainder of the back shoulder edge pressed in place. Press all other seams open.

Figure 11b shows this same step for the garment with a back facing. Note that the shoulder edges are identical in length. In this case, join the shoulder seam and press it open and then baste under ⅝ inch on the front and neck edges, clipping the back neck curve; do not press.

See Figure 12. Join the sleeve seams, being careful to assemble sections to obtain right and left sleeves. Press the seams open. See Figure 12a. Make ½-inch clips into the curve in the underarm area. Baste under ⅝ inch on the armhole edges, as shown. See Figure 12b. The turned-under seam allowance must be trimmed to ⅜ inch, but before this is done, notch positions must be marked on the turned-under edge. Put tailor's tacks on the edge (shown as dots on the sketch) directly across from the notch positions. Then trim the seam allowance to ⅜ inch.

INSERTING THE LINING

The most important thought to keep in mind is that seamlines in the lining must

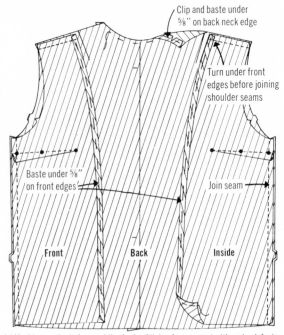

Clip and baste under ⅝" on back neck edge

Turn under front edges before joining shoulder seams

Baste under ⅝" on front edges

Join seam

Front   Back   Inside

(a) Machine method of assembling body of lining for garment with no back facing

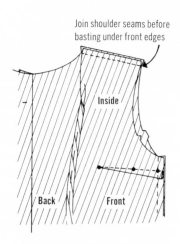

Join shoulder seams before basting under front edges

Inside

Back   Front

(b) Machine method of assembling body of lining for garment with a back facing

FIGURE 11

match corresponding seamlines in the garment. The rule of "seamlines matching" also applies at the front and neck edges because (in reality) a seam is involved (the lining to the inner edge of the facing or neck edge), but it is done with a lapped seam by turning under ⅝ inch on the lining and lapping over ⅝ inch on the inner edges of facings and neck edges.

The rule of seamlines matching is a most important one, but the strictest rules must be broken sometimes. Little inaccuracies of cutting and stitching seams and darts may result in a need to break this general rule. For example, the shoulder line of the lining should match the shoulder line of the garment in length, but if the lining is slightly shorter, as a result of little construction irregularities, it would be wiser to break the rule and make adjustment for the irregularity than to force seamlines to match if that would result in a misfit.

See Figure 13a. Insert the body of the lining in the garment. Begin by matching seamlines at both ends of the shoulder line. Lap the edge of the lining ⅝ inch over the inner edge of the front taking the following precautions:

1 Catch pins through the facing layer only; do not pin through all thicknesses to the outside layer of the garment. Put in as many pins as are necessary to hold the lining edge in a smooth line because this line is a very prominent one; if the lining fabric is very slippery, pins may be required at 1-inch intervals.

2 The lining should ease very slightly over the bust area, and a simple way to obtain the proper amount of ease is to hold the garment in a position that is opposite to wearing position; in other words, when pinning this area, hold the work in such a way that the lining takes the outside curve over the garment. This will result

in approximately ¼ inch of ease when the garment is in wearing position.

3 Note that the garment pictured in Figure 13a has a gradually narrowing facing. Most facings are shaped in this way as far down as the bust level. Some facings continue to narrow to the lower edge, as shown in Figure 13a, while others become parallel below the bust level, as shown in Figure 13b. If the inner edge of the facing is parallel to the front edge, make a cardboard gauge in the proper width and use it to ensure perfection of

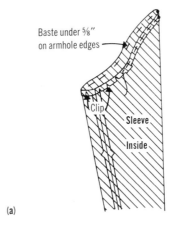

Baste under ⅝"
on armhole edges

Clip

Sleeve

Inside

(a)

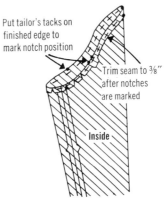

Put tailor's tacks on
finished edge to
mark notch position

Trim seam to ⅜"
after notches
are marked

Inside

(b)
FIGURE 12

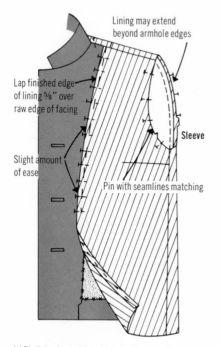

Lining may extend beyond armhole edges

Lap finished edge of lining ⅝" over raw edge of facing

Sleeve

Slight amount of ease

Pin with seamlines matching

(a) Pin lining in position with seamlines matching

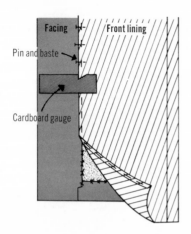

Facing

Front lining

Pin and baste

Cardboard gauge

(b) Check parallel lines for accuracy

FIGURE 13 To insert lining made by machine method

the line; the finished edge of the lining should lap ⅝ inch over the facing edge, but little irregularities of cutting and construction can be perfected by measuring from the finished front edge. Baste the front and neck edges to the facing layer only, with stitches sufficiently secure to hold the edges in proper position.

See Figure 13a to position armhole edges. The raw armhole edges of the lining must be pinned to the armhole of the garment with seamlines matching (the stitching line at the garment armhole to the ⅝-inch seamline on the lining). The directions for setting in regulation sleeves included trimming the seam to a ⅜-inch width. Therefore, if the seam was trimmed at that time, the raw edge of the lining will extend ¼ inch beyond the cut edge of the sleeve seam, as shown. Pin the armhole edges together with seamlines matching.

TO SECURE ARMHOLE EDGES
Figure 14 shows the construction for the garment with no shoulder pad, and Figure 15 shows the difference in construction if a pad is used. See Figure 14a. Hand-sew the lining to the armhole (permanent stitches that will remain) by working from the sleeve side and placing stitches just ¹⁄₁₆ inch outside the stitching line; stitches should be small and secured frequently with backstitches, particularly in the underarm area. It is important that these stitches be very close to the stitching line of the sleeve because the underarm area of the lining must be clipped (as the sleeve seam was clipped), and the clips must be made to a point very close to the stitching line. The lining seam will be trimmed to ⅜ inch, but before this is done, notch positions must be marked on the seamline. Put tailor's tacks on the seamline directly across from the notch positions.

See Figure 14b. Trim the armhole edges to a ⅜-inch width. If the sleeve seam has not been trimmed, trim all layers of the seam to ⅜ inch. If the sleeve seam has been trimmed, trim off the raw lining edges even with the sleeve seam. Make several clips into the seam-line at the underarm area between the notches.

Figure 15 pictures the one construction detail that must be done in a different manner if a shoulder pad is used. The hand stitches which secure the armhole edges must be done in two segments in order to leave a 3-inch span free, as shown. The lining should be left free for a 3-inch span at the transition point between the padded and unpadded portions of the edge, as shown. Therefore, the hand stitches in the upper part will secure the lining to the underside of the pad (not catching through the pad to the garment seam), and the hand stitches in the lower part are done in the usual manner, as explained above. This is a very important detail, for if the stitches were allowed to cross the edge of the pad, the difference in thickness would create a certain tautness that would be apparent from the outside of the garment. In every other way, the armhole seam is finished according to the directions accompanying Figures 13 and 14.

TO INSERT THE SLEEVE LINING

Figure 16 shows this step for the garment with no shoulder pad, and Figure 17 shows the difference in construction if a pad is used. See Figure 16a. Turn the sleeve lining wrong side out and slip it into the garment sleeve, wrong sides together. Pin the underarm area into position by matching the notch positions (marked with tailor's tacks) and the underarm positions; lap the turned-under edge of the sleeve ⅜ inch over the raw armhole edges, thereby matching arm-

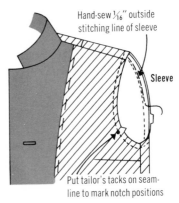

(a)

(b)

FIGURE 14 To secure armhole edge for garment without shoulder pads

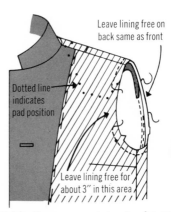

FIGURE 15 To secure armhole edge for garment with shoulder pads

hole seamlines and hiding the hand stitches.

The step shown in Figure 16b is the most difficult one because fullness in the sleeve cap must be eased to the armhole, and this is much more difficult with a lapped seam than with a plain seam. The worker must understand that the fullness will be evident and that this portion of the seam will not look entirely smooth and attractive.

Match the shoulder positions and lap

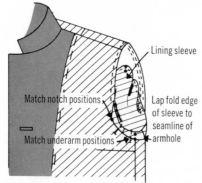

(a) Position sleeve in area below notches

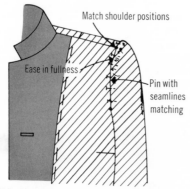

(b) Position sleeve in cap area

FIGURE 16 To insert sleeve for garment without shoulder pads

the turned-under edge of the sleeve ⅜ inch over the raw armhole edges, thereby matching seamlines and hiding the hand stitches. Pin the shoulder position and then pin the cap of the sleeve in place, easing in the fullness and distributing it properly (review the directions accompanying Figure 59 on page 278). Baste the sleeve to the armhole. The sleeve must be sewn to the armhole with hand stitches that are as attractive as possible and yet secure enough to withstand the strain this seam will receive when the garment is worn. A slip stitch (done in the manner pictured in Figure 21) would be most attractive, but the slip stitch will not withstand a great deal of strain. It seems wiser to favor a more utilitarian stitch such as a whipping stitch secured frequently with reinforcing stitches.

Figure 17 shows the one construction detail that must be done in a different manner if shoulder pads are used. Just as the lining was left free from the armhole for a short span in the transition area of the pad, so the sleeve lining must be sewn in such a way that stitches do not catch into the seam in that same 3-inch span. By lifting up the needle each time a stitch is taken in that area, one can feel that the stitches are catching into the lining layer only.

FINISHING THE LOWER EDGE OF THE LINING

See Figure 18. Put the garment on the figure, match center fronts, and pin carefully in position. An assistant will be needed. With one hand on the lining side, pin the lining and the garment together with a row of pins about 3 inches apart, placed about 5 inches above the finished edge of the garment; allow the lining and the garment to fall naturally and do not pull at the lining any more than is necessary to shift seamlines into matching positions. If there is a pleat or a vent opening in the garment, additional pins are required; see Figure 28 on page 322.

Sleeve hems are hung in the same manner. After the seams are shifted into matching position, the wearer should bend her arm to waist level close to her body and then bring it down to a hanging position; this allows the sleeve lining to settle into wearing position. Then pin the two layers together with pins about 2 inches above the finished edge of the sleeve.

Figure 19 shows the lower-edge treatment for all sleeves and for the great majority of jacket and coat designs; this is the lining attached to the lower edge of the garment. Some few garments (usually coats with style fullness and with linings that do not have the same amount of style fullness) have free-hanging linings, as shown in Figure 20.

See Figure 19a. Baste through all thicknesses along the pin line, as shown. Trim the raw edge of the lining parallel to the lower edge of the garment; ideal measurements are 1 inch below the finished edge of the garment for sleeves and jackets and 1½ inches below the finished edge for full-length coats. The lower edge of sleeves and jackets can be finished properly if the lining is only ½ inch longer than the finished edge, but the 1-inch measurement is preferred if there is sufficient fabric.

See Figure 19b. Turn up the lower edge of the lining, allowing ½ inch of the garment to extend, and pin the lower edge in place; match seamlines and catch pins into the hem layer only. Measure carefully to be sure the lower edge of the lining is parallel to the lower edge of the garment. Baste ¾ inch above the lower edge of the lining with stitches catching into the hem layer only. Do not press at this time.

See Figure 19c. Roll the fold edge of the lining to the outside, as shown (pin

if desired), and slip-stitch one layer of the lining to the hem layer. Be sure that the stitches do not catch into more than one thickness of the lining. Press the

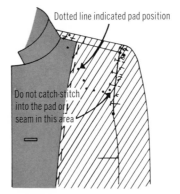

FIGURE 17 To insert sleeve for garment with shoulder pads

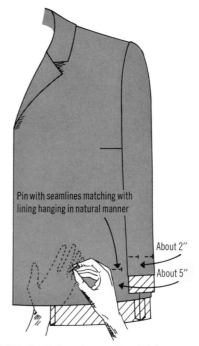

FIGURE 18 To hang lower edge of lining

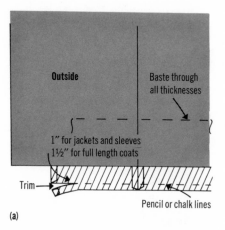

(a)

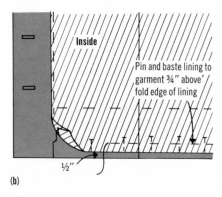

(b)

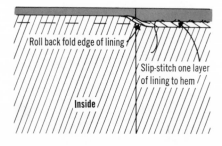

(c)

FIGURE 19 To finish lower edge of lining that is attached to garment

crease at the lower edge of the lining and remove the bastings. The lining will hang in the position pictured in Figure 19b, but because the stitches are above the lower edge, the lining can shift position without disturbing the hang of the garment.

For a free-hanging lining, see Figure 20a. Baste through all thicknesses along the pin line, as shown. Trim the lower edge of the lining, as shown in Figure 19a. Turn up the lower edge of the lining, allowing ½ inch of the garment to extend, and pin the edge in position with pins in the lining layers only, as shown; do not pin the lining to the garment.

Figure 20b shows the lining lifted away from the garment and reveals that the garment hem has been finished by one of the bound methods. Hem the lining separately, as shown, using a method appropriate for the fabric. Light-weight linings are best done by turning under and slip stitching, as shown in the sketch. If the fabric is heavy, a bound hem is a wiser choice.

See Figure 20c. Although this lining requires great freedom because it is not as full as the garment, side seams should be fastened together loosely with a swing tack about 1½ inches long. The tack should reach from the lining hem to the garment hem at a level such that it will not be visible when the garment is worn. The tack can be done with a hand crochet stitch or by doing the buttonhole stitch over several strands of thread.

TO FINISH FRONT AND NECK EDGES

See Figure 21. The front and neck edges are prominent lines as the garment is worn, and because there is relatively little strain during wearing at these edges (especially at the front edge, which is the most prominent), it is important that hand stitches be hidden. Stitches should not show, but because they are more apt to show in thin fabrics, it is usually better to use thread that matches the lining.

Fold the facing to the outside of the garment, as shown. The enlarged view shows the finished edge of the lining extending a scant ¹⁄₁₆ inch beyond the facing; this position makes it possible to slip the needle into a fold of the lining

so that stitches are very close to the fold edge but are hidden from view. After work is finished, remove the bastings and press the front and neck edges.

THE HAND
METHOD
OF
LINING

Before beginning work, read the special note on page 306.

PREPARATION OF LINING SECTIONS

See Figure 22a. Baste along the center-back line to hold the pleat in place for pressing. This should be done when

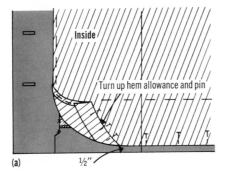

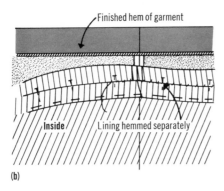

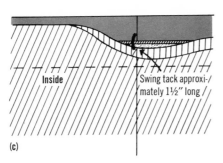

FIGURE 20 To finish lower edge of free-hanging lining

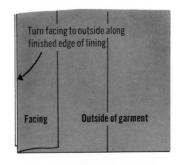

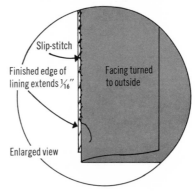

FIGURE 21 To slip-stitch finished edges of lining

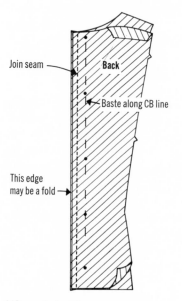

Join seam —

Back

←Baste along CB line

This edge
may be a fold →

(a) Prepare back sections

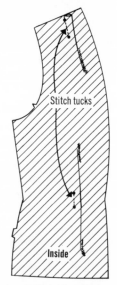

Stitch tucks

Inside

(b) Stitch darts and tucks in all sections

FIGURE 22 Preliminary steps for hand method
of lining

working with all fabrics except satin or
similar fabrics which might be permanently marked by pressing over a basting
thread; when working with satin, it is
better to hold the pleat in place for
pressing. If there is a seam at the center-
back edge, stitch the seam. Figure 22b
pictures a front-lining section with tucks.
Stitch tucks and darts in all sections of
the lining.

The pleat should be pressed at this
time; see the directions accompanying
Figure 9b and those with Figure 10 for
a discussion of the pleat and the bar
tacks that will hold it in place.

Figure 23 shows the preparation of
the lining sections for a typical princess-
line garment; the sections are prepared
in a similar manner for any type of design. In the hand method, one edge of
every seam is turned under, and the corresponding edge is left raw. The edge
nearer the front of each section is the one
that is turned under; for example, in the
side back section, the side edge is nearer
the front, so it is turned under, and the
remaining edge, which is nearer the
back, remains raw. Note that the back
shoulder edge is turned under, while the
front edge remains raw. It is well to assemble all lining sections flat on a table
in proper order, as shown, before beginning work. Baste under ⅝ inch on the
front edge and on the back shoulder and
neck edges, clipping the curve on the
back neck edge. Then baste under ⅝
inch on one edge of each corresponding
seam, as shown. Do not press.

TO INSERT SEPARATE LINING SECTIONS

The most important thought to keep in
mind is that seamlines in the lining must
match corresponding seamlines in the
garment. The rule of seamlines matching
also applies at the front and neck edges
because (in reality) a seam is involved
(the lining to the inner edge of the fac-

ing or neck edge), but it is done with a lapped seam by turning under ⅝ inch on the lining and lapping over ⅝ inch on the inner edges of the facing and neck edges.

The rule of seamlines matching is a most important one, but the strictest rules must be broken sometimes. Little inaccuracies of cutting and stitching seams and darts may result in a need to break this general rule. For example, the shoulder line of the lining should match the shoulder line of the garment in length, but if the lining is slightly shorter as a result of little construction irregularities, it is wiser to break the rule and make an adjustment for the irregularity than to force seamlines to match if that would result in a misfit. In fact, the greatest advantage of the hand method of lining is that it allows one to break rules more easily. See Figure 24 as an illustration of this important point and consider the width of the lining front at the waistline as an example. If all work has been accurate, the lining will lap ⅝ inch over the edge of the facing and will reach to the side

edge, so that the raw edge of the lining will be cut edges even with the pressed-open seam in the garment (seamlines matching); in that position, the lining will fit perfectly. The general rule of seamlines matching has been followed, and the results are perfect if all work has been accurate. However, if the front tuck in the lining was stitched just a bit too wide, the cut edge of the lining will not reach to the raw edge of the pressed-open seam without drawing up the garment somewhat; however, the rule can be broken very easily by allowing the lining to fall along the side edge in the position required for a proper fit. The great advantage of this method is that each seamline can be allowed to fit as required.

Breaking rules must be done scientifically, however. The worker must understand the general principle involved,

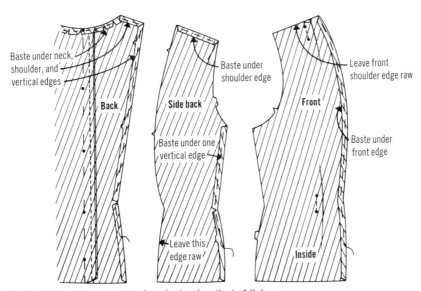

FIGURE 23 Preparation of lining sections for hand method of lining

she must know the general rule and the reasons why it is scientific, and she must look for the reason why the general rule is not satisfactory in her case. Only then is she prepared to break the rule scientifically.

TO INSERT FRONT-LINING SECTIONS

Figure 24 shows the front-lining section being inserted into the garment. Both the right and the left fronts should be inserted at the same time, and then both side sections, and so on to the back section, which is the last section inserted into the garment.

See Figure 24a. Insert the lining front and begin by lapping the front edge of the lining ⅝ inch over the inner edge of the facing, with seamlines matching at the shoulder. Lap the edge of the lining ⅝ inch over the entire front edge, taking the following precautions:

1 Catch pins through the facing layer only; do not pin through all thicknesses to the outside layer of the garment. Put in as many pins as are necessary to hold the lining edge in a smooth line because this line is a very prominent one; if the lining fabric is very slippery, pins may be required at 1-inch intervals.
2 The lining should ease slightly over the bust area; a simple way to obtain the proper amount of ease is to hold the garment in a position that is opposite to wearing position. In other words, when pinning this area, hold the work in such a way that the lining takes the outside curve over the garment; this will result in approximately ¼ inch of ease when the garment is in wearing position.
3 Note that the garment shown in these

sketches has a gradually narrowing facing. Most facings are shaped in this way as far down as the bust level, and some facings continue to narrow to the lower edge, as shown in these sketches. However, the facing may be parallel below the bust line. If the edge of the facing is parallel to the front edge of the garment, see the directions accompanying Figure 13b.

See Figure 24a to position the armhole edges. The raw armhole edges of the lining must be pinned to the armhole of the garment with seamlines matching (the stitching line at the garment armhole to the ⅝-inch seamline on the lining). The directions for setting in regulation sleeves included directions for trimming the seam to a ⅜-inch width. Therefore, if the seam was trimmed at that time, the raw edge of the lining will extend ¼ inch beyond the cut edge of the sleeve seam. Pin the armhole edges together with seamlines matching.

Pin the side seams together, seamlines matching, and then make tests for proper fit; standards of proper fit are included in Figure 24b. The lining should be just a little larger than the garment at the bust and waist levels, but the lining must be a "flat fit" (must be identical in width to the garment) at the lower edge. Pins can be removed to allow the lining to release or be taken in at the side-seam edge in order to meet these standards of fit. Do not do the permanent handwork shown in Figure 24b before reading the following paragraph.

The great advantage of the hand method is that any problems of fit in one lining section can be discovered before proceeding to the next. To benefit from this advantage, baste the two front sections in place and then test on the figure to see that the garment hangs properly and smoothly. If there are mistakes, they can be corrected now. As each piece is inserted, it should be basted and tested prior to doing handwork. Thus, because each piece is perfected as work progresses, it is simple to discover and correct problems because they will always be in the last piece inserted.

See Figure 24b. Armhole edges are treated in the same manner in the hand method and the machine method. The only difference is that the work is done in segments in the hand method: the front armhole is secured at this time, and the back armhole is secured later. For important detailed directions, see To Secure Armhole Edges on page 310.

Hand-sew the raw side edge of the lining to the side seam with stitches a scant $\frac{1}{16}$ inch outside the stitching line of the seam of the garment. End the stitches and fasten the thread $2\frac{1}{2}$ inches from the lower edge, as shown; this is an important detail, to be explained later. Hand-sew the raw shoulder edge of the lining to the shoulder seam of the garment in the same manner.

NOTE All the principles and directions given in great detail for the front-lining section should be applied when working with all remaining sections of the lining.

TO INSERT ADJACENT LINING SECTIONS

Figure 25 illustrates details for inserting all adjacent sections. Lap the turned-under side edge to the seamline of the raw edge and pin in place with the upper and lower edges even, as shown. Lap the turned-under shoulder edge to the seamline of the raw edge and pin. Pin the remaining raw seam edge to the corresponding seam on the garment, seamlines matching. Test for fit and make necessary adjustments. Baste both side sections in place and test on the figure before doing permanent handwork.

Figure 25b illustrates some techniques that are the same as those done

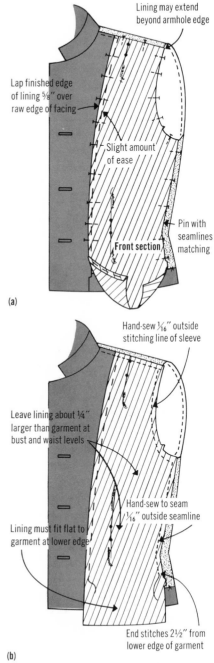

(a)

Lining may extend beyond armhole edge

Lap finished edge of lining $\frac{5}{8}$" over raw edge of facing

Slight amount of ease

Pin with seamlines matching

Front section

Hand-sew $\frac{1}{16}$" outside stitching line of sleeve

Leave lining about $\frac{1}{4}$" larger than garment at bust and waist levels

Hand-sew to seam $\frac{1}{16}$" outside seamline

Lining must fit flat to garment at lower edge

End stitches $2\frac{1}{2}$" from lower edge of garment

(b)

FIGURE 24 To insert front-lining sections

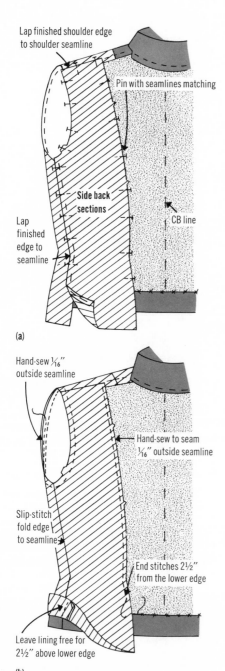

Lap finished shoulder edge
to shoulder seamline

Pin with seamlines matching

Side back
sections

Lap
finished
edge to
seamline

CB line

(a)

Hand-sew 1/16"
outside seamline

Hand-sew to seam
1/16" outside seamline

Slip-stitch
fold edge
to seamline

End stitches 2½"
from the lower edge

Leave lining free for
2½" above lower edge

(b)

FIGURE 25 To insert adjacent lining sections

on the front sections; hand-sew the arm-hole edges and the raw vertical seam edge in the same manner. A new technique is to do the handwork on the lapped seam. This seam should be slip-stitched in place (see the directions accompanying Figure 21 for more details). The side edge of the front was left free from the garment for a distance of about 2½ inches from the lower edge, and now work must be done in such a way that both edges remain free from the garment; note the lining edge flipped up. It is important that the lining be free from the garment up to a level about 2½ inches above the finished lower edge of the garment in order that the lower edge of the lining can be turned up for a hem. Every vertical seam in all lining sections must be handled in this manner.

TO INSERT BACK-LINING SECTIONS

The center-back section, the last section to be placed in the garment, is shown in Figure 26. All edges of this section (except the lower edge) have been turned under and must be lapped ⅝ inch over the corresponding edges and pinned in place. Baste, perfecting the fit, and test on the figure as usual. All edges will be slip-stitched in place according to the directions above.

All remaining steps of construction are the same as those of the machine method of lining. To insert the sleeve lining, to finish the lower edge of the lining, and to finish the front and neck edges, see the directions on pages 311 to 315.

PROBLEMS
OF LINING
A VENT
OPENING

The vent opening presents several problems because it is a construction detail in which a small mistake can create a serious problem. Because mistakes can be corrected by the way the lining is cut and handled, these directions are given in great detail. The only differences between these directions and the ones on the instruction sheet are that these include testing suggestions at several stages in construction and one section of the lining is cut after the lining is inserted (rather than before, as recommended in pattern directions).

Figure 27a shows the finished vent opening in the garment; detailed directions are not included because this construction is explained in sufficient detail on the instruction sheet. Note that the pleat is pressed in one direction so that one layer of the vent extension becomes a self-facing which is catch-stitched to the garment, while the other edge has been turned under on the seamline. Note that the weight of the vent extension is supported by horizontal stitches ⅝ inch

below the upper cut edge. This is usually done by machine, and these stitches must necessarily show on the right side of the garment; if the fabric is not too heavy, they can be done by hand.

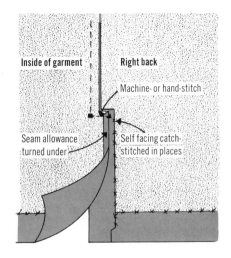

(a) Finished view of vent back construction

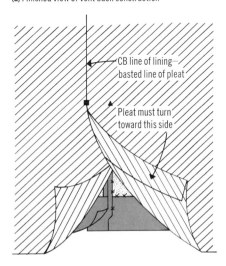

(b) Test lining in garment to determine direction for pleat

FIGURE 27 The vent opening

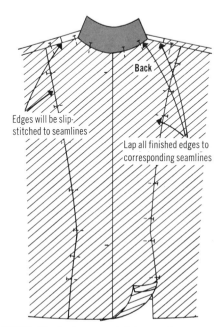

FIGURE 26 To insert back-lining sections

The seam and the vent are usually pressed in the direction illustrated in Figure 27; sketches on the instruction sheet picture the proper direction for each individual design. One mistake the worker might possibly make is to press the seam and the vent in opposite directions; the tests for the lining given below allow for correction of that mistake.

See Figure 27b. The pleat in the lining must be pressed in a certain direction, depending on the direction in which the vent is pressed. Before pressing the lining pleat, place the back lining in the garment wrong sides together and be sure that the pleat in the lining is pressed in the same direction as the seam and the vent in the garment. Note that both are turned toward the right-hand side of these sketches; had the vent been pressed in the opposite direction, both could be turned in that direction. After this test, press the pleat in the lining and put in the bar tacks.

See Figure 28a. The first step in finishing the lower edge is to pin the lining in position on the figure (shown on a basic garment in Figure 18). Additional pins are required to position the lining properly in the vent area. First of all, the fold edge of the lining pleat should be placed directly over the stitching line of the garment seam. In addition to the row of pins about 5 inches from the lower edge, pins should be placed right at the lower edge to match all seamlines in the lining to corresponding seams in the garment, as shown. A rectangle of pins, placed about 1½ inches outside the vent area, is needed to locate the lining properly in the entire vent area.

See Figure 28b. Baste along the pin lines, as shown. One edge of the lining extends in such a way that it covers the vent extension (the layer with the turned-under edge). Turn under ⅞ inch (the seam allowance plus ¼ inch) on the raw edge of the lining and lap it over the raw edge of the garment, allowing ¼ inch of the garment to extend, as shown. Pin and baste this edge in place.

Study all the directions accompanying Figure 29 before proceeding with work. This is the most difficult step in-

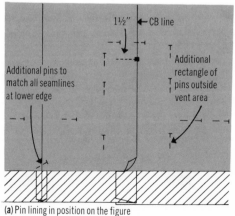

(a) Pin lining in position on the figure   (b) Pin one edge in position

FIGURE 28

volved with the vent opening because a slash must be made to a precise point and because there is no opportunity to reinforce the point as a precaution against raveling. Furthermore, this is the time when small irregularities of previous construction can be corrected.

A portion of the lining must be cut away. The pattern indicated a cutting line, but (if the cutting directions suggested in this book were followed) the cutting line was tailor-tacked, and the excess lining was not cut away; the cutting line is indicated with a line of dots on the sketch.

The square and triangle shown on the sketch are pattern markings that should match similar points on the garment. Study Figure 27a to see the position of similar markings on the garment. The square is at the end of the stitched seam; the triangle is on a line directly across from the square, ⅝ inch in from the raw edge of the self-facing. The point on the garment marked with a triangle in Figure 27a is the point that must correspond to the slashed corner in Figure 29a. The markings on the lining will be almost correct, and they would be in perfect position if all work done on the garment had been absolutely accurate. The sketch shows construction as it would be if all work had been accurate, but work should be tested for little irregularities.

The most important step is the slash shown. Make a slash through the lining to the pattern marking or to the point that is directly across from the end of the stitching on the garment and ⅝ inch from the edge of the self-facing; this is the point shown with a triangle in Figure 27a.

See Figure 29b. A section of the lining must be cut away, and the cutting line will be along the tailor-tacked cutting line if all previous work has been accurate. To test the cutting line for accuracy,

smooth the lining flat in the whole vent area and fold the lining to the outside, in such a position that the fold edge laps ⅝ inch over the edge of the self-facing, as shown. If all work has been accurate, the fold edge will be ⅝ inch from the

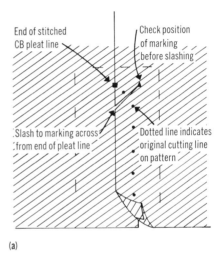

End of stitched CB pleat line

Check position of marking before slashing

Slash to marking across from end of pleat line

Dotted line indicates original cutting line on pattern

(a)

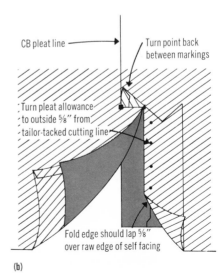

CB pleat line

Turn point back between markings

Turn pleat allowance to outside ⅝" from tailor-tacked cutting line

Fold edge should lap ⅝" over raw edge of self facing

(b)

FIGURE 29 Tests for accuracy of cutting line

tailor-tacked cutting line, as shown, but the lining can be adjusted to whatever position is necessary for a flat fit on the garment. The proper cutting line will be

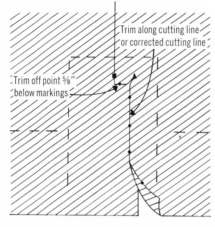

(a) Trim along cutting lines

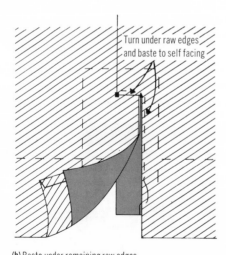

(b) Baste under remaining raw edges

FIGURE 30 Finishing lining for a vent opening

a line ⅝ inch from the fold edge of the turned-back lining.

See Figure 30. Trim along the cutting line or the corrected cutting line, as shown in Figure 30a. Note that the tip of the triangle has been trimmed away at a level ⅝ inch below the pattern markings. Figure 30b shows the lining edges turned under and basted over the raw edge of the self-facing. The hem of the lining should be turned up and finished before permanent hand stitches are done on these edges. When the hem is finished, these edges should be slip-stitched, as shown in Figure 21. One or two diagonal stitches placed over the lining edge right at the slashed corner will help prevent the corner from raveling.

THE NOVELTY HONG KONG FINISH FOR FACING EDGES AND LININGS

The Hong Kong finish is a novelty finish without being overdone and is attractive (the effect can be seen in Figure 32). It differs from the traditional method in that the inner edge of the facing is bound with the Hong Kong finish, and then the facing edge is lapped over the lining; in the traditional construction, the lining edge laps over the facing. Obviously, this is a subtle change, and yet it does give a very distinctive appearance.

This method is somewhat more expensive because of the extra yardage required for long bias strips to match the lining, it requires somewhat more time, and it results in a certain amount of extra thickness and stiffness at the facing edge. Disregarding the cost factor, which must be considered a disadvantage, the other two points may or may not be disadvantages. The person who sews for pleasure will not object to spending more time, and if the fabric of the garment is sufficiently heavy, the extra stiffness is no more of an issue than a corded edge on the traditional lining. It would be difficult to state that one method is better than the other; both are very attractive. This finish will probably not replace the traditional one, and yet it is a nice change of pace for the person who has done many linings.

See Figure 31a, which shows the Hong Kong finish applied to the facings for a garment with both front and back facings. Note that the lower edge has been left free and will be secured later. Directions for doing this finish accompany Figure 6 on page 00. If one plans from the very beginning of construction to do this finish, the inner edges of the facings can be finished more easily before the facings are attached to the garment.

If there is no back facing, this construction is somewhat more intricate, as shown in Figure 31b. When the Hong Kong finish is used, the finished edge should be at the seamline, and therefore the seam allowance at the shoulder edge of the front facing and the back neck edge of the collar should be trimmed away before the raw edges are bound. The binding must be applied in several segments, turning under the raw edges at corners.

Figure 32a shows the method of inserting the lining. If this method is used, the front and neck edges of the lining are not turned under. As the lining is inserted, the facing edges are flipped up, and the raw edges of the lining are catch-stitched to the interfacing of the garment. Either the hand or the machine method of lining can be used. The lower edge of the lining is turned up, while the facing edges are still free. The sleeve lining is done in the traditional manner.

Figure 32b shows the last step of construction. The facing edge is basted in position, and the free lower edge is slip-stitched. The edge of the facing will be slip-stitched to the lining layer only

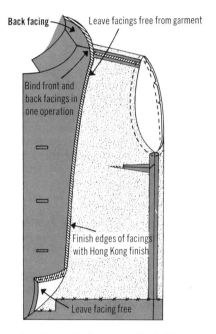

(a) To finish facing edges for garment with a back facing

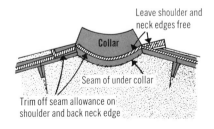

(b) To finish shoulder and neck edges for garment with no back facing

FIGURE 31 Treatment of facing edges for novelty Hong Kong finish

in a manner similar to that shown in Figure 21. The traditional slip stitch is done a scant 1/16 inch under the lining edge, but the Hong Kong finish requires

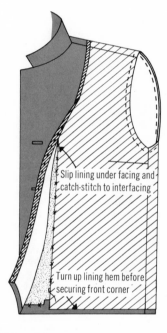

Slip lining under facing and catch-stitch to interfacing

Turn up lining hem before securing front corner

(a) To insert lining

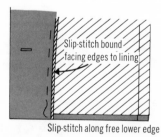

Slip-stitch bound facing edges to lining

Slip-stitch along free lower edge

(b) To secure facing edges

FIGURE 32 Treatment of lining for Hong Kong finish

stitches about 1/8 inch back from the finished edge of the facing.

MISCELLANEOUS LINING FEATURES

TO COVER AND ATTACH A GARMENT SHIELD

Purchased garment shields can be used in the tailored garment if they are covered with a layer of lining fabric. The shield can be removed for laundering, and the lining cover can be dry-cleaned or replaced with new fabric if it is badly stained. See Figure 33. Cut four sections of lining fabric, using the shield as a guide, as shown in Figure 33a; allow a 5/8-inch seam beyond the shield edges. Stitch two sections together along the concave curve in a 5/8-inch seam and clip the curve, as shown in Figure 33b. Place the cover over the shield with the right side of the lining outside and concave curves matching. Turn the remaining raw edges over the shield and baste in place. Figure 33d shows the shield in position in the garment. Whip the edges of the shield to the garment, catching the stitches through the layer of lining only.

TO INSERT THE DIOR CHAIN WEIGHT

See Figure 34. The chain is used to give additional weight for whatever purpose it might be needed, and therefore it can be used at any position along the hemline of any garment. The chains come in a length suitable for weighting the back of a jacket or coat and will reach across the back and extend a short distance on each side, on an average-size figure. Links can be removed, or more than one length can be used if a different length is required for particular purposes. Center the chain at the center-back line and place it over the garment hem close to the hand stitches which secure the lining and under the fold of lining, as shown. Hand-sew through the links with stitches catching into the hem layer only, being very careful that the stitches do not catch through to the outside of the garment.

The fold of lining will cover the

chain, but it will peek out as the jacket or coat is removed and will add an attractive professional appearance. The chain should be removed when the garment is dry-cleaned.

TO ATTACH A LABEL

See Figure 35. Labels provided by fabric or pattern manufacturers or personalized labels can be placed near the neck edge at the center back, as shown, or along the front facing or lining edge. Labels on ready-to-wear are frequently placed near the front in a prominent position that is ideal for advertising purposes, but they do detract from the garment in this position. The center-back position is preferred by most persons.

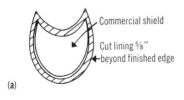

(a)

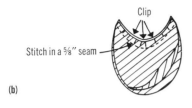

(b)

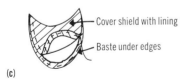

(c)

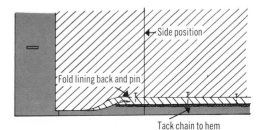

FIGURE 34 To insert a Dior chain weight

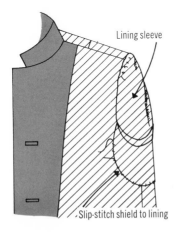

(d)

FIGURE 33 To cover and attach a garment shield

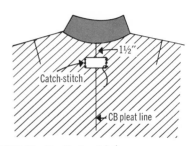

FIGURE 35 To attach a label

The label should be centered over the center-back pleat line and should be placed in a position that creates attractive proportions. If the garment has no back facing, a position about 1½ inches down from the neck edge will be attractive; if there is a back facing, the label will look more attractive placed closer (½ to 1 inch) to the upper edge of the lining. Labels are usually done with catch stitches that pass through the lining layer only; the stitches should be very small and very even. Slip stitches can be used if preferred.

INDEX